Feasting and Fasting

WITH LEWIS & CLARK

A Food and Social History of the Early 1800s

Leandra Zim Holland

*Proceed On! with
Lewis & Clark
Leandra & Chuck Holland
2/11/2004*

Old Yellowstone Publishing
Emigrant, Montana
2003

OLD YELLOWSTONE

D1212354

Credits: The majority of larger illustrations bear the credit alongside the illustration or within the caption. Other illustration credits, by page, are: cover and title-page, J. K. Ralston, courtesy: Jefferson National Expansion Memorial/NPS; back cover, R. L. Rickards – courtesy: R. L. Richards Western Art; 43, Pennsylvania Farm Museum at Landis Valley; 45, Herbert Manchester from *We Proceeded On;* 46, Pennsylvania Farm Museum at Landis Valley; 56, Frederick Pursh from Philadelphia Academy of Natural Sciences; 57, sketch by Jim Jokerst; 78, from Herbert Zim, ed., *Encyclopedia of Natural History;* 81, sugar loaf and nippers from *Tools* by Bobbie Kalman, Crabtree Publishing; and map from archives of Missouri Historical Society; 108, medal sketch from *We Proceeded On;* 152, US Forest Service, Northern Idaho, plant leaflet; 162, from *The Journal of Forestry;* 167, sketch by Jim Jokerst; 200, from Herbert Zim, ed., *Mammals;* 215-217, animal sketches by Jim Jokerst; 218, Audubon sketch from *We Proceeded On;* 219, Herbert Zim, ed., *Mammals;* 222-227, Herbert Zim, ed., *Fishes;* 229-232, from Herbert Zim, ed., *Gamebirds;* 235-236, from *Uses of Plants* by Melvin Gilmore; 237-238, and pencil sketches on 241-242, from *Cooking with Spirit* by Darcy Williamson and Lisa Railsback; 241-242 color sketches from *Wild Berry Book* by Katie Lyle.

Paintings by R. L. Rickards, a premier Lewis & Clark artist, appear throughout the book with attribution accompanying each illustration; courtesy of R. L. Rickards Western Art, Thousand Oaks, California. www.RLRickardsWesternArt.com.

Quotations and information from the Expedition, unless otherwise noted where presented, is from the *Journals of the Lewis and Clark Expedition,* Gary E. Moulton, editor, 13 volumes, published by University of Nebraska Press, 1983-2000. All such *Journal* quotations are presented in this book in *italics,* and unless the source can be easily determined from date and writer context, bear the inline superscript citation of "Jvv:ppp" where "vv" is the volume and "ppp" is the page. Similarly, quotations from key documents related to the Expedition taken from *Letters for the Lewis and Clark Expedition with Related Documents 1783-1854,* Donald Jackson, editor, 2 volumes, published by University of Illinois Press, 1962, bear the inline superscript citation of "Lv:ppp" where "v" is the volume and "ppp" is the page.

ISBN: 1-59152-007-X hardbound
1-59152-010-X softbound
Copyright: Leandra Zim Holland and
Old Yellowstone Publishing, Inc.
Emigrant, Montana 2003
www.oldyellowstone.com

Library of Congress Control Number: 2003110749

This book may not be reproduced in whole or in part by any means (with the exception of short quotes for the purpose of review) without the permission of the publisher.
Produced and designed in the United States of America by Farcountry Press, Helena, MT.
Printed in Korea.

To
my parents who raised me to be curious
MILTON and NATALIE ZIM
and
the memory of my uncle who motivated me to write
DR. HERBERT ZIM, *author and educator*
and
my husband CHUCK HOLLAND *who helped throughout.*

— Leandra Zim Holland, September 2003

To the loving memory of Leandra – writer, lecturer, historian,
seeker of wisdom, and compassionate friend to all
– this book is re-dedicated; all net proceeds from it will go to the
Leandra Zim Holland Memorial Research Fund, *administered by the*
Lewis and Clark Trail Heritage Foundation, Great Falls, Montana.

— Chuck Holland, October 2003

Acknowledgments

TWO HUNDRED YEARS AGO, Lewis and Clark found their Expedition supported by the efficiency, goodwill, and exemplary efforts of many. I am likewise indebted to my contemporaries, filled with the same spirit. This book would not have been possible without the dedicated researchers who have unearthed and edited the documents of the Expedition: Gary Moulton and his crew with *The Journals of the Lewis & Clark Expedition,* and Donald Jackson with *Letters of the Lewis and Clark Expedition* – the extent and importance of these works is evident in the many references listed in my notes.

I greatly appreciate the encouraging words from both Gary Moulton and James Ronda. Additional thanks go to Robert J. Moore, historian at the Jefferson National Expansion Memorial (the Gateway Arch) in St. Louis, for his review and suggestions; Jim Merritt, editor of *We Proceeded On,* for his helpful comments and publication of articles excerpted from this book; Lee Whittlesey, archivist of Yellowstone National Park, and Joe Mussulman, Lewis and Clark researcher and online editor, for their early encouragement; the late Don Nell, past president of the Lewis and Clark Trail Heritage Foundation, for his review; and to nutritionist Marilyn Peterson for her suggestions.

Other historians/librarians who unfailingly and generously answered questions are from the National Archives, the U.S. Army Records, Monticello, the Missouri Historical Society, James Holmberg at the Filson Historical Society, the North Dakota Historical Society, Janice Elvidge at Fort Clatsop, and the Great Falls Interpretative Center (especially Jane Weber, Sue Buchel, and Rebecca Young). Special thanks go to R. L. Rickards and Michael Haynes for supportive sharing of their Lewis & Clark art – please refer to www.RLRickardsWesternArt.com and MHaynesArt.com respectively for additional information and artworks.

My heartfelt gratitude goes to my dear friend, Cynthia Stewart Kaag, head of Science Library at WSU, for her continuing editorial assistance and enthusiasm; and to my husband, Charles Holland, for research backup, technical support, and untangling the word-processor snafus. And to all my cooking buddies from Bozeman and Great Falls, bless you. Finally, to the strong editorial and production staff at Farcountry Press – Kathy Springmeyer, Charlene Patterson, Jessica Solberg, and Shirley Machonis – who brought the book to a printed reality; Barbara Fifer for her expert proofreading of the *Journal* quotations; and to Merle Guy of Farcountry for his marketing perspectives.

To my readers: despite rounds of reviews, editing, and proofreading, there are bound to remain errors in both form and fact – please let me know at Leandra@LewisandClark-food.com.

Now, let's "Proceed on"!

Table of Contents

Introduction

ONE OF OUR MOST BASIC NEEDS IS FOOD. About this subject, entire libraries have been written – from cookbooks, to food science and nutrition, to histories. A major educational area of study, it encompasses the preparation of food, as well as the art, science, and business of food cultivation, distribution, and the economics of trade.

The Lewis and Clark Expedition, also referred to as the "Corps of Discovery," long ago captured the American imagination and has again received increased emphasis at its bicentennial. About this single endeavor hundreds of books, studies, and documentary presentations have been produced. Our national organization, The Lewis and Clark Trail Heritage Foundation, features a quarterly scholarly publication, *We Proceeded On,* which pursues serious research and environmental stewardship issues relating to the Expedition.

As can be imagined, food played a crucial role in the Expedition – from an unbelievable feasting with "food on the hoof" across the Great Plains, to the edge of starvation and involuntary fasting as the Corps crossed the Bitterroot Mountains from Montana into Idaho. However, despite its importance, and although several cookbooks with modernized recipes have been produced relating to the Expedition, no comprehensive studies of food or the food-related social history of Lewis and Clark have been published until now.

Part One: Food Culture of the Times looks at the background for the Expedition: from Lewis' White House days; to how food was preserved, packaged, cooked, and hunted; to quantities required; to food-related maladies; and to how the Army organized around food.

Part Two: The Expedition is chronological. It follows the Corps' day-to-day and week-to-week progress from a food perspective – hunting, gathering, cooking, eating, and socializing – both among themselves and with the native peoples along the way.

Reference Section: Foods, Meals, and Menus catalogues and discusses the main foods consumed, grouped in chapters by Meats, Fish and Fowl, Plants, and Beverages, followed by appendices summarizing the recipes, menus, foods eaten, and an analysis of quantities required.

While the intent of this book is to offer a complete discussion of foods rather than be a cookbook, recipes are presented throughout the text in context with the ongoing discussion when they can be derived from either the Expedition documentation or from closely related documents of the time. Other than as occasionally noted in the recipes, the ingredients and instructions are presented as they were at the time without modernization for today's kitchen. An index to the thirty-four included recipes and a discussion of known meal menus are listed in Appendix A; a listing of animals and plants documented as being used for food is given in Appendix B.

This book should not be viewed as a general history of the Expedition or a study of its members – there are numerous excellent works available on that subject: *Undaunted Courage* by Stephen Ambrose is compact, while The *Journals of the Lewis & Clark Expedition* in thirteen volumes edited by Gary Moulton is extensive and contains all the original text. A complete treatise on the animals and plants discovered along the way can be found in *Lewis & Clark: Pioneering Naturalists* by Paul Russell Cutright and *Lewis & Clark's Green World* by A. Scott Earle and James L. Reveal.

Quotations from the *Journals* and *Letters of the Lewis & Clark Expedition,* edited by Donald Jackson, (and only those entries) are in italics and are presented as written with no correction to spelling, grammar, or punctuation. In these quotations, [NB:...] are additions by the first editor, Nicolas Biddle. In keeping with the extensive use of *Journal* and *Letter* material, this book presents the Expedition in present tense – as the Corps saw it unfolding. Most *Journal* quotations are cited inline where they occur, but where writer and date of an entry can be determined from context, the citation is deleted.

Those interested in American food-ways of the 1800s, but with only a limited knowledge of Lewis and Clark, will find sufficient information in *Part Two: The Expedition* chapters to form a good image of what the Expedition encountered as it progressed across the continent and returned. Hopefully all readers will emerge with a greater appreciation of the vital role that food played in making possible the Lewis and Clark Expedition.

Leandra Zim Holland
Emigrant, Montana – Fall, 2003

Part One

Food Culture of the Times

Typical plantation kitchen from *The Williamsburg Cookbook*.

Courtesy: White House Association

The President's House, later The White House, from 1814 drawings used in its reconstruction following the 1812 British burning. Although the executive mansion in Washington was officially called the President's House throughout the Jeffersonian period, it was starting to be informally referenced as "The White House" well before that name was made official by Theodore Roosevelt in 1901.

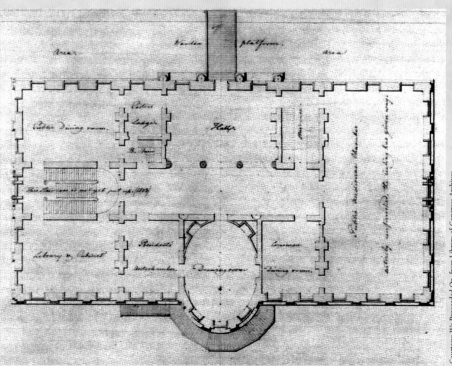

Courtesy: We Proceeded On, from Library of Congress Archives

Early 1800s President's House first floor floorplan showing the original Jefferson dining room.

Meriwether Lewis: White House Gourmet

February 6, 1802 – The President's House, Washington, D.C.

At 4:00 PM THE DINNER BELL RINGS SMARTLY, and the doors to the dining room open ceremoniously. It is a daily rite President Jefferson enjoys.

Meriwether Lewis, cutting a trim and fashionable figure in his hose and sculpted pantaloons, starched shirt and ornate jacket, shifts his weight. He is now secretary to his boyhood mentor, Thomas: Mr. President, Commander-in-Chief, Great White Father. As leader of an upcoming Expedition across unknown lands to the western ocean, Lewis is contemplating foreign relations with Britain, France, and Spain – all of whom hold substantial territories in the New World for which there is as yet no American counterbalance. Then there are the Indians. What sort of reception will his little Expedition receive? His mind pitches and rolls over the question of extra guns versus extra whiskey.

Before the guests arrived, the finishing details of the meal had been attended to by the kitchen help. The table is set not with one tablecloth, but two. A linen napkin rests in the center of each English bone china plate, and the silver glitters with the reflections of flickering candles. Flavorful aromas waft in the air, beckoning the diners.

Jefferson, a sophisticated and discerning eater, wants variety and has no less than eight dishes at any meal he eats alone; with company, the number of dishes increases significantly. For a small gathering such as he is hosting tonight, nine or ten different flavors and tastes will be adequate. He prides himself on his fine foods, a lovely table, excellent conversation, and, of course, superb wines.

Indeed, the table is a visual delight. Lewis' observant eye savors the nuances, for each dish or "cover" is placed for its eye appeal. There are large platters of fried beef, ham, mutton, cutlets of mutton or veal, a loin of veal, and fried eggs, all placed symmetrically top-to-bottom and side-to-side. Some of the food is served on smaller side dishes that are paired like twins and arranged in a dancing constellation between the gastronomic stars. Serving utensils and carving knives shine in complementary geometric array.

Amidst conversation, the guests enter and are seated. "One circumstance, though minute in itself, had certainly a great influence on the conversational powers of Mr. Jefferson's guests. Instead of being arrayed in straight parallel lines, where they could not see the countenances of those who sat on the same side, they encircled a round, or oval table, where all could see each others faces, and feel the animating influence of looks as well as of words." [1]

These dinners usually begin with a first course of soup, fish, or both. Tonight a plentiful tureen stands ready for the cheerful host, who ladles the rice soup into soup plates for his guests. As the guests finish, the covered bowl and their used china are whisked away, and roast beef and turkey are brought. The singular formality of the opening part of the first course retires with the tureen, and the atmosphere becomes more family-like.

Writing on manners of the time, Louise Beldon describes a typical meal. "The company then set to on the tableful of food. Whoever sat near the roast, game, and fowls was expected to carve and do a good job of it – seated. Women rivaled men as carvers, and their friends often urged them to sit near a platter that called for their skill. The carver ... placed a slice of meat or a piece of fowl on a plate ... [for]

whichever guest expressed a wish for it ... there followed a confusion of passing and of polite urging by host and hostess to 'try a bit.' "[2]

Guests wishing a drink could obtain it from the sideboard. First-time guests might notice that while Jefferson's sideboard contains expensive wine; the President later records, "malt liquors & cyder are my table drinks."[3] The wine is reserved for after dinner. Lewis, polite but somewhat detached, ponders alcohol for his troops. What kind; sources? How much to buy and what is the packing weight for a keg or barrel?

During dinner, a small taste disaster is underway. One guest, the Reverend Cutler, is taken aback by "a pie called macaroni, which appeared to be a rich crust filled with the strillions of onions, or shallots, which I took it to be, tasted very strong, and not very agreeable."[4] There is a polite and whispered murmuring with Lewis. "Mr. Lewis told me there were none in it; it was an Italian dish, and what appeared like onions was made of flour and butter, with a particularly strong liquor mixed with them."[a] It is not hard to imagine a slightly disdainful sniff preceding what is recorded next: "Dinner not as elegant as when we dined before."

Meriwether has dined often enough with his friend Thomas to acquire a sophisticated palate, although on this night the vegetable dishes so favored by the President are singularly lacking. As the appeal of the heavy meat dishes goes slack after robust eating, a pause occurs. And while Jefferson generally uses few servants, depending instead on a dumbwaiter elevator to move food and dishes to and from the preparation area below, a servant does come and clear the table down to the tablecloth, and in a whisk of gracious "French service," removes the soiled cloth too, revealing the fresh cloth, now ready for the next course.

Although the food and service are impeccable, the dessert course tonight does not follow the common English tradition of serving a veritable parade of desserts. Rather, the talented Presidential chef, Honoré Julien, a French freeman who was responsible for the legendary status of Jefferson's table, serves only two desserts:

"Ice cream very good, crust wholly dried, crumbled into thin flakes; [and] a dish somewhat like a pud-

ding—inside white as milk or curd, very porous and light covered with cream sauce—very fine."[5]

Lewis indulges in this ice cream dish often, for it is a signature dish of Jefferson's winter dinner parties. The novelty of anything frozen is enough to cause animated gossip, and the daring required to contrast it with hot meringue is simply astounding.[b]

But what of Jefferson's renowned wines? Dessert has been served, but dinner is not over yet. Again the table is cleared, this time revealing the bare wood. While serving as diplomatic attaché abroad, Jefferson had taken to the French custom of serving light fruit and cheese as dessert, and he has instituted it as a final but distinctly different course. And, in the continental style, conversation is the main focus of this course. One later guest notes, "Mr. Jefferson said lit-

Monticello kitchen with pastry chef at work.

tle at dinner besides attending to the filling of plates, which he did with great ease and grace for a philosopher, he became very talkative as soon as the cloth was removed." And another writes, "You drink as you please, and converse at your ease."[6]

As personal secretary to Jefferson, one of Lewis' responsibilities are to process the purchases for this famous wine cellar. The following year, just before leaving to meet Clark in the West, Lewis – behind schedule and furiously preparing for the Expedition – will be asked to essentially stop his preparations to send Jefferson's compliments for some wine that the President has finally received, and to arrange payment.

---

[a] Dr. Netta Davis, curator of the Culinary Collection at the Schlesinger Library at Harvard, notes that the word "liquor" often meant "pot-likker," the liquid which remained after boiling a food. Thus, a likely supposition is that the mysterious onion flavor might be attributed to potlikker, rather than some exotic alcohol.

[b] This dessert is very similar to today's Baked Alaska.

Thomas Jefferson Memorial Foundation

And the quality of wine demanded by Jefferson is highly extravagant even amongst his contemporaries: "... never before ... such a variety of the finest and most costly wines. ... His wine was truly the best I ever drank, particularly his champagne."[7]

And so it seems that there is nothing small or ordinary in this cosmopolitan world peopled by extraordinary individuals in adventuresome and tumultuous times. Even the cheese served at dessert is record-setting, and the inscribed card read, "The greatest cheese in America for the greatest man in America."[8] A New Year's present in 1802, the 1,235 pound cheese had been three weeks in snowy transit by sleigh from Cheshire, Massachusetts, and was described as being "as large as a burr millstone."[9] The President's public reception that New Year's Day

At Jefferson's table, wine is reserved for the final fruit and cheese course.

featured the Marine band playing and guests slicing off wedges of the Cheshire-style cheese. Regrettably the quality did not match the quantity. But it was gargantuan, and the politically sensitive Jefferson continued serving the cheese, meal after meal, for several years.

Certainly this grand scale of entertaining has gone far beyond Lewis' own plantation experiences. But, as with all forms of education, it makes its imprint. His choice of winter quarters in St. Louis with the wealthy river barons, his rhapsodic culinary description of the tiny candlefish in Oregon, and a plaintive *Journal* entry longing to be back in civilization are the soul songs of a highly erudite and civilized man – Meriwether Lewis, cosmopolitan gourmet.

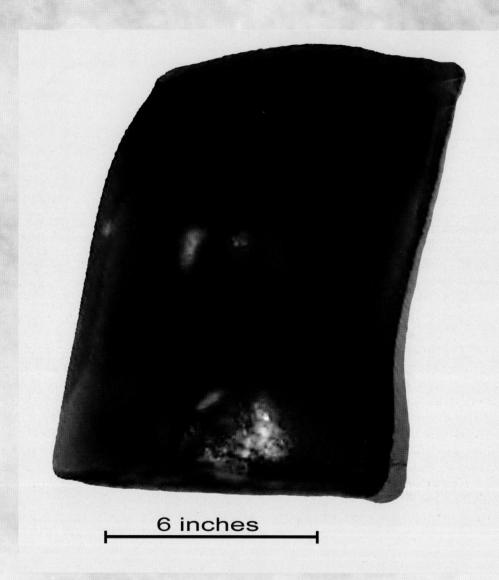

6 inches

Courtesy: C. Holland, digital photo processing

Modern preparation of a 9" by 12" slab of gel *"Portable Soup"* prepared according to the recipe in this chapter. For the Expedition, it was then cut into chunks and packed into tin canisters that Lewis purchased for this purpose.

Food Preservation in 1800

Completed packing fifty Keys of Port ...
& roled & filled them with brine ...
— CLARK, APRIL 17, 1804 [J2:205, a]

IN 1804, AS MERIWETHER LEWIS PREPARES the provisions list for his party about to cross the North American continent, his available preservation choices do not even include canning and bottling, which will cause a revolution in food technology within ten years. And even farther in the future are those mainstays of the modern army – the freeze-dried MRE.[a] So what works? How is food made storable and travel-worthy for up to two years with neither chemical preservatives nor bacteria-free, air-tight packaging?

Provisioning has always been the key to moving across vast terrains. Ancient Greeks loaded up skins of prepared barley meal and wine, reconstituting it with hot water for a satisfying meal, or with cold water for one less appetizing.[10] Genghis Khan is reputed to have equipped his fearsome horsemen with leather sacks of primitive yogurt which served as nutritious, self-preserving, non-spoiling meals.

By the end of the 1700s, ensuring adequate food supplies for long treks had not changed much since the Middle Ages. Napoleon, believing that "Armies travel on their stomachs," offered a handsome reward to the first person who made it possible for his armies to march long distances. A Parisian pastry chef, sometime pickle-maker, and brewer named Nicholas Appert won with his development of safe canning, and in 1809 walked off with fame and 12,000 francs, a veritable fortune at the time.[11] With canning as the first major technical advancement, food preservation was on its way. Just five years after Lewis and Clark began their trek, bottled soup was available. By 1810 it came in tinned, unbreakable containers.

But in 1800, American staples were still treated as they had been for thousands of years: the ancient Egyptians were air drying fruit and pulses (edible seeds of legumes, such as peas and beans), as well as sun-drying, pickling or salting fish.[12] Smoking food evolved alongside the dying campfire, and surprisingly fat also acted as a preservative. Using one, or perhaps even two of these methods combined, was simple and ultimately effective. In cosmopolitan St. Louis there were additional methods of preservation which probably produced foods that the Captains ate: pickling and sweet packs. Finally, there were the grains that required various degrees of preparation, drying, and storage.

So how do these techniques work? What determines which mode might be used? Several considerations enter into the final decision:

- ✦ What is the product: meat, legume, soft vegetable, or fruit?
- ✦ Urban (spices, sugars, jars, etc. available) or on-the-road with no supply lines?
- ✦ What equipment is available, either for preparing the food or storing it?
- ✦ How long will the process take from start to finish?
- ✦ Is extra weight worth carrying, worth the effort?

---

[a] Throughout the book, explanatory material will appear on the page as a footnote indicated by a letter; citation references from Jackson, *Letters of the Lewis and Clark Expedition,* will appear inline as superscripted *"L volume:page",* and from the Moulton edition of *Journals of the Lewis and Clark Expedition* as *"J volume:page";* other citations are flagged in the text with a superscript Arabic numeral and appear at the end of the book in *Notes.*

[b] Meal Ready to Eat – a plastic-pouch-sealed one-meal provision that can be eaten as is, or heated if facilities and time are available; with an outside pouch that also contains condiments, beverage mix such as coffee, and possibly a high-energy sweet item.

Boiling-down (Reduction) and Drying

In 1724, a method was developed whereby an evaporated and condensed broth could be dried into cakes. The process of boiling down the meats extracts the nutritious components and sterilizes the broth from any pathogens that might have been lurking. Whether exposed to the heat of an oven or even the sun, the secondary drying of the gel served to extract whatever moisture was left, thus making the "glue" into an inhospitable environment for opportunistic bacteria, molds, or other decay-causing organisms encountered during travel. After processing, the nutritive value is similar to today's bouillon cubes, but is far less salty and has about 30 Calories per tablespoon

This *"veal glue,"* as it was sometimes called, had been around for a long time. Casanova said he never left home without it.[13] His Majesty's Royal Navy supplied Captain James Cook with cases of this "portable soup" for his circumnavigation of the world in 1772. When reconstituting the soup, *The Lady's Home Companion* adds, "You are to use this by boiling about a Pint of Water, and pouring it upon a piece of the Glue or Cake, about the bigness of a small Walnut, and stirring it with a Spoon until the Cake dissolves."[14] Captain Cook added pea or "pease" flour (as in the nursery rhyme: "Pease Porridge hot. Pease Porridge cold ...") and felt it to be valuable food for sick sailors. A cake of the very soup Cook carried on that trip was analyzed in the 1930s (about 160 years later) and found not to have changed in any significant way.[15] But, it was still the same "small, oblong, flat cake, grayish white in color" looking just like "a slab of glue."[16]

There are many recipes for Portable Soup, all arriving at much the same end-product. The following recipe is derived from Ann Shackleford's recipe, circa 1767. It is the simplest and easiest:

PORTABLE SOUP[17]

"Take four calves feet; buttock of beef, twelve pounds; fillet of veal, three pounds; leg of mutton, ten pounds. Stew them in a sufficient quantity of water over a gentle fire and carefully take off the skum, pass the broth through a cullender."

The original recipe goes on to double boil the meat in a second batch of water, add the two liquors, skim off fat, clarify with five egg whites, salt to taste, and then strain through a flannel bag.

The emphasis on a filtered bouillon without chunks of meats or fats is to ensure a product that won't grow bacteria or go rancid. The use of egg whites clarifying a consomme was first codified by La Varenne, author of *Le Cuisinier François* (1651), and was considered something of a culinary innovation, far more discrete than egg shells or fish skin.[18]

The bouillon is further reduced until it is very rubbery. When it reaches that stage, it is either dried at low heat or put upon absorbent flannel until all the moisture has evaporated out – the only requirement being that it must be a consistency that doesn't change form when exposed to heat. A firm-in-the-fridge, concentrated, jellied consomme will melt if left out on a hot day. That is the perfect example of what the portable soup shouldn't do.[c]

Shackleford, discussing the use of the soup, adds: "please, add to the composition, fowl, leguminous roots, or spices, as a few cloves, a little cinnamon, pepper, &c."

Unfortunately, the emaciated men of the Corps didn't have the more nourishing version with Shakleford's suggested additions. But, perhaps even better than eating the soup is reading about it, and one of the keenest literary descriptions comes from *The Fortune of War* by Patrick O'Brian:

'Oh,' she said, and absently she took three spoonsfuls of the soup. 'Lord above,' she said, 'What is this?'

'Soup. Portable soup. Pray a little more, it will rectify the humours.'

'I thought it was luke-warm glue. But it does go down quite well if you don't breathe.'

Is portable soup worth carrying for thousands of miles? In 1729 governor William Byrd of Virginia recommended that "... if you shou'd be faint with Fasting or Fatigue, let a small Piece of this Glue melt in your Mouth, and you will find yourself surprisingly refreshed."[19]

Its portability (i.e. travel worthiness) rests in its description, "[It] ... may be carried around in the Pocket without Inconvenience."[20] Another tout claims, "These lozenges, or cakes, will keep good four or five years."[21]

The Philadelphia and St. Louis inventories are the sole mention of "*p.soup*" until it reappears only during pressing

---

[c] In a recent reproduction of this soup at the Lewis and Clark National Historic Trail Interpretive Center in Great Falls, Montana, calves feet were impossible to find. The meats were boiled down, and then four packets of Knox Gelatin were added as a substitution for this missing gelatin-producing item. Since there was also a time pinch, another shortcut was taken – the soup was clarified once only, and with a linen-weave hand-towel rather than with egg whites. These substitutions worked well; the reduced broth was a very tasty consomme.

need in September 1805, when the men are critically close to starving and the situation is dire. By then the soup has traveled for two years, three-quarters of the way across the continent; although not popular, it has preserved its food value.

Wet Cure

On April 3, 1804, Clark first notes that they are packing pork into barrels. The processing used is noted on April 17 when he writes, *"Completed packing fifty Kegs of Pork ... & roled & filled them with brine ..."* [J2:205] From this it is clear that they are not using a dry salt-pork preparation, but rather a water-diluted salt mixture and perhaps adding sugar or additional flavorings that would make it more palatable and not so harsh as straight salt. More to the point, however, is a comment taken from Mary Randolf's *The Virginia Housewife* that avers that if meat is left to stand in straight salt too long it "will certainly draw off the juices, and harden it."[22]

The brine used for pork might have been similar to the one Mrs. Randolf describes for beef; she recommends proportions that are about one pound of salt for ten pounds of meat.

This idea can be expanded a bit further. "Brine, also called wet cure or pickle, is a solution of salt, water, sugar, and often curing salts. Meat placed in a brine is preserved by reducing the moisture content and replacing the moisture by salt; and adding the anti-bacteria properties of nitrate/nitrite. Spices and other seasonings can be added to the brine for

Brined pork is a key expedition staple in which chunks of pork are packed into kegs with a preservative brining solution.

BRINING BEEF

Into a clean 30 gallon cask mix: "one pound of salt-petre[d], powdered, fifteen quarts of salt and fifteen gallons of cold water" stirring thoroughly until the salt is dissolved.[23]

more flavor."[24] There is no mention as to whether or not spices are added to the Corps' pork brine. They may not have been, as Americans were at the tail-end of a backlash against the over-spicing that had predominated for centuries to mask the odors and tastes of spoiled food, and which eventually became an acquired taste. Further, spices are expensive, especially in the quantities needed for 50 kegs of product.

The use of saltpeter was apparently controversial even in the 1700s, for Mary Randolf comments, "The generally received opinion that salt-petre hardens meat, is entirely erroneous: – it tends greatly to prevent putrefaction, but will not make it hard."[25] The frightening specter of putrefaction still warrants our attention. "If you decide to air-dry or cold smoke, curing salts must be used to prevent any possibility of botulism. During cold smoking and air drying the temperatures are ideal for the growth of bacteria, so the protection offered by curing salts is necessary for safety."[26] As with much of cooking, there is more than one way to get a desired result – an alternate is to pre-salt the meat and then add brine.

This is the first part of preserving meat safely. The second, and equally important part, is the issue of good cooperage, barrels that are sturdy and don't leak. As historian Bob Moore writes, "Meat stored in barrels of brine often spoiled, especially if the brine leached out of the barrels. Sometimes the meat turned rancid; sometimes it was full of maggots and

---

[d] Saltpeter (salt-petre, either potassium nitrate or sodium nitrate) was long used as a standard remedy to prevent meats from going bad. Saltpeter is no longer recommended by the USDA, being a potential carcinogen; but a variant, sodium nitrite is generally available in a packaged combination called "curing salts" (nitrite with sugar, salt, and/or other ingredients) to be used one teaspoon per 100 pounds of meat – Aidells, p. 343.

SALT MEAT PACKING, CIRCA 1776[27]

"After the meat has cooled, it is cut into 5 lb. pieces which are then rubbed well with fine salt. The pieces are then placed between boards, a weight brought to bear on the upper board so as to squeeze out the blood. Afterwards the pieces are shaken to remove the surplus salt, [and] packed rather tightly in a barrel, which when full is closed. A hole is then drilled into the upper end and brine allowed to fill the barrel to the top, the brine being made of 4 lbs. salt, 2 lbs. of brown sugar and four gallons of water with a touch of salt-petre. When no more brine can enter, the hole is closed. This method of preserving meat not only assures that it keeps longer but also gives it a rather good taste."

other pests."[28] A leaky bung-hole courts disaster, so imagine the care used in packing. All barrels upright and tight!

In whatever fashion Clark and his men brine their pork, it is mostly successful. On May 3, 1804, a month after the first pork went into the kegs, he records, *"Majr. Rumsey was polite enough to examine all my provisions Several Kegs of Pork he Condemed."* [J2:211] Considering the quantity of meat involved (3705 pounds) and the volatility of bacterial fermentation, losing only a few hundredweight of product (most likely less than 10%) is not bad at all.

Jerking – Air Drying of Meats

Air-drying and sun-drying are both best accomplished when the sun is high and the weather hot (and preferably not humid). It can still be used if the weather is cold, windy, and *dry*. And it can be supplemented by smoking if the air is water-saturated as found in summer humidity or in the cold and rainy/snowy winter months.

The word "jerky" comes from the Spanish word charqui and describes cutting meat into thin strips and then air-drying the strips until they resemble hardened shoe leather.[29] Lewis, with his gourmet tastes acquired at the White House, is suffering a bit at Fort Clatsop when he laments, *"some marrow bones and a little fresh meat would be exceptable; I have been living for two days past on poor dryed Elk, or jurk as the hunters term it."* [J6:186]

The process of jerking is so common that the *Journal* entries almost pass it by. Out of all the occasions that the Cap-

An 1832 upper Missouri sketch by George Catlin of Indians
sun-drying strips of buffalo meat, which might become pemmican.

George Catlin - courtesy: *We Proceeded On*

tains note jerking going on, only once (during the return trip) is there any mention of what steps are actually followed. It is Lewis who writes on April 8, 1806, *"exposed our dryed meat to the sun and the smoke of small fires."* [J7:94] The *Journals* reproduce a footnote added to Patrick Gass' journal by his original editor, David McKeehan, who writes "Jerk is meat cut into small pieces and dried in the sun or by a fire. The Indians cure and preserve their meat in this way without salt." [J10:16n2]

Jerking is probably the single most efficient means of preserving the abundant game that the Corps encounters, and Capt. Clark first notes this technique on June 5, 1804. The day before the hunters had killed seven deer, and after the luscious aroma of venison roasting over the fire had vanished, the excess meat was *"jurked."* [J2:227] Rancidity and spoilage, both constant threats, make it *"... Constant Practice to have all the fresh meat not used, Dried in this way."* [J2:294]

To Salt or Not to Salt

Air-drying is the primary form of preserving for Native Americans in 1800. Closer to civilization, the European approach might have been to enhance the process by using salts and/or a smokehouse to hasten the drying and to add an extra level of antibacterial safety. Along the trail there is much more air-drying of meat and no mention is made of either salt or curing salts. Several factors might be operating here: the paucity of salt, or the meticulousness needed to hand-apply salt to every square inch of the item being preserved. Considering the relative dryness of the American West, preserving with salt was not as much a necessity as on the moister East Coast. Clark comments on this as the Corps returns home after trekking through Montana and North Dakota leads to renewed recognition of how quickly things rot in sultry humidity: *"... halted ... to kill Some meat that which we killed a fiew days past being all Spoiled."* [J8:356]

Between the native and white cultures another difference becomes obvious: How to cut the meat? According to the *Cambridge World History of Food*, native women "cut the meat [buffalo] into strips, across the grain, in order to maintain alternating layers of lean and fat."[30] This fat would add to the caloric value of the meat and give an extra palatability. Think of a slice of bacon.

The Corps, on the other hand, would probably cut their meat with the grain, eliminating as much of the fat as possible. Imagine a piece of Canadian bacon. The chance of fat oxidation which would cause the meat to go rancid is reduced and hopefully the supply wouldn't spoil. It will also guarantee a cleaner pouch. Seemingly this is the traditional approach, for a pioneer recipe found in *Trail Boss's Cowboy Cookbook* reads, "Slice buffalo meat along the grain into strips $1/8$" thick, $1/2$" wide and 2-3" long." It also recommends to "drape them on bushes to dry in the sun."[31]

Smoking

Going back, there is the question of how to dry meat in one of the wettest times imaginable, the Fort Clatsop winter of 1805–06. The air is so saturated that it rains interminably, and air-drying becomes nearly impossible because water molecules in the meat can not osmose into saturated air. What will the Corps do?

One possibility is that they simply make the best of their shelter and try to keep the rain off the meat. However, rain implies temperatures that are quite hospitable to bacterial growth, albeit slow. With memories of their dysfunctional innards from eating dried fish the prior autumn,[e] they probably are exceedingly cautious. Lewis, on February 9, 1806, notes, *"fearing that our meat would spoil we set six men to jurking it."* [J6:290] Clark repeats the entry, adding, *"... which they are obliged to perform in a house under shelter from the repeated rains."* [J6:293] This sounds very much like a smokehouse, and indeed they built one at Fort Clatsop. It is a laborious process and the quantity of meat is such that the drying strips still hang over the spindly stick racks the next day, and the next, until pronounced *"done!"* four days later.

Safe preservation most likely comes from smoking the meat, for they certainly have fires for both cooking and warmth. Smoke adds flavor, but how does it cure food? An explanation lies in food chemistry. "Smoke is a very complex material, with upward of 200 components that include alcohols, acids, phenolic compounds, and various toxic, sometimes carcinogenic substances. The toxic substances inhibit the growth of microbes, the phenolics retard fat oxidation, and the whole complex imparts the characteristic flavor of burning wood to the meat."[32] In other words, smoking complements air-drying, gives the meat a different flavor (depending on the wood used), and is useful to cooks who need to have the meat ready to go at a certain time and can't rely on unpredictable air-drying.

Fat as an Anaerobic Preservative

Pemmican, the "Native American Power Bar," fueled natives, fur-trappers, explorers, and anyone who could put it in a pouch or pocket. While Napoleon was searching for

---

[e] See *Fasting Over the Rockies*, page 162, for details of the September, 1805, malady.

portable preserved food, Native Americans had already solved the problem. Unlike today's little individual power bars, pemmican was made up in large quantities, enough to last awhile. It combines air-drying of meat with the displacement of air by fat to seal out any extraneous bacteria or molds that might come floating by.[f] In addition to deleting something (water, by air drying) it added something (fat). The word itself is a phonic equivalent of the Cree term, pimikan, which translates to "manufactured grease."[33] In technique it is quite simple.

The Corps actually manufactures their own version of this native food, and, in the fall of 1804, Clark gives the Sioux recipe:

After the meat is dried, it is pounded until pulverized and then placed in a mixing vessel. Various kinds of berries

PEMMICAN

"Pemn is buffo meat dried or baked pounded & mixed with grease" [J3:118]

might be added to improve the flavor,[34] and as a counterpoint of sharpness against the next ingredient. Marrow from bones is melted until it reaches a liquid state, the high heat acting as a purifier for the grease. The sanitized fat is then poured over the meat particles, allowed to cool into a stiff paste, and then packed inside a rawhide sack. Another layer of pure fat is applied, much like sealing wax or paraffin is used to cap preserves, and this layer forms another anaerobic barrier that stretches the storage time.

Culinaria: The United States makes one more revealing statement about the rawhide container that obviously had confused unwary cooks: "All historical recipes for pemmican helpfully suggest that the bag must be made with the hair on the outside."[35] This power bar is apparently not terribly thrilling, and Clark not overly-enthusiastic, for he merely writes, *I Saw & eat Pemitigon ...* [J3:119]

The Corps encounters another variation on this theme: preserved whale blubber. The Tillamook tribes relish fresh

blubber, boiled. The Corps eats it that way in January of 1806. But for the sake of provisioning and future consumption, Clark writes that the Indians fillet the blubber into *"flickes"* or flitches (thin strips) that are partially rendered, then dried, and put away. [J6:183] As the pores shrink and close, the very nature of the oily meat causes an impenetrable, anaerobic self-seal. Later it will be reconstituted either by flame-roasting or boiling, either of which will unseal the closed cells and allow the blubber to plump up and become tender.[36]

Air-Drying of Grains

Air drying, or perhaps gentle heating near the coals, is so simple that a dried grain or legume usually doesn't elicit much interest. But what happens during the process of removing water from the plant that makes it safe for storage and later consumption? As drying progresses, the degenerative actions of the plants' own enzymes are put on hold and deactivated. On April 3, 1804, a number of the men are set to work on the dry provisions. *"I have meal mad & the flour Packed & repacked ..."* [J2:191]

A few days earlier, Clark started the preparation of the corn, *"I had Corn parched to make parched meal."* [J2:181] What, exactly, are they doing? Parching, and parched meal, are not common references today. Michael Caduto, in *Native American Gardening,* writes, "Parching corn softens and dries out the starches and gluten, making corn easier to digest. ... 1. Put dried corn meal or kernels in a dry fry pan over low to medium heat. Do not use oil. ... 2. Stir the meal or kernels until they are lightly browned."[37]

The bane of any air-dried product is wetness, which will reactivate slumbering compounds and once again begin the process of disintegration and spoilage. The only acceptable water is that which is purposely added as part of cooking. On May 14, 1804 Clark is poking around and re-estimating his quantity of provisions, but what really counts is his entry later that day: *"Some provisions on examination is found to be wet ..."* [J2:215] From this last entry in May when they are *"fixing for a Start"* until the last weeks of their return, regular and religious drying of wet provisions occurs. The Captains *never* allow wet provisions to remain in that state, even to the detriment of their timetable.

Sugar Preserving

A last form of food preservation, which the Captains probably encounter during their winter social visits in St. Louis, is sugar-preserving. It is used for fruits, fruit compotes, jams, and jellies. Lewis, during his time in town and around, keeps

---

[f] Lest we think this form of oil-preservation is extinct, the Lebanese still use this fat-preserving process with previously cooked lamb tails (they are quite meaty and are not docked or shortened as they are in the U.S.). British "potted shrimp," using butter as the oil, is another example.

his botanist's eyes open for plants and especially foodstuffs – apples, three types of cherries, both wild and cultivated gooseberries, and peaches. Since all of these are prized edibles and cane sugar comes upriver from New Orleans, apple butters, peach and gooseberry jam, and cherry compotes might easily grace local tables. These fruity luxuries certainly would not be inconsistent or unexpected considering the prosperity of the families like the Chouteaus or the Robidouxs. After all, Army Captain Amos Stoddard declares the residents to be living "in a style equal to those in the large sea-port towns."[38]

How to make these luscious sweet fruits stay that way? Harold McGee explains the intricacy of sugar and living organisms. "Another ancient technique for making plant foods, especially fruits, resistant to spoilage is to boost their sugar content to the point where microorganisms will be dehydrated by the osmotic pressure across their membranes ... and will be incapacitated or killed."[39] Thus, the food – fruit in this case – is preserved. A wax cap might be poured on top (anaerobic sealing), and voila! Impeccable fruit preserves.

Virginia or St. Louis – Preserving is the Same

Whether Lewis and Clark travel for over two years across the continent or stay home in settled Virginia or Kentucky, the food preservation techniques they use in daily life would not have been significantly different, simply better controlled. America at the turn of the nineteenth century is still using ancient methods for assuring safe and portable food supplies. The most common techniques are air-drying and/or smoking. Reduction and drying is a variation of this principle. Fat-preserving evolved along a different path but is also a minimal-cost method. Salting, brining, and sugar curing are commonly known techniques. Only after the 1830s, when canning factories become significant, will commercially preserved foods begin to change the old ways of "safely preserved and stored" and begin to offer a serious alternative on a regional, then national, scale.

As the men of the Corps hunt and eat their way across the West, they experience what the natives already know, the fullness of the American pantry in its primal glory. Thank goodness Napoleon's dream had not progressed far enough for Lewis to stock the Expedition with canned chicken soup or tuna in a tin.

From Musca Wine Pressing and Supplies, Ltd., Ottawa, Ontario, Canada

Barrels of various sizes were the Corps' most common container – these varied from the two-gallon (20 lb.) salt kegs to the five-gallon whiskey keg to the approximately ten-gallon "half-barrels" for flour and corn.

Pre-plastic Packing

An Outdoorsman's Nightmare

*... in attending to the security of my goods I was exposed to the rain
and got wet to the skin as I remained untill about twelve at night ...*

— LEWIS, SEPTEMBER 9, 1803

HOW TO PACK? In the days before self-locking plastic baggies, vacuum-sealing, and other advanced packing, one of the big problems was how to keep food and equipment dry. Lewis knows the fecund wet forests and rivers of the East but has no idea what will greet him as they travel to the Pacific Coast. All he knows is that they will be in boats on the water, and precautions must be made to ensure the safety of his goods.

What dictates the way they pack?

Which items go into what type of container? Imagine the riverbank piled high with gear, men standing around, arms crossed, waiting for orders. What comes first? The sergeants have already issued the men their own cups and spoons, items for which each of them is responsible and which are already being used on a daily basis. Each mess is responsible for its kettle, pots, cooking spoons, and the metal roasting spit. These will be used regularly. Clark and the Army's commissary agents are supervising the tons of food to be stowed after pre-packing and wrapping in 1800s style. The prevailing attitude runs: If something gets wet, learn from your mistake. This idea does not, however, stop the Captains from lamenting the damages ... and the *Journals* resound with these.

Four factors dictate the Captains' choices of packing materials:

✦ The need for easy access and portability.
✦ The ability to withstand crashing blows or dropping.
✦ The nature of the items being packed.
✦ Containment rather than waterproofing.

Easy access to frequently used items and the desire to carry lighter loads rather than heavier ones account for many of the packing decisions. The Captains' delicate instruments need to be tucked into a pocket, kept waterproof, and ready for use many times a day. Very easy. Do the men need to get at those cooking spoons on a daily basis? Yes. The mess cooks pack them in a small bundle that can be easily tucked into a boat or canoe and pulled out at mealtime. Bags of grain can be picked up and thrown over a man's shoulder. Goods wrapped in oilskin or an elk or buffalo hide can be folded into a large packet – portable, although the bundle would be bulky and awkward.

Do the men need to get into those heavy barrels (80-90 pounds) of pork each day? No. Then leave them onboard and tied down. How about the evening ration of grog? A small keg can be tossed ashore quite easily. Daily versus infrequent use is one consideration, weight another.

Breakability versus durability dictates packing to withstand hard knocks. Drop a sack of corn and the grains will shift and separate, and usually no damage is done. However, drop a bag of corked medicine bottles and the results will be far different. Metal canisters are used not so much for extreme strength, but because they can be sealed with wax, insuring waterproofing. For strength there are heavy, rigid wooden kegs and barrels bound with durable iron hoops; they provide maximum exterior protection.

The nature of the contents destined for the containers invariably plays a huge part in the packing decision. Anything liquid has to be carried in a keg or barrel.

15

Anything loose that can blow away in a flash (like flour) also goes into barrels; it is more easily confined that way. Corn kernels are heavy enough not to be whisked away unless the wind is blowing up a storm, and can be stored in either bags or sacks, tucked into barrels, or both. Cook pots are durable and waterproof but need to be secured from washing away in case of capsizing or the canoe being swamped.

Nature's Water Hazards

Water is a fascinating topic, and throughout the trip the journalists write continuously of it – usually with annoyance, often with trepidation, sometimes in robust and healthy fear. Water: it is essential – without it, there is no "roadway." But, the current drags the boats over snags[a] nearly ripping holes in them; undercut banks collapse under the coercion of water and threaten to capsize; rain in unimaginable quantities nearly sweeps them away. Even the start of the Expedition is wet – while on the Ohio with rain coming down *"in such torrents that I found it necessary to have them bailed out [the pirogue and canoe] freequently in the course of the night; in attending to the security of my goods I was exposed to the rain and got wet to the skin as I remained untill about twelve at night."* [J2:76] Cruzatte and his men run waterfalls the natives deem unpassable, water rots their provisions, precious gunpowder is ruined. This love/hate relationship with water dominates the text as does the awe of extreme weather, usually some manifestation of water on yet a grander scale. Water, then, is both essential and the enemy. And waterproofing is one ultimate overriding consideration in staying alive. Two different types of water hazards exist; both must be protected against:

- The power of water to carry unsecured items away.
- Moisture getting into/onto items which causes rot or rust.

So, what storage containers are used on the trip? Jefferson, the avid wine collector, would have thought of glass and cork immediately and, in fact, small corked bottles are used in the Captains' pharmaceutical kit. But glass is not appropriate and too fragile for river running. George Rogers Clark is decanting his whiskey from a keg – even hard liquor isn't sold in bottles. Lewis is quite clear about what he wants, his storage needs appearing in his List of Requirements.[L1:69-75] Many of these storage items are acquired in the bustling city of Philadelphia as a precaution; Lewis doesn't know exactly what is available out West. Still, the majority of the barrels and kegs do come from St. Louis.

---

[a] Called sawyers because they appear to saw up and down in the river. Tom Sawyer – a later river rat – was named for these snags.

> ## FOUR TYPES OF WATERPROOFING
>
> <u>Two types of soft wraps or tarps:</u>
> - Oilcloth wraps and bags
> - Animal products – skins and internal membranes, such as bladders
>
> <u>Two types of hard containers:</u>
> - Wooden containers: barrels, kegs, casks, trunks, and boxes
> - Metal canisters

Oilcloth

Oilcloth is their all-purpose waterproof fabric and has myriad uses.[b] Lewis specifies *"20 yds. Oil linnen for wrapping and securing Articles,"* *"10 yds [Oil Linnen] of thicker quantity for covering and lining boxes. &c."* [L1:71] His list also specifies: *"15 Oil Cloth Bags for securing provision."* [L1:72]

Lewis' request for such heavy-duty fabric falls into the realm of upholstery, and on June 15, 1803, Richard Wevill presents his bill for fabrics, tents and their manufacture, *"Oiling all the Linen & Sheeting – 150 Square Yards @2/6"* for which he charges $52. [L1:90]

No sooner have they left Pittsburgh than Lewis is forced into buying a canoe, two paddles, and two poles for $11 to lighten the load in the pirogue, which is leaking badly and *"had nearly filled."* Lewis stops to dry everything. Then he continues with a grateful statement, writing, *"the articles were not as much injured as I had supposed."* [J2:71] So, is the oilcloth treatment effective? Yes and no. The *Journals* record, *"the stores in the canoes being well secured with oil cloth I concluded to let them remain on board and directed that the water which they maid should be bailed out of them occasionally throught the night, which was done – they still leaked considerably notwithstanding the repairs which I had made on them ..."* [J2:72] The oilskin covering is considered adequate despite their leaky canoe. However, *"had the articles well oiled and*

---

[b] Oilcloth, according to *The Encyclopedia of Textiles*, page 568, is "material which is treated with linseed-oil varnish to give a patent leather effect." The professional formula for oilcloth gives details about boiling the oil. It is heated to 375°F and then the pigment is added. "The heating continues until the temperature reaches 525°F and held at this temperature for nine hours or until the oil reaches the proper viscosity. It is then allowed to cool overnight to about 250°C [480°F] and is ... thinned to coating consistency."[40] Oilcloth manufacture is both time consuming and demanding of a certain amount of skill.

put up in oilcloth baggs and returned to the casks in which they were previously were." The ever-cautious Captain is double-protecting his gear, first in oilcloth – which can leak – and then stowing it in a barrel which should be almost impervious to water damage. If anything, his goods would potentially float away and be lost forever before they would be ruined.

Bagging It

Lewis is paying meticulous attention to detail, for the upholsterer is instructed to number all the bags and tents. To his logical mind, no time is to be wasted guessing where to put an item; each has its proper bag and each bag its proper place. But the bags themselves are not just for storage; they are also for carrying.

On June 1, 1806, there is a shopping catastrophe, both on the part of the Corps and the natives who are anxious to deal. Charbonneau and Lepage are out when their horse, laden with merchandise, falls into the river carrying all their valuables on its back. It is swimming for the other shore, anxious for land, when the white men signal a native to shoo it back. He is a cooperative sort and hustles the horse back across the river, but everything is lost; no trade goods survive despite drying. *"the indians at the village learning of their errand and not having a canoe, made an attempt esterday morning to pass the river to them on a raft with a parsel of roots and bread in order to trade with them; the indian raft struck a rock, upset and lost thir cargo; the river haven fallen heir to both merchandize and roots, our traders returned home with empty bags."* J7:322

A few days later, on June 7, there is another reference to bags as the Indians and a few corpsmen are trading native ropes for little odds and ends the Corps finds dispensable. But rope isn't the only objective, *"they were also directed to procure some bags for the purpose of containing our roots & bread."* J7:343 The bags mentioned are native crafted and quite useful, but Lewis is disappointed and unhappily reports, *"they procured a few strings but no bags."* J7:344

Animal Products

For animal products the Captain is even more specific than he was with the oilcloth. He wants and specifically designs a quality backpack for his troops.

> *Materials for making up the Various Articles into portable Packs*
> *30 Sheep skins taken off the Animal as perfectly whole as possible without being split on the belly as usual and dress'd only with lime to free them from the wool;*

> *or otherwise about the same quantity of Oil Cloth bags well painted*
> *Raw Hide for pack strings*
> *Dress'd letter [leather] for Hoppus Straps*
> *["hoppas" has been identified as an Indian term for knapsack.]* L1:74-75

The ability of sheepskin to endure is one of nature's little miracles, as is seen from medieval manuscripts written on vellum.[c] The skin is tough, waterproof, and is an admirable product for a water-shedding backpack.

With customary frugality and inventiveness, early farmers found another benefit in the animals they raised: the use of the bladder as a container. It is perfect in many respects: watertight, thin, flexible, and as a nonpermeable membrane it can hold water in or hold water out. In his March 6, 1803, letter to Jefferson, the astronomer and surveyor Andrew Ellicott writes a small dissertation on the topic, and concludes, "It will be a necessary precaution to have the Chronometer, with its case, tied up in a bladder when not in use,– it will privent its being injured if by accident [if] it should be thrown in the water by the overturning of a canoe ..." L1:25 Obviously a bladder would not be an appropriate storage bag for large items or even food, but it is deemed superior for small valuables.

But the bladder is not the only membrane used. For a one-meal duration, Charbonneau uses the "gut" as a technically and mechanically good means of holding diced sausage meat together while cooking.

Metal Canisters

For durable packing, metal canisters are preferable. Not only do materials such as gunpowder need to be kept absolutely protected from moisture, but so also do some of the food-stuffs – for example, tea and the portable soup.

Both tin and lead canisters are manufactured specifically for the Expedition. Lead is destined only to hold gunpowder. When the contents are used up, the entire container is melted down to make shot. This process keeps the two Expedition blacksmiths busy melting lead into appropriately sized ammunition.

The *Camp Equipage* document written in Lewis' fine hand[41] notes that tin canisters are destined to hold the portable soup. Thomas Passmore of Philadelphia manufactured the tinware and his bill of May 19, 1803, charges 25 cents each for 32 canisters, for a grand total of $8.00. L1:79

There has been some notion among Lewis and Clark

---

[c] Vellum is the processed skin membrane of a sheep, separated from the wool.

Lewis uses lead canisters like the one picture here as gunpowder containers – when empty, the containers are melted into shot.

Courtesy: R.G. Montgomery

research writings that lead canisters were used for the portable soup, and this brings up the unhealthy prospect of lead poisoning. The studied use of tin by Lewis reflects a sharp recognition by the Colonials that lead poisoning, a leading cause of "dry bellyache,"[42] is caused by the proximity of food or drink to lead. As a curious teenager Benjamin Franklin had heard the diatribes against lead in liquor stills and knew of the first anti-lead legislation in the New World by the Massachusetts Bay Colony in 1723, forbidding "leaden heads or worms" in liquor manufacture.[43] From his scientific tutelage in Philadelphia, Lewis most certainly understood the risks of lead.

The use of metal containers turns out to be critical. On one disastrous day, August 6, 1805, a canoe overturns and the medicine box, rifle ammunition, and other articles are lost; Private Whitehouse barely escapes being ground to death between the canoe and the bottom of the river. Lewis rejoices that his man is still alive, but says, *"to examine, dry and arrange our stores was the first object ..."* He describes the circumstances: *"a part of the load of each canoe consisted of the leaden canestirs of powder which were not in least injured, tho' some of them had remained upwards of an hour under water."* By comparison, other powder *"which we had in a tight Keg or at l[e]ast one which we thought so got wet and intirely spoiled."* This is bad news for wooden keg security. Continuing, he offers a suggestion as to why this unhappy event has not turned to total catastrophe, *"this would have been the case with the other had it not have been for the expedient which I had fallen on of securing the powder by means of the lead hav-*

ing the latter formed into canesters which were ... well secured with corks and wax." [J5:53]

On October 14, 1805, Drouillard's canoe strikes a rock and everyone is pitched overboard. The canoe sinks. The entire party scrambles to save whatever they can, from the sunken canoe being dragged along by the current to articles floating by. It is a grievous loss, but *"fortunately the lead canisters which was in the canoe was tied down, otherwise they must have been lost as the Canoe turned over ..."* [J5:271] Nonetheless, the results are not totally satisfactory, *"our loose powder was also in the Canoe and is all wett ..."* [J5:272]

The added precautions of corking, sealing with wax, double wrapping, and tying everything down can be compared to adding suspenders to your belted pants, and perhaps adding some twine through the belt loops, too. When traveling wild and rocky rivers, it is definitely worth the time and effort involved.

Wood Goods

Kegs and barrels are normally made by the village cooper, a strong, muscular guy who cuts wood into staves, steams them, and then bends the pliable wood into softly curved, uniformly sized ribs that are shaped into a barrel. The barrel staves are held in place by circular rings around the outside of the container, and finished at both ends with a round, wooden, flat disk set into a notch around the inside of the end of the staves. The rings may be bent wood, wire, or for added strength, riveted metal hoops.

Lewis doesn't need to know the specifications for the cooper's ware.[d] He simply orders *"6 Kegs of 5 Gallons each ..."* and additionally *"6 Kegs bound with iron Hoops"* [L1:72] To simplify the idea of what each type of container can hold, it is easiest to assume the following:

◆ A barrel holds 160 lbs.
◆ A half-barrel holds 80 lbs.
◆ The kegs noted above hold 5 gallons, which is about 40 lbs.

---

[d] Today, we are unfamiliar with the size of barrels, so it is useful to illustrate by measuring the inside dimensions and then convert them to volume, or possible weight of the food contained.[44]

Consider, for example, the formula for a keg or barrel – the interior volume (cubic inches) for barrel or keg:

$V = .262 \times H \times (2 \times D^2 + d^2)$ where;

V=volume, H=height, D=diameter at widest width, and d=diameter of narrowest width.

Lewis' whiskey kegs 15" x 12" (diameter) with likely inside measurements of 13" long by diameters of 9"-11":

$V = .262 \times 14 \times (2 \times 11^2 + 9^2) = 1100$ cu.in. [about 5.0 gal.]

Think 5 gallons of milk; or a 5-gallon paint bucket.

There are frustrations however. Lewis makes the assumption that needed barrels and kegs can be bought when they arrive at St. Louis and is caught short. He will later rue this, writing Clark under the shadow of imminent departure, *"Not a kegg can be obtained in St. Louis nor are they to be expected from Mr. Contractor, we must therefore do the best we can."* L1:180

Back on the riverbank at Camp River Dubois in 1804, the Captains have tons of goods to be loaded onto the keelboat. Imagine loading barrels and barrels of pork with their added weight of wood and iron. Heave aboard bulging bags of Indian trade goods. Groan under the heavy weight of corn and know that all of this is packed or double packed for safety.

Are there failures? Yes. From start to finish, the techniques aren't perfect by any means, and while some containers are watertight, others aren't. But the Corps has the best pre-plastic packing available. Early in the Expedition, storage is not going well. On September 17, 1803, the keelboat pilot informs Lewis of an upcoming bright and sunny day and the commander resolves to *"open & dry my goods which I had found were wet by the rain on the 15th ..."*

Nor does the Corps ever get it quite right; the water is always a greater force. Equally dismal days occur on a regular basis throughout the entire trip. Nothing is sacrosanct from the ravages of water. Consider this report:

> *... found on opening the goods that many of the articles were much Injured; particularly the articles of iron, which wer rusted very much my guns, tomehawks, & knives were of this class; I caused them to be oiled and exposed to the sun ...* J2:83

Hunting, skinning, and the vital task of butchering and cutting food all depend on these tools. To the Corps, everything is necessary to the primary task of survival. Drying takes all day, and after that Lewis writes, *"all the articles that would admitt of that mode of packing to be put in baggs of oil-cloth which I had provided for that purpose and again returned to their severale casks, trunks, and boxes ..."* J2:84

Canoe drenchings and sinkings are not the only catastrophes. Foods and supplies loaded on horseback are no more reliably safe when it comes to the issue of waterproofing. The very careful Clark gets caught on July 5, 1806, trying to find a safe place to ford the West Fork of Clark's River. Young Shannon finds a good spot to cross and most of the party makes it across in fine fashion. However, their senior officer reports, *"the water running over the back of the 2 Smaller horses only. unfortunately my trunk & portmantue ... got wet, also an esortment of Medicine, and my roots."* What

Various sizes and styles of barrels available today.

they have is something a little more than bare necessity; Clark is carrying a whole trunk (loaded with souvenirs, as it turns out) and his personal insurance against starvation: roots. Doing what is always done, they stop to dry the wet goods.

By the end of the trip, everyone is much the wiser. On July 24, 1806, on the Yellowstone, Clark takes a risk and *"had all our baggage put on board the two Small Canoes which when lashed together is very Stu[r]dy ..."* The canoes are forever taking on water; loaded with eight adults and a baby, the freeboard is less than desirable. This makeshift raft is quite susceptible to taking a drubbing; indeed, shortly thereafter they arrive at a good size riffle where, *"the Small Canoes took in a good deel of water which obliged us to land a little above the enterance of this river ... to dry our articles and bail the Canoes."* Not wanting to repeat the process over and over, ingenious Clark resorts to a new trick: *"I also had a Buffalow Skin tacked on So as to prevent the waters flacking in between the Two canoes."* J8:217 These two canoes that Clark tied together carry Shields, Gibson, Bratton, Labiche, Charbonneau, Sacagawea, baby Pomp, York, and the Captain down 2400 miles on the Yellowstone River and then the Missouri to where the canoes are abandoned only two days before the Corps reaches St. Louis.

If water is the enemy, then the diligence of the Corps and the effiency of their storage methods are worthy opponents. Despite losses from items washed away, or rotting from an inability to dry promptly, these honorable oilcloths, bags, barrels, bladders, and metal canisters are sturdy solutions to one of nature's most vexing problems.

Michael Haynes

Army garrison life circa 1803 involved a boring routine of fatigue duties, drills, strict discipline, and a monotonous diet.

Army Messes

... provision for one day will be issued to the party on each evening after we have encamped; the same will be cooked on that evening by the several messes ...

— LEWIS, MAY 26, 1804

WHEN BOSTONIANS THREW THEIR TEA PARTY in 1775, there was no army – only militia from the individual colonies, long on privates, short on officers. Later, when there were thousands of troops to be fed, the overwhelmed General Washington literally *begged* for provisions. To ensure that food – so necessary for fighting and surviving – was distributed fairly, a sergeant was appointed to command a number of messes[a] and issue orders through these messes. Psychologically, the most poignant aspect is that men who eat together will look out for each other in battle, and afterwards – such is the bonding.

Traveling without a Mess

By Jefferson's presidency, the United States Army was institutionalized and structured. Lewis and Clark were both military men, savvy to the ins and outs of all the regulations, procurement procedures, and commands. In 1803, when the eastern journey begins, Clark is out west, and as yet has no men to command.

Lewis has only seven army privates ("transfers" who are assisting in bringing the keelboat down while they themselves are on their way to another posting), one river captain, and "three young men on trial."[45] There is no need for a formal mess structure. As they travel down the Ohio, Capt. Lewis eats or visits with the "establishment" in the little villages while his men head straight for the tavern. The normal distinction between enlisted men and officers is clear.

In October, 1803, just outside of Clarksville, Kentucky, the little cadre meets up with Clark and the recruits he has gathered.[b] There is still no organization – they are basically just getting by and getting on to St. Louis. After establishing camp at River Dubois, more men continue to arrive, including Drouillard with eight Army transfers, and organization becomes imperative.

The Mess at Wood River Camp

By January 4, 1804, a mess order is in place. Before Lewis and Clark go to a ball in St. Louis, on February 20, 1804, they issue a *Detachment Order* placing the Corps under the supervision of Sergeant Ordway. Sergeant Floyd is appointed quartermaster, responsible for both provisions and liquor: *"Floyd will take charge of our quarte[r]s and store and be exempt from guard duty untill our return, the commanding Officer hopes that this proof of his confidence will be justified by the rigid performance of the orders given him on that subject."*

Since food is not particularly important yet, the only touchy subject is alcohol – doling it out to the troops. Ten days later, the *Detachment Orders* issued on March 3, 1804, are a stunning review of every bit of malfeasance that rowdy, disrespectful, undisciplined young bucks can pull off:

- ✦ Disobeying orders of February 20, as left by the Captains, read before they left.
- ✦ Refusal to mount guard.
- ✦ Refusal to accept commands from the duly appointed Sgt. Ordway.
- ✦ Inciting *"disorder and faction."*
- ✦ Visiting the local whiskey shop.

---

[a] A *mess* was the smallest organizational Army unit – typically 6 men who prepared food, ate, and worked together. Two messes normally formed a squad of 12 men, lead by a sergeant. Squads were sub-units of a Company: 48 men in Washington's time and 60-80 men by 1803.

[b] These nine are often referenced as the "Nine Young Men from Kentucky."

Surprisingly, their punishment is relatively mild compared to what will come in the spring as they travel up the Missouri. For now the Captains are being lenient with the men they hope to have with them, despite their obnoxious behavior. The offenders are confined to camp for ten days. Ordway is re-confirmed as commander when the Captains are absent.

Organizing The Messes

As spring arrives and the Corps is readying itself for the up-river trip, Clark draws up a Detachment Order on April 1, 1804, dividing the men into squads that are further divided into two messes each. Sergeant Ordway continues to be in charge of the duty roster.

Squad 1	8 men	*Sgt. Nathaniel Pryor*
Squad 2	9 men	*Sgt. Charles Floyd*
Squad 3	9 men	*Sgt. John Ordway*

"Sergeants, with equal Power (unless when otherwise specially ordered)."

In each squad the first mess will have four privates, with the remaining men in a second mess. Since two of the three squads (numbers 2 and 3) have nine men, the second mess has one additional mouth to feed. To keep each mess self-sufficient, the best hunters are evenly divided between the messes. Clark's slave, York, has no military role and as a slave his orders are to serve his master's wishes – he is associated with the mess composed of the Captains and inter-preters (Drouillard and later the Charbonneau family). In all, it must be a relief to Clark, who the next day happily notes, *"all mess arranged."*

After Parade, the sergeants are ordered to take the cook-ing gear, *"Camp Kittles and other Public utensels,"* and divide

A tin cup and a spoon are the only utensils.

Courtesy: R.G. Montgomery

them up among the men. This includes the nests of pots, spits on which to roast meat, axes for chopping firewood.

Mundane dispersals continue. On April 6, 1804, Clark be-gins equipping his men with the necessary supplies: *"give out Knives Tomahawkes &c. &c. to the men ..."* Even after they have set out up the Missouri, Clark is still doling out the goods, *"Gave out tin Cups & 3 Knives to the French hands ..."* [J2:237]

Bonding of the Messes

By May 26, Lewis is tinkering with the mess structure and orders that the six small groups be re-amalgamated into three groups, each under their own original sergeant. These three messes man the keelboat, a "bonding" sort of exercise for the permanent party.

The French engagés (hired on just for the first summer up the Missouri to the Mandans), rowing and keeping time with their oars to the songs they are singing, form their own mess. They become the permanent crew for the red pirogue. Corporal Warfington – who will return the keelboat to St. Louis – now has a mess under his command, the non-per-manent men manning the white pirogue. Lewis has beefed up the number of men to forty-five. This expanded Corps has two separate functions: a larger presence in the face of dread-ed Teton Sioux they will be passing upriver, and helping haul provisions that won't fit into the nearly overloaded keelboat.

The Duty Roster

Not only are the keelboat sergeants in charge of their mess-es, they personally have important navigational duties on-board. Two almost incidental duties relate to the messes. The Sergeant-at-the-Helm is responsible for steering and *"seeing that no cooking utensels"* are left on deck, nor is baggage to be left in disorder. The Sergeant-at-the-Center has, as one of his duties, that *"he will attend to the issues of sperituous liquors; he shall regulate the halting of the batteaux through the day to give the men refreshment ..."*

Since the sergeants are responsible for so much of the Expedition's safety and ongoing progress during the day, at night they *"are relieved and exempt from all labour of making fires, pitching tents or cooking, and will direct and make the men of their several messes perform an equal propotion of those duties."* [J2:258] As if their jobs during the day onboard the ves-sels are not enough, they are not finished at night. They must write, for they are charged with journal-keeping, which is one of the most tedious and demanding jobs of the entire Expedi-tion. (Some of this pain is alleviated by copying.)

The French chief of the engagés, patroon Jean Baptiste Deschamps, who will later return from the Mandan country to St. Louis with the keelboat, is charged with the proper loading of the pirogues during the trip up the Missouri and seeing to it that the goods are "kept perfectly free from rain or other moisture ..." For food products, rifles, and powder, this is a particularly sensitive issue.

Feeding the Messes

Finally, Lewis spells out the food orders: *"provision for one day will be issued to the party on each evening after we have encamped; the same will be cooked on that evening by the several messes, and a proportion of it reserved for the next day as no cooking will be allowed in the day while on the ma[r]ch ..."* This is a definite instruction, but also one subject to change. As the Corps moves along during the trip, other more appropriate feeding schedules evolve. Hunters away from the Corps eat when hungry and save game for those coming along. As winter arrives, hot cooked breakfasts are the order of the day, and other mealtimes are adjusted.

Rations Issued

When the Revolutionary War ration was established by Congress on November 4, 1775, "the soldier was issued his ration uncooked each day – Later to be prepared by himself over the glowing ember of the campfire." A U.S. Army file on supplies details the rations allocated (for one man, one day), beginning in the exceptionally cold winter of 1775.[46]

1 lb.	Beef
1 lb.	Flour
7 oz.	Peas
2 C.	Milk
1 oz.	Rice
1 qt.	Spruce Beer

By 1800–1810 a daily ration looked like this:

1¼ lbs.	Beef or ¾ lbs. of Pork
18 oz.	Bread

a gill (½ C.) of Spirits: rum, whiskey, or brandy

Other dried products, such as cornmeal and beans, are supplements. Lard could be added. Beverages are tea or coffee. Other food issues per hundred rations include a gallon of vinegar to prevent scurvy[c] and two quarts of salt.[47]

In comparison to the rations cited above, the Corps has no access to milk – that particular item goes by the wayside when they move out of dairying country. Nor do they carry rice, primarily a Southern product – local corn is the substitute mainstay. They carry a small quantity of beans as well as a large quantity of flour, but in the end the overwhelming bulk of their diet is protein from game. Grog or whiskey is doled out by the Sergeant-at-the-Center at the Captain's command, and the messes adhere to the standard army unit of a gill of spirits per man per day.[d] Finally, Lewis defines the rotation of meals:

> Day 1: *lyed corn and greece*
> Day 2: *Poark and flour*
> Day 3: *indian meal and poark*
> *and in conformity to that ratiene provisions will continue to be issued to the party untill further orders.— should any of the messes prefer indian meal to flour they may recieve it accordingly — no poark is to be issued when we have fresh meat on hand.—* J2:258

Hewing the Line

It pays to look at common military practice of the day to see how closely the Captains are hewing the line. As seen above, Lewis plans on stopping for the evening and cooking dinner at the end of the day. Under the General Orders for Fort Wayne, Indiana (1802)[48] the commissary issues food at 9 AM and the cooks serve it as the midday meal at 1 PM. This pattern allows for a considerable intake of fuel which will sustain the troops throughout the remainder of the day. Lewis' idea of eating is to keep the Expedition moving and minimize travel disruption. A mid-day stop does allow re-heating food cooked the evening before.

A more significant point of departure is the Army ruling which frowns upon, even forbids, hunting even when food is short.[49] Most commanders apparently preferred not having their armed soldiers shooting through neighborhood forests, something not quite in keeping with tight military discipline and regimentation. This is ignored by the Captains who want their men to hunt. Clark is continually sending two or three men out to bring back meat.

Functioning of the Mess

The purpose of the mess, then, is to provide enough hands to make feeding the group as simple a process as possible, and to promote bonding among the men. In explicitly spelling out the functions of the mess, the Captains issue a joint statement on July 8, 1804.

> *In order to insure a prudent and regular use of all provisions issued to the crew of the Batteaux in future, as also to provide for the equal distribution of the same among*

---

[c] Scurvy is discussed further in *Nutritional Maladies*, page 55.

[d] A gill, pronounced *jill*, is a historic liquor measure and is ¼ pint = ½ cup = 4 ounces. See also "Liquor" in *Beverages*, page 246.

the individuals of the several messes, The Commanding Officers Do appoint the following persons to receive, cook, and take charges of the provisions which may from time to time be issued to their respective messes ...

The Captains then name Thompson as cook for Floyd's mess, Werner for Ordway's mess, and Collins for Pryor's mess. These cooks are to insure,

judicious consumption of the provision which they receive; they are to cook the same for their several messes in due time, and in such a manner as it is most wholesome and best calculated to afford the greatest proportion of nutriment ...

Finally, they are to decide what proportion of food is to be eaten at each meal and to be responsible for all the cooking equipment. The cooks are then explicitly exempted from any further duties around camp, *"those duties are to be ... performed by other members of the mess."*

Water has to be drawn at the river or a stream and hauled

Cooking fire and stew kettle.

up to wash with and to cook with – even if it isn't very tasty. Fuel must be cut or gathered. The hunters are doing their job bringing in the meat. And what do the mess cooks do? It is hot, dirty work cooking over a campfire, especially if ashes and coals are being blown by the winds. After the raw rations are doled out – or the meat brought in – cooking commences. With the fire set and glowing, a kettle of water ready, the pot of pork 'n' mush or fresh meat and flour stew is put on to boil. If it's cornmeal mush, it has to be stirred continually so it doesn't lump up or burn. The adjacent recipe is a close approximation for the Army ration of Indian meal and pork.

Not all cooks are the same, and unhappy eaters complain. Thompson, one of the original cooks, fails to impress and his mess deploys him to other duties, selecting Weiser as their new chef. [J2:427] Charbonneau, the translator who joined the Expedition at the Hidatsa villages, is esteemed for his boudin blanc and the men willingly slice and dice for him. Even the mess composition changes as need be. On August 28, 1804, the Captains apparently realize that they have not covered the crews in either pirogue, and direct that each group elect a cook. They have the same duties and exemptions as the previously appointed *chefs-du-pot.*

What Time's Dinner?
Or Breakfast, for that matter?

Lewis' orders specify three meals a day: breakfast, dinner, and supper. Breakfast time varies depending on the weather. If it's fine weather, the Corps starts out soon after dawn and stops around 8 or 9 AM to eat; Lewis actually specifies *"8 A.M. our usual time of halting"* during summer hours. [J5:61]

PORK AND CORNMEAL STEW[e]

6 oz.   salt pork, cut approximately ½" x ½" x 1"

4 T.   bear fat – (or pork fat or oil)

⅓   onion, chopped

1 C.   coarsely ground cornmeal

4-5 C. water

1 tsp. dried sage

De-rind salt pork and slice. Heat fat in kettle. Add meat, and stir on moderate heat until lightly browned, then add onions and continue to saute. As these cook, make a cornmeal/water slurry (1:1) and add to the pot after the onion turns translucent. Add 3 cups of water, then add sage, stirring until smooth. Cook for approximately 15 minutes, adding more water if necessary. Stir regularly, every 2-3 minutes. Serve in a tin cup. Serves 6

---

[e] This recipe results from many trials, adjusted until it looks like what the Corps' army stew in 1805 might have been. The ingredients are authentic except for cultivated onions substituting for wild ones. This is one of the Bicentennial favorites and is very easy to cook. One caution is to use a stone-ground cornmeal – the difference between old stone-ground texture and current homogenized texture is what really makes the difference. Although it can be a supper dish, it makes a favorable breakfast, especially if topped with an egg.

If it's cold, the Captains may delay departure. On May 3, 1805, *"the morning being very could we did not set out as early as usual; ice formed on a kettle of water 1/4" thick."* An early breakfast is a psychological soother; hungry people tend to snap and snarl when under duress.

Later in August, 1805, when the troops are near the end of their rope (literally and figuratively as they pull the dugouts upstream), Clark again changes the breakfast rule and feeds his men before they start working. The *Journal* entry for the August 11 reads, *"This morning Capt Clark dispatched several hunters a head; the morning being rainy and wet did not set out untill after an early breakfast."*

For the main dinner, Lewis says they halt and dine at about noon, *"our usual time of halting for that purpose."* [J4:102-3] This is consistent with military custom of the day, which has a two-three hour dinner break somewhere between noon and 2 PM to cook and eat. Cooking fires are generally made only at this dinner meal, and for reheating mid-morning breakfast leftovers cooked earlier. In particular, fires were to be avoided in the still air of early morning in Indian territory as the smoke would rise un-diffused and could be seen for miles.

Finally, supper is eaten in the evening. It is often a leftover meal, but it may have been cooked when the Corps halted for several days, as at the Great Falls portage. It is also a "hospitality" meal when native visitors arrive.

Guess Who's Coming to Dinner?

Most military men take eating as a fueling operation rather than a dinner party. The Corps' messes are often short a member or two who are out hunting. Sometimes the hunters are out for days, and the mess has to rely on provisions or what other hunters bring back, and wonder what's become of their comrades. The hunters, meanwhile, cook for themselves and bring back what they can.

During their stay near the Mandan villages in the winter of 1804–05, hunting parties come and go, often taking half the men out at one time. The same holds true during the winter at Fort Clatsop, 1805–06, as the men fan out in their search for game. After re-crossing the Rockies and returning to Montana in June, 1806, the Corps splits up and the several smaller parties become less structured with everyone assuming the role of a "generalist."

Finally, from a social standpoint, several native families might drop by and be invited to dinner. Or, consider what happens when an entire village of Lemhi Shoshone needs feeding. The number of mouths to be fed might be just half the party (16 or so), all of the party (32) plus a village, or just Lewis sitting by himself at camp waiting for the portage party. So when it comes to planning, "Guess who's coming to dinner?" is always a great question to ask. And the answer might well be ... guess!

R. L. Rickards - courtesy: Rickards Western Art

"Lining a canoe" is the process of raising or lowering a canoe through rapids with ropes – a very exhausting and dangerous process.

Nutrition in Extreme Environments

Under certain conditions, such as work performed in extreme environments, the physical demands of performing military duties approach, or may even exceed the physical demands of training that endurance athletes experience.

— UNITED STATES ARMY

FEEDING HUNGRY MEN IS REWARDED by seeing them continue, alive and well, to the next day, the next round of life.[a] These basic needs are then pushed to their limits by extreme environments.

Three different climates and terrains are considered here as extreme: hot, cold, and high mountain elevations. Hot climates for the Corps include the muggy, humid areas along the Missouri and the hot, dry climes of the West. Freezing-cold occurs in the northern climatic zones and up in the mountains. Going to altitude is a stress because the Corps is going up and down mountains, and their bodies must make more serious adjustments than if, for instance, they were based in a mountainous region and had become adapted. In order to assess the Corps' nutritional needs in stress situations, a contemporary Army manual, *Nutritional Guidance for Military Operations in Temperate and Extreme Environments*, is compared for reference.[b]

Heat

Heat is a factor that cannot be avoided. Clark writes on June 30, 1804, *"rested three hours, the* [sun or day?] *being hot the men become verry feeble."* Again, *"the men were verry much overpowered with the heat."* [J2:338] The major solution to heat stress is to stop and rest, and have plenty to drink. Because they are on the water most of the time, this need rather nat-

urally takes care of itself. But not all the time. In August, 1805, Lewis, too, becomes dehydrated. He is *"exposed to the intese heat of the sun without shade or scarcely a breath of air,"* as well as having taken a dose of purgatives and then walked eleven miles. No wonder he feels the need for water. It is a virulent combination, all bad. *"We then hurryed to the river and allayed our thirst."* [J5:26] Another time the men *"were suffocated nearly with the intense heat of the midday sun"* and in the expected desert thermal shifts they find, *"the nights are so could that two blankets are not more than sufficient covering."* [J5:30]

Heat and Nutrition

Heat increases the sweat rate. As the body literally drips precious fluid out from within, vital minerals and salts wash away. Working in exceptionally tough conditions, "maximum sweat rates can exceed the body's ability to absorb fluids. In hot environments, sweat rates of 1.5 quarts per hour or more are not unusual." Furthermore, the normal thirst mechanism doesn't kick in, and the body continues to deplete its supplies. And that isn't all – the appetite fails as well. "Soldiers typically reduce their food intake by as much as 40% during active operations." The manual continues, "military personnel living and working in temperatures ranging from 86° to 104°F (30° to 40°C) may require up to 10% more calories to do the same amount of work as they would under more temperate conditions." The body needs more but stalls out and takes in less.

The weather diaries alone show us that these conditions are continuing and even disabling at times, but the Corps

---

[a] Fundamental food requirements are examined in detail in *Appendix C: Food Requirements*.

[b] All quotations and data in this chapter come from this Army manual.

simply toughs it out. The Captains do their best to minimize the men's discomforts whenever possible, but of course they must proceed on.

Cold

The winter of 1805 and the trek over the Bitterroots are particularly vicious. In North Dakota, men's body parts freeze, and conditions in the mountains of Idaho and Montana are not much better. In between these two horrible spells of frozen wasteland are the mountain-fed streams and rivers. Capsizing in cold water in the midst of a terrible storm with rain and extreme wind chill or towing canoes up icy mountain streams are also body-rattling and require greater energy than simply being dry and paddling a canoe in cold weather.

The Canoe and White Water states that if you are well fed and happen to capsize in 48° to 56°F (10° to 15°C) water, you can survive for up to two hours. It goes on to note that "Hypothermia is particularly dangerous to white water canoeists in the early spring when the water is close to the temperature of melting snow."[50] Of course, this is exactly the time that the Corps' flotilla is on the water in all three years.

Winter arrives early, on September 16, 1805, and the Expedition awakens covered in two inches of snow. Clark must have been awake even earlier for he notes that it has been snowing for at least three hours before daybreak. Whitehouse writes that those without moccasins wrap their feet in rags, and the whole party continues "*not having anything for to eat,*" [J11:318] through the endless ridges of snow-covered mountains. At noon, Clark calls a halt to feed the horses (at least) and "*worm & dry our Selves a little ...*" It is so horribly bad, the tough army man confides, "*we are continually covered with Snow, I have been wet and as cold in every part as I ever was in my life, indeed I was at one time fearfull my feet would freeze ...*" [J5:209] He no doubt remembers the bad day of January 9, 1804, when the ice broke as he started to cross a pond. "*my feet, which were wet had frozen to my Shoes ... exceedingly Cold day.*" He probably also remembers he was "*verry unwell*" the next two days.

Whitehouse probably remembers the prior May 1 and being forced to sleep out on the shore of the Missouri River, where he and another man were "*obleged to lay out all night without any blanket.*" [J4:100n1] as Lewis reports. Whitehouse himself is a little more frank, "*it being verry cold I Suffered verry much,*" [J11:142] all this a consequence of extremely strong winds preventing them from returning to camp. Flying, wind-driven spray may have left the two men in damp clothing, another disagreeable, dangerous factor. It was 36°F (2°C) after sunrise the next morning, and there is no way of knowing how far the wind chill dropped the temperature during the night.

On June 17, 1806, during the first attempt at a return trip through Lolo Pass, Lewis pauses at 6,000 feet elevation and, totally deflated and discouraged, declares that "*we found ourselves invelloped in snow from 12 to 15 feet deep ... my hands and feet were benumbed.*"

Arctic Nutrition, Preventing Hypothermia – "Food is an ally."

The greatest risk in extreme cold is freezing to death. Nature builds in one preventative – shivering – as a warning and a means of keeping the human engine humming along. Shivering helps keep the blood flowing and muscles warm. High caloric intake helps keep the body warm in the first place. Dense fatty foods that sustain energy and high carbohydrates for quick energy are needed. After shivering comes the dangerous condition of hypothermia, when the body can no longer manufacture enough heat to keep the engine turning, when normal mechanisms for fending off cold are overwhelmed in the face of severe and dangerous environmental conditions. The current Army guidelines stolidly state, "food is an ally often overlooked against the cold. Remember that food ultimately fuels the heat-generating shivering response. A lack of critical metabolic fuels limits shivering."[51]

What are the contemporary Army Guidelines? And how did the Corps do compared to them?

Camping along the Missouri. Eating together improves digestion.

R. L. Rickards – courtesy: Rickards Western Art

Eat together. A time of sociability and relaxation increases food intake.

Eating with their regular mess buddies is something the Corps does. At Fort Mandan, mealtime was a pleasant time for all. In the Bitterroots they have no shelter, but they sit around their campfires trying to get the portable soup down. The mess units are probably even more critical at this point when gathering firewood requires more hands, and they need multiple fires for the more than thirty people wanting to huddle around for warmth.

Provide hot, palatable food. Hot food and hot beverages provide a warming sensation and taste better than cold provisions. This improves morale and satisfies appetites. Adequate rations at the garrison become inadequate when the troops are exposed to the cold, and men should increase their intake from 3200 Cal up to 4500–5000 Cal, while a woman's ration should go from 2400 to 3500 Cal.[c] Sacagawea, probably still nursing, would have required far more than 3500. The Army's suggested caloric increase for cold is 25–50%.

This standard for human satisfaction, hot and palatable food, is something that comes and goes in the annals of the journey. Feasting and fasting. During the winter of 1803–04 there is plenty of food at Camp River Dubois. The next winter at the Mandan villages alternates between meat and no meat, but there is always an underlying security blanket of corn. By the time winter storms arrive in 1805–06, food is in short supply and sometimes is nonexistent. Would the privates count hot portable soup as palatable? No. Colt? Yes.

Eat regular meals, and hearty snacks at 2-hour intervals. Eat before going to sleep. Whenever possible the Corps eats regular meals, which seemingly are huge. Pemmican or jerky are the snacks of choice. Fruit is picked if available, but this would only be when marching or paddling in the right season and in the right locale.

Consume no excess caffeine and avoid alcohol. The Captains are carrying fifty pounds of coffee, but the *Journals* don't mention its use. Clark views it as a treat rather than a daily habit. During the winters of 1803–04 and 1804–05 liquor is handed out regularly, part of the daily ration and also as anti-freeze once an afflicted man makes it back to camp. By the Fourth of July, 1805, the liquor is gone.

Lower salt intake. Salt increases body's water requirements. If the Corps has salt, they salt their meat. Why would they do anything different? Nutritionists point out that salt, if not accompanied by adequate water, may lead to dehydration. The extra water is needed for the body to flush out excess salts.

At Altitude

Nothing has prepared the Corps for the vastness and height of the mountains and the sheer physical toll these towering obstacles take on the body. Red blood cells and the transport of oxygen to muscles and the brain become important, the Army advises, "Red blood cell count increases at altitude so that the blood can carry more oxygen." Proceeding to higher elevations successively diminishes the amount of oxygen available, and this can make for measurable short-term and long-term memory disruptions. Good thinking goes askew; there is a lack of clarity, a poor quality of rational thinking.

Cautions for Operations at Elevation

Weight Loss. Today's Army warns, "Almost all persons going to altitude lose weight. This weight loss is a combination of body fat and lean tissue, and at very high altitudes the weight loss is incapacitating. The loss of insulating fat decreases tolerance to cold temperatures. Accompanying the weight loss are fatigue, loss of strength, and psychological changes such as decreased mental alertness and morale. All these can contribute to accidents and failure to accomplish the mission."

Furthermore, the human energy requirement goes up by 15–50%. As the men wander in the wilderness and use up their provisions, their food supplies diminish by the day. A host of other food-related problems crop up. In an unusual paradox, as gross bodily activity increases the appetite decreases. According to environmental medicine research, "many mountaineers report an aversion to fat and a preference for carbohydrates." If this is the case, the men may have had trouble with Lewis' last-chance provisions: bear grease and tallow candles.

Low Carbohydrate Intake. Military nutritionists count low carbs as a dietary danger. Having their corn or flour provisions in the mountains might have saved the troops and their commanders from tumbling down the mountain like sticks in a bag of skin. The glucose from the carbohydrates does two things: 1) it replaces depleted

---

[c] The unit Cal (capital "C")is used in this book in accordance with nutritional convention, and is equivalent to the more scientific unit 'kcal', or 1000 calories (the heat required to raise 1 kg of water 1°C). Everyday usage (on packages, etc.), confuses these units, specifying "calories" when what is actually meant is kcals. This book will only use "calorie" (lower case "c") when the generic meaning of "food energy" is intended; not as a measurement.

glycogen stores in the muscles and 2) prevents those muscles (protein) from being internally cannibalized for energy. Lastly, sugars are easier to digest than protein.

Low Blood Sugar. Related to the former problem is what may be the most relevant issue confronting the men as they struggle along: low blood sugar. Army nutritional orders follow this dictum: "A low carbohydrate diet can result in low blood sugar. Low blood sugar causes confusion, disorientation, and lack of coordination; these conditions can be extremely dangerous when combined with oxygen deficiency." What the starving men are eating is a diet devoid of carbohydrates – portable soup and horseflesh. The recommended balance is about 70% of the calories being carbohydrates. The Corps has none to speak of in the Bitterroots and must wait until they get to the other side of the Rockies before native roots come into their diet.

From Environmental to Physical Extremes

Such hugely disparate environments are serious factors as the Corps progresses, but the physical extremes to which the men are pushed cannot be underestimated. A list of their energy-burning, calorie-consuming activities would fill a whole page, single spaced. However, the major physical stresses, those endured over the entire trip are walking, weight-lifting and hauling, and canoeing.

Marching, Walking, Moving Along

Walking at 2 mph burns 160 Cal/hour. The Corps travels fast, and walkers cover a minimum of 15 and a maximum of 30 miles a day. Ten hours covers 20 miles and burns 1600 Cal. This is over and above the basal metabolism. Bear in mind that a good portion of the journey from St. Louis to the Pacific Coast and back is walked. The Corps has access to only a few horses during the winter spent with the Mandans. They hunt on foot, walk beside canoes when they can't paddle, walk from the Lemhi Shoshone territory to other side of the Rockies, and then hunt on foot all through the winter of 1805–06. The time spent on land is considerable, especially considering the daily work of setting up camp, chopping and hauling in firewood, and dragging in the hunters' kills.

Weight Lifting and Hauling

At least one of the Captains and one hunter are usually walking, carrying guns and then meat back to their camp or canoes. A forequarter of elk might weigh 40 pounds, a buffalo hump around 30–35 pounds. Transporting 600 or 800 pounds of meat or finished jerky is not inconsequential. During all of the portages until they are in the Rockies, the Expedition is carrying, pushing or pulling a huge weight (tons, in fact). A dugout weighs about 500 pounds for a small, thin 27-foot canoe to 1000 pounds for a longer, thicker version.

Extreme lifting burns about 400 Cal per hour. The portages often take a full day, several days, or in the case of the portage at Great Falls, almost two weeks, working all day. When portaging, the men are probably lifting and carrying for a minimum of 8 hours, for an approximate caloric burn of 3200 Cal, plus 10% specific dynamic action to process the food, plus 1700 Cal basal metabolism, which equals a daily total of 5220 Cal.

Canoeing and Boating

Analysis showed that the members of the Corps needed about 5115 Cal/day to meet their strenuous activities. And, "les voyageurs," the Expedition's engagés, are not accustomed to being hungry and out of fuel. Very early in the Expedition, *"the French higherlins Complain for the want of Provisions, Saying they are accustomed to eat 5 & 6 times a day ..."* [J2:306] These boatmen are nutritionally correct: the Army currently advises that best results come if you can "maximize glycogen replenishment by consuming carbohydrates withing 30 minutes of completing intense activity.

Foul weather on the Columbia north shore near the Pacific. Energy needs are pushed to the extreme by both temperature and fatigue.

R. L. Rickards - courtesy Rickards Western Art

They can also enhance recovery by eating small carbohydrate snacks while working."[52] The commanders are not privy to this twenty-first century wisdom but they always try to have plenty of jerky on hand. The protein does not, however, provide instant energy like the carbohydrates will. Perhaps the native population intuitively knew this, adding berries to the road-worthy pemmican.

Energy Aspects of Boating

Moving the boats themselves is the major work of the privates, and it is useful to get some sort of grasp on sizes and tonnages carried (in addition to the weight of the men). The first flotilla consists of:

Keelboat	12 tons of cargo	27 men plus the Captains and York
Red Pirogue	9 tons of cargo	8 voyageurs
White Pirogue	8 tons of cargo	6 escort soldiers

Rowing or poling upriver, against the prevailing current, and fighting for control of overloaded rowboats occupies the party as they begin the voyage up the Missouri to the Mandan villages. At other points they are hauling the vessels upstream on rope tow lines.

Preparing to depart from Fort Mandan in the spring of 1805, the Pacific-bound crew hollows out six dugout canoes. Over the entire trip, they will make fifteen of these cumbersome but useful vessels. An early description of the Iroquois dugouts, made by roughly the same techniques as the Corps used, described them as "miserable vessels, little more than logs of pine rudely hollowed out and pointed at bow and stern. So heavy were they, so easily water-logged, and so ill-adapted for portaging ..." Manhandling these quarter-to-half-ton crafts requires a considerable amount of energy, since they lack the trim finesse of the birchbark canoes of the East or the native canoes found at the Great Rapids of the Columbia where the *"Indians who arrived last evining took their Canoes on their Sholders and Carried them below the Great Shute ..."* [J5:369] Furthermore, this doesn't consider the efforts put into subsequent bailings and ultimately the weight-lifting involved in unloading sodden goods to dry.

Yet it is not totally the size or nature of the canoe that dictates calorie expenditure. The simple size of the paddle also decrees the amount of energy plowed into paddling a canoe. Short and narrow – 4-foot long by 4-inch wide – paddles are extremely efficient in maneuvering the canoe with as little resistance as possible. The shorter length makes the paddle lighter, and requires less energy to get from the forward pull stroke to the beginning of the next stroke.[d] Along with this, the voyageurs would paddle a relatively quick cadence, avoiding the "speed up and slow down created by the slow cadence of a large paddle, which would have been extremely wasteful of energy."[53]

Nutritional Intake Under Stressful Conditions

The French-Canadian voyageurs used small narrow paddles and paddled like crazy, very very fast, about one stroke per second. There is no journalistic evidence about the Expedition's paddling rate, but Paul Kane, a traveling artist, noted that when a rest-stop appeared, the emaciated canoeists "did little but eat and sleep. The rapidity with which they changed their appearance was astonishing. Some of them became so much improved in looks, that it was with difficulty we could recognize our voyageurs."[54] In other words, this isn't easy work or even hard work; it's "bloody hard." While the Corps didn't canoe frenetically all the time, they did spend a lot of time in the cold mountain waters of the northern rivers, towing the boats or pirogues. All of these activities are a quick means to dissipate energy, burn calories, and build up a big appetite.

If the emaciated French did nothing but eat and sleep and changed appearances so drastically in three days, weren't they eating an awe-full amount? This would tend to support the idea of gorging, of ingesting huge quantities of food when it was available. The Captains find this same tendency to eat as much as possible among their own men. On July 31, 1805, (near Three Forks, Montana) game is becoming scarce. Lewis, with some aggravation, writes, *"nothing killed today and our fresh meat is out when we have a plenty of fresh meat I find it impossible to make the men take any care of it, or use it with the least frugallity."* With a shrug of the shoulders, he finishes, *"tho' I expect that necessity will shortly teach them this art."* The body looks out for itself, and dictates: eat when you can, for you never know when your next meal will arrive.

---

[d] Today's paddles generally are 5 feet long or "up to your nose."

R. L. Rickards - courtesy: Rickards Western Art

Nature's bounty. The Corps' hunters provide 90% of the Expedition's food needs from game, birds, and fish.

Hunting – Tools of the Trade

we eat an emensity of meat ...
— LEWIS, JULY 13, 1805, GREAT FALLS

I T IS CLEAR THAT THE AMOUNT OF FOOD required for the Expedition can not be carried. Rather, the Corps must hunt as they go to provide the *"emensity of meat"* noted by Lewis. Throughout the journey, the hunters have their work cut out for them.

Types of guns used

Working men need the tools of their trade, and one of the greatest considerations Lewis faces in Pennsylvania is armaments. Cutting-edge technology in firearms is of prime importance – powerful weapons that will quell the greatest of Indian threats and accurate, easy-to-use guns for hunting.

Harpers Ferry rifles of the period: (top) 1792 contract rifle of the type retrofitted for Lewis, and (bottom) the model 1803; from the Virginia Military Institute archives.

Otherwise no one eats. The weapons he orders are exemplary, the best of that time. He brings along an amazing airgun (discharged by a civilian and looking as if it had killed a woman spectator on the first day of the westward journey), which turns into one of the most impressive signals of American supremacy. Tribe after tribe sees it; it makes a great show. But what are the hunters using?

From National Archives

Harpers Ferry circa 1803 with armory along the river.

When Lewis arrives in Lancaster, Pennsylvania, in the spring of 1803 he immediately writes Jefferson on April 20 regarding such issues as recruitment, keelboat building, and armaments. *"My Rifles, Tomahawks & knives are preparing at Harper's Ferry,"* and, in a breath of relief that follows any successful dealing with a contractor, he notes they *"are already in a state of forwardness that leaves me little doubt of their being in readiness in due time."* [L1:40] Lewis has ordered the best of both rifles and knives. They appear as virtual lifesavers in later diary entries.

For the men of the Expedition, Lewis has fifteen new rifles obtained from the Army's Harpers Ferry armory, a 54-caliber muzzle-loading flintlock.[a] The barrel is short, less than three feet. The "Nine Young Men from Kentucky" recruited by Clark bring their standard of the day, the

Kentucky long rifle. These Kentucky long rifles are a combination of a traditional hefty and accurate German design (the Jäeger, which arrived in Lancaster Valley, Pennsylvania, in 1709, and migrating to Winchester, Virginia, as early as 1729) and a lighter-weight, more delicate English fowling piece, combined with "the two piece, brass hinged patch box."[55] The ability to carry patches at hand, a quite necessary part of loading, makes this rifle eminently user-friendly. It is a German/American invention, and its heyday appears to have been 25 to 30 years after the American Revolution.[56] Additionally, all soldiers detailed to the Expedition carry an older, less technically advanced gun, a Model 1795 musket,[57] a smoothbore flintlock that doesn't have the same accuracy or distance as either the Kentucky rifle or the rifled-barrel weapon from Harpers Ferry.

Ammunition is a lead ball, propelled from the barrel by an exploding charge of gunpowder.[b] If the user runs out of lead balls, then sticks or stones can also be stuffed down the barrel and shot out like balls. (While Shannon did this with a stick early in the trip, the Captains view this as a gun-ruining technique when they see natives loading up with pebbles on the Pacific Coast.)

Ammunition Policy

Lewis is quite clear: no waste. *"we killed a couple of young gees ... but as they are but small game to subsist a party on of our strength I have forbid the men shooting at them as it waists a considerable quantity of amunition ..."* [J4:426] By August 8, 1805, ammunition supplies are being reserved for large game such as deer and antelope, despite *"great quantities of beaver Otter and musk-rats."* If they are passing up beaver, it is a tipoff to the degree of concern attached to the need to conserve ammunition. As a cautious military commander, Lewis knows that having cached some lead and powder for the return trip, what they now have must last to the Pacific, over the winter, and the return. There are no other sources or substitutes for these critical survival items.

Recruiting the Hunters for the Job

Hunters actually have two jobs, the obvious one of hunting and a second task that goes along with tracking. Equally important is being a *"spy"* or a *"scout."* If you have your eyes to the ground following tracks, part of the skill is to see small signs of passing – broken twigs, bits of bone left behind, mocassin prints.

"When descending the Ohio it shall be my duty of enquery to find out and engage some good hunters, stout, healthy, unmarried men, accustomed to the woods, and capable of bearing bodily fatigue in a pretty considerable degree ..." The issue of finding a capable hunter sounds as easy as rolling off a log, especially in a time when everyone hunts. But the Captains must have been hard to please, for they appear to be eternally dissatisfied. Even when Drouillard – the premier hunter of the Expedition – pulls into camp, Clark is fussing.

Dear Captain,   Cahokia, December 17th 1803
Drewyer arrived here last evening from Tennessee with eight men. I do not know how they may answer on experiment but I am a little disappointed, in finding them not possessed of more than the requisite qualifications; there is not a hunter among them. [L1:144]

Perhaps there are reservations on both sides, for a week passes before Drouillard decides to accompany the Expedition, and he never does sign on as a member of the Army. He remains a private contractor, his own man, but he comes along *"at the rate ofd [offered]"* – $25 a month. [J2:141] A hunter, paid $300 a year instead of the $60 for privates, is quite valuable. [J2:85]

Who Actually Does the Hunting?

The two Captains are fine hunters and regularly supply meat, particularly as they walk the shores alongside the canoes. George Drouillard – a metis, or of mixed French-Canadian/Shawnee heritage – is hired on as an interpreter and hunter, and fulfills his job admirably. Clark's slave, York, hunts. John Colter, another legend of the West, is on the list, as are George Shannon, John Collins, and brothers Reubin and Joseph Field. Excellent hunters. Private William Bratton hunts as well as being a blacksmith.

---

[a] Conventional research has listed these rifles as Harpers Ferry Model 1803 rifles. However, other recent research suggests that while the lock mechanisms were from the not-yet-delivered new 1803 model, the barrels and stocks were cut-down from 1792 contract rifles. Resolving this, and other such equipment issues, is beyond the scope of this book.

[b] The "charge" can either be: (a) a measured amount of gunpowder poured down the barrel from a powder horn, then held in place by a piece of wadding tamped down the barrel, or (b) a pre-packaged load of gunpowder rolled into a cylinder in powder-paper, carried in a hunter's pouch, and tamped down the barrel in one operation. A few grains of additional powder are poured into the flash-pan on the rear-end side of the barrel (and which leads through a small flash-hole into the barrel chamber); the flint-edged hammer is pulled back to cocked position; the rifle is aimed; and the trigger pulled to release the hammer. The flint springs down, striking against a metal edge on the pan and producing a spark; the pan-powder ignites with a flash into the barrel; and the main powder explodes, driving out the lead ball.

George Gibson, Richard Windsor, Hugh McNeal, and Peter Weiser also go after game, although not as frequently. Out of thirty people, at least fourteen are hunting at one time or another.

Hunting and Blacksmithing

From what we know, Lewis worries more about finding hunters than finding blacksmiths on his trip from the east. Clark, too, is working the frontier, scouting around for the keen shot with an adventuresome heart. But "smithies" are vital; these men are essential for all metalworking on the Expedition. They are the ones who will repair broken guns: Field *"injured his gun"* [J10:106] when he jumps off a steep bank into the water to escape three grizzlies chasing him. They will melt lead canisters down into ammunition and manufacture specifically sized balls for all of the different guns being carried, a precision that is vital. If one of the traps breaks, the "smithie" will repair it.

Getting Going, Going Hunting

As the Expedition boats begin their haul up the Mississippi, the entries describe ducks that aren't bagged, wounded deer which escape. Even Clark misses. The hunters aren't quite up to snuff yet. And what would one of these men be taking with him as he heads out of camp? He'd have his rifle and a gun sling, a powder horn or pouch, some of the *"best rifle powder"* to be found, rifle flints, little lead balls and brush and wire to clean the barrel. Only one or two hunters go out if game is abundant.

Perhaps it is the bitter cold of late winter 1803–04, or hunters out and lost, but there is no further mention of hunting until April 1804. As per Jefferson's suggestion, the Corps draws its supplies from the quartermaster. Both the dangers of winter and the vagaries of hunting are minimized, and the only shots fired are those that help the men improve their aim. Practice is part of the camp life, a ritual that steadily strengthens eye and arm and fosters good-natured competition which will slowly convert to teamwork.

Later, during winters on the road (1804–05 and 1805–06) when game is scarce or meager, almost the entire Corps turns out. They hunt with the Mandans and the Lemhi Shoshone, but they do not actively hunt with any other tribes. During the journey, several groups of hunters may go in different directions, especially when very little is being brought back and the party needs to scour a wider area. The hunters often leave game where it's shot, and go back to camp to report where it was left; different men are sent to bring it back.

Perils of the Hunt

Lost!

Perhaps the men aren't the best shots, and sometimes they aren't the best navigators. But remember these troops are not carrying maps, nor do they have any two-way communication devices. They are navigating by the sun, watching the sky for weather, and generally using superb skills to keep their orientation in relationship not only to the party but also in the direction of animals on the move. Dealing with getting lost, especially in a land of grizzlies, and finding yourself totally alone in a vast wilderness is a terribly frightening matter, and requires great courage.

Locating the Lost

Hunting Horns. Hunters do get lost, and are actually expected to – for hasn't Lewis brought with him four sounding horns? These are to be sounded so that the men can locate their position by echo-location of the human sort. September 5, 1803: fog, then rain. Lewis frets, *"my canoes which had on board the most valuable part of my stores"* [probably his navigational equipment, medicines, etc.] *"had not come up, ordered the trumpet to be sound and they answered."* [J2:72] Using the horns is far easier and safer than sending men out to look for one another. Guns are often fired for the same reason.

Discharge of guns and firing the swivel gun. *"Soon after we came too we heard Several guns fire down the river, we answered them by a Discharge of a Swivile on the Bow."* [J2:263] Accustomed to this form of communication, the men are able to discern how far apart they are, as well as an approximate time it will take to close the distance.

Whooping. Sound carries, and when ammunition runs low or the sound of guns might cause problems, the men whoop. The usually self-conscious Lewis resorts to this method on several occasions, *"struck the river about 3 miles above them; by this time it was perfectly dark & we hooped but could hear no tidings of them."* [J5:45] On June 23, 1805, Lewis writes of *"hooping as we went on in order to find the hunters ..."*

Sending Help. The Captains even send out a capable "older" hunter to find the young George Shannon on more than one occasion. The *Journals* reflect the anxiety and tension when a man slips away from the security of the fold.

Who Gets Lost?

The canoeists don't get lost. In almost every case it is a hunter who is lost, a man who has gone too far and is suddenly in dire straits. These men are forced back onto their own resources, onto their own reckoning and ingenuity. It is a terrific psychological stress. And it affects the group. If these men disappear and their crew has no hunter, other hunters must fill in. In the plains this is not so tough; Drouillard and one Captain are probably enough. In sparse game areas, it's a hardship.

But the Corps hasn't even left Camp River Dubois before men go missing. On January 11, 1804: *"one man McNeal <lost> out last night, he Sepperated from the hunting party about 7 miles from this place, he returnd this evening Sgt. Ordway was also lost all night."* As they begin their trip up the Missouri River, Joseph Whitehouse gets lost first thing out and *"we deturmined to proceed on & leave one perogue to wate for him."* [J2:263] Even more distressing in this shakedown start of the Expedition is the loss of two of their best hunters. *"Drewyer & Shields came over to the opposit Side to day at SunSet we sent across & brought them over, they had been absent 7 days Swam many creeks, much worsted."* [J2:269]

This record of being lost for a week is topped by eighteen-year-old George Shannon, who goes missing for seventeen days, over half a month.

Hunting Injuries
On July 12, 1805, successful hunting produces two buffalo and three deer. Three men under Sgt. Pryor are dispatched to bring the meat in. Carrying those immensely heavy, bloody bundles is so tearing on the muscles that Pryor dislocates his shoulder in the process, and they reset it on the spot. Lewis opines, *"it was replaced immediately and is likely to do him but little injury; it is painfull to him today."*

On another day, *"Drewyer missed his step and had a very dangerous fall, he sprained one of his fingers and hirt his leg very much."* [J5:45] On the whole, hunting accidents are relatively rare. Axe handling is far more dangerous.

Finally, the most catastrophic hunting injury occurs as the Corps is returning through Montana. One-eyed Cruzatte mistakes buckskin-clad Capt. Lewis for an elk and shoots him in the buttocks, seriously wounding the shocked Lewis and incapacitating him for a good portion of the final float.

Overall Hunting Strategies
When setting out from Fort Mandan, plains animals should be there for the taking, but the Corps is having a hard time, and on April 12, 1805, Lewis writes, *"the country ... had been recently hunted by the Minetares, and the little game which they had not killed and frightened away, was so extreemly shy that*

the hunters could not get in shoot of them." In fact, game that week is very short, an involuntary fasting is relieved only by beaver and a hare.

As they travel across the northern Great Plains, the natural abundance of game makes it quite easy for one or two hunters to bring in sufficient buffalo, elk, or deer. When scarcity becomes apparent, a change of tactics ensues. More men are put on the hunting detail, as Clark describes. *"Sent out the hunters to hunt in advance as usial. (we have Selected 4 of the best hunters to go in advance to hunt for the party. This arrrangement has been made long sinc)."* [J5:199]

Approaching Sacagawea's home territory on July 22, 1805, the Corps is split in two – Clark takes a group ahead to hunt, the other comes along with the canoes. Clark is not pleased with the hunting, complaining mildly that, *"These men were not Suckessfull in hunting killed only one Deer."* Belatedly he notes that more game is brought in his absence: two deer, an elk, and an antelope. It is barely enough. By August 29, the *"emensity of meat"* has so dwindled that Lewis is rejoicing in a little meal of venison, *"a great treat to me as I had eate none for 8 days past ..."*

As the Corps is waiting out the winter of 1805–06 at Fort Clatsop, nearly everyone is involved in hunting. The game is poor as well as scarce, and the troops scour the surrounding areas for red meat. Even selecting a site for making salt is governed by *"the probibillity of game in that direction, for the Support of the Men, we Shall Send to make Salt."* On December 8, Clark's focus is that the little army construct trails, so that *"men out hunting might find the direction to the fort if they Should get lost in cloudy weather."* Navigating by the sun is not working in a rainy, foggy coastal climate. At any given time it is possible that a good number of men are out in the near-freezing rain, tromping through bogs, hunting.

Specific Hunting Techniques
As any hunter knows, there are tricks of the trade. The Native Americans had their own particular methods, such as antelope pens and buffalo jumps, but these are used by people staying in one place for a while. The Corps is proceeding on, and their techniques must match the pace of travel. The standard method, of course, is simply to shoot the game.

With vast numbers of game, there is little call for finesse, but sometimes something so simple as being upwind or downwind needs to be considered. *"we could not git near them before they Smelled us and ran off."* [J9:180] Sometimes other methods are used, some involving physical traps or snares, some involving vocalizations imitating the game being hunted.

Some Grizzly Strategies

The most enraged grizzly they encounter is wounded near the river on May 14, 1805, when six canoeists decide to make short work of the sleeping giant. The tables are turned as the wounded monster nearly overtakes them, two fleeing to the canoe, the others hiding. After reloading they fire again, and the infuriated male nearly catches the two men racing for their lives into the river. More volleys finally bring the bear down; it takes a total of eight balls to kill him. Lewis is both relieved and appalled at the near miss from *"ruinous injury."*

On June 27, 1805, Drouillard and Joseph Field are out hunting and dodging hailstones, and they later return with nine elk and three grizzly – but it is the grizzly that once again gets the headlines. *"... one of the bear was the largest by far that we have yet seen; the skin appear to me to be as large as a common ox."* Man, devious creature that he is, devises a new tactic to deal with this immense foe. Drouillard lodges himself in a tree and begins whooping. The aggressive grizzly charges from the bushes and makes straight for him – *"when he arrived at the tree he made a short paus and Drewyer shot him in the head."* The hunters have figured out that the grizzly, unlike the black bear, doesn't climb [c] and secondly, that a shot to the brain is the only sure-fire way to kill one. Drouillard is evening up the odds while playing it safe. Lewis has earlier, on May 10, remarked on the difficulty of this particular shot: *"this becomes difficult in consequence of two large muscles which cover the sides of the forehead and the sharp projection of the center of the frontal bone, which is also of a pretty good thickness."* [J4:141] In other words, be a darned good shot. Luck won't supplant accuracy. Caution, in this case, is more than admirable, *"the fore feet of this bear measured nine inches across and the hind feet eleven and 3/4 in length & exclusive of the tallons and seven inches in width."*

Beaver Traps

Each mess relies not only on the carbohydrate provisions that are doled out for the day, but also upon fresh protein. Several members of the Corps carry beaver traps – John Colter carries a steel trap, and Drouillard has several. These effective, vicious, lethal snares are set out at night, to be collected in the morning before the canoes depart. While food wars are extremely unusual, on one occasion the shortage of edibles seems to have prompted a heated dispute over a

[c] This is refuted by Yellowstone National Park, which in *Yellowstone Today* (Spring 2002) reports in an article titled "If You Encounter a Bear" on page 7, "All black bears, all grizzly cubs and some adult grizzlies can climb trees." Now that's an *awful* thought.

R. L. Rickards - courtesy: Rickards Western Art

On May 14, 1805, the Corps learns that an enraged grizzly is very hard to kill.

beaver caught *"in 2 traps by one hind foot and one fore foot. they belonged to 2 owners. they had Some difference which had the best rite to it."* [J9:133]

While caching goods before crossing the Rockies, Ordway records an oversight that might actually have been a bit of subconscious wishing. *"we burryed 3 traps which was forgot when we made the Deposite yesteday."* [J9:166] But this doesn't mean that all the traps are stowed. Up in Shoshone territory, the beaver meals continue, including one caught in a trap on August 19. Some stalwart beaver-eater wasn't about to cache a valuable dinner tool and it is Drouillard, the hired hunter, who must retrieve it for the beaver carried it two miles downriver.

At Fort Clatsop in January, 1806, Drouillard catches a large, fat beaver, on which Lewis (alone) *"has feested sumptiously."* [J6:197] Clark then dreams of catching many more, hoping to lure them into his kettle with a recipe of his own design. Perhaps he is rankled over Meriwether's solo consumption of the delicacy. Not all recipes are for foods. In fact, the word has its origin in the Rx of medical prescriptions

Trap similar to the Corps' beaver traps.

and concomitantly; it is "a list of materials and directions for preparing a dish or a drink." But it can also mean "a procedure for accomplishing or achieving something." Clark's recipe for beaver trapping is both a list of materials and a procedure, with the intent of achieving something, in this case another beaver for dinner.

BEAVER BAIT

January 10, 1806. *"this bate when properly prepared will entice the beaver to visit it as far as he can Smell it, and this I think may be Safely Stated at ½ a mile ... To prepare beaver bate, the Caster or bark stone is taken as a base, this is generally pressed out of the bladder like bag which Contains it, into a phiol of 4 ounces with a wide mouth; if you have them you will put from 4 to 6 Stone in a phial of that Capacity, to this you will add half a nutmeg, a Dozen or 15 grains of Cloves and 30 grains of Sinimon finely pulverised, Stur them well together, and then add as much ardent Sperits to the Composition as will reduce it to the Consistancey of mustard prepared for the table, when thus prepared it resembles mustard precisely to all appearance. When you cannot precure a phial a bottle made of horn or a light earthern vessel will answer, in all Cases it must be excluded from the air or it will Soon lose its Virtue; it is fit for use imediately <as So> it is prepared but becoms much Stronger and better in 4 or 5 days and will keep for months provided it be purfectly Secluded from the air. when Cloves are not to be had use double the quantity of allspice, and when no Spices can be obtained use the bark of the root of the Sausafras; when Sperits cannot be had use oil Stone of the beaver adding mearly a Sufficient quantity to moisten the other materials, or reduce it to a Stiff paste. it appears to me that the principal use of the Spices is only to give a variety to the Scent of the bark Stone and if So the mace vineller, and other Sweet Smelling Spices might be employd with equal advantage."*[d]

---

[d] Greg Muellich, a trapper and member of the Lewis and Clark Honor Guard, describes a sample of this at his workshops as musky, perfumey, and "very effective" for luring beaver into the trap. Clark was on to something.

Other Means of Securing Meat

Newfoundland dog
in the time of Lewis' Seaman.

Sick the Dog On 'em: Lewis paid a hefty $20 for Seaman, an immense price in 1803, and he more than got his money's worth. This faithful Newfoundland is not only a constant companion and watchdog, but also a fine retriever. The dog fetches squirrels along the Ohio River, *"as many as each day I had occation for ..."* [J2:79] and he continues this fetching game until the squirrels give out – the dog never does. In fact, Seaman is excellent at catching little things, *"great numbers of gees with their young which are perfectly feathered <but> except the wings which are deficient in both young and old. my dog caught several today, as he frequently dose."* [J4:411] He pursues beaver, *"we came to for Dinner at a Beever house, Cap Lewis' Dog Seamon went in & drove them out."* [J2:350] The doughty dog almost dies in pursuit of a beaver when he is bitten by one and suffers a

York transporting a deer back to camp.

severed leg artery. But, like everyone else on the trip, the dog is tough. He lives and goes on to bring in yet bigger animals. Even antelope are no match for him, especially when he can trap one swimming, *"my dog caught one drowned it and brought it on shore."* He brings down a pregnant antelope, but Lewis discounts the effort; the prey wasn't up to her usual snuff. From all evidence, Seaman is indeed the water dog, *"Drewyer wouded a deer which ran into the river   my dog pursued caught it drowned it and brought it to shore at our camp."* [J4:383] What a well-trained dog – bringing home the meat.

The Espontoon: This all-purpose spear is used in a number of ways. It is used by the hunter as a gun rest to steady his aim, and Lewis finds it *"very serviceable to me in this way in the open plains."* [J4:294] He also throws or jabs with it, bringing in a number of animals caught at close range, such as a *"verry jentle"* wolf that Clark speared. [J4:219] As for the porcupine that is *"clumsy and not very watchfull"* – Lewis merely touches it with his spear, but he certainly uses it to beat a rattlesnake to death on May 26, 1805.

The Setting Pole: Normally used to push the canoes upriver, this is generally a willow branch, *"seldom seen larger than a mans arm ... white light and tough ... generally used*

Lewis with an Espontoon.

Michael Haynes

... in preference to anything else." [J3:455] On July 19, 1805, deep into the Gates of the Mountains, one of the privates is struck by a hunger attack and quickly uses his setting pole to get an otter, normally a speedy little animal. It goes on the dinner menu.

Bleating: Another technique is vocalization – the men "bleat" like the game they're hunting as a lure, especially like a fawn calling its mother.

Processing the Meat – Getting the Knives Out

Big metal knives are a huge draw: as Indian trade-goods and as carried by the Corps. Fifteen dozen are packed for Indian trade. They come in two sizes: the larger is a hunting knife with a bone handle and a blade of almost six inches; the smaller has a stag (or horn) handle and is more of a paring knife with a shorter three-and-a-third-inch blade. In a box of necessary stores, Lewis packs twenty-two dozen of the hunting knives and thirteen dozen of the smaller ones. [J3:499-500] Obviously the Corps carries enough knives to make each man self-sufficient.

Gutting

Once game is killed, blossoming bacteria counts demand that the animal be gutted immediately. It is a chore that falls to the hunter, and it is a bloody, messy task.[e] A skilled hunter can accomplish this field-dressing in about five minutes.

Tools used for this purpose are carefully guarded, *"many of the articles were much Injured; particularly the articles of iron ... knives were of this class; I caused them to be oiled and exposed to the sun ..."* [J2:83] Technology has not advanced yet to rust-free steel.

---

[e] Jesse Mains, a contemporary hunter in the South, describes this job: "Every time I down a deer I like to keep the liver, sometimes the heart as well. When dressing the critter out, only open the body cavity as far as the sternum, or bottom of the rib-cage. Then cut the diaphragm away, reach up in, cut the windpipe/veins, and pull out the critters engine works. I also don't split the pelvis when field-dressing, cut around the anus and carefully work the connective tissues around the 'pipes' loose inside the pelvis. It takes some patience, but once you get it right you'll be able to pull the tubing out from the front cleanly. It helps to tie the anus as soon as you have cut it loose. I usually just pull off a strip of basswood bark from a sapling or a thread from my hunting shirt. After this is done, you can carry the liver/heart in the body cavity as you drag said critter back to camp with less likelihood of loss/soiling. If it [the weather] is warm, it keeps flies and dirt from the hams, which are opened up when you split the pelvis. I open the brisket and pelvis when the critter gets hung up for cooling." He then hangs the deer, head down, to drain the blood away from the meat. The men hang their bagged game as well, but it is usually more to keep it away from predators than for improving its quality.

Transporting the Carcass

The troops are strong as young oxen. They can literally throw a deer over their shoulders and walk with 80 pounds of meat draped over them. Lewis does this on May 5, 1805, *"in the course of my walk killed a deer which I carried about a mile and a half to the river ..."* When Pryor dislocated his shoulder, the carcass (of a buffalo) had been quartered, each man again carrying about 60-80 pounds, but a quarter doesn't drape comfortably, hence another possible factor in the injury. If the carcass is too heavy to be carried on the shoulders (as is elk), another method is to use a pole and sling the animal under it, using lashing to secure the forelegs together and the hind-legs together.

There are a number of different ways the Corps handles the transport. When an animal is killed near camp, or near the riverbank where the Corps is paddling, the gutted carcass is simply left by the hunters – apparently the mess cooks will deal with it. The hunters, probably Drouillard or a Field brother, proceed on in search of more game. The canoes come along, the carcass is spotted, picked up, thrown into the boat, and dinnertime eventually rolls around.

Near central Montana on May 24, 1805, Clark kills a buffalo cow in the evening and they leave two canoes and six men behind to dress the meat. The butchers do not overtake the advance party that night. This implies that there is more work than expected, or possibly that the butchers may have stayed overnight and had a nice barbeque – *"game is becoming more scarce."*

On other occasions, the hunters do all the processing on the spot, from gutting to butchering, to finally fileting and drying. This is exactly what Shannon is doing when it appears he is lost the second time. On June 25, 1805, Lewis sends Frazer out to retrieve Drouillard and his meat, and that evening they *"arrivd with about 800 lbs. of excellent dryed meat and about 100 lbs of tallow."* Here two jobs are being merged, and even a cook is drafted to help in the transport. This remote processing can, of course, only happen when there is plenty of firewood or the air is exceptionally dry.

Guarding the Meat

One of the biggest problems for the entire Expedition is keeping their meat safe from the rest of the food chain. At Camp River Dubois, the crows consumed most of the illicit hog meat hung in the forest. On the prairies the biggest competitor is the wolf, and wolf packs make continuing predations on the meat. The only way to foil them is to build a very tall scaffold and hope that it is higher than they can jump. With less construction effort, the hunters *"hung the meat and skins on the trees out of the reach of the wolves."* [J4:280] But their efforts are not always successful: *"... examined the meat which Capt. Clark had left, but found only a small proportion of it, the wolves had taken the greater part."* [J4:326]

As if the wolves aren't enough to worry about, the problem can be bigger. On June 27, near White Bear Islands, at the head of the portage route, Lewis comments that *"a bear came within thirty yards of our camp last night and eat up about thirty weight of buffaloe suit [suet] which was hanging on a pole."* Seaman, good guard-dog that he is, is hysterical. The food chain competition is particularly intense with wolves, bears, and panthers.

Shooting – Cautions around Indians

When searching for the Lemhi Shoshone, both Captains are exceptionally cautious about the presence of the Corps and telltale noises. On July 19, Clark's advance party finds *"Several Indian Camps which they have left this Spring."* He is

Due to the presence of wolves and other scavengers, Indians used pole scaffolds to keep marauders away.

Karl Bodmer - Joslyn Art Museum, Omaha, Nebraska

mindful, and Lewis writes a few days later: *"having deter-mined to hunt and await my arrival somewhere about his pres-ent station was fearfull that some indians might still be on the river above him sufficiently near to hear the report of his guns and therefore proceeded up the river about three miles and [not] finding any indians nor discovering any fresh appearance of them returned about four miles below and fixed his camp near the river ... they set out in different directions to hunt."* J4:412

Likewise, when approaching the Lemhi Shoshone, Lewis is under extreme pressure not to scare his only-hope people away. Not only does he refrain from shooting, lest it *"should al-larm and cause them to retreat to the mountains and conceal themselves,"* J4:398 but he uses food as a sign that he is peaceful.

Hunting Problems on the Coast

While the Great Plains hunting can be almost too easy, the difficulty in procuring meat at the Pacific almost prompts vegetarianism. On December 8, 1805, Clark describes a search for elk: *"Saw a gange of Elk ... rafted the creek, with much dificulty & followed the Elk thro, emence bogs, & over 4 Small Knobs in the bogs ..."* Not content with this, he con-tinues, *"and maney places I Sunk into the mud and water up to my hips without finding any bottom on the trale of those Elk."* It is not easy going any way he looks at it. He further describes this "rainforest" hunting:

> in those Slashes Small Knobs are promisquisly Scattered about which are Steep and thickly Covered with pine Common to the Countery & Lorel. we made a Camp of the Elk Skin to keep off the rain which Continued to fall, the Small Knob on which we Camped did not afford a Sufficiency of dry wood for our fire, we collected what dry would we Could and what Sticks we Could Cut down with the Tomahawks, which made us a tolerable fire.

Indian Techniques Encountered

One of the first native hunting techniques the Captains ob-serve is the Cheyenne boys' method of killing the excep-tionally fleet antelope. They simply wait until the animals are swimming a river, and then swim among them, *"Killing them with sticks and then hauling them to the Shore."* For a simple technique, it's very effective. Clark observes fifty-eight carcasses on the riverbank. J3:176

Two other tactics are also common. One is a camouflaged corral, *"formed of timber and brush ... on one side of which there was a small apparture, sufficiently large to admit an Antelope; from each side of this apparture, a curtain was extended to a considerable distance, widening as they receded ..."* J4:42 away from the enclosure. Essentially it is an antelope chute, de-

Alfred Jacob Miller - Joslyn Art Museum, Omaha, Nebraska

A native technique safer than shooting individual buffalo was to drive a herd of buffalo over a cliff, killing many; these were "buffalo jumps."

signed to control the animals entering and keep them mov-ing forward toward the trap. Clark dubs a nearby stream *"Goat Pen Creek."*

The third type of hunting strategy is using cliffs as a buf-falo jump, a relatively safe and ultimately efficient means of procuring huge quantities of meat which was used initially in the pre-horse era. By forcing the animals into headlong flight over a cliff, the Blackfoot or Atsinas avoided break-aways, had less chance of being gored, and saved on weaponry, be it lost arrows or even bullets. This technique was not used frequently, as it yields huge quantities of meat, and being an indiscriminate killer can be quite wasteful in violation of native philosophy.

Other native techniques they see include a dead fall or snare, used for wolves, racoons, and fox. *"a long pole which will Spring is made fast with bark to a willow, on top of this pole a string"* J5:340 On January 15, 1806, Clark devotes his win-tery day to describing native hunting tools, *"the gun the bow & arrow, deadfalls, pitts, snares, and spears or gigs."*

A final, distinctly native strategy is to collect buffalo car-cases of animals that have floated downriver or fallen through thin winter ice. In either case, the carcasses have been de-composing a while, and the stench is *"most horrid."* J4:216 The Captains dub one area in Montana *"Slaughter house Creek."* J8:246n The natives enjoy this meat pudding when opportunity allows.

The Hunters' Bane: Being Attacked

Grizzlies are at the top of the wilderness food chain. At the lowest level are the mosquitoes and sometimes it's not clear which is worse:

> *"Musquetors excessively troublesome ... I find it entire-ly impossible to hunt in the bottoms, those insects being*

So noumerous and tormenting as to render it imposseable for a man to continue in the timbered lands and our best retreat from those insects is on the Sand bars in the river and even those Situations are only clear of them when the Wind Should happen to blow which it did to day for a fiew hours in the middle of the day." J8:280 *The next day, "I assended the hill with a view to kill the ram. the Misquetors was So noumerous that I could not keep them off my gun long enough to take Sight and by thair means missed."* J8:281

This brings to mind an early form of pest repellent. Having no 24% DEET (the five-hour wipe-on with an almost nofailure risk), the men use their only remedy, *"greesing themselves"* with bear fat slathered on thick.

Not only are Clark and the Corps miserable, but so are the local animals. Red-headed William's temper is probably up when he writes, *"I killed five deer and the man with me killed 2. four others were killed in the Course of the day by the party only 2 of those deer were fat owing as I suppose to the Musquetors which are So noumerous and troublesom to them that they Cannot feed except under the torments of millions of those Musquetors."*

The Exemplary Hunters

If any one thing needs to be said for the hunters, it is that these men carry the lives of their compatriots on their shoulders, providing food and nourishment during times when it is often thought impossible to find anything. Yet they manage to find game, working long and awful hours in the worst of weather and in unknown terrain. The Captains often record pity and sympathy for their tough, uncomplaining hunters in such a state. Being a hunter, under all these circumstances, is a tribute to the men themselves, their endurance, and their willingness to persevere.

Michael Haynes

Sacagawea and Jean Baptist ("Pomp") as mother prepares a small cooking fire – from Michael Haynes' artist's collection.

Cooking Techniques

She made a Kettle of boild Simnins [pumpkins], beens, Corn & Choke Cherries with the Stones which was paletable ... Considered, as a treat among those people.

— CLARK, DECEMBER 23, 1804

THE *JOURNALS* ARE NOT FILLED WITH mouth-watering game recipes or dazzling treatments for native vegetables. Instead, they reveal some cooking techniques, a scattered but comprehensive list of edibles, and a number of broad recipes with no measurements. Reading through the eleven volumes is like reading a culinary mystery: here a clue, there a clue. The solution is an impressionist picture, and regretfully there is no grand or tangible feast at the end of the story.

Much that we would like to know was so taken for granted that it wasn't mentioned, and this isn't all that surprising. Today a person would write, "made a breakfast of ham and eggs" and never think of listing the coffee or toast or elaborating the details. Human nature tends not to elaborate on a procedure it takes for granted. What the *Journals* offer are small hints, often just one sentence which leads us to an impression, a reflection in a dark mirror.

Furthermore, the daily entries by Ordway, Gass, Whitehouse, and the Captains don't always agree. During the spring abundance, the various *Journals* are at odds over what is brought in and eaten, and this basically reflects 1) the mood of the writer and 2) what each mess is cooking. These same discrepancies occur often enough to note them – when, for instance, the men are starving in the Bitterroots and it is critical to know what they actually ate. Later, on December 7, 1805, at Fort Clatsop, Clark itemizes *"pork"* on his inventory. Where did that come from? They supposedly had eaten all they had with them early in the Bitterroots – pork has been off the menu for three months. Perhaps Clark did not mean "pork," but meant "meat" and wrote "pork" without thinking. There are no answers. Mysteries abound.

What did the kitchen look like? Archaeological Evidence.

The only heat on the trip is a fire, and flickering flames heat both men and food. The fire pits (one for each mess and one for the Captains) are circular, constructed with a ring of stones around the outside perimeter to keep the fire from being blown out, or blowing away and starting a prairie or forest fire. A few more rocks are also placed inside the outer ring, to balance cookpots away from the hottest fire area.

There are times when accidents happen – sometimes this can tell us a story. Ken Karsmizki is an archaeologist devoted to the Lewis and Clark story who has spent more than twenty years tracking where the explorers might have camped or stayed for any duration (such as the area near White Bear Islands, during the Great Falls portage in Montana). His research has located evidence of a fire circle, and that site also shows a set of pot leg marks which are baked into the soil.[58] He speculates that a cast-iron pot of spilled soup "set" those marks and left a clear outline of where the pot had rested; he also believes that those same legged cookpots were put off to the side of the fire, resting on rocks with coals underneath – a slow-cooker, if you will. However, as the equipment inventory does not list any cast-iron

Dutch ovens and legged kettles.

ware, it is speculative as to whether this was a "legged kettle," a "spider" (cast iron fry-pan with legs), or a "Dutch Oven" with a lipped lid to retain coals on top for baking or roasting. The sole clue comes from Whitehouse's reference to caching a *Dutch Oven* on June 11, 1805.

Further excavations have found an encampment spot with a butchering area slightly away from the camp. Then come three fire circles (think sergeants' messes 1, 2, and 3). At the end of that row is an equipment area. Finally, protected behind the line of the messes, sandwiched between the troops and the riverbank, is one lone fire circle. This is probably the Captains' mess where York and Charbonneau prepared meals for Lewis, Clark, Sacagawea and baby Pomp, Drouillard, and themselves.

But during rainy, snowy times on the trail, how do the mess cooks protect their cook fires? Desperation often leads to improvised solutions. The *Journal* inventories record 40 yards of thicker quality oil linen *"to form two half faced Tents or Shelters."* There certainly was never any intent to have cooking fires contained within cloth confines; but in drenching rain, perhaps these tent sections served as impromptu mess kitchens.

During the Corps' three winter encampments, the forts are built to provide each mess unit with at least a one-room bunkroom/workroom/kitchen, all heated by a fireplace. Now imagine the pouring rain at Fort Clatsop, and cooking salmon or whale blubber in your bedroom. A separate "smokehouse" room serves as an auxiliary to the kitchen functions, used for making jerky and preserving meat supplies as they come in.

Stoking up the Fires

The entire meal process is time-consuming. Firewood has to be gathered, and this is not always an easy task. In one episode of Captain Lewis cooking at White Bear Islands, he says he collected his wood. Then he says, *"Shields and Gass returned with a better supply of timber than they had yet collected tho' not by any means enough."* [J4:334] Lewis is certainly not out scrounging wood, since he says the other two men are searching far afield. Rather, he is selecting the pre-collected wood and building his fire. It takes the labor of three men to build one fire. The wood situation also influences where the Expedition camps for the night. *"This evening we encamped, for the benefit of wood, near two dead toped cottonwood trees ... the dead limbs which had fallen from these trees furnished us with a scanty supply only, and more was not to be obtained in the neighborhood."* [J4:208] This scarcity of firewood will crop up over and over, and the *Journal* entries make much of the problem.

Fuel Substitutes

When wood is unavailable the privates go searching for other prairie fuel. Anything that will burn is gathered. There are buffalo-chips, which some wag later christens "anthracite of the desert,"[59] sagebrush, hackberry bush, willow, and – over the entire trip – a host of other burnables. It is worth noting that the twiggy substitutes burn quickly and a great quantity is needed; the denser wood logs burn more slowly and are relatively long-lasting. To get a real sense of the difficulty the fuel situation poses, consider Lewis' situation on August 10, 1805. His little party is moving fast, thirty miles a day. The Captain commissions Drouillard to get some meat for breakfast; he then builds a fire and waits. He waits an hour and a half by his estimation. Three times during his wait, he writes, complaining about the lack of wood, stating that they are reduced to using dry willow brush – the largest fuel in sight – which is quickly consumed. The Captain is very busy collecting twigs during his long wait, and he becomes hungrier and more irritated each time he goes out.

After the Expedition crosses over the Rockies, the extremely barren landscape of the Columbia plateau leads to outright theft. Until this time, the Corps has been impeccable in their behavior toward the natives. Clark writes, *"we have made it a point at all times not to take any thing belonging to the Indians even their wood. but at this time we are Compelled to violate that rule and take part of the Split timber we find here bured for fire wood, as no other is to be found in any direction."* [J5:272] So critical is the fuel situation that it has a decidedly negative impact on the men. *"we Could not Cook brakfast before we embarked as usial for the want of wood or Something to burn."* [J5:314]

Exploring on a ten-mile sidetrip up the barren Columbia plains, Clark observes natives *"drying fish & Prickley pare (to Burn in the winter),"* [J5:301] Just as the Plains Indians and early pioneers gathered buffalo-dung, the locals adapt to what they can use successfully. They are given to knocking over and drying a nasty form of prickly pear, as well as sun-drying fish (oily, combustible, and probably smelly when burning). But this is a treeless land. The heavier wood used for fish scaffolds and lodge construction is floated downriver from the mountains after parties of native men travel great distances to harvest trees. Burning wood is unnecessary when alternate fuels are at hand.

Until late in 1805, the Corps has purchased only food. Now their trade goods go to fill an unanticipated need. They are *"obliged to purchase wood at a high rate."* The lack of wood is aggravating – *"last night we could not Collect more dry willows the only fuel, than was barely Sufficient to cook Supper, and not a Sufficency to cook brackfast this morning."* J5:315 Eventually the situation is so bad that they have to start out on a frosty morning without a warm-up breakfast or campfire; there is nothing burnable. On October 21, 1805, at the end of a long day after paddling forty-two miles, they are reduced to a new low, *"landed at 5 Lodges of Pierced noses Indians at 4 miles where we encamped and purchased a little wood to boil our Dogs & fish … fortunately for us the night was worm."* It becomes a new pattern: buying dog, fish, and just enough wood to cook a meal. Seeing their trade goods disappearing, they hope not to need nighttime fires for warmth.

Only after the climatic zone softens into the moister Pacific region does the fuel situation ease up. Clark, the consummate frontier woodsman finally writes, *"the only wood we could get to burn on this little Island on which we have encamped is the newly discovered Ash, which makes a tolerable fire."* J5:357

First the Wood, then the Fire

After enough fuel is gathered, a few more minutes are involved in lighting the tiniest twigs (tinder) by striking a flint against steel, or perhaps using a spark from a gun flintlock held close to the fine tinder. The common match had been invented just recently but was relatively unknown and certainly not in mass production. While Lewis may have been given some of these unusual "lucifers," in St. Louis, the best assumption is that they used flint and steel. Clark was trying to buy more flints as they returned to Mandan country in 1806.

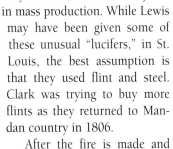

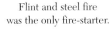
Flint and steel fire was the only fire-starter.

After the fire is made and burns down to coals, cooking can commence. Raw meat does not cook up immediately, so this was a good time for the men to relax from their labors, pick thorns from their feet, stitch moccasins, or merely rest.

Finally Dinner Can Begin: The Mess Cooks

The cooks work so hard that normally they are excused from other duties. They are always excused from guard duty, as they are still working when the rest of the Corps is done for the day, and in winter they are up early getting breakfast ready as the men awaken. The cooks are morale boosters,

making the best of what the hunters bring in, trying to keep everyone full and happy.

Only on rare occasions do the Captains cook. On June 26, 1805, at the Great Falls portage camps, while Charbonneau cooks at lower portage camp, Lewis takes on the responsibility at the upper camp – *"to myself I assign the duty of cook as well for those present as for the party which I expect again to arrive this evening from the lower camp. I collected my wood and water, boiled a large quantity of excellent dryed buffalo meat and made each man a large suet dumpling by way of a treat."* Lewis is likely to have been disappointed as he finished this tasty dumpling and meat stew, for no one is there to eat it. The men finally arrive for dinner late in the evening, dragging in two more canoes and even more baggage. His "treats" were probably similar to the dumplings in this traditional recipe.

SUET DUMPLINGS[60]

| ½ lb. | suet | 1 tsp. | salt |
| 3 C. | flour | 1 C. | cold water |

Finely dice suet, mix with flour and salt. Gradually add water until mixture forms a ball. Shape into 2" dumpling balls. Place in stew and cook until done (approximately 25 minutes at a simmer) – makes a dozen dumplings.

More surprisingly, on July 1, Lewis is found helping Drouillard with a very messy cooking chore, for the two of them *"completed the opperation of rendering the tallow; we obtained about 100 lbs."* Frying great greasy hunks of fat down to oil is quite beyond what a Virginia gentleman would normally do, but behind this task is perhaps Lewis' idea of using the result to caulk and waterproof his pet project: the iron-frame-boat covering.

A Few Notes on Kitchen Equipment

Cooking Gear – There is strong evidence that the inventories do not show all the cooking equipment carried on the Expedition. When the *Journals* note a meal of *"roasted"* or *"broiled"* meat, it is highly unlikely that the cooks threw the meat on the coals, but the record is strangely silent about what tools they actually are using.

Standard "barbeque" equipment of the day could be manufactured by any blacksmith: two upright supports to hold a pointed cross-rod over the fire. Meat could either be threaded

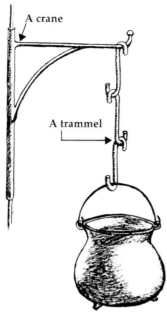

A crane

A trammel

Crane and trammel s-hooks
support kettles in fire places.

onto the rod directly or be hung by trammels or "S" hooks, shaped just like the letter, the bottom of the "S" hooking the meat or pot while the top of the "S" hangs over the rod. The advantage of the S-hook is that the meat can be seared directly over the heat, and then slid away to the side of the fire for slower cooking. Threaded meat is more troublesome to move, and the rod must be turned to keep the meat from burning. Many of the rods actually had a handle on one side, just for this turning function. On other spit rods, the blacksmith loops the metal back on itself, forming a circle at the end. A hefty stick could be inserted into this and used as a turn handle.[a] Also, the brass kettles with the thin, half-circle handles could be hung from the rod by trammels allowing a soup or stew to cook over the fire. Probably this gear was so standard it went unnoticed, or perhaps it was made by the Camp River Dubois blacksmith.

By the time the Corps reaches the Pacific coast, many cook pots have been lost out of capsizing canoes or washed out to sea by merciless storms. On November 21, 1805, Clark purchases some replacements: tightly woven baskets used for stone-boiling foods.

In addition to the non-inventoried cast-iron ware discussed above, there are other utensils which go unmentioned. The inventories don't list long-handled stirring spoons used to keep the cornmeal and flour-thickened stews from burning. Even if they had very thick potholders, the cooks aren't going to be pouring from a red-hot kettle, a disaster of unwanted spills and burns waiting to happen; yet no mention is made of ladles for serving these dishes or the portable soup or long-handled forks for securing or stabbing chunks of meat. No plates are indicated; the men are issued

cups for drinking or eating soups and stews. But certainly cups aren't the right equipment for holding a very large slab of barbeque or even a fried trout. The troops probably end up carving their own plates from wood, the old wooden trencher found in European history. Forks have yet to be accepted by most Americans, and it is only later that they will make their way onto the table.

The Beloved Knives – The long, red-handled knives are multi-purpose. They can be used for butchering, cutting meat at a meal, and much more. The following episode demonstrates what fine quality they are.

Much of what is now Montana is the terminal end of glaciers, and they deposited an extremely fine glacial or alluvial till that makes an extremely compacted, difficult, and slippery soil. Up the Marias River, constant rain on June 7, 1805, turns this "gumbo" soil into a slick lubricant and Lewis nearly slides over a ninety-foot precipice. Windsor, directly behind him, also slips and finds himself hanging in space, grasping the slick hillside for all his life is worth. He is saved only by Lewis' calm instructions and the aid of his hefty knife, which all the men carry. He literally carves not meat, but mountain, and works out a foothold to salvation. That same day other men in the party are carving footsteps into the bluffs so they can continue towing the boats when the water becomes too deep. Those great knives, so hefty and strong, literally cut a path for the Expedition.

The Food Inventory: What it tells us about the Corps' Meals

From the inventories of food and equipment taken, the following emerges:

♦ Baking, as in cakes and cookies, isn't done. Easily portable leavening has not yet been invented, nor do they take a huge quantity of sugar. There are no baking pans, although a covered kettle could suffice. In some moment of inspiration, someone might have made a mix of flour, sugar, egg, and water, making something like a pancake.

♦ Dairy is a rare commodity, mentioned only in the spring of 1805, when the men are gathering goose eggs. When found, the ratio of men to eggs is something like ten-to-one. Since these finds are unusual, they are not significant except as a different item eaten.

♦ Carbohydrates are limited to whole corn kernels (parched corn), cornmeal, and flour. Any other sources are acquired on the road. In parts of the West, with native help, the starches are plentiful – first in the form of camas, then wapato, cous, and other bulbs/roots.

[a] The Lewis and Clark Honor Guard in Great Falls, Montana, uses his setup and also keeps the meat securely in place on the rod by anchoring it with wrought-iron forks about two feet long.

◆ Meat, in the form of brined pork, is a backup supply – hunted fresh game will provide most of the meats.

◆ As for seasonings, the Captains both write of using salt and pepper in cooking, although Clark is probably the only man on the entire trip who doesn't care a whit about salting his food. As far as any other seasonings, the *"spicies assorted"* from Philadelphia are noted only in Clark's beaver bait (page 38).

◆ Coffee is brought along, but mentioned once in two years.

Changing Recipes, Changing Tastes

Understanding the Corps' food is difficult, for what was acceptable in 1800 is no longer acceptable or even appreciated. Classic wildlife recipes have disappeared altogether from the American cookbooks and the 1997 *Joy of Cooking*, yielding to new times, abandoned earlier favorites. Farewell, "muscrat with creamed celery." Goodbye ole frontier friends: possum, beaver, porcupine. Live well. Science also throws a noose around old standbys – so long, lard! Finally there is a shrinking use of the pantry of native American edibles, triggered by a modernized food industry, an increasingly cosmopolitan array of foods, and a highly urban culture which brings freeze-dried backpacking meals into the wilderness.

The recipes discussed throughout this book are plain and simple, and many can not be exactly replicated at home unless there is a game and native vegetable supplier at hand. But, in most cases, a close approximation can be made with the substitution of similar, but more available, modern ingredients.

European-style Recipes – A recipe, in Virginia terms, usually involves not only ingredients but measures, the sequence of steps/additions, the time and temperature for cooking. Recipes, by their nature, can be exacting or loose, or characterized by a number of ingredients used (many twenty-first century recipes call for twenty to thirty ingredients, quite complicated). All dishes listed in the *Appendix A: Index of Recipes* can be prepared at home. Classics from the Eastern seaboard such as Fish House Punch or Biscuit de Savoye have precise measures. The closest a trail recipe comes to following this pattern is Lewis' very complete description of boudin blanc, which lacks only precise measures and the cooking time.

Trail Recipes – Recipes, if you can call them that, for foods cooked on the trail are vague. They have no precise measures, no steps to follow in cooking, and no cooking times. But they are authentic. And not all meals are cooked from fresh ingredients. Once a food has been preserved, how will it be used? Will it be eaten "as is" like pemmican or jerky? Or, reconstituted while being cooked – like corn, beans, or jerky-soup? Or, washed and then cooked like brined pork? All of these questions interplay with what foods the Captains want eaten and which cooking technique the mess cooks will use.

Indian Recipes – Ethnographically, the journalists record many native cooking techniques and even jot down impressionistic recipes. But very few native women west of the Mississippi even contemplated the possible variety of plant seeds, spices, recipes and resultant finished dishes existing in Europe, and imported to the new colonies. (The exception would be the "stolen" ones who sought refuge and returned home or those who were traded into a white family.) The Indians measure their variety in types of corn, squash, and beans they choose to grow, each subspecies with its own special set of taste nuances. The women's food preparation is traditional and basic. The measure of "a cup" is duplicated by another type of measure, that of "a double-handful" and despite the odd phraseology, it leads to an authentic and reproducible dish. Look at the food, feel it with the fingers – that's kinesthetic learning, the frontier and native style found here.

Cooking Methods

Boiling Down

Boiling is an old and honorable cooking tradition. The sheer act of raising the temperature and evaporating the water out of a substance causes a condensation and concentration. Both sugaring, done in the early spring of 1804, and salt-making, in 1805–06, involve boiling down and condensing. The men appear to have no problems in handling either of these similar processes and the end-products turn out exactly as they want.

Diane Haker - courtesy: Mountain Arts

Camp River Dubois sugar-making team labors over kettles of boiling sap. Fifty-six gallons of sap make ten pounds of sugar.

Boiling: Cooking with Water

Boiling can be the simplest means of cooking. Put a food in hot water and it cooks. This easy-cook method is the start of the Lewis' favorite meal, the boudin blanc. The water is not intended to be part of the meal. However, if the food is cooked and served with the accompanying water or broth, we think of it as soup. If a thickener is added, the dish becomes a stew. At least 14 different soups are recorded in the *Journals*. Several are vegetarian, some are strictly meat, and at least two are a combination.

VEGETABLE SOUP IN THE MANDAN STYLE[b]

2 C. butternut, acorn, or kabocha squash
1 qt. vegetable stock
1 C.   corn kernels – re-hydrated parched corn
1 C.   dried cherries, seeded
¾ C. white beans – cooked, then measured
          (salt and pepper to taste)

Peel squash and cut into 1" cubes. Simmer the stock and add the squash; cook for 20 minutes. Add the corn and cherries; continue cooking for 10 minutes. Before serving, add the white beans to heat through.
Makes 8-10 servings.

Soups

Vegetable soups are made from vegetables, roots, and berries. One example is made as a welcoming present for Captain Lewis, representative of the Great White Father, by the Teton Sioux. Ordway records, *"they Gave Capt. Lewis Some fine Soup made of what they call white apples."* [J9:69]

Soup, for the natives, is a proper gift of welcome. Later, at Fort Mandan on December 23, 1804, not only do Chief Little Crow's wife and son carry corn down to the Fort, but his wife also prepares a special soup for the Captains. *"This Dish is Considered, as a treat among those people."* From his apparent lack of enthusiasm, Clark appears to be unimpressed.

---

[b] The only *Journal* hint of an actual Mandan recipe is *"a Kettle of boild simnins [pumpkin], beens, Corn & Choke Cherris"* [J3:261] which is shown as *Mandan Winter Stew* on page 115. This adaptation, from similar recipes of the era and the materials available to the Corps, was served to 100 people in Great Falls, MT, in 2002, and a good majority liked it, thought it good. Note: if parched corn is not available, fresh corn cut from the cob can substitute.

On August 26, 1805, on the same day that a Nez Perce woman sends her baggage horses on with a friend while she stops to give birth to her baby and then catches up in about an hour, Lewis issues *"a pint of corn to be given each Indian who was engaged in transporting our baggage and about the same quantity to each of the men which they parched pounded and made into supe."* When the Corps first encounters the Nez Perce, they comment upon the camas bread and also note a camas soup. [J5:222] It is not clear if they consume this at one of the meals they are invited to, or if it is simply a culinary note. Clark is served another kind of soup while visiting the Clatsops, a berry soup. The local berry is the salal, a deep purple coastal fruit. An earlier edition of the *Journals* has roots added to this soup.[61]

Meat soups are made also along the trail, from a variety of animals and birds, and usually *"Supe"* of this sort is prepared for the sick. Many foods are traditionally used as medicine, and readily digestible soup for bodies out of order has been prescribed for millenia.

An example is squirrel soup, which is made just as the expedition is about to embark up the Missouri. Clark writes, *"Priors is verry Sick I sent out R Field to kill a squirel to make him Suip."* [J2:183] Earlier, going up the Mississippi, Lewis had brewed a heath hen (grouse) soup *"for my friend Capt. Clark who has been much indisposed since the 16th [Nov. 1803]."* [J2:101] Again, the health giving properties of a *"rich soope"* of buffalo are touted when Sacagawea falls ill at Great Falls and this nutritional booster is noted on June 17, 1805, as she is recovering. As the Corps stumbles out of the Rockies and is afflicted with disastrous gastrointestinal disorders in late September, 1805, Clark orders up the old standby. *"Provisions all out, which Compells us to kill one of our horses to eate and make Suep for the Sick men."* [J5:244]

Two soups are noted with a mixture of meat and vegetable; the first is an elk and wapato soup made for a sick Clark on December 3, 1805. The second is a soup made from breadroot (or white apple) and meat as the Corps is on its way home and back in what is now North Dakota. Familiar plants begin to reappear, and this is one of the few occasions where the men are allowed to dig their own vegetables. The root is an old favorite of the engagés: *"pomme blanche."* The men must have been excited for they *"dug great parcel of the root ... which they boiled and made use of with their meat."* [J8:288] Clark dislikes this combination, again finding the French ways with food unsuited to his palate, but he goes on to observe that the natives also *"use this root after it is dry and pounded in their Seup."* [J8:288]

Mandan soup ladle and bowl.

Boiling as a Cleansing Method

Boiling water is also a means used to leach undesirable properties out of certain foods. The acorn is a prime example. As one of the more difficult foods to deal with, this nut is a tight, compact little bundle of tannin and other indigestables, which often leads to the acorn being deemed poisonous. One food authority cites only twenty-seven of the sixty indigenous species as being edible.[62] The acorns are generally pounded, and then leached several times in water to remove unwanted toxins or bitter flavors. With this is mind, it is no wonder that despite the Corps' familiarity with acorns, and eating them, the men do not prepare the nuts themselves.

Boiling to Preserve Moisture

Boiling is also a cooking technique that enhances or preserves moisture in foods that might otherwise dry out in a harsh contact with heat, such as roasting. The cooks are ready to go after the Captain *"purchased a little wood to boil our Dogs & fish."* [J5:315] This is not a combined stew – rather, each ingredient is cooked separately. Each of these foods will benefit from not contracting and drying out, and much of the internal oil will remain in the flesh if the water is kept at a low temperature on the side of the fire.

About ten thousand years ago the earliest ancestors of the native American cooks devised a boiling technology; archaeologists date it back to Archaic times. These progenitors, not having metal, found that food could be cooked by placing it into water-filled, tightly woven baskets into which hot rocks from the fire are dropped. After a time, the water boils (from the internal heat of the rocks) and cooks the food. The fresh (undried) baskets that the Corps sees are made from beargrass and reinforced with roots of the western red cedar.[63] These baskets speak of weavers' skills in creating tight, waterproof items that do not leak and can withstand stone-boiling. Clark reports that he *"Saw them boiling fish in baskets with Stones ..."* [J5:347] This quick-cook is more than adequate. Also, in referring to the burial practices of the Chinook natives, Clark observes *"Basquets of which they*

make great use to hold water boil their meet &c. &c." are included in the funerary offerings. Either he has been told of, or has seen, meat being cooked the same way as the fish. A large piece would cook slowly, so it might have been cut down to smaller, quicker cooking sizes.

On the return trip home, the Expedition stops at what is now called Jackson Hot Springs, located in Beaverhead County, Montana. Clark is quite curious about this natural feature and conducts his own little experiments. *"this Spring contains a very considerable quantity of water, and actually blubbers with heat for 20 paces below where it rises. ... too hot for a man to endure his hand in it 3 seconds. I directt Sergt. Pryor and John Shields to put each a peice of meat in the water of different Sises. the one about the Size of my 3 fingers Cooked dun in 25 minits the other much thicker was 32 minits before it became Sufficiently dun. ... [the water was] a little sulferish."* [J8:170] The eaters make no complaints about any sulphur flavor.

Stews

The last type of "boiling" technique is for stews. The deer stew recipe below substitutes domestic onions for wild onions but is authentic in approach and ingredients:

DEER STEW A LA CORPS

1 lb.	deer, cut into bite-size pieces flour, salt, pepper dredging mixture
2-4 T.	bear fat (pork fat or your oil of choice can be substituted)
½	red onion, chopped
1 pt.	pearl onions, peeled and halved
3-4 C.	water (boiling preferred)

Dredge the deer meat in a flour/salt/pepper mixture. Throw the meat into a heated pan with hot fat. Brown, turning regularly, and add the chopped red onion. Add up to ¼ cup of the leftover dredging mix and stir to make a smooth roux. As the browning completes, add at least 3 cups of boiling water, stirring until the flour/water mixture is smooth and not lumpy. If it looks too thick, add more water. Cook for approximately 30 minutes, stirring regularly, adding more water if necessary. Add the pearl onions and cook for another 10 minutes or so.

Serves 4 as a main course.

Dredging versus a Roux

Continental cooking uses a roux (a mixture of fat and flour) to thicken a soup into a stew. For example: "The turkeys are cooked rather simply, and the sauce is thickened with a roux of pork fat and flour; but at the end he [La Varenne] adds, 'If raspberries are in season, throw a handful on top.' "[64] The colonial French, and indeed the coastal colonists, know this type of cooking well, but they might also use dredging flour, as in the preceding recipe. The measurements there are for the modern cook; the mess cooks would have tossed in whatever they had and used a kinesthetic approach, adding more (flour, in this case) where necessary.

Roasting, Broiling, Barbeque

Despite the orders of the day to boil their meals, the men like their meat cooked over a fire. Several different words describe the barbeque process, *"broiled"* or *"roasted"* being the most common. All sorts of meat goes over the fire, the *Journals* never record a burnt dinner, and invariably everyone is happy. Sergeant Ordway records, *"About noon we killed a fat Bull and took out the hump ... we broiled the hump and eat a hearty meal of it."* [J9:175] These humps can weight at least 30 pounds and would require a while to cook, even if cut into three or four pieces (a 9-pound roast takes about an hour and a half). This would indicate that the meat would need continuous turning to avoid becoming charred, indirectly pointing to the need for a lever on the spit to accomplish this. As an aside, but still on the topic of turning the meat, Clark mentions a *"turnspit dog."* This is a true curiosity, one known from Renaissance times: *"A type of small dog ... trained to walk on a treadmill to furnish power to a turn-spit."* [J6:3n5] Another reason to keep man's best friend around.

Other examples: *"Some of our party killed a fat dog, which they had got from the Indians at the last Village that we passed through. They roasted & eat it in the Evining – "* [J11:338] Salmon also gets the flame treatment: *"one of the young men took his guig and killed 6 fine Salmon two of them were roasted and we eate ..."* [J5:233]

The Expedition may roast their meats, but the Clatsops prefer to roast their vegetables and the Captains find this to be a new culinary experience. Boiling vegetables is a long-standing American tradition (descending from the British cooking style) that cooks the food simply. Roasting, especially for foods that have a higher sugar content, brings out the sweetness and actually can slightly caramelize the crust, adding yet another flavor dimension. Lewis is experiencing this phenomena when he writes about roasted thistle root, *"it becomes black, and is more shugary than any fuit or root*

that I have met with in uce among the natives ..." [J6:226] Camas bulbs are also roasted on the embers, *"like a potato,"* Clark notes on December 27, 1805. Bracken fern, giant horsetail rush, and even acorns are roasted.

Smoking

Smoking is usually considered a means of food preservation, but extra flavor is also imparted by a fine wood smoke. Many different types of woods (apple, hickory, oak) add this extra nuance, this extra layer of taste complexity, to open-fire smoking of food. *"We fleece all the meat and hang it up over a Small Smoke ..."* [J6:127]

Frying

Frying certainly is not the Army's endorsed method of cooking, but it is a favorite. Coming down the Ohio, Lewis makes many meals of black squirrels and comments, *"they wer fat and I thought them when fryed a pleasent food."* [J2:79] Even at the very beginning of the trip, lard is bought: *"1 keg of pork fat,"* [J2:203] and this soft, flavorful fat would have been used for cooking. The constant rendering of grizzly fat indicates more frying and it is used in the second stage browning of

Courtesy: C. H. Holland

Meat spit roasting and stew simmering over fire.

COOKING TECHNIQUES ∂⟩ 51

the boudin blanc sausage. Fish, another candidate for frying, shows up on October 26, 1805, *"giged a Salmon Trout, which we had fried in a little Bears oil ..."*

Baking

There is no evidence that the men actually baked anything other than one lonesome buffalo-berry tart. Some of the cornmeal or flour might have been mixed with water and patted into flat breads or ash cakes, and while these old-time breads are edible, they are not inspiring. Their virtue is in the chewing, something to rip into, far more substantial than the soft texture of a mush or a stew.

Plain-Style Cookery

The Corps' cooking techniques get the job done. They reflect a plain frontier cookery that treats food as a fuel, not a gourmet experience. The entrées are adequate, and keeping the hungry young bucks fed is a full-time job of the hunter and a hot, arduous one for the cooks. Except the rave reviews for Charbonneau's charcuterie (the boudin blanc), none of the dishes mentioned shine with culinary brilliance. The men indeed enjoy many of the foods they eat during their two year tour of the New American Pantry, but rather than great cooking, this is more a case of very hungry young men and tasty, fresh ingredients.

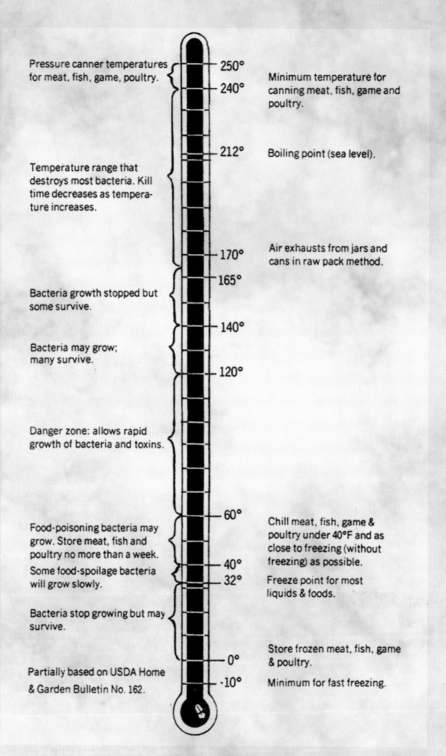

Pressure canner temperatures for meat, fish, game, poultry. — 250°

240° — Minimum temperature for canning meat, fish, game and poultry.

212° — Boiling point (sea level).

Temperature range that destroys most bacteria. Kill time decreases as temperature increases.

170° — Air exhausts from jars and cans in raw pack method.

165°

Bacteria growth stopped but some survive.

140°

Bacteria may grow; many survive.

120°

Danger zone: allows rapid growth of bacteria and toxins.

60° — Chill meat, fish, game & poultry under 40°F and as close to freezing (without freezing) as possible.

Food-poisoning bacteria may grow. Store meat, fish and poultry no more than a week.

Some food-spoilage bacteria will grow slowly.

40°

32° — Freeze point for most liquids & foods.

Bacteria stop growing but may survive.

0° — Store frozen meat, fish, game & poultry.

Partially based on USDA Home & Garden Bulletin No. 162.

-10° — Minimum for fast freezing.

USDA recommended cooking and storage temperatures for meats, fish, and poultry.

Nutritional Maladies

*I am verry unwell the drid fish which is
my only diet does not agree with me ...*

— CLARK, DECEMBER 2, 1805

IN 1803 THE LEADING PHYSICIAN of the time is Dr. Benjamin Rush, with whom Lewis studies. Rush can only hope to stave off what horrors might be lurking in the waters, plucked from bushes, or growing unchecked in the intestines. He is all too familiar with the drama of death-in-waiting. The good doctor sends off a letter of admonition to Lewis on June 11, 1803, and of the eleven cautions prescribed, seven relate to what goes into or out of the body:

✦ "When you feel the least indisposition, do not attempt to overcome it by labour or marching. Rest in a horizontal posture. Also fasting and diluting drinks for a day or two will generally prevent an attack of fever. To these preventatives of disease may be added a gentle sweat obtained by warm drinks, or gently opening the bowels by means of one, two, or more of the purging pills."

✦ "Unusual costiveness [constipation] is often a sign of approaching disease. When you feel it take one or more of the purging pills."

✦ "Want of appetite is likewise a sign of approaching indisposition. It should be obviated by the same remedy."

✦ "In difficult and laborious enterprises & marches, *eating sparingly* will enable you to bear them with less fatigue & less danger to your health."

✦ "The less spirit you use the better. After being *wetted* or *much* fatigued, or *long* exposed to the night air, it should be taken in an *undiluted* state. 3 tablespoons taken in this way will be more useful ... than half a pint mixed with water."

✦ "Molasses or sugar & water with a few drops of the acid of vitriol will make a pleasant & wholsome drink with your meals." L1:54-55

As it is, the issue of bacterial contamination and food safety plagues the party in their trek across the West. If Lewis followed these particular prescriptives, the Expedition might never have reached the Pacific. Looking in retrospect at the Expedition's food handling, their kitchen and supplies are indeed at great risk. Today's food safety experts warn that serious food-borne illnesses bloom and spread under many different conditions, at least in these five major arenas:[65]

✦ Improper holding and storage temperatures for food
✦ Inadequate cooking
✦ Improper hygiene
✦ Contaminated equipment or cross-contamination
✦ Food from an unsafe source

Given these guidelines, the Corps of Discovery (as well as most trappers and other frontier folk) should have died off before they got halfway to the Pacific. Of course refrigeration, antibacterial treatments, meat thermometers, and federal regulations were unknown at the time.

If credence is given to current knowledge, then it is surprising that the men experienced as few episodes of stomach ailments as they did. Perhaps immune system defenses were stronger in 1800. Their terrifically healthy bodies only yielded to these factors when they were loaded one on top of the other, since virtually 100% of the time they had at least one or more of these negative attributes present.

Dehydration and Malnutrition

Despite being near water for most of the journey, dehydration is a risk for the Corps and dry overland treks (such as the Great Falls portage or the high mountain desert of the Bitteroots) are taxing and dangerous. While some lost inventory list may show all the men equipped with canteens, the *"sportsman's flask"* that carries liquor is the only one mentioned. The men were supposed to keep hydrated with either their cupped hands or tin cups thrust into a stream. Under these circumstances, drinking enough water is nearly impossible and dehydration is a clear certainty. From the Army manual cited earlier, two more contemporary guidelines specify:

Do not consume protein snacks. Eating huge amounts of protein requires extra fluids to metabolize the amino acids, and if water is not available, this will trigger dehydration. An indicator of this condition is dark yellow urine to brownish urine. Army guidelines suggest "pale yellow" or even "clear and copious" as the color to shoot for. The 1800s Army manufactures high-protein jerky and pemmican, standards of the day.

Do not eat ice/snow or drink cold water. Enhanced bodily sensitivity to the cold makes drinking ice water an unpleasant chore and the soldier therefore doesn't drink as much as he should. At altitude, the troops must find fuel and make a fire to melt snow into drinkable water. According to the Army's current assessment, "It takes an exorbitant amount of time and fuel to melt snow in sufficient quantities (it takes 40 minutes to melt 4 cups of snow to make a cup of water)."

The Cold Water Mystery

Water, usually so life-giving, can cause problems when coupled with overexertion. On June 26, 1805, Lewis reports that Private Whitehouse arrives totally fatigued and thirsty, drinks *"a very hearty draught of water and was taken almost instanly extreemly ill."* Whitehouse says, *"I expect by drinking too much water when I was hot. I got bled &c"* J11:212 This afflicted journalist notes another man going down with the same complaint. This curious malady can be linked to overexertion, overheating, and dehydration. Once this trio gets into a vicious cycle, it's hard to get the body back on an even keel.

Overexertion – All of the cold water mysteries happen when the men have been working to the maximum and their condition is aggravated by overheating. When these two problems coincide, an imbalance of electrolytes (potassium/sodium/calcium/magnesium) occurs, the minerals lost though copious sweating – an unfortunate result since they are influential in preventing dehydration and overheating. As they are depleted, the body gets more and more out of balance, and there are potential risks (the extreme being death due to heat stroke or dehydration).

Dehydration – Looking carefully at the situation, Whitehouse has a stomach capacity of little less than a quart (a short liter). Walking and working in a hot dry environment, he becomes dehydrated, lips and skin dry, but absorbed in what he's doing, he forgets to drink. The thirst sensors in the brain are not particularly sensitive. Maybe he's away from the river at this point. Then, suddenly terribly thirsty and back at the river, he downs several big cups of cold water. He might feel a little discomfort from putting very cold water into his overheated body. The recommended athletic prescription is to drink tiny, almost continuous, sips. A little in, a little out. Think of the stomach as balloon, with a very narrow stem that empties into the intestine. If the stomach is rather empty, putting three-fourths of a quart in (those three thirsty gulps) can make the stomach painfully full, for the pressure is outward and remains quite uncomfortable even as the stomach slowly empties. While the large and small intestines keep the water moving and spilling down the tract, the stomach may actually shrink back on itself as the water travels on.

Another time, Lewis says, *"[Clark] suffered excessively with the heat and the want of water, at length he arrived at a very cold spring, at which he took the precaution of weting his feet head and hands before drank but notwithstanding this precaution he soon felt the effects of the water. he felt himself very unwell shortly after but continued his march ... [he] was so unwell that he had no inclination to eat."* J4:431

Clark's disinclination to eat is the result of his over-filled stomach (from the water) collapsing. An imbalance of potassium to sodium may also confuse the body which is trying to return to its correct mineral balance.

Overheating – When overheated, the body loses electrolytes through sweating, beginning the nasty complication of dehydration, not to mention steaming the brain. Cooling the outside body is a precaution. Medical wisdom in 1800 observed that if the whole body was overheated, cooling the extremities would reduce the temperature of the blood being circulated. As cooler blood mingles with overheated blood, the core body temperature will gradually drop to normal. Clark is following common wisdom, although he apparently is so overheated that his efforts are futile. Current practice goes further, cooling the head and the heart.

Malnutrition and Near Starvation

Great hunger intrudes on the Expedition more times than anyone expected. Game animals are unavailable; supplies are gone. Hoped-for feasts and unexpected generosity are wishful thinking, vanishing like a flash in the reality that faces them. The saving grace for the Expedition is that they have benefactors like the Mandans who feed them, the Nez Perce who offer salvation from starvation, and other tribes who donate generously.

What exactly are the symptoms of starvation? With fewer calories to burn, less work gets done. The metabolic rate decreases; the bowels begin to atrophy. The intestines can't handle anything, as the previously healthy cellular lining gets thinner and thinner. The Corps' lack of food may have been coupled with the possible anorexia that sets in at altitude: *"we melted what we wanted to drink and made or mixd a little portable Soup with Snow water and lay down contented."* [J11:317] Either the onslaught of starvation, altitude anorexia, or symptoms of both combined helps explain the horrible state the men's bodies are in as they come off the Rockies. Their immediate sickness upon eating seriously complicates everything. It has been suggested by a dietitian at the US Army Research Institute of Environmental Medicine that history has put too much blame on the Nez Perce fish or the camas. Perhaps their twelve-day illness is due to the body's own responses to the withering of the digestive/intestinal system.[66]

"Wasting away" used to be a common phrase. On the physical side there is bodily fatigue, lassitude, inability to even move. The immune system begins to fail. Natural defenses fall and are overwhelmed. The *Journals* record incidence after incidence of skin ailments, aches, pains, and other maladies. *"Boils and imposthumes [abcesses] have been very common with the party Bratton is now unable to work with one on his hand; soar eyes continue also to be common to all of us in a greater or less degree."* [J4:138]

Clark, who is as tough as they come, has no shame in writing of his physical ailments, of having a body out of order. His comments are matter-of-fact and informative, his candor admirable. Psychologically, starvation first prompts a mental hysteria, with frantic or determined scrambling to alleviate the problem. If a solution is unavailable, the weakened body can slip into inaction, the mind into confusion and depression. Finally, there is defeat and death. The visionary but dictatorial spirit of Lewis, who knows nothing other than success, and the practical, problem-solving nature of Clark tend to negate these possibilities. The men know and trust that Clark will bolt down the mountain to find game for them, and will buy dog as long as he has fishhooks to trade. Lewis will bring them home. The men feel they are in good hands.

More Gastrointestinal Complaints

Scurvy

Scurvy is a Vitamin C deficiency. For the Corps it could have been described as "chronic partial Vitamin C deficiency." J. Gerarde's *Herbal* (1633) gives this picture, "... the Scurvie ... this filthy, lothsome, heavy and dull disease, which is very troublesome and of long continuance. The gums are loosed, swolne, and exulcerate, the mouth greevously stinking; the thighs and legs are withall very often full of blew spots, not much unlike those that come of bruises," and on it goes.[67]

Scurvy was the scourge of nations attempting long sea navigation, and epidemics were recorded worldwide from ancient times up until the nineteenth century. The vinegar issued by the U.S. Army was a preventative, as were the lemons and limes that cured British sailors ("limeys") of the disease.

The lack of citrus on the American frontier leads to a ration of 4 quarts of vinegar per 100 rations, which is 128 ounces per 100 days,[68] or 4 teaspoons per man per day. The only mention of this remedy is on January 16, 1804, when Clark records that he settles with Rumsey for *"750 rats. of Soap Candles & vinager."* However, after leaving Camp River Dubois, the vinegar is not mentioned. Was is consumed before they left St. Louis?

Since the Corps carries no vinegar, what would prevent scurvy? Fruits and berries have a high Vitamin C component; this is one natural protection. Even wild greens such as cattail, lamb's quarter, and miner's lettuce have high concentrations.[69] On June 14, 1805, before the berries have really

Miner's lettuce

Used with permission of photographer James Reveal

become abundant, *"two men with the Tooth ake ..."* Do their teeth hurt from loosened gums, an early sign of scurvy? If so, the upcoming berries will solve that problem.

Philadelphia Prescriptions, Native Woman

In June 1804, Sacagawea, their best hope for a successful meeting with the Shoshones, is in danger of dying from a female disorder that causes a virulent infection. Charbonneau, probably not thrilled with a severely invalided wife and a four-month-old baby, contemplates returning home. All the medicinals have failed so far, but then Lewis remembers the curative springs found in Virginia. "Taking the waters" is an old term, and its efficacy is duly noted as the sulphur waters of the spring are administered to the young mother. Several doses later, *"she is free from pain clear of fever, her pulse regular, and eats as heartily as I am willing to permit her of broiled buffaloe well seasoned with pepper and salt and rich soope of the same meat ..."* J4:303 Since they will be leaving the area of the sulphur springs, a man is sent to secure a cask of water. The medical reports on Sacagawea follow a format that automatically links pain, fever, and eating habits into one whole, *"she eats hartily and is free from fever or pain."* J4:306 This is good news where appetite and health are equated.

The young mother, meanwhile, is feeling so much better that she ventures out, ready to resume her normal life. *"she walked out and gathered a considerable quantity of the white apples of which she eat so heartily in their raw state, together with a considerable quantity of dryed fish without my knowledge that she complained very much and her fever again returned."* Lewis is clearly agitated at his patient's show of initiative, and glowers – not at her, a mere woman-child, but at her husband who is clearly responsible for his wife's behavior; Lewis continues, *"I rebuked Sharbono severely for suffering her to indulge herself with such food he being privy to it and having been previously told what she must only eat."* J4:309

Lewis clearly and unequivocally believes that the raw vegetables are not beneficial, at least in the quantity she ate nor would he prescribe fish over a

Prairie turnip

good healthy cut of meat. Granted, she has been improving with the waters, soup, and buffalo protein, and maybe she just overdoes her body's need for variety. Whatever the case, it is a setback, and food is clearly the cause, at least according to the Captain. But the native girl may have been eating the prairie turnip as a medicinal: it has diuretic properties, which might help flush away the toxins of her illness.

Again she improves and immediately goes out fishing. She obviously is craving fish, and the dried fish was an answer to that need. While she is drinking the mineral waters, so are the buffalo – much to Lewis' consternation. From this story there are two things a cook needs to know: (1) sulphur apparently doesn't affect the flavor of the meat, and (2) as Will Rogers used to say, "always drink upriver from the herd."

Trichinosis

The Trichinae parasites are an ancient enemy opportunistically hiding in some hosts, awaiting a new host. Historically this may have led to religious prohibitions against pork, which formerly was a serious carrier of the disease. Today it is not so fatal as it might have been in olden times; the current mortality rate is something like 4 to 5% of those initially infected, so it is still of some concern. Trichinosis is carried primarily in carnivores or scavengers eating dead meat; bears and pig are well known as host animals. The great meals of grizzly really came onto the menu near Great Falls, Montana.

The symptoms of trichinosis include a high temperature, deep muscle aches, hemorrhaging under fingernails, and puffy eyes. What distinguishes trichinosis is the rather quick life-cycle of this invader. In the first 7 to 10 days these parasites cause a dramatic reaction in the gut, resulting in severe diarrhea. It is here that they are laying their eggs, causing a larval infection of the intestine. And then the adult form of the ingested worms goes on to create havoc in the blood-laden muscles of the host as well as the lymphatic system.

After a 10- to 30-day onset period – and this would be near Three Forks, two weeks away from from Great Falls – the worms may have begun to migrate throughout the body, producing a series of flu-like symptoms, the "dangerous" phase. The lymphatic system is vulnerable: there is a transient sore-muscle syndrome with deep muscle aches and high temperatures. On Saturday, July 27, Lewis writes of his friend, *"Capt Clark arrived very sick with a high fever on him and much fatiegued and exhausted. he informed me he was very sick all last night had a high fever and frequent chills & constant aking pains in all his mustles."* Clark describes an even

Grizzly bear – like the pig family, bears are trichinosis carriers.

deeper aching in his bones, causing speculation that he had, "a better than 50-50 chance that such transient symptoms are those of trichinosis."[70]

A longer cooking period prevents trichinosis – the USDA recommends cooking possible host meat to a temperature of 160-165°F for at least 15 minutes. But, if the men are really hungry and the mess sergeants are cooking away, there might have been a tendency to cook the meat to "the juicy stage," decidedly undercooked. Rare meat uses less fuel and reduces the effort in gathering it. Fifteen minutes at that higher temperature might have resulted in a dry meat, not too desirable, not what the men want to eat.

Since these symptoms do not reoccur, it's likely that the infection is cast off, and further re-infection on the outbound trip is not encountered because of the change of diet in the Rockies and then on to the Pacific Ocean.

Seawater and Dried Fish

Although the men's bodies go into violent full rebellion against dried fish when the Nez Perce introduce them to it, they eventually become accustomed it. However, there is a new round of complaints as the waterlogged, storm-battered Corps tries to cook their dried pounded fish under extreme conditions. By late 1805, they have passed into the estuarial zone where the Columbia River meets the tidal swells from the Pacific, and the bogs and marshes are brackish. Even if they cannot see the ocean for the thickets, they can hear the constant crashing of the waves upon the shore. Clark, as usual, is listening to his men and moves immediately to correct what is becoming a serious problem. *"Several men Complain of a looseness and gripeing which I contribute to the diet,*

pounded fish mixed with Salt water, I derect that in future that the party mix the pounded fish with fresh water ..." [J6:97]

Sea water or even brackish water is not a healthy drinking or cooking liquid. A potent brew, it contains a whole new host of bacteria and a pantheon of minerals. It's no wonder that the men's bodies react with diarrhea and gut cramps. Three days later, on December 2, Clark himself complains bluntly, *"I am verry unwell the drid fish* [reconstituted with bad water] *which is my only diet does not agree with me and Several of the men Complain of a lax, and weakness."* Given his gut feeling that all is not well, he resolves to move camp to a place where meat can be obtained. No matter what the medical diagnoses would have been, the indisposition is incapacitating. On December 3, *"the men Sent after an Elk yesterday returnd. with an Elk which revived the Sperits of my men verry much, I am unwell and cannot Eate, the flesh O! how disagreeable my Situation, a plenty of meat and incaple of eateing any – "*

The immediate remedy, the health-coaxing medicine, is soup. As luck would have it, a great canoe comes by. The Indians are carrying wapato intended for sale to the Clatsops, and they stop to see if there is a quick sale at the white men's camp. Clark trades off a fishing hook and it appears that Sacagawea readily prepares a kettle of soup, the equivalent of something like beef broth and potato, in this case elk broth and wapato. Unknown to Clark, his purchase is totally serendipitous. The inadvertent druggists have just traveled by with the right prescription, for pharmacologically the roots of the wapato, or broad-leafed arrowhead, are routinely used by the natives for relieving indigestion.[71] *"those roots I eate with a little Elks Soupe which I found gave me great relief I found the roots both nurishing and as a check to my disorder."*

Intuitive Medicine

What is most amazing is that all these people live through ailments that might fell a good portion of the population today. The two Captains certainly save the day with their medical intuition and goodly doses of herbal remedies, while the inadvertent doctorings with native foodstuffs are fortuitous. Although all are certainly blessed with hearty constitutions and exceptionally strong bodies, it still is a miracle that, with the exception of Sgt. Floyd who died early of probably incurable appendicitis, they all come back alive ... and in fine physical condition.

The primary territories of major American Indian nations against a modern map of the 48 contiguous states.

Bill Stroble, courtesy: Dontom, Inc.

Native Relations
Food, Hospitality, and Diplomacy

The Corolla of the Indian Tobacco as prepared for the purpoe of Smoking ... is mixed with a small quantity of Buffaloes Tallow ... It is esteemed a great delicacy among these people, ... who visit them for the purpose of Traffick ...

— Lewis, Fort Mandan Journals miscellany J4:466

One of the more overlooked aspects of Anglo-American and native relations is the dependence of the newcomers (be they initially from Europe or later from the East Coast) on the local people for food. When John Smith, a soldier of fortune, claimed a peninsula on the James River in 1607 and founded Jamestown, it was only a short time before the colonists were relying on the Powhatan tribe for food. The newly arrived eaters needed help – is this plant edible or poisonous? This same reliance on native wisdom repeats itself when Lewis forbids his men to pick the staple root camas and tells them to trade only with the Nez Perce, who knew which camas was safe (the one with the blue flower) and which was deadly (the white flower). After all, if the plant has gone to seed, and the flower disappears, which is which? The Indians have both gathering and hunting wisdom. The Expedition follows the model of their Virginia predecessors, relying on local tribes for information and often sustenance.

Enabling Trade
Lewis, representing American commerce, leaves Philadelphia with literally tons of trade goods. He is toting a veritable store of attractive gifts, many appealing to vanity (glass beads, brooches, cheap rings) while others are more practical (bolts of colorful fabrics, buttons, and sewing needles). There is good reason for local people to be beaming. Jefferson's man also carries everyday items centering around catching food, preparing food, and cooking food, as well as hard goods like axes and tomahawks. They will simplify the chore of dealing with forests and make light work of chopping firewood and kindling. Warriors might have other ideas for using them, but at present Lewis is sticking to the President's injunctions about promoting peace. The oilcloth bags also protect 2800 fishhooks, brass kettles, and eleven-dozen red-handled knives so beloved by the Indian men. This is a wedge into the market dominated by the British, who are the only traders with such knives.

Brightening the Chain of Friendship – The Native View of Trading
Yes, there is pleasure in new items, and yes, there is prestige in upgrading. A satisfied man might give that old fishing weir to his brother-in-law and walk down to the river with a fishing line sporting tough metal fishhooks. But more to the native point of view is the singular idea that appropriate trade goods and diplomatic gifts should be reflective of a mutual concern, a respect for what the other person or tribe needs.

The European model of giving prestigious gifts to an emperor or king is singularly absent. Tribal chiefs do not have galleries devoted to ticking clocks (as did one Chinese emperor) nor do they astonish their subjects with egg-sized diamonds and a dazzling crown for every occasion (as did the British). Leadership is not an entrée into huge wealth and its continuing enterprise through generations. Rather, diplomacy embraces reciprocal gift-giving on a far smaller scale, one designed to "brighten the chain of friendship."[72]

Seeking Understanding
But trade is not the only object. The Captains are loaded with questions that will help the westward-bound population

(and their leaders back East) understand "most everything" they need to know about their newly acquired, but unknown, territory and the lands and people beyond.

Dr. Benjamin Rush, who mentors Lewis at the President's request, puts together an extensive collection of questions. He sends these to his friend Jefferson, but only after first posing many of them in an oration before the American Philosophical Society in Philadelphia titled "The Natural History of Medicine Among the Indians of North-America." L1:50 For this group it may have been intellectual curiosity, but the practical-minded would see other values to the information being sought.

Rush is investigating many conditions arising from nutritious foods, or lack thereof. He wants to know if the Indians have goiter (iodine deficiency). How long do they live? At what age do the girls begin to menstruate? (This is linked to nutrition.) What is the provision of the children after being weaned? Do they ever use voluntary fasting? What is the diet, the manner of cooking – and times of eating among the Indians? How do they preserve their food?

Rush's questions, others posed by Dr. Caspar Wistar, and perhaps some by the well-intentioned but notorious prevaricator Dr. Benjamin Smith Barton, reach Clark out west. He combines and embroiders them into what he loves most, a list. The food-related topics are numerous.

Clark's List of Questions L1:157-61

"Morrals" category questions:

♦ Do they use any liquor or Substitute to premote intoxication, besides ardent spirits?
♦ Are they much attached to spiritous liquors, and is intoxication deemed Crime among them?

It is not clear exactly what triggers the question on substitutions to promote intoxication, but humans are quite prone to experiment with mind-altering drugs, alcohol being the least. In Mexico, peyote was a standard. Jimsom weed was used extensively. These and other hallucinogens were part of the native cultures, although not so much along the routing of Lewis and Clark as in the more southerly Meso-American cultures. Apparently tales gleaned from the Spanish mentioned these religious legacies and in their relative isolation on the eastern seaboard, Rush and friends felt it would be useful to find out if they were true. Alcohol is already a given, and seemingly Clark interprets the question "is intoxication a crime?" to be one of morals. In a surprising similarity to today's worry, the 1800s thinkers are wondering, "are drugs and liquor something to be concerned about"?

Agriculture and Domestic economy has a lengthy list:

♦ Do they obtain by the Cultivation of the soil their principal mantainence?
♦ What species of grain or pulse do they cultivate?
♦ What are their implements of husbandry, and in what manner do they use them?
♦ Have they any domestic animals & what are they?
♦ Do their men engage in agriculture ...
♦ How do they prepare their culinary and other domistic utensils and what are they?
♦ At what time do they usually relinquish their hunt and return to their villages?
♦ What are the esculent [edible] plants, and how do they prepare them.
♦ What are those that are Commonly used by them?...
♦ Of what does the furniture of those lodges Consist, for the accommodation of the necessary avocations of human life eating Drinking & Sleeping.

Fishing & Hunting exacts another, shorter list:

♦ Do those furnish their principal employment?
♦ How do they persue, and how take their game?
♦ What are the employments used for those purposes — how prepare & in what do they use them?

War raises one unsettling question for men who are about to go into potentially hostile territory:

♦ Do they eat the flesh of their prisoners?
Humans have long memories and store away warnings they think might be useful in the future. Although cannibalism is not a noted human trait, it does exist. An earlier French tale tells of a party of emissary Ottawas preceding a French trading mission and being eaten by the river-controlling Winnebagos.[73] For American traders going upriver into unknown lands, this could be disquieting.

Customs & Manners Generally continues on a friendlier note:

♦ Have they any & what are their festivals or feasts.
♦ What is the cerimony of reciving a stranger at their Village?
♦ When publickly recived at the Lodge of the Chief of the Village is there any Cerimony afterwords necessary to your admission in any other Lodge.

It is not only the Captains who are to answer these queries. These same questions are copied and then forwarded to others who will hopefully add to the new accumulation of knowledge. In a letter dated January 4, 1804, Lewis writes to his new acquaintance Auguste Chouteau in St. Louis, "Sir: I have taken the liberty to add to this, additional questions *of a mixed nature relating to Upper Louisiana, your answers to which will be extremely gratifying, and very gratefully acknowledged.*" L1:161

White Man's Milk and Diplomacy

If this is a diplomatic mission, greeting tribes on behalf of the Great White Father, then his delegated hosts should bring all the necessary trappings to the gathering. Reports from the West already describe the manners and ceremonial behavior expected: the offering of tobacco for a peace pipe, a sip (or more) of white man's milk (Indian name for hard alcohol), and a bestowal of gifts – all rigorously defined by the recipient's chiefly status within the tribe. The protocol is diplomatically visible and rigid, based on political power. Smoking the pipe is mandatory, and hard liquor has informally woven itself into part of the ceremony.

Hard Liquor to Natives:
A Destructive Business Strategy

Alcohol addiction was part of a planned trading strategy introduced by fur trader Duncan McGillivray of the North West Company, a loose confederation of British merchants based in Montreal. He actively promoted alcoholism as a means of enticing the natives to return again and again to his establishment, bringing with them skins and pemmican for trade. "Drunken Indians" and "Indian alcoholism" began with demon rum, for "when a Nation becomes addicted to drinking, it affords a strong presumption that they will soon become excellent hunters."[74]

On the frontier, alcohol is the new beverage of choice for many tribes, and its lure is irresistible. However, some tribes are not snared. The *Journals* describe two polar extremes in this issue. The Arikaras held two misgivings, as Clark noted: "*The Ricareis are not fond of Spiritous liquers, nor do they*

apper to be fond of receiving any or thank full for it ..." Nicholas Biddle, Clark's first editor, added that the Captain told him, "*they say we are no friends or we would not give them what makes them fools.*" J3:183

On the other hand, "*the Ossinniboins [Assiniboine] is said to be pasionately fond of Licquer, and is the principal inducement to their putting themselves to the trouble of Catching the fiew wolves and foxes which they furnish, and recive their [liquor] always in small Kegs.*" J4:38 Lewis goes even further, reporting that the tribe supplied the "*British estabishments on the Assinniboin river with the dryed and pounded meat and grease,*" as well as skins mentioned by Clark. "*these they barter for small kegs of rum which they generally transport to their camps at a distance from the establishments where they revel with their friends and relations as long as they possess the means of intoxication, their women and children are equally indulged on those occasions and are all seen drunk together. so far is a state of intoxication from being a cause of reproach among them, that with the men, it is a matter of exultation that their skill and industry as hunters has enabled them to get drunk frequently.*" J4:34-5

The native taste for rum now aids the British fur establishments, which welcome the easy trade of keg liquor for the much harder to acquire meat and grease, with its highly labor-intensive nature. The pemmican is then made available at the trading posts where the companies, "*are enabled to supply provision to their engages ... without such resource those voyagers would frequently be straitened for provision, as the country through which they pass is but scantily supplyed with game, and the rappidity with which they are compelled to travel in order to reach their winter stations, would leave therm but little leasure to surch for food while on their voyage.*" J4:35 The Assiniboine are, however, thrifty enough to use the wood from the kegs as firewood, thus leaving behind only the hoops as evidence of their passing.

Tangible Diplomacy

Always lurking is the doubt that if this little band of white men angers the natives, disaster is just a step behind. Clark, the "people person," works to assuage anything which has even the tiniest potential of going awry. Back at Camp River Dubois in 1803 he notes, "*Three Indians Come to day to take Christmas with us, I gave them a bottle of whiskey ...*" Lewis, in a document from April 1804, notes he is loading "*20 G Whiskey for Indians.*" The gifts of whiskey seem to produce the desired result: harmony and even a transitory friendship. "*a Camp of Kickapoos on the St. [starboard] Side   Those*

Rindisbacher, circa 1820

Trading-post alcohol addicted many tribes to trade; and it has caused untold misery in drunkenness and alcoholism.

Indian Presents

5ᵗʰ White Wampum
5ᵗʰ White Glass Beads mostly Small
20ᵗʰ Red Do: Do. Asorted
5ᵗʰ Yellow or Orange Do. Do. Asorted
30 Calico Shirts
12 Pieces of East India muslin Hanchurchiefs
Striped or check'd with brilliant Colours
12 Red Silk Hanchurchiefs
144 Small cheap looking Glasses
100 Burning Glasses
4 Vials of Phosforus
288 Steels for Striking fire
144 Small cheap sizers
20 Pair large Do.
12 Groces Needles Asorted Nᵒ 1 & 8 Common points
12 Groces Do. Asorted with points for sewing leather
288 Common brass thimbles — part W. office
10ᵗʰ Sewing Thread asorted
24 Hanks Sewing Silk
8ᵗʰ Rea lead
2ᵗʰ Vermillion . at War Office
288 Knives Small such as are generally used for the Indian
trade, with fine blades & handles inlaid with brass

Courtesy: National Archives

Lewis' list of goods for "Indian Presents."

Indians told me ... by the time I got to their Camp they would have Some Provisions for us ... Soon after we came too the Indians arrived with 4 Deer as a Present, for which we gave them two qts. of whiskey ..." J2:245

As the Corps travels, they engage in brief diplomatic/ trading relationships, generally positive with the exception of the Teton Sioux confrontation. It is only when they reach the Mandans that food, the primary need after breathing, reveals its many different aspects. Dancing, fiddling, and gift-giving are terribly important in the realm of diplomacy, as they engender good will, happy times, and a soul full of intangible and beneficial emotions. But food is critical: The need for it prompts forays out to hunt, elicits digging explorations, or necessitates trade; thus creating a variety of food interactions between very different cultures.

Intuitive, Basic Hospitality

Eating, or perhaps its antithesis hunger, prompts a constant, underlying thread of hospitality. This is the absolute and most reassuring greeting from all natives. The initial impulse is to feed a stranger in their midst. There is no exception to this rule throughout the Expedition. It is a universal so accepted that it is done without reservation, done unless there is some exceptional evidence to the contrary. Withholding food is to show extreme displeasure, even hostility.

People view food in two distinct fashions. It can be fuel, eating to exist, or it can be a social event. In the fuel case it is usually consumed as rapidly as possible and with the least distraction. Beyond this primal function, however, food has a variety of social functions ranging from sociability to displaying social status. At its deepest level, food is a divine commodity, a blessing and divine gift from the Universe, a viewpoint expressed throughout the native cultures. Nowhere do the Army journalists reveal any such leanings. So, what will happen when these secular, food-for-fuel travelers meet with tribes who have never before seen white men? This all-encompassing question revolves around the relationship of food to politics, food to hospitality, and finally trading for reciprocal benefit.

Smoking the Pipe

Diplomacy centers around smoking a ceremonial pipe stuffed with a mixture of tobacco held together with a little buffalo tallow. As a matter of practice, Lewis says, *"The Corolla of the Indian Tobacco as prepared for the purpoe of Smoking by the Mandans, Ricacas, Minetares & Ahwahhaways, in this State it is mixed with a small quantity of Buffaloes Tallow, previous to charging the pipe — It is esteemed a great delicacy among these people, they dispose of it to their neighbors the Assinouboins & others who visit them for the purpose*

Peace Pipe by John F. Clymer, 1979, courtesy: Clymer Museum of Art

The Corps smokes the pipe with a native tribe on the middle Missouri in summer 1804 – the pipe is presented to the four winds.

of Traffick with whom they obtain a high price ..." J3:466 Sharing peace with trading partners involves sharing tallow-rolled tobacco with its changed flavor, a different smoothness than what is expected in the original tobacco. This is an unusual use of a food product.

A level of diplomacy beyond traditional greetings and smoking together includes eating, which when done as a group signifies nonaggression, cements relations and imparts good will. Big family and community meals nourish both the group, and the individual – in mind, body, and soul.

Hunting Together

Guns and hunting go together in such a successful fashion that the Corps is quite popular as meat-providers. They are invited to go with the Mandans December 7 and 8, again in January, and finally out together, again, in reprisal against the Sioux incursion. Hunting enemies, this time. With the rifle's superior firepower, distance, and accuracy, the troops are able to safely bring in much more meat than the native men who must take far greater risks closeup to bring in buffalo with bow and arrow. Acknowledging this disparity, it is easy for the Captains to be generous and share meat, a gesture that costs them little and is repaid with good will.

Bartering Food and Services

When the Corps' traveling emporium opens, there are trinkets to be traded, but the Captains soon realize that they must ration their goods for the next year's journey. With an early supply of enticements gone, they must conjure up services that can be exchanged for tomorrow's dinner as they need to preserve their own rations for the trip ahead.

Two types of service come to mind and are put to use: blacksmithing and medicine. A most desired skill is blacksmithing, turning out hatchets and battle axes, which only the white men can do. Lewis also puts his own medical knowledge to work – "*a womin brought a Child with an abcess on the lower part of the back, and offered as much corn as She Could carry for Some medison, Capt Lewis administered &c.*" J3:260 Medical treatment is especially valued by people who have tried their own healers and not been cured.

Gifts of Food as an Initiative in Fostering Friendship

As a guest, one is honored with friendship and nothing more is expected. Friends, on the other hand, want to give back.

Food is "the little something" a visitor would bring, just as today a hostess gift is in order. The type of food demonstrates (by uniqueness like meat, or quantity as in corn) the status of the donor and might even advance the cause of the giver, hopefully in the form of favors or services now, or perhaps at a later date.

Everyone has a part in "brightening the chain of friendship." Shining with pleasure in giving gifts that are appreciated, everyone has an expectation – that of being liked, and perhaps even being cared for, protected, or in some manner, raised in status above that of a total stranger. Friends – how to become one? Give something. Give again. And again.

Food Shared in Friendship Without Trappings

Inviting a visitor to share a meal is an intuitive gesture and can engender terrific ill will if the host is negligent in his duties. Most cultures frown on throwing guests out or implying they should go home because it's mealtime. Of course there are mitigating circumstances, such as no food, but that too can be shared, as will be seen later with the Lemhi Shoshone.

Communal meals are a constant thread woven throughout human history, and literature records lavish Roman banquets, medieval festivals abounding with food and wine, even Meriwether Lewis dining with Jefferson and his Congressional colleagues. The native oral traditions describe the first "Thanksgiving" meal and celebrate potlatches.

For the Expedition, food and diplomacy are inextricably linked, forming a diplomatic buffer, a hospitable gesture, a means of establishing friendships. Eventually, and quite realistically, the group of thirty-plus outwears its welcome. Hosts realize they cannot continue giving. The villages become marketplaces, and food is actually purchased with trade goods. However, good will remains essential as the Corps almost always has greater needs than their native hosts, placing the Captains in a precariously weak bargaining position. That the critical trade for food continues time after time is a tremendous tribute to both the good will of the natives and the perseverance of the Corps.

In the end, even with the confrontations, no man of the Expedition was scalped or even wounded – something which was quite feasible. Looking back at the gifts of food, perhaps there was even more good will involved than has generally been credited.

NATIVE RELATIONS — A DIFFERENT VIEW
PIERRE, SOUTH DAKOTA — AUGUST 2001

The Sioux invite members of the Lewis and Clark Trail Heritage Foundation to come to a program they want to share. They use the event as a means to explain their side of the story, one not in the *Journals*.

It is seven generations later, a time that their medicine men had predicted would be the generation to make peace – which they are doing. Oral tradition has passed on a very different perspective of events from those recorded by the Captains in the *Journals*. Now, two hundred years later, an elder tells the Teton Sioux version of the meetings:

Their forefathers had been watching the keelboats and canoes coming upriver. Their keen-eyed men had seen things that disturbed them, actions disturbing to their collective soul. These white-Americans killed animals for no purpose [specimen collecting, measuring]. They killed doe deer, while the Sioux preferred to kill bucks so that the females could live to produce more of their kind. They watched as animals were killed, and only part was eaten [as in buffalo hump and tongue] – this was disrespectful to the animal which had given its life, and disreputable for the eater to be so ungrateful and wasteful. Nor did the white-men appear to have any understanding or reverence for the cosmos of the Native World. If they couldn't understand these basic principles regarding man and nature, how could the tribe even attempt to articulate their position, or bridge the cultural gap?

This is the bridge we can cross today, remembering that there are always two or more views to any story.

Part Two

The Expedition to the Pacific and Return

The Corps of Discovery route from St. Louis across the unknown territory to the Pacific and return.

R. L. Rickards - courtesy: Rickards Western Art

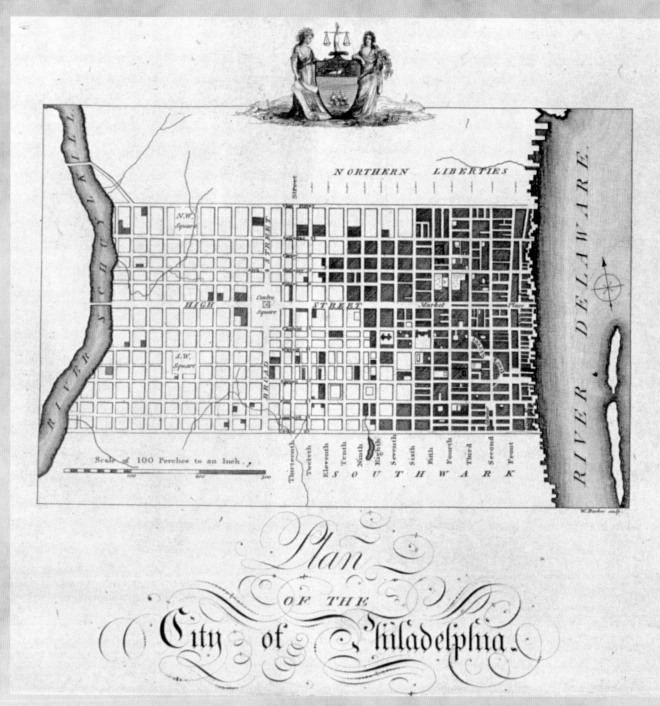

Map of the City of Philadelphia circa 1803 when Lewis prepared for the Expedition.

Shopping in Philadelphia
Spring and Summer, 1803

You will be pleased to purchase when requested by the Bearer
Captain Meriwether Lewis such articles as he may have occasion for ...
— JOSHUA WINGATE, MARCH 14, 1803 [L1:76]

WHAT DO YOU BRING ALONG for provisions when you're going into the unknown? Even today, as exploration goes undersea and into space, the strongest, luckiest, and best prepared – those who gather the most information and are best equipped – are the most likely to be successful. If the Expedition is military, as President Jefferson proposes, is it an incursion expecting conflict, or is it primarily for the sake of exploration, with surprises thrown in?

Exploring, by its very nature, is all about leaving your own culture behind and traveling to some far-away realm where the environment and its inhabitants are unpredictable or unknown at the time of departure. Despite their U.S. Army designation, Lewis' Corps of Discovery has no luxuries of backup supplies or personnel. After the initial planning and preparation, carried on back east and then again in St. Louis, the Corps is left to its own fate without further intervention.

Supplies in Hostile Territory

Normally, the military confronts hostile parties, and in pursuing the goals of war, the conquest of enemy territory is desirable. Armed hostilities demand supply lines and backup personnel. However, Jefferson's explicit orders forbid any interactions that would alienate the native populations. Stealing food – the old military standby of "foraging" – is eliminated as an option. For the Corps, the "civilized" world and its supplies all end in St. Louis. While frontiersmen believe that hospitable Indians will trade, the Corps must still attempt to be self-sustaining.

Determining What to Order

In the 1600s, the earliest forays into the American wilderness went inland from the Eastern seaboard – a few daring and adventuresome colonists stealthily crossing hostile terrain, past tribal encampments, seeking to avoid all contact. Ten to twelve men was the average size of such parties. Three previous unsuccessful attempts to reach the Pacific remind Jefferson it won't be an easy act to pull off. In fact, the frontier General George Rogers Clark (one of William Clark's older brothers) tells Jefferson that *"Large parties will never answer the purpose. They will allarm the Indian Nations they pass through. Three or four young Men ... might perhaps compleat your wishes at a very Trifling Expense."* [L2:656] Yet twelve is the number Jefferson proposes to a questioning Congress.[L1:10]

This dream of an overland western trade route is truly Jefferson's and the proposal does not bring forth approval and accolades, even from the President's own cabinet. Levi Lincoln, his Attorney General (1801–04), takes the opportunity of the President's letter to respond in a blistering burst of negativity. It all will be, in his words, "hazardous," "perverse," "hostile"; he fears a "malignant state of the opposition," "failure, or serious disaster." He knows, "from my ideas of Capt. Lewis, he will be much more likely, in case of difficulty, to push too far, than to recede too soon."[L1:35]

So Jefferson uses the old colonial trick on Congress and hopes to sneak the proposal through with fewer men, and less noticeable expenses – a political smoke and mirrors act. Lewis composes a short list of supplies. Lacking any rationale for a larger party (at least at the present), the quartermaster of the Expedition submits sums for a twelve-man party in his "Estimates of Expenses." This is an obtuse list of categories with what must have been a reasonable set of figures, for Congress appears satisfied with the fairly nominal figure quoted – $2,500. This is not, however, anywhere near what the final costs of the Expedition will be – many of which are covered by Presidential letter.

Of the $2,500 estimated cost, Lewis lists eleven categories of expected expenses. Seven, detailed below, might possibly turn into food or items relating to food: [L1:8]

Arms & Accoutrements extraordinary 81

For the pay of hunters guides and Interpreters 300

    Guns and ammunition (hunting and self-defense), and certainly the best hunters to be found. These are not strict food costs but are associated necessities.

Camp Ecquipage 255

    Equipage includes kettles, mess kits, tools, tents, and packing materials including oilcloth.

Medecine & packing 55

Provisions extraordinary 224

    Lewis doesn't mean champagne and caviar. Instead, the fledgling commander is envisioning the portable soup he will order, and alcohol – *"Indian spirits."*

Materials for making up the various Articles
into portable packs 55

    The portable packs are an early equivalent of our backpack and might be loaded with personal items and food.

In silver coin to defray the expences of the party
from Nashville to the last white settlement
on the Missisourie 100

    Silver coins pay a baker or a farmer for food as they journey down the Ohio, serve as back-up purchasing power for more supplies if they are not available from the quartermastering services at Kaskaskia or Cahokia, and pay for towing the keelboat over shoals.

It is obvious from this list that the categories are general and unrefined; no Congressional Committee today would give it half a thought. There is very little information, and it is a scratchpad start; much further detail and tightening is going to be necessary. After all, here Lewis is describing all the supplies necessary for a two-and-a-half-year trip in 57 words, while most of his later specimen descriptions will run at least 100 words for a single bird or berry.

During the two months of May and June 1803, while the President's secretary is preparing for the West and studying with several tutors in Philadelphia, he is working strenuously on dual tracks. While learning more of botany, medicine, and celestial navigation, he is also upgrading, refining, and implementing his inventory of purchases in the East. What supplies and equipment does he feel will be necessary for the Expedition to succeed? It is a balancing act between the known and unknown, between optimistic trust and the knowledge that supplies in the frontier town of St. Louis will be available, and the almost-paranoid compulsion to carry every possible item. We can track his process through a document which appears several months later, an accounting of bills, of "Supplies from Private Vendors" detailed by Israel Whelan, "Purveyor of Public Supplies" [L1:78]

Costs: 1804 versus Today [75]

Looking at Lewis' purchases, it is useful to get an idea of what he was paying in today's money. That seems simple at first – the official U.S. Department of Commerce's Handbook of Labor statistics CPI (Consumer Price Index) table from 1803 to 2002 shows that the cost of living has increased by a factor of 12 – that is, on average something costing $1 in 1804 will cost $12 in 2002. But a further check of some of Lewis' purchases – flour, pork, beef, whiskey, and cinnamon – reveals major discrepancies: while the price per ounce of cinnamon (then a medicine) has increased by just over the prescribed 12 times, the price of bulk flour has gone up only 8 times, common-grade whiskey 11 times (pre-taxes), and the various meats from 15 to 30 times. So, what is the value-of-money index?

It gets even more confusing when salaries are examined. The Corps' privates were paid $5 per month and given all needed supplies, clothing, and subsistence. Today's army privates are paid $1200/mo and receive clothing and subsistence – a factor of 240 times more. And, while today's equivalent pay is only an educated guess, Lewis' 1804 salary of $40 per month as Expedition leader would likely be about 150 times more today. But, unlike cost of goods, pay rates are significantly driven by the value of the work produced, especially with industrial labor; and in that arena, technology and productivity have increased the value of each labor hour by between 5 to10 times compared to 1804, with the greatest gains in the lower paying jobs. If this productivity gain is divided out, the resulting pay-related inflation factor becomes 24 to 30 times – much closer to the cost of goods inflation factor.

What can be concluded? First, that CPI comparisons

over centuries are only vaguely meaningful. Second, that while there may be an underlying "value-of-money" index,

Costs in 1803 versus 2003

	$-1803	$-2003	Factor
Flour/lb	.040	.42	11
Beef/lb	.035	3.50	100
Pork/lb	.048	3.00	60
Whiskey/gal	1.25	37.50	30
Salt/lb	.035	.48	14
Rifle/ea	15.00	500.00	33
Private/mo	5.00	1350.00	275
Lewis/mo	40.00	6250.00	156
Listed CPI	45	540	12
Total Cost	$35,000	$1,000,000	30

its visibility is highly distorted by the amount of either productivity-gain or scarcity influencing any particular product.[a] And finally, if a single 'value-of-money' index from 1804 to 2002 is sought, considering both goods and labor, it is most likely in the range of 25 to 30; more than twice the official CPI index. That is, a total Expedition cost in 1803–06 of $35,000[b] would be equivalent to about $1 million today. What a bargain we all received: Such an Expedition mounted in the early twenty-first century would spend more than a million dollars just in the "feasibility study"!

Purchase and Haul

For planning purposes, there is the sharply defined black-and-white of the known world. This encompasses the American East Coast, moves down the newly settled areas of the Ohio River, and culminates in the bubbling cultural gumbo

[a] For example: (i) flour production has been highly automated, and this reduces the cost per pound below what overall price-inflation would suggest; (ii) meat production has benefitted only slightly from productivity and may be one of the better true measures of inflation; and, (iii) labor has benefitted greatly from productivity and has amplified hourly-wage rates from 5 to 10 times what basic inflation would suggest.

[b] Various researchers have placed the total government expenditures for the Corps, including the salaries and bonuses of the Army men, in this range.

of St. Louis. Beyond the Missouri, all that is known comes from word-of-mouth from traders out at civilization's edge who have first-hand knowledge of native cultures both near and sometimes far. As the horizon grows gray and indistinct, all tribes merge under the great fringed blanket of "Indian," and there is no surity about supplies or anything else. Are these distant natives unforeseen enemies and as quartermaster should the Captain order extra tomahawks for his men? Or should they be wooed as spontaneously invited guests with additional rations of whiskey given to potential allies? Will his Expedition be trading beads for food, or will the food supplies be adequate? In the obscure nothingness of the unknown, meticulous planning and self-sufficiency is the last resort, their best hope.

The initial preparations in Philadelphia involve extraordinary detail. Mail carriers ferry a two-way stream of letters from the East to far-flung Army posts and even to the buckskin-wearing, wealthy river men in St. Louis. Many of these men and their trapper/traders have two families: one native, one in town. Their information is good.

Buying and carting is a burdensome chore – ask any traveler. So what prompts Lewis to buy back East when supplies are available farther west? Three factors are at work here. First, there is an assurance of fine quality. For guns, Harper's Ferry production is top of the line and customized. Lewis fiddles with the Army standard and improves upon it. It's a military purchase, and every effort is made to turn out the product flawlessly and on time.

Next, Lewis can see the product and assure that he has it in hand. It's the old wisdom of "a bird in hand is worth two in the bush." And, finally, there is accountability. Lewis can visit the merchant's store and get his worthy opinion of when, where, and why. On the frontier, where the suppliers are French or Spanish, and where Indian war parties cut trade lines, nothing is quite so sure. The time between order and delivery is unpredictable and can be interminable. It is best to count on an assured supply, particularly if there is no certainty that it can be bought or manufactured on the frontier in the desired time-frame.

Lower expenses might be a third reason to buy in the East. If manufacturing houses are competitive in Philadelphia, why not buy at the lowest price? Such prudence will fall within military guidelines, please the President, and silence Congress. Lewis knows that fish hooks are not manufactured on the prairies. Buy *"4 groce"* and bring them – they are not terribly heavy. Beads for trade with the Indians are an import from China via Europe – pack and ship. The cost of brass kettles is surely going to be higher on the frontier than where they're manufactured in bulk. The effort of carrying the purchased goods is less than the cost of buying them in St. Louis.

Eastern Purchases

Lewis' first estimate of expenses is a rough outline of what becomes a definitive *"List of Requirements."* L1:69-75 Purchase orders go out to at least twenty-nine different merchants, all of whom present their bills to Israel Whelan, purveyor of public supplies – who finishes his job and abruptly resigns in August, 1803.L1:76 Before retiring, Whelen compiles a finalized *"Supplies from Private Vendors"* L1:78 totaling $2,323.77. The quartermaster of the Expedition has spent almost all of his allocated $2500 and he hasn't left town yet. His Corps will expand from twelve to a peak count of forty-five, and he still has two and a half years and ten thousand miles to go. Staying within budget is not likely.

What are all these items listed under *"Expenses"* L1:69-99 that will in a month's time become a mountain of supplies to be moved?

Under the original outline, Lewis starts with *"Mathematical Instruments."* The completed list contains many items which are quite useful to someone looking at the culinary aspect of the trip. There is writing paper and ink, which will be the journalists' mainstay and inform curious historians two hundred years hence. There is sealing wax (which later appears sealing canisters from water damage), a set of brass money scales used to weigh specimens and foodstuffs, and lastly, a two-volume set of Linnaeus' natural species classification book. Using these relatively new scientific books, the science-commander will describe and tentatively apply a name to newly discovered plants (the official function he leaves for botanists back East). He uses these precious books as a naturalists' bible, identifying and determining what is and isn't food, contemplating new edibles served by the natives.

As all the men are to be well armed, the next grouping is *"Arms & Accoutrements."* Included in this category are the fifteen rifles from the Harpers Ferry armory [c] and twenty-four heavy-duty knives that can carve slabs of meat. Most of the gear is high quality, such as the 200 pounds of "best rifle powder" (used in conjunction with 400 pounds of lead), and 500 of the "best flints" for gun locks. Twenty-four pipe Tomahawks are included for good measure.

"Camp Equipage" L1:70 is where food-related items begin,

---

[c] These rifles are discussed in *Hunting*, page 21.

Lewis' ledger of "Camp Equipage" purchased in Philadelphia in the summer of 1803 – National Archives.

Courtesy: National Archives

although some of the items sound like weapons. For instance, drawing knives used in butchering, axes for cutting firewood or constructing a smokehouse, could – in an emergency – fall under the category of Arms.

6	Copper kettles (1 of 5 gallons, 1 of 3, 2 of 2, & 2 of 1)
25	falling axes
4	Drawing Knives, short and strong
4	Groce fishing Hooks assorted
12	Bunches Small fishing line assorted
1	lb. Turkey or Oil Stone
1	Iron Mill for Grinding Corn
20	yds. Oil linnen for wrapping & securing Articles
10	yds. " " of thicker quality for covering and lining boxes. &c
24	Iron Spoons or table spoons
24	Pint Tin Cups [without handles as customary]

30   *Steels for striking or making fire*
100 *Flints for "   "   "   "*
2   *patent chamber lamps & wicks*
15   *Oil Cloth Bags for securing provision*
4   *Tin blowing Trumpets* [To communicate at a distance or to signal lost hunters]

Most of these items are self-explanatory and simply give an idea of what is being taken along.[d]

Kettles

As quartermaster, Lewis orders copper kettles. Then he decides that he wants nesting camp kettles, *"brass is much preferr'd to Iron, tho both are very useful to the Indians size from 1 to 4 gallons."* [L1:75] By the time he is finished, still more changes have transpired. Received from Benjamin Harberson & Sons: 14 brass kettles ($10.67) and a black tin saucepan ($1.50). Eight of the kettles are put into the *Indian Presents* list, six are listed in *Camp Equipage* as *Copper* and altogether weigh 28 pounds. Another reference describes *"6 Brass kettles from one to five gallons* [a nest of kettles], *$15.18"* From this description, it sounds like they may have twenty brass or copper kettles, no iron kettles, and one tin saucepan. The tin saucepan weighs three-quarters of a pound, not too substantial but perhaps useful when traveling away from camp.

So, what can be determined from all this? There will be six messes cooking during the trip up to Mandans and through that winter, and four messes thereafter. The messes will not have standard size kettles, but the Corps will have the convenience of carrying nesting pots, a space-saver. Varying sizes also means that a gallon or two of leftover stew need not be stored in a big 5-gallon kettle, but will fit more compactly in smaller pots, which can then be nested into a larger one, providing more waterproofing protection. But what of the legged kettle impression found by archeologist, Ken Karsmizki? Those are generally from cast iron kettles.[e] Did Lewis buy some iron legged kettles in St. Louis?

Corn Mills

On April 30, Jefferson is still ruminating about some mapping advice but begins his note to Lewis on a different tack, *"I think we spoke together of your carrying some steel or cast*

Corn mill. This one is modern, but similar to 1803.

iron corn mills to give to the Indians or to trade with them, as well as for your own use." [L1:44] This is the first mention of corn as a staple provision, for a mill would only be useful if dealing with large quantities of the grain, particularly for recipes such as porridge, cornbread, or a sweetened pudding dish. This particular mill weighs 20 pounds, and costs $9.00.

Two other mills are purchased separately and billed as *Indian Presents*. Each weighs about 26 pounds, and costs $10.00. [L1:94] Speculating about the six-pound weight difference: either the Indian presents are a bit more substantial, or possibly they are just bulky and lacking in sophistication. On October 29, 1804, an *"excellent, large"*[76] iron corn mill is given to a chief. A second corn mill (either the remaining 26 pounder or the lighter 20 pounder) is cached in Montana on June 11, 1805. This leaves one remaining mill, and there is no further record of it, ever.

Culinary Items Purchased

Culinary equipment purchases made in the East fall into two categories: *"Indian Presents"* and *"Camp Equipage."*

Most of the *"Indian Presents"* are sheer fluff – showy glinting beads, vibrant scarlet cloth, fashionable combs, looking glasses, etc. – definitely vanity items, exotic gifts that have a magnetic appeal. Despite the prestige aspect, many gifts are truly useable and welcome. The culinary items destined for the tribes form only a small portion of the total inventory, and are more pragmatic and less flashy. Consider these labor savers: butcher knives (48 for $5.33), standard knives (11 dozen for $25.17), burning glass (for starting fires), brass kettles, corn mills, fishing hooks (2800 for $8). Nice, useful presents. Finally there is the diplomatic peacekeeping symbol: tobacco. A linguistic surprise awaits the careful reader who will note the metamorphosis of food descriptors: 130 rolls of Philadelphia *"pigtail"* tobacco, also referenced as *"carrots"* or twists of tobacco.

The Corps will carry pint cups and spoons for each person, kitchen gear, and tools for getting the raw product and preparing it for the pot. Hunters will use the drawing knives (to gut animals) and anyone fishing will have access to fishing gear (125 large hooks, assorted fishing lines, a pre-tied set of lines and hooks). Someone, presumably Lewis, gets a sportsman's flask.

---

[d] Oilcloth is covered in the *Pre-plastic Packing,* page 16 and a brief explanation of hunters' weaponry is found in *Hunting – Tools of the Trade,* page 33.
[e] Archeological findings of Ken Karsmizki are further discussed in *Cooking Techniques,* page 43.

Food Goods

When Lewis leaves for St. Louis, he has with him all the food items he intends to order in the East. From what he's not carrying, it's obvious that he has full confidence that he can get anything and everything he needs either on the way (to sustain them on the downriver trip) or from the military commissaries during the upcoming winter, as suggested by Jefferson.

Here is his shopping list, annotated with what he actually obtains:

Provisions and Means of Subsistence [L1:72]

> 3   bushels of Allum or Rock Salt
> Lewis did not buy this.
>
> 6   Kegs of 5 Gallons each making 30 Gallons of rectified spirits as is used for the Indian trade
> Lewis actually buys 30 gallons of Strong Spt. Wine.
>
> 6   Kegs bound with iron Hoops
> These become the kegs to hold the "Spt.Wine".
>
> 150   lbs. Portable Soup
> Lewis is delivered 193 pounds.
>
> Spicies assorted

The few spices Lewis actually purchases are not used in cooking and are never mentioned as seasonings for anything; they are from a druggist along with the Expedition's other medical goods: "2 oz. Nutmegs - 75¢; 2 oz. Cloves - 31¢; and 4 oz. Cinnamon - 20¢." [L1:81] Mostly forgotten is the 1800s use of spices as curatives: cinnamon bark relieves diarrhea and nausea and is useful for digestive problems; cloves have antiseptic and anti-parasitic properties and also act as a digestive aid;[77] nutmeg or mace is a tonic, a narcotic, a somatic and anti-emetic.[78] Their only reference in the Journals is by Clark in a recipe for Beaver Bait. [J6:197] [f]

As to the "Rectified spirits," they become "Strong Spt. Wine" in the final inventory. But what is "Strong Spt. Wine"? Brandy is a fine example – made from grapes first fermented into wine, its alcoholic content is then increased by distillation. Since this purchase is obtained from David Jackson, druggist, we can carry this supposition one step further. Brandy has a long tradition of being a medication, a relief, and a refresher. Think of a St. Bernard plowing through the snow going to a traveler's aid – a small keg of brandy strapped around the dog's thick furry neck. Lewis' bill for thirty gallons is $70, approximately $0.47 a bottle (in today's 750ml size). As such it is considerably more expensive than

the whiskey later purchased in St. Louis for an equivalent of $0.25 per bottle.

Finally there is the "Portable Soup." For the Corps of Discovery this is an emergency ration, much as supplies are stocked in case of hurricanes, tornadoes, or earthquakes. Lewis has become aware of this dried soup and writes to General William Irvine concerning it on April 15, 1803. Records show that on May 30, 1803, Israel Whelan for the United States writes payment for "193 lbs. of Portable Soup at 150 Cents (for a total of) $289.50." The 150 pounds of ordered soup has turned into a billable 193 pounds of delivered soup. Francois Baillet, the cook/provisioner, is probably the person who packs the finished product into the separately ordered tin canisters.[g]

In the end, the Expedition's edible provisions from Philadelphia are tallied at $360 for soup and liquor. This is just the start of food shopping; the bulk of the prepared provisions will be obtained in St. Louis: Two Tons for the winter at Camp River Dubois, and Eight Tons taken with the Expedition when they leave in May 1804 – altogether costing more than $2,000.

Lewis, behind schedule in getting his provisions and departing, is personally bulldogging the suppliers and apparently doesn't have time to correspond. He is hurrying off to Harpers Ferry when he is seen by two different army officers who report sighting him to Jefferson. Jefferson's April 23 letter reaches him and reads, "I have not been able to hear any thing of you since Mar. 7." [L1:43] Then, possibly figuring that all is lost for the winter of 1803–04, the Monticello planter suddenly remembers a small task or two that he asks his personal secretary to attend to. "Will you be so good as to call on Doctr. Bollman with my compliments & pay him for some wine sent me? I suppose it will be about 12 Doll. But it must be whatever he says. I will also thank you to purchase for me a Leopard or tyger's skin, such as the covers of our saddles were cut out of." [L1:43] It is as if all thoughts of the Expedition have flown from the President's mind, and he is simply asking his secretary to go about town running errands.

Philadelphia, May 29, 1803: Lewis writes back to Jefferson, expressing the hope that he will be leaving on June 6 or 7 for Washington, "for all the articles have been either procured" or are nearing such a state. He has been extremely busy, but has found time to pay the wine seller and "I have also purchased a Vigogna Blanket, of which I hope you will approve," noting that "The Tiger's skin you requested I have not

---

[f] See Hunting, page 38 for a discussion of Beaver Bait.

[g] See "Portable Soup" in Food Preservation (page 8) and a discussion of using the Portable Soup in Fasting Over the Rockies (pages 158–9).

been able to procure, those I have seen appear to be too small for your purpose, perhaps they may be had in Baltimore if so I will get one at that place."

Documents from this time detail a flurry of commerce, bills, and credits. Lewis is free to request articles he cannot find in the public stores and does so; the United States pays $1,000 for additional items. The edgy Captain is now in high gear, and impatient to be going. Eventually, all of the Expedition equipment, some 3,500 pounds of it, [L1:53-54] is to be loaded aboard the keelboat (*"at least 60 feet in length her burthen equal to 8 tons"*), and one large wooden pirogue. But getting that keelboat completed is another story in frustration. Even with astute planning, the expected departure date is severely off-schedule. Lewis is forced to hustle horses and wagons to cart the goods. He progresses on, no doubt doubly furious and distraught at the destruction of his perfect timetable.

The Fourth of July – 1803

In 1803, no patriotic celebration is bigger than the nation's birthday. It is still a glorious, uplifting, yet poignant, event in national life. On this hot summer day, Meriwether Lewis stands in the sunshine, smelling the green grass of the garden, ready to leave the very next day. His expedition, if successful, will add to the continued wealth and glory of the fledgling nation; at worst, their failure will be more of the supreme self-sacrifices made. Jefferson, Commander-in-Chief of the Corps of Discovery, has invited scores of guests to the President's house to celebrate. The stories and even images of those violent, blood-drenched days of patriotic sacrifice are still fresh in their memories, and many invitees personally knew the combatants or their families.

The festivities of the day are described by Samuel Harrison Smith, founder of the first national newspaper in the United States, who covered the events of the capital during its early years. He is the son of an army colonel who fought in the Revolution and later signed the Articles of Confederation. Smith, an avid patriot, writes home to his wife Margaret on July 5:

> Yesterday was a day of joy to our citizens and of pride to our President. It is a day which you know he always enjoys. How much more he must have enjoyed it on this occasion from the great event that occasioned it. The news of the cession of Louisiana only arrived about 8 'clock of the night preceding, just in time to be announced on this auspicious day. ... This mighty event forms an era in our history, and of

itself must render the administration of Jefferson immortal. [79]

As cakes and punch are served, imagine the days of preparation by Jefferson's chef and staff. Here are two recipes typical of the time which may have been served on that 1803 Fourth of July – the first, Biscuit de Savoye, is one of Jefferson's cakes as chronicled in *Thomas Jefferson's Cook Book*; and the second, Fish House Punch, is a long-standing "secret" recipe of the Schuylkill River Fish House Club in the Philadelphia area and likely known by the Philosophical Society.

BISCUIT DE SAVOYE[80]

6	eggs
6 T.	sugar
I	orange rind, grated
6 T.	flour, sifted
⅛ tsp.	salt

Separate eggs and beat the yolks until lemon colored and light. Add the sugar and the grated orange rind. Beat well; add flour mixed with salt. Beat the egg whites until stiff and dry. Fold into the first mixture. Butter a cake mold and dust with sugar. Turn the mixture into this and set in a slow oven. Bake from thirty-forty minutes, until the cake shrinks from pan.

FISH HOUSE PUNCH

I	bottle dark rum (750ml)
9 oz.	cognac
4 oz.	peach brandy
4 oz.	simple syrup
5 oz.	fresh lime juice
5 oz.	fresh lemon juice
I	block ice, for serving

Place the ice into a large punch bowl, add the rest of the ingredients, and allow to chill for approximately one hour. After the ice melts just a bit, it serves 16 4-ounce cups.

Jefferson's Instructions to Overwinter in St. Louis

Letters between the governmental dignitaries have been flying thick as flocks of passenger pigeons. One of Jefferson's messages reaches Albert Gallatin, his Secretary of the Treasury, who responds on April 13, 1803, acknowledging that time is liable to defeat the party before it gets going and suggesting a remedy. He suggests that the commanders should *"try and winter with the traders <u>from that quarter</u> who go to the farthest tribe of Indians in the proper direction. A boat or canoe might be hired there (at the Illinois) to carry up to that spot a sufficient quantity of flour to enable him to winter there with comfort so that his band should be fresh & in good spirits in the spring."* L1:34

It is obvious that Gallatin believes the *"quantity of flour"* will bring contentment and satisfaction. Food out west, as the Corps will find in Illinois, is based on an agricultural society. Common knowledge of the 1800s relies on some assumptions: dairy products – butter, milk, eggs – are available and might be used with that flour to produce some variety in daily cooking. It will all depend on who's cooking.

By April 23, 1803, the President bleakly notes that the delay of a month now *"may lose a year in the end."* L1:43 It's apparent that Jefferson has already foreseen a winter layover in the vicinity of St. Louis. Clearly, all provisions ordered by Lewis will have to be adjusted for a half-year longer stay within civilization's reach, and more purchases can be expected. The chits for these may make it back to Washington and may arouse Congressional interest.

There is nothing that can be done except reconcile themselves to a lost season. In Jefferson's practical response written November 16, 1803, he instructs, *"your winter might be passed in gaining much information by making Cahokia or Kaskaskia your head quarters, & going to St. Louis & the other Spanish posts that your stores &c would thereby be spared for the winter, as your men would draw their military rations ..."* L1:137 It is a military solution to civilian contractor's delays.

After numerous delays, the keelboat is finally completed near Pittsburgh.
On August 31, 1803, Lewis starts down the Ohio River in the new boat.

Jim Adams/Keelboat reconstruction by Butch "Mr. Keelboat" Bouvier

Down the Ohio – Up to St. Louis

September-December, 1803

Dear Sir,
... on the morning of the 31 st [August] *that my boat was complete,*
she was instantly loaded, and at 10 a.m. the same day I left Pittsburgh ...

— LEWIS TO JEFFERSON, SEPTEMBER 8, 1803

Down the Ohio

The tiny military contingent of twelve that leaves Pittsburg on August 31, 1803, is on familiar ground. They know where they are going, have supplies for their present needs, and are secure with re-provisioning at stops they will make on their way down the Ohio River. That is the easy part. The difficulties lie in heavy loads and low rivers.

No one anticipates that delays in starting will turn a float down a normally swift, deep river into a back-breaking, calorie-burning, push-and-haul trip over a riverbed now drying to record lows. Lewis' hopes for a speedy transit are dashed on the sandy bars of the receding river and snared in gnarly "riffles" composed of tangled driftwood and river rubble. Short delays turn into even longer delays as all the packed gear is off-loaded so the privates can shove the heavy, beached-whale of a keelboat along. Then there are more delays as the goods are reloaded after reaching deeper water. But, the river notwithstanding, the original and most insidious delays are due to alcohol.

Too Much Booze, or Broken Promises, Drunken Brawls

On September 8, Lewis writes to Jefferson about the aggravation of being *"moste shamefully detained by the unpardonable negligence of my boat builder."* [L1:121] He is sorely disappointed.

On my arrival at Pittsburgh, my calculation was that the boat would be in readiness by the 5th of August; this term however elapsed and the boat was so far from being finished was only partially planked on one side. In

this situation I had determined to abandon the boat and to purchase two or three perogues and descend the river in them, and depend on purchasing a boat as I descend, there being none to be had at Pittsburgh; from this resolution I was dissuaded first by the representations of the best informed merchants at that place who assured me that the chances were much against my being able to procure a boat below.

In other words, Lewis is forced into the strategy of "buy where you can," especially if it appears that there are no reputable or reliable sources for the purchase ahead. Construction of the keelboat is far off schedule, almost a month behind the projected completion date. Lewis' letter goes on to report that the boatbuilder promises a renewal of swift work, *"however a fews days after he got drunk, quarrelled with his workmen and several of them left him, nor could they be prevailed on to return."* Lewis is in the middle of a labor dispute and time is passing. *"I threatened him with the penalty of his contract, and extracted a promise of greater sobriety."* The builder continues *"to be constantly either drunk or sick"* and Lewis takes over management, attempting to hurry the process along, *"alternately presuading and threatening."* The frustrated, offended military officer concedes nothing works – he is helpless.

When Lewis finally departs, late, it is without the enthusiastic physician, reputedly another chronic alcoholic who wanted to join the Expedition at Wheeling, West Virginia, who never appears at the appointed hour of departure. [J2:75]

Lewis' problems with both alcoholics are just the beginning of a zig-zag path with road-signs pointing to "grog" and "white man's milk" and "whiskey!" Determined to allow his privates some rest and relaxation after the backbreaking toil of moving the keelboat down a river with less than a foot of water, the Captain pulls in at old, established Marietta (Ohio), founded in 1788. Lewis entertains the postmaster but such social amenities aren't quite what the young bucks have in mind. The town, and its alcohol, proves too much a temptation. No doubt written in disgust, the September 14, 1803, *Journal* entry reads, *"Set out this morning at 11 oClock was prevented seting out earlier in consequence of two of my men geting drunk and absenting themselves. I f[i]nally found them and had them brought on board, so drunk that they were unable to help themselves ..."* It's worth noting that heavy drinking on the frontier was common at this time.

Rain and riffles set the tone. The season is changing and it is a tough day on September 12 when Lewis, at one point, orders his men to *"cut a channel through the gravel with our spade and canoe paddles and then drag the boat through ... , we came 20 miles this day."* The travails in getting the keelboat downriver are important because of the physical exertion, the burning of calories, and the subsequent implications for food quantities needed. Sometimes the labors involved are too great for the men and in yet another letter to his commander, *"On board my boat opposite Marietta, September 13, 1803,"* Lewis writes with sardonic irony, *"Horses or oxen are the last resort: I find them the most efficient sailors in the present state of the navigation of this river, altho' they may be considered somewhat clumsey."* L1:124

This weight-lifting, pulling, hauling drama is so difficult that Lewis is constantly trying to assure a plentiful supply of food. Being near farmhouses offers this small contingent a chance to purchase food from the local populace anytime they come upon a village or farm. The Captain barters a few pounds of lead for some corn and potatoes, knowing that his hungry troops will be waiting for food to be cooked, meals to be eaten. The shakedown part of the journey is so busy and exhausting there is no need to plan variety in the meals (not sanctioned by Army regulations anyhow) or even a leisurely bit of fishing. Even the sight of fish, however stirring, is put aside. *"we fixed some spears after the indian method but have had too much to attend to of importance than gigging fish."* They are not hungry enough to attend to the plentitude of shovelnose sturgeon, bass, northern pike, catfish. J2:71

The Bread Crisis Rises

Not all crises are alcohol driven. On September 8, Lewis notes, *"my men were much fatiegued and I concluded it would*

better to give them a days rest and let them wash their cloths and exchange their flour for bread or bake their bread in a better manner than they had the means of baking it while traveling ..." Lewis dines with the locals. And he plays host, inviting his acquaintances for an after-dinner stroll: *"in the evening they walked down to my boat and partook of some watermellons."* J2:75

But the issue of the bread rises. The keelboat and canoes are seven miles downstream when the two-day fiasco begins.

I was now informed that by some mistake in the contract between the Corporal and the woman engaged to bake the bread for the men at Wheeling that the woman would not agree to give up the bread being 90 lbs. and that the bread was left I instantly dispatched the Corpol. and two men for the bread and gave him a dollar to pay the woman for her trouble ... J2:76

It is no wonder that the baker woman wants payment, for bread-making is, as always, a hot and time-consuming procedure. And it is made more complex by one singular factor. Powdered yeast hasn't been "invented" although it is available when skimmed from the "barm" or foam on top of beer. In *American Cookery*, the first published cookbook in

LONDON-STYLE BREAD[83]

To make white bread the London way.

"You must take a bushel of the finest flour well dressed [108 cups], put it in the kneading trough at one end ready to mix, take a gallon of water (which we will call liquor) and some yeast; stir it into the liquor till it looks of a good brown colour and begins to curdle, strain and mix it with your flour till it is about the thickness of a good seed-cake; then cover it with the lid of the trough, and let it stand three hours, and as soon as you see it begin to fall take a gallon more of liquor, and weigh three quarters of a pound of salt, and with your hands mix it well with the water, strain it, and with this liquor make your dough of a moderate thickness, fit to make up into loaves; then cover it with the lid, and let it stand three hours more. In the meantime, put the wood into the oven and heat it. It will take two hours heating. When your sponge has stood a proper time, clear the oven, and begin to make your bread. Set it in the oven, and close it up, and three hours will just bake it."

Baking bread or hardtack in 1800
is a labor-intensive, hot, slow job.

North America, Amelia Simons adds *"emptins"* to her bread, this being defined as "leavings of fermenting ale or barm, replenished from time to time, adding flour, to serve as yeast; effectively, a sort of *sour dough*,"[81] clarifies the facsimile's editor, Karen Hess. Citing Englishwoman A. Edlin's 1805 *Treatise on the Art of Breadmaking,* food chemist Harold McGee writes that Edlin preferred the beer froth to the "everlasting yeast," a method using starter taken from old dough, which produced "a disagreeable sourness" that then had to be neutralized by adding potash.[82]

To get some idea of the physical nature of the work, go no further than Hannah Glasse's bread recipe (1774), listed on opposite page, which uses barm.

Today the Wheat-Montana Bakery uses 1¼ pounds of flour for a 2-pound loaf. Given that figure, Lewis' men must have left approximately 72 pounds of flour to be made up into, perhaps, 45 two-pound loaves. That would comprise the 90 pounds of bread the Captain recorded.

With the London-style Bread recipe, the baker woman must have been running a series of steps to produce 45 loaves, a commercial scale far larger than that used to make a single loaf baked in a Dutch oven. She probably started the first batch of dough rising. Next, she would prepare the bake-oven: "a large brick or stone structure, either free-standing outdoors or built next to or within the fireplace, used for baking many things at one time; a fire was built inside to heat it, and when the oven was hot enough, the fire was raked out, the food put inside, and the oven closed with a heavy door."[84] Our best analogy today would be a pizza oven. Following the fire-making, she would have started a second batch of dough. The first batch would be punched down and started for the second rise, then baked while the second batch was on its second rise, and a third load was started up for its first rise. It probably was a dawn-to-dusk job, perhaps even longer.

On September 10, Lewis wrote, *"I should have been able to set out at sunrise, but the Corporal had not yet returned with the bread— I began to fear that he was <miffed> piqued with the sharp reprimand I gave him the evening before for his negligence & inattention with respect to the bread and had deserted; in this however I was agreeably disappointed, about 8 in the morning he came up bring with him the two men and the bread ..."* [J2:76-7] Getting a supply of bread isn't simple!

Should all else fail, Lewis has *"bisquit"* with him in the heavily leaking pirogue, *"my bisquit was much injurd I had it picked and put up into these baggs – this work kept [me] so busy that I ate not any thing untill after dark, being determined to have every thing in readiness for an early start in the morning ..."* [J2:84] Lewis' biscuit to is not the light fluffy quick-breads we consume; it is hardtack – unleavened wafers common to the Army and Navy in those times. The following recipe is attributed to Naval Commander George Vancouver, explorer of the western coast of America in the early 1790s:

HARDTACK OR BISCUIT[85]

2 C.	whole wheat flour
1 C.	water
1 tsp.	salt
1 T.	butter

Make into a ball. The dough will be tough. With a rolling pin, roll out until the dough is ⅜" thick. Cut into 4" diamonds. Bake at 450°F for 25-30 minutes.

With the issue of bread falling away, the Captain notes an interesting phenomena. It is early fall and the gray squirrels are actually migrating from one side of the Ohio to the other. Lewis supposes the climate may be prompting the swim, but this seems unlikely. On the other hand, he observes mast, which seems to be abundant, referring to nuts being used as food. *"... the walnuts and Hickory nuts the usual food of the squirrell appears in great abundance on either side of the river— I made my dog take as many each day as I had occation for, they wer fat and I thought them when fryed a pleasant food."* [J2:79] Seaman, a Newfoundland, is a good retriever: he kills and brings the little critters right back to his master. Lewis does not mention squirrel in the other men's supper arrangements, but he is fond enough of them himself to go ashore and shoot some while his men are struggling with the boat.

The Falls of the Ohio and on to the Mississippi

On October 14, 1803, Lewis pulls his little flotilla into Louisville, Kentucky, a brawling raw frontier town of 800 at the upper end of the Falls of the Ohio where he is joined by William Clark. The next day, the keelboat is piloted through a mile and a half of churning rapids that comprise the Falls of the Ohio to arrive at Clarksville, Indiana Territory, where William is staying with his older brother, General George Rogers Clark. A manly slap on the back, a welcoming handshake and hug, and the three men are no doubt happily engaged in discussing this magnificent dream that is about to unfold. General Clark, a mighty drinker, would likely decant his "corn-likker" whiskey from its keg and pass the bottle along, serving glass after glass of that uniquely American, western-frontier liquor.

And so from October 16 to 27, Lewis and Clark remain in the Louisville/Clarksville area making preparations, staying in the Clark family home. And here, just beyond the Falls of the Ohio, these rugged Army men sip their whiskey in peace, eyes gleaming in anticipation of what lays ahead. They eat heartily – on blue and white Stafford bone china – the British diet of meats, bread, and perhaps apples. Although the apples planted by Johnny Appleseed in the Ohio River Valley just two years earlier are yet too young to produce fruit, the earlier French settlers had carried their precious fruit trees with them.

Specimen or Dinner: The Gigantic Catfish

There is no further mention of food until November 16, and even then it is not clear if their find is food, a specimen, or both. Upon their return from a morning's mapping to measure the width of the river, both Captains *"were a little surprised at the apparent size of a Catfish which the men had caught in our absence altho we had been previously accustomed to see those of from thirty to sixty pounds weight ..."* After taking the dimensions of it (including a length of 4 feet, 3¼ inches), Lewis goes on to the final tally after figuring five pounds for, *"The loss of blood, its lying out of the water six hours in the sun, & waistage from the circumstance of being obliged to weigh it in small draughts not having any method of weighing entire may be estimated at, at least, Total weight— 128 [lbs]. I have been informed that these fish have been taken*

in various parts of the Ohio and mississippi weighing from 175 to 200 lbs. weight which from the evidence of the subject above mentioned I have no doubt is authentic" [J2:89-90]

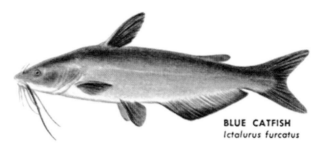

BLUE CATFISH
Ictalurus furcatus

On November 16, 1803, Lewis' crew catches a 128-pound giant Blue Catfish in the lower part of the Ohio River.

Catfish is a standard item on the menu, but there are no further clues as to the fate of this monstrous fish. Was it chilly enough in November that the mess cooks saw fit to fire-roast slabs of catfish? Did they make fish stew? There is no journalistic mention of other "eats" that day except *"a heath hen or grows which flew of[f] and having no gun with me did not persue it ..."* This is not a bird in the pot, so fish might have been the next best thing. Or, they may have been eating Army-issue pork and corn.

Jefferson's Salt and Wheat Mandates

The imprint of Thomas Jefferson's mandates appears in items that seem like simple nutritional observations. Nineteen years before, in 1784, he was the American ambassador to the court of Louis XVI and Marie-Antoinette of "Let them eat cake" fame. In this international arena, Jefferson became aware of two national traumas scarring the French joie d'vive in the 1780s. There were the salt arrests of 1780 and "the flour war,"[86] of 1784, the year he arrived in tree-lined, elegant Paris. And then, finally, the shortages of grain and bread in 1788–89 became one of the sparks that ignited the French Revolution.

Jefferson, the democrat, wished nothing like this on his fellow citizens. He would have his countrymen seek free access to salt on the American continent, looking especially for inland sources to sustain those living away from the coastal waters. Never should the horrors which were so fresh in his mind to be visited on his beloved country.

Salt: Dreadful to Drink, Savory to Eat

Jefferson has been sending out requests for any geographic data he can get, especially for natural resources that might be invaluable to the young, growing country. William Henry Harrison, then Governor of the Indiana Territory, forwards a map commissioned by the Spanish, done by a Mr. Evans. While a useful aid, this chart of the upper Missouri has incongruities that spring forth like the water it's purported to describe. It reports, *"On the declivity of a little hill, there are five holes of about a foot and a half diameter, by two of depth always full, without ever overflowing a drop, very salt. If we take away this salt water, it fills immediately; and at about ten feet lower, there comes out of this same Hill, a Strong Spring of pure & Sweet water."* Another section reveals, *"At a distance of about 18 Miles from this low land are found mines of meneral Salt, almost at the surface of the Earth. The Savages who know it perfectly, are found to employ leavers to break it and get it out of the Ground."* [L1:141]

With salt plentiful in the twenty-first century, the question arises: Why this fixation with salt supplies? And, later in the trip, how serious are the men's grumbling about the lack? Mammals are attracted to the taste and flavor of salt. It helps regulate metabolism and blood chemistry, but is lost along with other necessary minerals as they sweat. It is chemically important to overall health and well-being, as well as being a flavor enhancer. This is the simplest explanation for wanting salt. Lewis leaves St. Louis in 1804 loaded with bushels of salt, and men at the oceanside salt camp manufacture three more bushels before leaving Fort Clatsop in 1806. It's an ongoing need.

Knowing Jefferson's desire to locate these inland salt sources, Lewis listens to reports and believes he is near some water source that will lead to the *Saline of Mississippi*. Despite a logical discrepancy between the muddy but fresh nature of that river and salinity, he is indeed near a source of salt. *"this landing is the place that Boats receive Salt from the Saline Licks ... and is worked at present to great advantage ..."* [J2:118] If Jefferson was hoping that Lewis would find new sources, he is already too late. The displaced French settlers coming in from the northeasterly Acadia and emigrants from Montreal at the beginning of the 1700s incorporated the salt springs as useful and prominent features of their first establishments in the territory. [J2:119n5] Sensing financial opportunity, their private use expanded into manufacture of a trade item, a culinary supply. The technique is simple: boil the salty spring water down until it evaporates and only the mineral deposits remain. Buying salt for the Expedition will not be difficult.

Wheat, Milling, and Bread

Soils conducive to growing wheat and running streams to power flour-grinding mills were, as noted above, a priority of Jefferson for the infant America. The Corps of Discovery is to find rich soils for farming, streams for mills, and worthy stones for grinding. There are Dutch descendants from the Atlantic States who are *"of <sober,> temperament, laborious and honest people,"* and they specialize in a technology interesting to the President: milling. Just after turning from the Ohio into the Mississippi in November 1803, Lewis notes two gristmills and a sawmill. [J2:108]

From City of St. Louis archives

The wind and water mills that Lewis sees in 1803 had already closed and began to fall into ruin by 1820 as other mechanical power and more extended commerce took over.

These great mechanical grinding stones are crucial to local communities needing flour and grain for common household foodstuffs such as bread, cakes, gravies, pie shells, etc. But bread is not just for homey, domestic use – it is the mainstay of armies. In 1780 the Continental Congress had issued an appeal for quotas of flour and pork to support the ragged armies fighting for independence. Like their military predecessors, Captain Lewis will soon be storing flour into keg after keg, and Clark putting aside tons of pork. The Army staples haven't changed. And while the mills are there and corn can be ground mechanically, Clark will have his restive, troublesome men occupied with grinding cornmeal by hand. No need to pay these local millers.

But the establishment of gristmills is significant. Both Lewis and Clark make diligent notes on rocks they observe as well as milling facilities, *"this stone appears to possess excellent grit for grind stones."* [J2:115] For the purposes of commerce and supplies, Lewis notes that Cinque Hommes [Five Men] Creek *"has a considerable number of inhabitants on it, and as many as three gristmills."* [J2:116] Later, on December 5 just below Cahokia, Clark notes *"above a rock forming a worft [wharf] into the river 200 feet … this Rock appears to be Composed of Grit well calculated for Grind Stones …"*

Onward to St. Louis

As the Expedition begins its haul up the Mississippi, the entries describe ducks that aren't bagged and wounded deer that escape. The hunters aren't quite up to snuff yet, and Clark isn't supervising. He has been ill for a week, and on November 22, they do the best they can to provide some nourishing chicken soup, frontier-style. Lewis writes, *"saw some <u>Heth hens</u> or grows [grouse]— one of my men went on shore and killed one of them, of which we made soome soup for my friend Capt. Clark …"* The Captain acknowledges that he thought of the bird as a specimen as well, *"this bird shall hereafter be more particularly discribed."*

On November 23, Lewis calls a halt at Cape Girardeau to pay his respects to the Commandant and deliver letters of introduction to facilitate the Expedition's overwinter stay. His sought-after commandant is the French-Canadian, Louis Lorimier, whose store and goods were burnt to the ground by General George Rogers Clark in 1782. [J2:109n2] Lewis is invited to dinner; Clark, down by the river, is not.

What foods Lewis might have been served that night is hinted at by Captain Amos Stoddard, the first American commandant of the newly acquired territories of the Louisiana Purchase. The food list is quite enough to live comfortably on, "wheat, corn … maple syrup. They annually export considerable quantities of beef, pork, lard, smoked hams and some peltry. They also cultivate various kinds of fruit, small grains, and garden vegetables."[87]

Lewis is quite taken with his host's family. Lorimier's wife is a dignified Shawnee woman, and the couple have several teenage children, *"the daughter is remarkably handsome & dresses in a plain yet fashionable stile or such as is now Common in the Atlantic States among the respectable people of the middle class."* Despite the hostess' eclectic but colorful mix of Native and French garb, Lewis is quite at home. He extolls the evening, *"The Comdt. pressed me to stay to supper which I did, the lady of the family presided, and with much circumspection performed the honours of the table; supper being over which was really a comfortable and desent one I bid the family an afectionate adieeu –"* [J2:108] Lorimier is such a gracious host that he has a son escort the Captain back to Girardeau, some three miles away. The grouse soup hasn't helped Clark and he is still unwell.

The upstream journey on the Mississippi is not terribly exciting. The little flotilla passes keelboats from Louisville bound for Kaskaskia, loaded with kegs of whiskey and dry goods. For the first time one of the hunters goes missing. Nathaniel Pryor, one of the better hunters, gets lost and stays lost, much to Lewis' consternation. No amount of blowing the hunting horns or firing shots seem to reach his ears. They set off without him, [J2:105] in what will be a pattern for dealing with the lost. Fortunately, Pryor re-appears after two days, *"much fatiequed with his wandering and somewhat indisposed."* [J2:110] This is the first time, but it will not be the last in the journey which follows, that a hunter strays from the reach of the party, his new family. As time progresses and the terrain becomes less known, the worries will become more vexing, more anxiety provoking. Is there a sense of relief among a group just beginning to be cohesive? Probably not, for the Corps is still a tumble of strangers.

The Sugar Loaf

The following day is rounded out with a different, one-of-a-kind celebration. Just as the sunset's rosy pink rays splash high on a smooth rocky dome, the men come to the Grand Tower, a feature that Clark sketches as *"Tower Rock, the Sugar Loaf, and their keelboat anchored"* near shore.[88] In this new land, geographical features are often dubbed with names relating to their shape and form, identified with foodstuffs (which *Sugar Loaf* amply demonstrates), or with an abundance of edibles that form part of the wayfarer's diet.

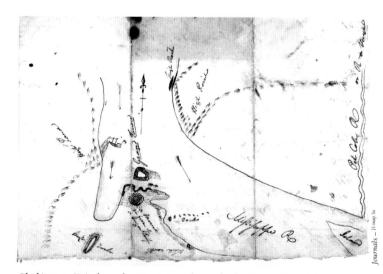

Clark's map (3a) along the Mississippi shows the keelboat adjacent to Tower Rock and "The Sugar Loaf."

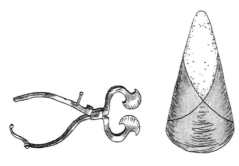

Sugar as sold in loaf form; and sugar nippers to crack off chunks to use.

Sugar refining had not yet made the step toward the white crystalline uniformity seen today, which is a result of mechanical centrifuging.[89] Their large-crystal brown sugar is similar to the raw sugar now available, but with a greater residue of dark, sticky molasses.

The *Old West Baking Book* amply describes the sugar loaves brought in from Cuba and sold throughout the country. The humidity and tropical heat during shipping further coalesced the sugar into great lumps or domes, and rather than fight nature, the sugar factories simply shaped the product into "loaves" which were shipped from the Caribbean. "Sugar augers or specially designed sugar nippers were necessary to break apart the hard loaf or cone. Then the chunks were pounded fine. Sometimes placing pieces through a coffee grinder proved faster."[90] This was just plain work, and costly to boot.

However, this particular rocky dome holds far more allure than that. *"This seems among the watermen of the mississippi to be what the tropics or Equanoxial line is with regard to the Sailors; those who have never passed it before are always compelled to pay or furnish some sperits to drink or be ducked ..."* [J2:112-3] For travelers coming up the Mississippi, this is indeed a voyager's landmark.

As the Expedition continues its laborious way up the Mississippi, Lewis goes on ahead to the fair-sized village and military establishment at Kaskaskia, population approximately 500. He departs on December 5, traveling north two days by horseback to reach Cahokia (about 55 miles north) situated on the riverbank across and just downstream from St. Louis, on December 7. The following day, December 8, he presents himself to the Spanish commandant of St. Louis, and returns to Cahokia the next day to meet his party, which has progressed upriver to the town. [J2:118n1] The mail service is functioning quite regularly, and during the time Clark stops in at Cahokia for provisions – and receives a letter from William Henry Harrison. Clark is caught without his ledger, and he notes his purchases for the day on the front of

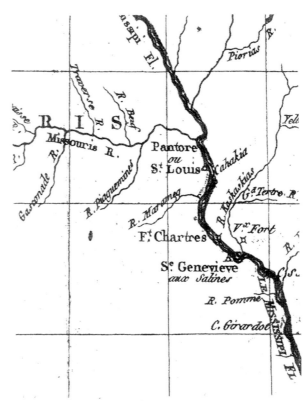

Map of 70 miles of the Mississippi River from Girardot to above St. Louis and the Missouri confluence.

the envelope: *"100 rations Bread & Med. 1050 Whiskey. 1 Barrel extra."* [L1:135] This is all we know about provisioning at this point, for on foods, the *Journals* are silent.

Realizing that his most urgent task as commander is to interact with the local people – the politicos, the merchants and suppliers, those savy in the ways of the native tribes – Meriwether Lewis hands the military command of Camp River Dubois over to William Clark. He relinquishes his constant presence and bows out of journal-keeping – until the following year when the Corps departs for the unknown West.

Known journals of the Expedition are those kept by Lewis and Clark; three sergeants: Gass, Ordway, and Floyd; and Private Whitehouse. "Robert Frazer kept a journal, but it has been lost. Sergeant Pryor should have kept a journal, and some think that he did. And there is some evidence, at least as remembered by his descendants, that Alexander Willard kept a journal."[91] But no other journals have ever been located.

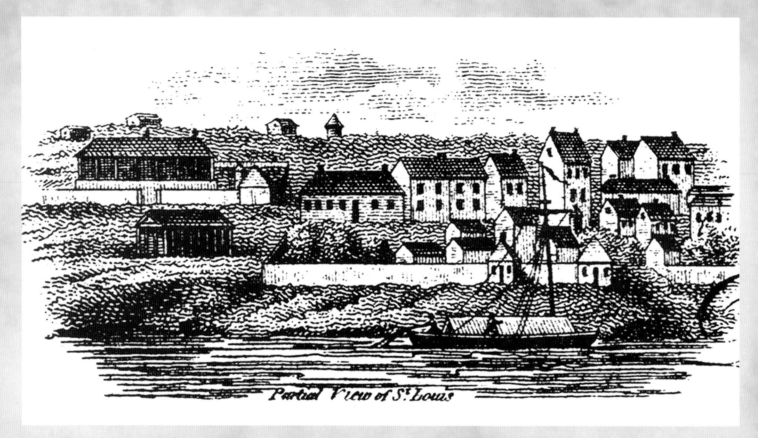

View of St. Louis from the Mississippi River circa 1814 from an engraving which appeared on a 1818 banknote.

Wintering Near St. Louis

Camp River Dubois: November, 1803 – May, 1804

The forests are filled with about fifty species of indigenous animals;
among which are the buffalo, two kinds of elk, two kinds of deer, the roe,
the bear, the beaver, the otter, two species of fox, a species of the goat,
... the raccoon, the opossom, the rabbit, and seven kinds of squirrels.

— AMOS STODDARD, 1803

The Countrey about the Mouth of Missouri is pleasent rich and partially Settled
... the Bottom is extensive and emencly rich for 15 or 20 miles up each river ...

— CLARK, MAY 1804

THE RICH, BUSTLING VILLAGE OF ST. LOUIS appears in 1803 as a shining vision on the horizon to the little flotilla coming up the Mississippi. With a population of about 200 homes, it is the largest French mercantile port north of New Orleans, and its gleaming, whitewashed buildings glow in the sunshine. Situated near the strategic confluence of the Mississippi, the Missouri, and the Illinois Rivers, this is the open gate through which liquor, flour, Indian trade goods, and a host of other commodities pour even as great bales of furs float downriver. Traveling by water is the speediest and least dangerous form of transportation through this Indian-occupied, undeveloped wilderness.

A mere forty years before, there was nothing at this spot but a great green forest atop a rocky bluff. Then, in 1763, a French grant of monopoly for the Indian fur trade on the Upper Missouri went to Maxent, Laclède and Company of New Orleans. So important was this financial windfall that Pierre Laclède, one of the two merchant partners, immediately embarked on the lengthy voyage upriver from the Gulf of Mexico. His winter reconnaissance produced three results: he chose an eminently propitious site, visualized and drew up a master plan for the company headquarters, and

lined up the French-Canadian laborers to begin working on it the following spring.

By the end of 1803 when Lewis arrives, this forty-year-old settlement is a prosperous boomtown, its leading citizens dedicated to trading, accumulating great wealth and power, and living a conspicuously fine lifestyle. The tenor of the town is quite cosmopolitan, with trade goods coming in from Britain, France, the Caribbean, and Spain. "River Baron" families such as the Chouteaus, the Robidouxs, the Gratiots, and the Cerrès all import French wines, bone china, and other luxury goods, and "at least 56 family heads possessed books ... before 1804 there were some 2,000 to 3,000 volumes in private libraries."[92] The Missouri Historical Society holdings list a book held by a dedicated cook of this period, *The Science of Cooking* published in Paris in 1776 – a fine example of practical, and perhaps avante guard, entertaining notions held by one of the French wives.

Surrounding this mercantile hub are settlements like Cahokia (with an American military detachment), Florissant, St. Genevieve, and St. Charles. While St. Louis prospers, the little villages that the Corps is passing have quaint nicknames indicating a different economic fate. The French, with their wicked humor, dub old Ste. Genevieve, "Mis-erre" or "Misery." Carondelet is doubly nicknamed, being called either "Vide Poche" (Empty Pocket) or "Pain de Sucre" (Sugar Loaf) for an Indian mound renamed after a more appealing sweet. Even St. Louis does not escape – it is "Pain Court" meaning "short of bread." There is a running joke in the area that the powerful merchants are so busy with trade that they have all but forgotten about farming and have lost their touch with the land. They are rich but breadless.

Several years earlier, threats of Indian hostilities and a general lack of dedicated farmers among the inhabitants failed to provide proper care for the "common fields" farming area originally located just beyond town, and the crops didn't flourish. Emergency supplies had to be shipped in. A situation six years earlier in 1797 illustrated the problems faced by the merchant/contractor/provisioner Auguste Chouteau in supplying the American garrison. He "was unable to meet the demand expected and supplies were rushed up from New Madrid at the mouth of the Ohio River. So great was the disruption that the Spanish minister in Philadelphia contracted with a Baltimore firm to send barges down the Ohio River with huge quantities of wheat, rice, corn, salt meat, and whiskey."[93] The speed and broad extent of Chouteau's trade connections, as well as the large-scale availability of provisions are impressive. Since St. Louis' inception when teenage Auguste Chouteau worked building the outpost, he had matured along with the town into its elder statesman, and is now the wealthiest and most influential of the fur trading river barons. His son, Pierre, welcomes Lewis.

There is no town gazette to record what happened the winter of 1803–04. Old diaries, letters, accounting ledgers, and histories provide us with pieces like a jigsaw puzzle coming together to form a ragged-edged but vivid picture. Physical items such as silver, kitchen ware, cloth and furniture, can lure our imaginations, tune our inner ear to the music and whispers of parties past. Most revealing, however, are the descriptions penned by Captain Amos Stoddard, representing the johnny-come-lately Americans as officer-in-command at the transfer of Upper Louisiana. Nothing escapes him. He writes pertinent and detailed histories of the area's recent past, probes the current political maneuvers, and lovingly describes this "new" land and its peoples as a treasure to be held and cherished. If the *Journals* are sparse, or even silent, regarding Lewis' activities during that winter, we are able to fill in much of what he and Clark experienced by going to these other sources.

The Social/Political Scene – River Barons and Voyageurs

At Lewis' arrival, the Spanish are formally in control, although the town is decidedly French in tone. At the upper end of the society are the families that control the trading houses, the River Barons. They occupy large stone houses behind fieldstone fences, live in rooms furnished with European furniture on polished hardwood floors, eat off imported china and drink French wines from crystal goblets.[94] From the sheer necessity of controlling the fur trade, these merchants forge deep and lasting links with their Native American contacts. Trade and mutual respect, an admiration for native ways ... all are interwoven. These strapping, bearded giants among men appear at social gatherings in buckskins, letting their French wives shine in fashionable silks or demure cottons.

Laclede-Chouteau house in St. Louis, circa 1803.

Courtesy: Jefferson National Expansion Memorial/NPS

On the lower rungs are French families living in the "American bottom lands," whose tough, compact men are the voyageurs plying the rivers, bringing home their pay at the end of a trip. They are, *"absent from their families or homes the term of six twelve or eighteen months and alwas subjected to severe and incessant labour, exposed to the feroscity of the lawless savages, the vicissitudes of weather and climate, and dependant on chance or accident alone for food, raiment or relief in the event of malady."* [J2:241-2] Their attitude seems to be that the old men, women, and children at home can take care of business, eh? Those French men, strong of constitution and disposed to travel, become the engagés, the boatmen working the pirogues up the Missouri for the Expedition.

These folk are, to the core, wholly French. They have their sweet and flowing mother tongue and a love of music and the sensuality of singing and dancing. Catholicism with its full calendar of Saints' days (and therefore feast days) blends with a lusty sociability and joie d'vive, all coupling with an agrarian lifestyle to blend seamlessly into a heaven on earth.

On "Three Flags Days," March 9 and 10, 1804, the combined forty-two year colonial periods of St. Louis end – initially the French, then a few years of the Spanish, and finally, briefly the French again. The Spanish flag goes down, and the French flag is raised as an honor to the tough, hardy settlers who never really recognized Spanish ownership of "their" land. Finally, the emblem of France is pulled from the grey wintery sky and the Americans raise the Stars and Stripes and own all of the Louisiana Territory.

The Little Town of St. Louis

To visualize this village of several hundred houses,[95] this "emporium of trade" as Stoddard calls it, a contemporary map drafted by Antoine Soulard and dating to about 1805 helps with the physical orientation. Three long broad streets are set back from the banks of the Mississippi, designed to provide close access to the town's source of wealth – trade. There are a few warehouses, but no mercantile offices – business is conducted in the owners' homes. Chouteau's water mill, several wind mills used for grinding wheat, a distillery, and an orchard are shown. Streets are given simple descriptive names such as Church Street ("Le Rue de L' Èglise") and Barn Street, barns being important for the storage of grain.[96] One street, "Rue Barrera,"[97] carries the name of a local baker who lives on the street and produces wonderfully yeasty, early-morning aromas.

A typical family would have a number of little structures on their property. There might be a henhouse (poullallier), an outdoor kitchen (cuisine) with a built-in oven, and a milk house (laiterie). There might be a water well, a pigsty (cochonnière), and perhaps a pigeon house (pigeonnier), something still found in France today. And in the growing town with no green-grocers, a garden is a necessity, and fruit orchards are common. At the end of the growing season, agricultural produce would be stored or overwintered in an outdoor cellar called a caveau.[98] Refrigeration doesn't exist.

The property of Swiss-born merchant Charles Gratiot is described in his "Land Envelope" found in the Missouri Historical Society: nine acres of gardens, orchards, and even more ambitiously, a mill and his very own distillery. Gardening and the cultivation of vegetables, originally in the commons, has moved into the individuals' own backyards, in this case near his 36' x 52' stonewalled mansion.[99] Orchards of sweet peaches and winsome apples yield ample fruit. Traditional crops include corn, beans, wheat, buckwheat, rye, oats, barley, cotton, flax, and tobacco. Caring for the land and its crops is a vital occupation, and the slaves are necessary components to surviving well.

Business enterprises in town include masons, carpenters, and joiners and blacksmiths. Blacksmiths ply their trade working on firearms and their repair, and in construction of kitchen utensils like drinking cups, plates, pots, and the heavy ironware built into kitchen hearths. The cooperage trade turns out barrels for the storage of goods and food.

Food Management

The entire industrial concept of fresh food production, shipping, and marketing as we know it is basically nonexistent, and anything being shipped must be preserved before it is ready to travel.

Homegrown produce is brought from garden to stove in a few brisk steps. For everyday eating by the kitchen fireside, cooks and homemakers might use earthenware pieces thrown by Joseph Eberlein, a potter who began production around 1795.[100] An ancient cooking method, still seen today, uses heavy clay pots gently cradled against each other and almost submersed in boiling water inside a huge kettle – cooking several dishes for dinner at the same time. One traditional French dish prepared this way is a daube, or braised meat.

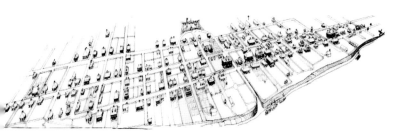

A perspective map of St. Louis in 1804 created by Jefferson National Expansion Memorial Historian, Bob Moore, from available historic maps and information taken from J. Thomas Scharf's 1883 book, *History of St. Louis City and County*, volume 1. Buildings shown are from recorded verbal description, historic artist sketches, or early photographs and reflect all buildings existing at the time.

DAUBE À LA MONTIGNY-EN-VEXIN[101]

2 lbs. beef
1 veal knuckle
1 slice ham, fat and lean
1 onion
1 carrot, large
1 calf's foot; or 1 T. unflavored gelatin
   white wine

Chop ham, carrot, and onion very very fine. Cover the bottom of the *cocotte* (earthenware or Dutch oven or roasting pan with cover) with the ham/carrot/onion mixture, and over it place the beef and veal. For jelling, add: either a calf's foot on top of the meats, or 1 tablespoon unflavored gelatin dissolved in 3 tablespoons white wine. Then add a mix of ⅔ white wine and ⅓ water to cover the meat, "so that the beef bathes well in it."

Let it cook, very slow, in the pot for six hours. Let it cool, skim the fat, and put it into a cool place; for this daube must be served cold in its jelly, the next day.

The French author/chef Amy Carley says that "this *daube* is best braised in an earthenware *cocotte* just large enough to hold the meat." It can also be cooked in a braisière (braises translates to "live coals"), or a Dutch oven with coals on the top of a raised-rim lid.[a]

The Food-related Businesses

St. Louis has few food-related commercial ventures. There are maple sugar works (sucreries), and salt works, based on the "salines, which yield a sufficient quantity of salt for the consumption of the inhabitants, and some for exportation."[102] There is also grain-milling and bread-baking, two trades that go hand in hand. A number of Frenchmen have mills where grain is processed by a horse-driven grindstone. Wealthy Joseph Robidoux's eight-horse operation (1802) is probably the largest in the area. For the producers of flour, the next step is to consolidate the operation and bake bread as well. Robidoux does just this, building a large, two-story bakery behind his mansion on the grandiosely named La Grande Rue Royale.[103]

Not to be outdone by the French merchants, an aspiring Spaniard named Manuel Lisa establishes himself by building "a water mill to make flour as fine as that of the Anglo-Americans,"[104] which he tells the Spanish government will stop the outward transport of grain and add value to the city. On May 29, 1800, Señor Lisa proceeds with his plan and hires Juan Gatzeze as his baker.[105] Lewis will have dealings with Lisa while over-wintering in St. Louis.

Clark at Camp River Dubois

While Lewis begins his duties as Presidential appointee, attending to business and socializing in St. Louis, Clark arrives at Camp River Dubois (Wood River Camp) on December 12, *"nearly opposit the Missouries."* He immediately sends out hunters even as the weather diminishes – *"the N W wind which had been blowing all day increased to a <u>Storm</u> which was accompanied by Hail & Snow, & the wind Continued to blow from the Same point with violence."* However, he determines to stay, for the woods are home to bountiful game, and the hunters bring in turkeys and opossums as evidence. The choice of River Dubois is not accidental, nor is it Clark's serendipitous find. The Spanish governor has recommended yet another location, but Lewis, writing to Jefferson says, *"other considerations of more importance had induced me to assign myself a different position ... (provided it answered the description I had received of it[)], the mouth of a small river called Dubois ..."* [L1:147] There can be little doubt that the hunting opportunities played an important part in the choice of winter quarters.

So what could persuade Lewis to politely decline the Spanish commandant and offer such inducements that he straightaway sends Clark to the wooded spot? Listen to the admiring words of Stoddard:

> The forests are filled with about fifty species of indigenous animals; among which are the buffalo, two kinds of elk, two kinds of deer, the roe, the bear, the beaver, the otter, two species of fox, a species of the goat, the mind, the raccoon, the opossom, the rabbit, and seven kinds of squirrels. ... [There are] ducks, three kinds of teal, the wood-cock, the plover, the pheasant, the partridge, the quail, the pigeon, the prairie hen, or grouse, the wild goose and turkey. Here the lovers of sport may be gratified at all seasons

---

[a] By the time Julia Child reintroduced this ancient classic, it was reinvigorated by soaking the meat in wine for three days, then larding with bacon, and finally finishing with garlic, herbs, tomatoes, and onions. The process of evolution is still at work in the kitchen.

of the year; and epicures can be at no loss for variety and delicacy of food.[106]

It is worth noting that Clark chooses to keep his troops together as a single unit. They do not stay at Army posts at either Kaskaskia or Cahokia, nor in a village. They are kept out of the mainstream of society, away from social interactions, away from distractions to military life and its disciplines, out at a distance where they will rely (more or less) on their hunting skills and, he hopes, start to form a team.

Bob Moore, historian at Jefferson National Expansion Memorial, points out several of the difficulties in maintaining adequate provisions for the troops. Apparently there is a delicate balance between having enough food and what to do if scarcity exists, for "many officers were thoroughly opposed to having their soldiers hunt under any circumstances." In opposition to this stand, "it was the duty of the officers to make certain that the health of the men was not impaired either by eating spoiled meat or by letting the storehouse run low on staples."[107]

If these contradictory positions in military policy are the case in 1803, the Corps' isolation is even more understandable, for the Captains *want* their men out hunting. Additionally, bringing in a fat deer or a brace of turkeys could help avoid more unnecessary food bills. This party is already over-budget; and Clark's bitter experience with trying to recover monies owed his brother George leaves him with a profound distrust of the new government when it comes to reimbursement.

Camp River Dubois or Wood River Camp.

Courtesy: We Proceeded On

At Camp River Dubois, Clark has three key job functions: one short-term, two long-term. First, he must get the men under winter shelter, i.e. construct the log buildings and fireplaces. Then he must unify the group and get some stiffer military training and discipline into the troops. Finally he must fill the position of quartermaster to keep his men eating. Quartermastering out at Wood River means making

a list and checking it twice, for his requests are forwarded by horseback messenger to Lewis, who, in turn, sends them on to the commissary at Kaskaskia about fifty-five miles downstream. Arrangements are then made for military requisitions to be sent up to Cahokia and finally transported to Camp River Dubois. Ultimately, in the spring, Clark will take over a major part of coordinating the provisioning for the rest of their journey.

A week after Clark arrives at River Dubois with his small party, Lewis sends two messages of import, two days apart. On December 17, 1803, he advises Clark that George Drouillard[b] and the eight men from Tennessee have arrived at Cahokia and that he is sending them on. The commander frets about not having a whipsaw to use for constructing the huts and is working on getting one, and adds that, *"You can obtain corn for the horses by application to Hennebury or any person who has the care of Morrison's farm."* [L1:144] Somehow or another, the Corps has gotten horses (on loan, perhaps from the military outpost at Cahokia, but definitely not on the list of equipment needed). This makes it easier to ride elsewhere for supplies, mail, etc. Surprisingly, there is no mention of using the horses to bring back heavy game.

More Mouths to Feed

A second letter – two days later, on the December 19 – is to Jefferson, *"I made a selection of a sufficient number of men from the troops of that place (Kaskaskias) to complete my party, and have made a requisition on the Contractor to cause immediately an adequate deposit of provisions to be made in Cahokia ..."* [L1:145] Records show that Lewis has picked up ten new men, six of whom will continue on as part of the permanent party.

The new group coming into Camp River Dubois is at least a full mess unit, perhaps two. The number of mouths to feed has increased greatly, and using a nominal five pounds of food per man per day, it comes out to be at least another fifty pounds per day, or close to 350 pounds per week for the new Army men. Moreover, the hunters are going to have to change their style: the type of game they've been bringing in (turkeys and opossums) don't weigh all that much, so the goal will be to look for the larger game – deer, bear, and so on.

---

[b] George Drouillard is consistently spelled "Drewyer" in the *Journals*. Drouillard, of mixed Shawnee and French heritage, is hired by the Captains as an expert native-language interpreter and as lead hunter. His story is written in *Sign Talker* by James Thom.

Eating at Camp River Dubois

Stocking up at Wood River begins with social calls from two independents: farmer Samuel Griffith and a Mr. Gilbert, salt trader. Although no transactions are recorded, it appears that these men are making their introductions. Perhaps their visits are purely social, but both are involved with the business of food and are likely hoping that not all provisioning will be done through military channels.

Meanwhile, Lewis, in St. Louis, is doing his part of the quartermastering, for on December 19 Clark writes, *"The Waggons Came with provisions this evening."* There is no record of what is on those wagons, but military subsistence is usually pork, corn, and flour. The food is stored, and Clark commandeers the carts for hauling logs to speed up construction of their cabins. On December 21, the wagoner collects $3 from the Captain and departs. But whatever the supplies sent up on the December 19, Clark is not totally happy. Four days later he sends a man to *"Mr. Morisons farm for a Teem & corn, which arivd about 3oClock, a raney Desagreeable day."* The commissary wagons obviously had to leave before the job was finished, returning to Cahokia for further deliveries. The privates are exhausted from hauling logs in the freezing cold, and Clark is bringing in help to speed up the work. Less hefting of logs and reduced exposure to the inclement weather will help with their caloric expenditure. As for the corn, it fueled either the men or the horses.

Local Suppliers

Meanwhile, Mr. Griffith, who dropped in on the December 16, reappears a week later, *"down from his farm with a Load of Turnips &c. as a present to me ..."* There is some strategy going on here, for it appears that Griffith is hoping to subtly coerce the Captain into *buying* the turnips, and thus establish himself as a supplier. It works. The next day (December 24) Clark records, *"Cloudy morning, I purchase a Cargo of Turnips for 3/ – a bushel of Mr. Gririffeth."* These common roots simmering in the pot are the only vegetable mentioned during the winter of 1803–04. Now there is a supplier and perhaps they are cooked as he might fondly remember them from Virginia. Here are several different presentations typical of the time.

The helpful Mr. Griffith is proving useful, and Clark continues with the aside that he is sending Shields with the farmer *"to purchase me some butter on the other Side of the river ..."* It is an overnight affair; Shields returns on Christmas Day with a cheese and four pounds of butter. If the Captain is hoping for a fine cheese, he is likely to be disappointed. Stoddard has addressed the quality of local dairy

> ### MONTICELLO TURNIPS[108]
> ### 3 VARIATIONS
>
> 1) Peel and boil until tender as many turnips as desired. Mash through a colander. Add butter, salt, pepper, and a little milk, and stew for fifteen minutes so as to dry them, or
> 2) *Cooked with sugar.* Peel turnips, cut in pieces, and put them in a vessel with a spoonful of butter, half a cup of brown sugar, and a pint of hot water. Stew until tender.
> 3) At Monticello we used to have turnips dressed with cheese. [a variation on #1]

products, declaring that the "cheese ... is of an inferior quality." When compared with the noted lack of quality in Jefferson's gigantic cheese, it appears that American cheese-making is still in its infancy.

Christmas, 1803 – New Year's Day, 1804

Clark, the only journalist in Camp River Dubois in 1803, records: *"Christmas 25th Decr: I was awakened by a Christmas discharge <of> found that Some of the party had got Drunk <2 fought,> the men frolicked and hunted all day, Snow this morning, Ice run all day, Several Turkey Killed   Shields returned with a cheese & 4 lb butter, Three Indians Come to day to take Christmas with us, I gave them a bottle of whiskey ..."*

Roast turkey probably graced the table, perhaps with a corn mush glistening with tasty butter. No information tells whether their flour was made into biscuits, or if sliced or slivered cheese was used to add flavor and roundness.

It is not a totally delightful day from Clark's point of view. Another brawl, and worse yet, after taking their bottle of whiskey, the Indians went off *"after informing me that a great talk had been held and that all the nations were going to war against the Ozous [Osage?] in 3 months ..."* This bad news contradicts the peace policy the Expedition is promoting. The only good news is that, *"Drewyear Says he will go with us, at the rate ofd [offered?] ..."* The Expedition has hired its best hunter and interpreter.

Locals provide other foodstuffs. On New Year's Day, 1804, Clark writes: *"Snow about an inch deep Cloudy to day, a woman Come forward wishing to wash and doe Such things as may be necessary for the Detachmt ... A Perogue Passed Loaded with Salt & Dry goods. Jos: Vaun offers to let the Contrator have Beef at 4$ pd. or 3$50 Cents in money, Pokers hake,* *the Nut is Sheshake, a plant growing in the ponds with a large broad leaf, stem in the middle of the leaf in french Volies ... one Man offers to sell pork ...*"

Meat is available, and Jos. Vaun appears to know that he can supply the troops through the commissary contractor but offers the beef for less if Clark pays cash – this might appeal to the cost-cutting needs of a quartermaster. Pork is offered to Clark straightaway, without considerations of the military provisioning system. Then there is the pond-nut from the American (or yellow) lotus. The seed from this beautiful aquatic plant is seen in Missouri and points west. It is a tasty treat, this *sheshake*, a food staple for the locals as well as competitors farther down the food chain. Clark, mangling the language, calls it *Volies*, some sort of approximation for the French *graine de volaille*. Someone, traveling through on land or perhaps by pirogue, is carrying these nuts. Is he selling the nuts as a merchant? Or is it a personal supply – a potential windfall?

The idea of beef apparently appeals to the Captain, for on January 3, two days after the idea is planted, the *Journals* record that "*Comy [commissary] Kiled a Beef & ...*" The military man orders from within his designated supply line while outside it is 10°F and "*Excessive Cold after Sunset.*" Perhaps the weather is prompting the need for good, hot meals.

Other people fortuitously appear. On January 2, "*Cap Whitesides Came to See me & his Son ...*" and from the date of his military service (Battle of King's Mountain, 1780) this old soldier is probably another friend of Clark's brother George. William Whiteside has traveled upriver from his station 35 miles south, and if it is commerce he is seeking, he achieves his goal. Clark reports a "*purchase 12 lb Tallow for 6/– of Whitesides, who Sold the Beef to the Com: [commissary] at 3$ pr. Hw.[hundredweight].*" [J2:150] There appears to have been some price-cutting going on – the first offer of beef is for $4 per Hw, then drops to $3.50, and finally Whitesides comes in at $3. The market economy is working well. Clark's gauge of the market is exact. Capt. Stoddard puts this $3 per hundred-weight market price squarely within the range of what was being asked in 1803, noting that at times the price would drop to $2.50.[109]

A closer examination of the sale is interesting in terms of what a cow is worth. Cattle in the 1800s are somewhat smaller than the twenty-first century version. Raising of cattle (and pigs) requires very little effort: They are turned out to browse on grass in the summer, and they subsist quite well on rushes and cane in the winter. "It is common for a farmer to own from a hundred to a hundred and fifty head

of cattle, and as many swine."[110] A cow might have weighed 600 pounds prior to slaughter, but the end result of useable meat might come in at 300–400 pounds. At $3 per Hw, Whitesides turns a profit at $9–12 per animal.

A local French family drops in, trading onions for some tin Clark can spare. [J2:153] Ramey, the liquor merchant/bootlegger who has been warned off, still "*gives me much trouble*" fumes Clark on January 9. Victualing on the frontier has its ups and downs.

An Arctic Winter

At least the trouble with the log cabins is done. They are built, and what follows is a dreadfully cold winter. Thermometers are showing temperatures hovering near zero, seldom rising higher than 23°F. [J2:166] It's cold enough for their porter beer (4% alcohol content) to freeze and break the bottles.[c] The cabins are not chinked early in the winter, and on one such day Clark notes that at 4 PM, the time of day when the most solar heat has collected, "*the Thmt.r in a corner of a warm room was 20 D. above (0)*" [J2:150] The human body has to work hard to stay warm. Although these are tough outdoorsmen, it is still shockingly cold, so much so that when Clark goes to explore the Cahokia mounds, he returns and in amazement finds, "*my feet, which were wet had frozed to my Shoes*" [J2:154] and he deems the day "*exceeding Cold.*" Not only is ice running on the river, but frigid high winds are blowing sandstorms off the islands and adding a ferocious wind chill factor. Clark takes to his sickbed the next day, attributing it to "*the Ducking & excessive Cold.*" It is under circumstances like these that those calorie-laden stews and cornmeal puddings heavy with fat are literally life-savers. The caloric expenditure of the body to preserve its core heat is tremendous.[d]

To make matters worse, Ordway and McNeal are lost and forced to sleep out overnight. They return the next day, January 11. These men do not have high-tech winter wear, thermal socks, or sleeping bags rated to -20°F. Neither, however, becomes sick. But, being inside poses its own threats. Clark, still sick from exposure, awakens to find "*My chimney got on fire ...*" [J2:155]

Country Sociability

In some respects Wood River is an open house. Local Americans come a'calling, a Reverend Bagley comes with potatoes

---

[c] See also "Malt Liquors – Beer and Porter", page 251.
[d] See *Appendix C: Food Requirements* for detailed calculations.

and fowls, which prompts Clark to trade. A Mr. Cummings appears on behalf of the contractor bringing meal and brandy. Some women (pretty young things eager to flirt?) pay a social call. On January 30, 1804, Lewis makes his first trip to the camp, accompanied by the merchant John Hay and sheriff John Hays. More food supplies roll in: butter and milk from two other men, Cane and Hanley.

Despite the visitors, Clark, as commander of the little military outpost, is wearing down and he has cabin fever. On January 15, he writes to his brother-in-law, Major Wm. Croghan. *"I have not been from Camp to any house since my arrival here."* But the conscientious commander of Camp River Dubois doesn't leave; he has duties requiring him to stay at camp. A younger William Clark had come to St. Louis in 1797, hoping to clean up brother George's finances, and he had enjoyed its social life. But now no ladies grace his table, nor do servants come forth with the course after course that any well-bred family would serve. Dinners consist primarily of game or Army rations, and there is no well-polished table with those heady conversations amongst educated diners. It probably doesn't occur to the minds of those young soldiers who are equally miserable in the monotony of an Army camp. Clark rues his lack of social contacts; he is lonesome. He has no one with whom he can discuss the momentous changes taking place *"... It is hourly expected that the American's will take possession of the other side of the Mississippi.*[i.e., the Louisiana Purchase completion]*"* L1:164

Clark is actually spending a goodly part of his time quelling alcoholic brawls and binges in camp, trying to form the men into a functional group. So this redheaded Captain endures his military training obligations; he's made of the same iron as his brother George. Purveyors may come and go but other than that, life is humdrum except for the Louisiana handover, which occupies the increasingly bored Clark. Finally his tolerance for isolation and those immature privates wears thin and he informs the insensitive, or perhaps unappreciative, Meriwether that he's due for a leave – which he takes.

By February 18, Lewis is at Wood River and Clark is gone. Meriwether jots a note to his friend. *"Nothing of any moment has occurred since you left us ..."* except the visit of a principal chief of the Kickapoo nation and a business visit by an agent of Elijah Galusha, the contractor for Army rations, *"with whom some little arrangments were necessary."* Lewis is given to understatement when it comes to business.

Those Rowdy Wild Guys
The little military contingent that camps out above St. Louis

probably is pegged as strangers, transients, or even rowdies. Under any of these guises, it would be difficult to start up a social life, especially if you are confined to camp. There are no down-the-road settlements, no blushing pretty things, only an indiscrete bootlegger. The local residents have their own established lives, and it probably would have taken a jolt of curiosity to bring them down to the rough soldiers' quarters. So what will relieve the winter boredom? Christmas of 1803 demonstrates the prevailing spunkiness which characterized the Corps. Clark writes: *"I was wakened by a Christmas discharge <of> found that Some of the party had got Drunk <2 fought> the men frolicked and hunted all day, Snow this morning, Ice run all day"* Drinkin', fightin', & frolickin'!

During that first winter of 1803–04, Clark is challenged to bring the little band of Army privates into a reliable, self-sufficient Corps. And, while the initial selection of men may have brought an above-average quality of soldier to camp, there was a general lack of quality of Army men in 1803. Bob Moore's considerable research on the subject indicates, "Officers and sergeants were frequently slapped or struck by enlisted men; men commonly talked back and reported for duty drunk; there were brawls, injuries, and murders. As punishment, men were whipped, branded, heads shaved, thrown into 'black holes' and chained to cannon balls without effect on their bad behavior. Lewis and Clark had a really good bunch. Even Collins seems like a pollyanna."[111]

Moreover, both Captains are chagrined by the poor hunting skills the privates display. Hunting has always been a manly pursuit, challenging and immensely physical. Clark encourages several men at a time to go out but emphasizes the command that *"No man shal absent himself from camp without ... knowlege and permission,"* simultaneously issuing the order that *"hunting excurtions ... will not extend their absence to a term by which they may avoid a tour of guard duty ..."* J2:175 He is helping them sharpen their talents and discipline as they provide fresh meat; it is the beginning of a regime of self-sufficiency.

From the privates' point of view, hunting is a welcome escape from camp, and the men enjoy the physical activity, the sport of it, and a certain gustatory satisfaction with bringing in a variety of game. On January 5, 1804, the lure of hearty meat is too much for the hunters. When they spot a pig, it is with nostrils already smelling sweet roasting pork, teeth ready to sink into moist, succulent mouthfuls. They skin it, and in some lapse of mental capacity, they leave most of it. Not content with pilfering, they resort to lying ... calling it bear meat. When the honorable Clark gets whiff of the operation, he takes immediate action: *"I send out Shields to enquire in the neighborhood whoes hog it was & inform me.*" [J2:152] It is a full two days later when a French family comes, does a little trading, and then complains that it was their hog that lodged in the cookfire. On January 9, Clark takes Collins, one of the two men, *"to the place he found a Hog Skined & Hung up, the Crows had devoured the meet ..."* and so it is a loss all 'round. In order to improve community relations and punish men for drunkenness and fighting, Clark has the miscreants fix up the house of a widow-woman who is doing laundry for the Corps.

Successful hunting and military fighting implies being a good shot, and few things on the frontier match being an able marksman with a good gun. Clark encourages his men to practice their shooting skills, and on New Year's Day, 1804, he sponsors a little impromptu contest. *"Several men Come from the Countery to See us & Shoot with the men ... I put up a Dollar to be Shot for, the two best Shots to win Gibson best the Countery people won the dollar ..."* By April 28, all the practice is paying off. Clark proudly writes, *"Several Country men Came to win my mens money, in doing So lost all they had, with them."* The Corps improves consistently – on May 6 Clark is probably gloating when he writes, *"Several of the Countery people In Camp Shooting with the party all git beet and Lose their money ..."*

Hospitality among the Elite

While the privates maintain one type of social life, the Captains (particularly Lewis) move in more elite circles. Two sorts of hospitality are extended to travelers. To people passing through, the offer of a meal is extended – restaurants do not exist. A fine example of this sort of courtesy is the dinner Lewis enjoyed at the Lorimier home in Cape Girardeau. Congeniality extends beyond the enclosures of one's house; presents are often sent home. Clark writes that a kindly Mr. Ducett *"made me a present of rivr Catts & Some Herbs."* [J2:237]

For those who intend to stay a while (as the Captains do for six months), lodging is provided by some host in town, as hotels do not exist. Both of the commanders stay with one of leading citizens of St. Louis, and find the Chouteaus' hospitality so gracious that they comfortably call this place "home."

Celebrating the Louisiana Purchase

On March 10, 1804, a one-time bang-up festivity engulfs St. Louis: the long-expected handover of the Upper Louisiana Territory. Without this real estate transfer, the Corps of Discovery would be operating on quicksand, spies in a foreign country. With the official declaration, they instantly become ambassadors of the Great White Father. On a fair but cloudy afternoon the temperature will rise to just 32°F and bundled dignitaries will gather at Government House to complete the official paperwork making America into a nation spanning three-quarters of a continent.

What do we know of the celebrations? Very little, directly. Lewis is not writing, nor is Clark, despite the fact that the signing is the tangible legitimization for the doughty little crew of American explorers to begin trekking across the great wilderness. It is of interest because, for once, both esteemed Captains appear to be together in St. Louis, on social and political business.

What is known of the day is directly attributable to Amos Stoddard. "The number of souls in my jurisdiction is about twelve thousand. The country is beautiful beyond description. The lands contain marrow and fatness. St. Louis contains about 200 houses, mostly large and built of stone, it is elevated and healthy, and the people are rich and hospitable."[112] There is no stinting in the entertainments for such a momentous occasion, and the citizens of St. Louis love parties. Stoddard is royally entertained by the upper echelon of society and Lt. Governor Carlos Delassos throws a dinner honoring the new governor. This is followed by a public dinner and a ball. Laces and ribbons bedeck ladies in their finest, the gentlemen stride about in elegant gear, tables all but disappearing under gleaming bowls and platters of food. The great hearths blaze and crackle, fiddles sing and there is dancing and gaming. Liquor and music ebbs and flows in a happy tide of good will.

The new commandant, not to be outdone socially, arranges an equally elegant public divertissement to be held at his house, again a dinner and ball. It must have been a fabulous event for, as the host wrote, "the expense amounted to $622.75 cents."[113] By comparison, note that John Colter, a Corps private, is paid $5 a month.[114] How is the former Army officer able to afford this? "I am in hopes that the Government will remunerate me for this expense."[115]

He hasn't had the experience of government harassment over bills that hounded George Rogers Clark. In the end, sympathetic, good-natured William Clark comes to Stoddard's rescue. However, in 1813, Clark writes his nephew, "Majr Amos Stoddard I am informed is dead. He owes me $200. cash which I lent him at St. Louis in the year 1804 to pay for a public dinner he was allowed for in his publick accounts by the Government. I wish you to inquire ... and if possible to procure it for me."[116]

Meriwether Lewis' signature is on the formal papers of the transfer; Clark helps out an Army compatriot, the new governor. The Captains are part of the festivities as the vast territory of Louisiana is adopted into the United States.

The Balls

Social calls and festive balls are almost obligatory among the convivial French. Clark himself wrote (in 1797), *"In the evening went to a ball given by Mr. Cl. Shoto where I saw all the fine girls and buckish Gentlemen."*[117] These grand affairs are alight with partying, fine foods, music, and dancing. Lit by candlelight, firelight, and perhaps grease lamps, chilled but welcome guests entering the house would be greeted with fiddle music, perhaps French jigs or if the American influence is felt, "Jeffersonian tunes" predating 1800.[118] There might be manly diversions such as shooting while dinner is being prepared, betting before the meal (or after), and arguing about horses, politics, or whatever makes a man mad! Best yet, all of these entertainments figure large as a regular part of the social life in St. Louis. No event is too small, nor any too large.

There are four balls during the 1804 season: Lewis attends one on February 14, and both Captains attend a Saturday bash on April 7, *"Set out at 7 oClock in a Canoo with Cap Lewis my servant york & one man at 1/2 past ten arrived in St Louis, Dressed & Dined with Capt Stoddard, & about 50 Gentlemen, a Ball Succeeded, which lasted untill 9 oClock on Sunday ..."* Their eager eyes and receptive noses would relish the scene and wafting aromas of tables filled to overflowing with the best foods available.

Foods for the Banquet Table

There are the gamey riches of the forest, fine free-ranging herds of cattle and swine. All of these meats would have appeared primarily as roasts, with their charcoal caramelized smells filling the room with lush abandon. Smoky marbled hams would be resting on platters. Some of the tougher cuts of meat might have been cooked into finely seasoned stews, appropriate for winter, although this would be distinctly "homey."

What summer crops would have been put aside to grace those tables? Apples, pears, plums, cherries, and peaches might have been dried or sugar-preserved, particularly the peaches from trees that "are generally so loaded with fruit as to break down."[119] Although Monticello-type rich, sweet desserts were not common, at a ball they probably appear.

George Heriot - courtesy: National Archives of Canada/C-000040

This George Heriot watercolor showing "A Dance in the Chateau St. Louis" actually takes place in Canada, but could as well be in St. Louis.

CLAFOUTI WITH CHERRIES[120]

¾ lb.   cherries, not pitted
3   large eggs
1   large egg yolk
⅔ C.   sugar
⅓ C.   flour
2 C.   milk
2-3 T.   unsalted butter, melted

Preheat oven to 350°F. Wash cherries and pat dry, then put aside. Combine eggs, egg yolk, and sugar. Blend until smooth. Add flour, mixing a couple of tablespoons at a time, making sure there are no lumps. Add milk, ⅔ cup at a time, whisking. When batter is smooth, stir in melted butter. Scatter cherries in the bottom of a well-greased 10" pie plate, 1½ inches deep. Pour the batter over the fruit, and bake for about an hour, or until the clafouti is puffy and slightly golden. Transfer to a wire rack. Serve warm, at room temperature, or chilled.

Courtesy: Pennsylvania Farm Museum at Landis Valley

This re-creation of a well appointed early 1800's kitchen hearth has a clock-jack spit, a spider pan, and a toasting rack.

A classic French dessert is named clafouti and can be made with fruit, in this case cherries.

There are *"esculent roots, and culinary vegetables."* Cucumbers, melons, and berries would have been finished by December when the Corps arrived, although pickles are a cupboard regular. Breads and baked goods would be made from wheat and corn, perhaps even corn pudding.

Cooking at Home[121]

For the wealthy, the summer heat of Missouri dictated a cookhouse removed from the house, just as it did in Virginia where Jefferson's slaves worked a separate kitchen. This outbuilding also meant no odors or grease would be carried throughout the house. Open fireplaces were equipped with "cranes" located at both sides of the hearth – these metal rods pivoted and could swing in or out allowing the temperature in the pots to be controlled by their placement over the fire and allowing the cook to stir the food without reaching over open flames. A stationary bar of iron bolted to the top of the fireplace would be used to hang kettles, or if attached to a "clock jack" could be turned by a wind-up mechanism (similar to the ones used in winding clocks) that would turn the rod, an early style of rotisserie. Safety measures included long rods with a hook on the end to remove handled pots or kettles from the cooking hearth, and long-handled spoons for stirring. Many frying pans, called "spiders" if they stood on legs, had long handles as well.

A well equipped kitchen would have had a mortar and pestle or a grinder (or both), a butter churn, an apple press, and a rotary apple peeler. There would be a spice mill and a sugar cutter to break off pieces of the hard, cone-shaped sweet. Bread was toasted in a fireplace rack made by the smithy. There would be a variety of wooden utensils ranging from buckets to spoons, and a rolling pin for making pastry. Fine foods could be turned out with these simple tools. The pride of a wealthy merchant or fur-trader's kitchen would be an "real" stove imported from New Orleans by the traders Clamorgan, Loisel and Co.[122] A fireplace was ordinary; a cookhouse out back was quite well-to-do; but a stove with metal cooking plates – extraordinary!

Local Alcoholic Beverages

Alcohols and hard liquors were manufactured locally, some distilled on the homeowner's property. Clarissa Dillon, writing about Eastern distilling, says, "The peaches are manufactured into brandy, and some of the farmers annually distill four hundred gallons of this spirit; an excellent substitute for foreign distilled spirits, the expense of which in a great measure prevents the use of them."[123] Windfall apples are also gathered to make brandy in the same manner as the peaches.

She continues, "Because both the peach and apple brandies were double distilled, they were <u>very</u> potent. As such, they might have been acceptable to the [Army] officers."[124]

The following brandy process from Pennsylvania is typical of the times and is likely the process used around St. Louis:

PEACH OR APPLE BRANDY[125]

"They make brandy from peaches here, after the following method. The fruit is cut asunder, and the stones are taken out. The pieces of fruit are then put into a vessel, where they are left for three weeks or a month, til they are quite putrid. They are then put into a distilling vessel, and the brandy is made and afterwards distilled over again. This brandy is not good for people who have a more refined taste, but it is only for the common kind of people, such as workmen and the like."

An early 1800's kitchen preparation table with spider pans, morter and pestle, mixing bowl, rising basket, rolling pins, and hot-pads.

Courtesy: Pennsylvania Farm Museum at Landis Valley

Fruits are not the only ingredients used in making home-distilled, higher-proof alcohol; traditional grains and corn found their way into the vats as well. Table wines were equally desirable.

Whiskey is also distilled from rye and Indian corn, which is most disposed of to the Indians ... [and] the country is filled with wild grape vines of a large size; some of them are seven inches in diameter, six feet above the ground, and they run to the tops of the tallest trees. They bear grapes of a tolerable flavor, especially when fully exposed to the sun; and it is said that, in 1769, the settlers in the Illinois country made a hundred hogsheads [100 hogsheads = 25 tons[126] or 6250 gallons] of good wine from them. The grape vines imported from France and the south of Germany, and cultivated at St. Louis, flourish extremely well.[127]

This early introduction (far before the recorded 1769 harvest) of European grapes into mid-western American soils proves the current obsession with micro-climates and resulting flavors to be a well established trend with a multi-century history on the North American continent.

Shopping in St. Louis
December, 1803 – May, 1804

*I have meal mad [made] & the flour Packed & repacked,
also Some porkie packed in barrels.*

— CLARK, APRIL 3, 1804

As WINTER 1803–04 IS ENDING, the great issue facing both Captains is provisioning. How much carbohydrate do they need to take for their trip? Are there other emergency rations to provide some insurance for surviving if it becomes impossible to live off the land? How much can the keelboat and pirogues carry? For that matter, are there enough boatmen? In mid-February the Corps is still short of boatmen and Lewis writes to Clark, begging him to ask around for more boatmen. When the Corps leaves Wood River on May 14, 1804, Clark has onboard all provisions and equipage, rowed by 22 men on the keelboat, 8 French in the large pirogue and 6 soldiers in the second pirogue.

Clark scribbles endless lists, calculates weights and volumes, and then recalculates again. Lewis forwards the shopping lists on to the commissary. The paper trail found in the *Journals* is dismal, and according to Old Military and Civil Records at the National Archives "Military records for this time period are often fragmentary because many of the original records were lost when Government buildings in Washington, D.C. were ransacked and burned by the British Army in 1814."[128]

Suppliers in St. Louis

Supply lines to St. Louis appear to be good. While going down the Ohio in the fall of 1803, Lewis stops Guy Bryan, who is coming back upstream, to ask about river conditions ahead. Bryan, of Philadelphia, specializes in supplying fur trappers in Kaskaskia and has made himself exceptionally well-to-do. [J2:70n1] More goods from another *"distinguished*

merchant" [J2:104n5] come into view on November 22, 1803. Lewis writes that they *"overtook two keels from Louisville bound to Kaskaskias loaded with dry goods and whiskey, belonging to Mr. Bullet of Louisville –"* [J2:101]

Throughout the winter, the *Journal* entries report of various merchants and their agents coming and going. In a December 17, 1803, letter to Clark from Cahokia, Lewis passes on information regarding the local supply line:

- ◆ William Morrison, a well-known merchant in Kaskaskia, partner and partial owner of a store in Cahokia, owns several plots of farmland in Cahokia; and Patrick Hennebury, farm manager for Morrison, is an appropriate person to ask regarding supplies. [L1:144-5]
- ◆ Elijah Galusha, and his partner, Dr. Catlett, contractor for army rations.
- ◆ Major Nathan Rumsey, officer in charge of area provisions. [L1:168]

The military camp at Wood River is a good customer but difficult to reach. There is a continual line of communication, with regular deliveries. Galusha's agent appears on January 15, having had a miserable delivery trip up to the Corps headquarters. *"at Sun Set Maj Rumsey the Comsy [commissary agent] arrived with Some provisions in a waggon of Mr. Todd ... a Cold night the Wag: in passing the Lowr Prarie which was Covrd. with Ice Suft [sufficiently] Stong to bear the teem but not the waggon which caused it to be dift.[difficult] to pass."*

This short advisory on ice conditions raises the question: What did they do with the goods in the wagon? Again, it appears to be the infamous unload-and-reload weight-lifting contest. The only difference between these energy expenditures now and those they endured coming down the Ohio is the battle to fend off freezing temperatures. Despite ice on the river, merchant activities continue, even on New Year's Day: *"a Perogue Passed Loaded with Salt & Dry goods."*

A Grocery List

A quick catalogue of goods from Kaskaskia is worth a look. Looking at the dates, these purchases cover a period from December 16, 1803 to March 31, 1804 – a total of 105 days: [L2:429]

1351	Comp[lete] Rat[ion]s from	
	16 Decr. 1803 to 31 Jany 1804	195.89
36	Rats. Whiskey	1.62
[100	lbs –] 88⁸⁄₉ [rats.] Flour	4.00
1800	Com. Rats. in Feby &-March	261.00
283	Rats. Whiskey	12.74
286	³⁄₄ lbs Flour–254⁸⁄₉ Rats.	11.47
6	quarts Salt	.69
155	lbs.–137⁷⁄₈ Rats. Flour	6.20
120	lbs.–96 Rats. Beef	4.32
219	Rats. Whiskey	9.85

*For sundry articles provision delivd. to him
at the Camp ... on 31st March 1804 including
Kegs & bags to contain them.* 1170.25
Transportation (2 entries) 27.50
　　　　[Total] $1703.53

This is very hefty grocery shopping, and already the Corps is substantially over budget. If Congress was having any trouble with the modest expenditures back in Philadelphia and Harpers Ferry, it is fortunate that the bold commanders will be long gone before wind of this purchase makes it East.

What can we learn from this? "Complete Rations" are defined by Lewis in the three day rotation as being pork, corn (in the form of meal, or lyed), and flour. Supplier Elijah Galusha is sending up 1351 rations, which for 30 men is about 45 days. Flour seems to be in demand for the quantity ordered up is an extra 344 rations, in addition to the complete rations. Salt is going for 11¢ a dry- quart, or 3¹⁄₂¢ per pound. Beef is an extra treat, above and beyond the pork. Finally there are 538 rations of whiskey, almost 17 gallons assuming the Army standard gill-a-day ration. This will hold 30 men for about 18 days – nowhere near the 105 days covered; there was obviously more whiskey bought elsewhere.

Not only is hunting keeping the troops fed, but there are also fortuitous finds. On March 25, Clark notes the river has risen 14 inches the previous night, and the warming weather is wakening nature's domain *"the men find numbers of Bee Trees, & take great quantities of honey."*

Preparing to Leave

While the Corps has relied on the local citizens for their everyday culinary necessities – butter, vegetables, etc. – it is now time for a shift in commodities and particularly in quantities. Clark, like the good quartermaster and traveler he is, senses it is time to begin the big preparations for the upcoming trip. Some of the corn supplies must have been delivered earlier, because on March 26 he begins to work the food supply, *"I had Corn parched to make parched meal, workmen all at work prepareing the Boat ..."* The next day, *"all hands parching Corn &c ..."* On April 2 – the eighth day that this job is still interminably grinding on: *"men makeing Parched meal."* It is with great relief that this duty terminates, and on April 3 the Captain starts packing the food in readiness for their ascent up the Missouri. *"I have meal mad & the flour Packed & repacked, also Some porkie packed in barrels ..."*

On April 1, *"Dr Catlates Boat arrived with provisions ..."* What seems incongruous is that a medical doctor is delivering groceries. But Dr. Hanson Catlett is in partnership with merchant/trader Elijah Galusha and is also surgeon's mate for Amos Stoddard's Army company at the St. Louis garrison in 1804 – so he is both working for the Army and supplying the Army. The question of a conflict of interest doesn't even arise. The three Captains (Lewis, Clark, and Stoddard) have been in close military contact, and certainly Galusha's people have performed their commissary function admirably. It is a cozy relationship. Obliquely what it points to is the lure of prosperity enticing a surgeon's mate to deal in supplies.

Packing the Supplies

So what is being packed up in St. Louis? On April 15, 1804, Clark writes, *"Mr. Wolpards Boat came up to day at 2 oClock under Sail, Left St Louis at 8 oClock a.m."* It is a six-hour transit upriver. This is apparently a charter designed to get the tons of pork, biscuit, and personal amenities such as soap and candles to the Corps. The Captains are busily noting contents of kegs and barrels to be loaded, and generally trying to put their pre-departure chaos into order. On Monday, April 16, Clark writes that he is packing away:

1	Keg of Hogs Lard
1	bag of Coffee 50 w
2	[bags] Sugar
1	[bag] Beens
7	bags of Biscuit
4	Barrels of Biscuit
2	Boxes of candles
44	Kegs of Pork packed w.3115
6	Half barrels of pork (ditto) w 590"

Clark orders the preparation and packing of 3,700 pounds of pork into 50 kegs and half-barrels.

The next day Clark is still working on his pork: *"packing Pork to day Completed packing fifty kegs of Pork ..."* Lewis now is fretting about what appears to be an issue of missing pork: [J2:199]

> *740 lbs Pork bone extracted*
> <u>*603 lbs of Bone*</u>
> *137 difference*

This issue never appears to be resolved. There are still discrepancies with Clark's account, for he has not mentioned some items that show up in another of Lewis' financial records: [J2:200]

4175	*Complete rations @14½ Cents*	*605.37½*
5555	*Ration of flour at 4½ cents*	*231.97½*
	[should be 249.97½]	
25	*Cask Corn @ 50 Cents*	*12.50*
12	*[ditto] Salt @ 3$*	*36.–*
100	*G. Whiskey @ 128 Cents*	*128.00*
10	*bus Corn fo I. [Indians?] –*	*50.00*
20	*G Whiskey [ditto] –*	*25.00*
4000	*rats. pork @ 4½ cents*	*18.00*
123	empty kegs [= Lewis' 4 entries]	90.00
	TOTAL [as corrected]	1376.85

On the April 19, a Thursday, the weather and packing are

still unsettled. Goods are delivered and Clark signs off on the receipt. And so there are lists and more lists, mixing itemizations such as the number of rations, gallons, casks, kegs, dollars, cents, pounds by weight and in British currency, bags, barrels, and just about any other measure imaginable. To help make sense of these orders and receipts, this jumble of accounting and finances, a scientist and financial expert has compiled a list of what quantities are taken aboard.[129] Just the gross weight is astonishing:

The Saint Louis Food Stockpile

- 6,000 pounds (3 tons) Corn, hulled, meal, and parchmeal
- 4,000 pounds (2 tons) Flour and Bisquit
- 3,700 pounds (1.75 tons) Pork
- 700 pounds Hogs Lard and "Grees"
- 100 pounds Dried Peas and "Beens"
- 750 pounds Salt
- 112 pounds Sugar
- 50 pounds Coffee
- 193 pounds Portable Soup
- 120 pounds Candles (Sept.1805: emergency rations)
- 120 gallons Whiskey

Freight weight: eight **TONS** of food. And this is not all the food that the Corps will need. In fact, it is only 10% of the total needed. Lewis actually writes to Clark saying that he doesn't think they can accommodate anymore goods being stored aboard the keelboat, which has a carrying capacity of between 10–20 tons including crew and gear:

◆ The starches themselves – corn, flour, peas, and beans – weigh in at about 10,000 pounds or 5 tons.

Gary R. Lucy - courtesy of the Gary R. Lucy Gallery, Inc.

Gary Lucy's painting *Lewis and Clark: The Final Briefing at St. Charles, May 21, 1804* depicts the Missouri River's banks with the Captains checking over the eight tons of provisions and other supplies.

- Meats and oils are 4400 pounds (almost 2½ tons). The ratio of carbohydrate to protein is about a 2½:1, a British-style pattern.
- Surprisingly they take sugar. There is no mention of its use in the *Journals*. Do they use it to make sweet corn-meal as a dessert? To add juice and flavor to berries? To sweeten coffee?
- Coffee: A topic covered in *Beverages*, page 249.
- Whiskey: A gallon will serve 32 men their "gill a day" ration. From St. Charles upriver, there are 45 men; and from Fort Mandan westward, there are 31 men. The 120 gallon whiskey supply, at Army rates, will last only the first 90 days, not even to the Mandans – clearly, there will have to be rationing.

Still More Shopping

But there is still more shopping to do, for Lewis apparently has arranged that he and Clark will go downriver with Pierre Chouteau. The Captains' incoming visitors have more interesting ways of announcing their arrival than ringing a doorbell: *"at three oClock a Cannon was herd up the Missouris. Soon after Mr. Choteau arrived with 22 Indians, we Saluted them and after Staying one [h]Our, Cap Lewis & myself Set out with them to St Louis, where we arrived before night."* The next three days, April 22–24 are devoted to shopping in town. This probably is time spent with the commissary supply people, for on the 26, *"Mr. Hay arrived."*

The following day, April 27, Clark is *"prepareing to pack up Indians goods."* And it appears that Clark is not alone in his supervisory task. *"Mr. Hay packing up all hands at work prepareing."* [J2:206] It is difficult work, because three days later (April 29, 1804) *"Mr. Hay Still packing up goods ... Wolpards Boat arrive from St. Charles."* Although the *Journals* give no explicit insight into what Woolford is doing, he apparently goes to St. Charles, returns, stays around, and then departs in the company of Mr. Hay. It's possible that he is a subcontractor hired on to help bring the vast mountain of supplies. This job is labor intensive and certainly calls for the troops to be drafted like a chain-gang, passing the goods hand-to-hand onboard. The next day's entry is optimistic: *"mr. Hay nearly finish packing up goods ..."* This is grunt work, but the United States Army is behind it; Clark is not doing it alone. Finally, on May 2 – *"Mr. Hay, Wolpard, & leave Camp to St Louis at 12 oClock."* If the usual punctuation "&c" is meant here, it implies that there are more than the two men mentioned, possibly more manpower involved.

Preparing to Depart

With the cool and pale sunlight of spring breaking up the great sheets of ice, melting the solidly locked crystals from their shimmering blue-white hardness until they relinquish and free the river, the season changes into the promise of spring. Winter doldrums are shed. During that harsh winter season, during that time when his young bucks subconsciously are preparing for a trip that might never bring them home, Clark in his wisdom knows that all is not work and heeds the ancient poetic rhyme which declares,

> Our minds need relaxation, and give way
> Unless we mix with work a little play. [130]

During the winter, men played games, sung, and had shooting contests. Women came visiting.

So, as the land warms, the gardens begin growing. The men are grateful that Arctic temperatures and blizzards are behind them and Clark, mindful of the change of seasons, sees anew a world that was frozen over when he arrived.

> *The Countrey about the Mouth of Missouri is pleasent rich and partially Settled ... in the point of the Bottom is extensive and emencly rich for 15 or 20 miles up each river, and about 2/3 of which is open leavel plains in which the inhabtents of St. Charles & potage de Scioux had ther crops of corn & wheat.* [J2:218]

Again, on May 17, after the expedition, without Lewis, has entered the Missouri River and moved up to St. Charles: *"receved Several Speces of Vegatables from the inhabitents to day."* This is good news for President Jefferson, agriculturalist. Lewis then analyzes the Frenchmen's view of tilling the soil:

> *a small garden of vegetables is the usual extent of their cultivation, and this is commonly imposed on the old men and boys; the men in the vigor of life consider the cultivation of the earth a degrading occupation ...* [J2:241]

And so, the Corps is almost ready to leave for their two-year journey. But in those last days of Spring, 1804, the Captains have been very, very busy.

On the Way – Buying Continues

Even after the Corps has left Wood River and moves up to St. Charles, the merchants still visit, either on business or in friendship. Clark says that on May 18, a Mr. Lyon delivered 136 pounds of tobacco from the Chouteau firm. Clark sends Drouillard along with a message for Lewis, who still has not joined the Corps. Not only is tobacco arriving, but so is liquor, although not earmarked for the Corps and apparently headed upriver. *"Two Keel Boats arrive from Kentucky to day loaded with whiskey Hats &c ..."* The merchants are heading

Gary Lucy's painting *Lewis and Clark: The Departure from the Wood River Encampment, May 14, 1804* depicts the Corps as it sets out for St. Charles to final loading of supplies.

into their busy season. Clark is handing out yet more supplies, *"tin Cups & 3 Knives to the French hands ..."*

Trading with merchants continues as far as the Mandans. Clark reports on November 22, 1804, *"... Corn in ears which Mr. Jessomme, let us have did not get more than 80 bushels ..."* J3:239

On the Way Home: 1806

Lest we think the merchants plying the fur trade routes out of St. Louis are forgotten as the Corps makes its way homeward in 1806, the following correspondence shows how much the Expedition values luxuries. William Clark to Sgt. Nathaniel Pryor:

Camp on the River Rochejhone
115 miles
below the Rocky Mountains
July 25th [23rd] 1806
Sir:
You will with George Shannon, George Gibson & Richard Windser take the horses which we have brought with us to the Mandans Village on the Missouri. When

you arrive at the Mandans, you will enquire of Mr. Jussomme and any british Traders who may be in neighbourhood of this place for Mr. Hugh Heney ... As maney of the remaining horses as may be necessary you will barter with the traders for such articles as we may stand in need of such as <u>Flints</u> three or 4 Doz. <u>Knives</u> ... <u>Pepper, Sugar & Coffee</u> or <u>Tea</u> ... 2 small Kegs of Sperits ... L1:313-4

Of note is Clark's willingness to communicate with British traders, a nationality not on the Americans' favorite list, but who are the most likely people to find in this region. Hugh Heney, an American with the North West Company, probably has everything Clark wants. And every item required is related to food. Flints for guns and fire-making, knives, seasonings, beverages, and – after a year of abstinence – liquor.

But the plan does not work – their horses are stolen and the river is the only way to return. Nonetheless, the dream is there. The comforts of home-cooking preceded by a drink or two haven't been forgotten. All that is left is to arrive back home in St. Louis, where "civilization" ends ... and begins.

This painting by L. Edward Fisher depicts the keelboat and two pirogues proceeding up the Missouri.

L. Edward Fisher - commissioned by and used courtesy of The Missouri Bankers Association

Up the Missouri to the Mandans

May – October, 1804

... a large fire was made on which a Dog was Cooked,
& in the center about 400 wt of Buffalow meat which they gave us...

— CLARK, SEPTEMBER 26, 1804

As the Corps leaves St. Louis behind, the world as they know it begins to fall away. While not totally isolated from their own culture, the men begin to encounter new and interesting situations as they move deeper into native territory. It is, for all intents and purposes, a shakedown cruise. They have lessons to learn, adaptations to make. While the confrontation with the Teton Sioux will be the most dramatic episode involving the Corps during this segment of the trip, several incidents will illustrate other dangers which could have had dramatic repercussions for the Expedition, as well. But in the first three months there are several causes for celebration.

July 4, 1804 – Heading Up the Missouri

On Fourth of July, 1804, about 960 miles away from St. Louis (near today's Atchison, Kansas), the day dawns with a clear, blue sky and in every direction fields of *"Leek Green Grass"* are broken by stands of trees shading running springs of fine water. *"We fired a swivel at sunrise in honour of the day."* (Gass) The day *"proved very warm,"* writes Whitehouse. *"we left off rowing and went to Towing the boat, but the sand was so hot, that it scalded <out> our feet, some of the Men left the tow rope, and had to put on their Mockasins to keep their feet from being burnt."* Joseph Field is bitten by a snake, *"but not dangerously,"* concludes Gass. Sergeant Ordway pens, *"we passed a creek on the South Side about 15 yards wide. comes out of the large prarie, and as it has no name & as it is the 4th of July, Capts. Name it Independence Creek."* Clark notes that, *"Groops of Schrubs covered with the most delicious froot is to be seen in every direction ... we Din[e] (on corn)"* and *"we Closed the [day] by a Discharge from our bow piece, an extra Gill of whiskey."*

Clark's Birthday – August 1, 1804

William Clark was born on August 1, 1770, in Caroline County, Virginia. Although the Corps doesn't recognize Clark's birthday, William doesn't forget his most important day and treats himself to a gourmet special. *"This being my birth day I order'd a Saddle of fat Vennison, an Elk fleece [strip of fat] & a Bevertail to be cooked."*[J2:433] He also orders dessert of local fruits. Clearly he is among the believers that "God helps those who help themselves," and he isn't waiting for some cook to remember the Captain's birthday – he orders right up.

CLARK'S BIRTHDAY COMPOTE

"a Desert of Cheries, Plumbs, Raspberries Currents and grapes of a Supr. quallity"

Lewis' Birthday – August 18, 1804

Meriwether Lewis was born on August 18, 1774, in Albemarle County, Virginia. His thirtieth birthday in 1804 is an unsettling day to say the least. Reed, a deserter who has stolen a public rifle and ammunition, is court-martialed, dismissed from the permanent party, and sentenced to run the gauntlet four times in lieu of 500 lashes. By the end of the day, only a party could enliven their spirits. Clark apparently organizes a little celebration for Lewis on this birthday. They *"had a Dance which lasted untile 11 oClock, the Close of Cap Lewis Birthday. a fine evening"* The men were served, *"an extra Gill of Whiskey."*

Oh, my innards!

On August 23, 1804, Captain Lewis, the scientist, is doing a bit of chemistry/geology, trying to determine what minerals are present on some nearby cliffs. It is more than a matter of pure curiosity: the men under his command are sick and ailing. His co-Captain is of two minds regarding the mysterious cause. It is either *"cobalt,"* J3:9 known by its beautiful blue color, or *"arsenic."* J2:500 In an interview several years after their return, Clark tells Nicholas Biddle (the *Journals'* first editor) that Lewis,

> was considerably injured by the fumes and taste of the cobalt, and took some strong medicine to relieve him from its effects. The appearance of these mineral substances enable us account for disorders of the stomach, with which the party had been affected since they left the river Sioux. We had been in the habit of dipping up the water of the river inadvertently and making use of it, till, on examination, the sickness was thought to proceed from a scum covering the surface of the water ... [131]

This poisonous scum was probably dust blowing or washing down from the bluffs. As a consequence, the men are instructed to agitate the surface of the water and thrust their cups deep, and after following this precaution, eventually their stomachs calmed and their skin eruptions and boils went away.

Cobalt (Co) is a rare heavy metal, used today in making a variety of things from super-alloys in aircraft engines to magnetic recording media; it's not something to be swallowed. It can produce a variety of symptoms from "staggers" in sheep grazing off cobalt-laden plants, to a dramatic fall in white-blood-cell count when related to radiation poisoning (Co_{60}), and may even produce vaso-constriction of the right coronary artery. However, none of these appalling conditions sounds like an upset stomach.

Arsenic, on the other hand, is an infamous toxin causing human death. Besides its ill-famed uses, it has been used in ceramics and paints, and its toxic properties lead to its use as an ingredient in pesticides. Symptomatically it is best known for "severe gastric distress," known to Victorian doctors as "gastric fever." [132] A heavy dose of arsenic can produce death in several hours.

Arsenic sounds like the most likely culprit, but cobalt

might have been involved, as well. Whatever the case, the Captains haven't learned their lesson yet about putting foreign substances in the mouth. On September 9, Lewis reports that Clark is walking on shore and discovers *"a bittuminus matter resembling molasses in consistance, colour and taste – "* and it issues from *"a blue earth."* Now, having been sick from what was originally assumed to be cobalt (blue), it doesn't seem too reasonable to be putting a sticky, coal-like substance originating from a blue earth into your mouth. Yet Clark does – the goo tastes like molasses and no one gets sick. Being a gourmet geologist is dicey.

But being sick doesn't come just from rare elements that shouldn't be part of the diet anyway. Stomachs are prone to rebel violently if their normal routine suffers disruption, and certainly drinking water is a major factor. *"Several of the men complaining of Great thirst –"* And since just-plain-water is the antidote to dehydration, that commodity is precious.

Several days before, the geological color of the area had been *blue*, and the mineral springs that break out from this *"Bluff of Blue earth"* have a peculiar taste, *"like salts."* J3:50,51n9 The salty aspect of this area prevails. On September 10, Clark is writing about *"a large Salt Spring of remarkable Salt water much frequented by Buffalow, Some Smaller Springs on the Side of the hill above less Salt, the water excesiv Salt ..."* Lewis, too, remarks on a *"bold salt spring of strong water ..."* By October 19 they still are having trouble with the midwest waters. *"all the Streems falling from the hills or high lands So brackish that the water Can't be Drank without effecting the person making use of it as Globesalts ..."* In other words, the gastric distress continues straight through to the intestines, causing diarrhea in a day when toilet paper hasn't been invented. The finicky nature of the stomach when traveling is well known. Here are the first instances of major upsets which foreshadow the most serious digestive problems coming, almost a year later, out of the Rocky Mountains.

The Teton Sioux

The earliest overtures between the Corps and the Indians feature food and reciprocity with the Teton Sioux. On September 25, *"we gave them Some of our Provsions to eat, they gave us great quantites of meet."* J3:112 Edibles usually indicate a positive outlook, a willingness to see how things will go. Are they friendly? The show is off to a felicitous start. Then it falters.

The Sioux's taste runs to "White man's milk," or "rum milk of great father" which means alcoholic spirits. The Americans and French are accustomed to this beverage and have been since times immemorial. But the natives' systems

When the whiskey bottle is empty, the Sioux chiefs want more.

are unaccustomed to this new substance, and it is tantalizing, quick-acting, and explosive. An argument could have been made not to trade alcohol with the locals (as the Spanish forbade a trade in guns), but such is not the case. Clark records giving *"1/2 a wine glass of whiskey which they appeared to be exceedingly fond of ..."* [J3:111] Although wine glasses were not the stemware we see today, half a glass might be three ounces – a stiff shot. Elsewhere he revises the quantity down to q quarter glass. But no mention is made of leisurely sipping during the afternoon while smoking a peace pipe – it's probably "down the hatch." With this in mind, it is no shock when he records, *"they took up an empty bottle, Smelted it, and made maney Simple jestures and Soon began to be troublesom ..."* The Captain records they even sucked the empty bottle. It shouldn't require a visionary to predict what might happen: there's a little trouble coming. Clark assumes one of the chiefs is feigning drunkenness and has rascally intentions. From there, everything is downhill, much like a bar brawl with both sides ready to fight. With disaster looming, the Captains move the keelboat upriver and post *"a guard on Shore to protect the Cooks,"* more to guard the keelboat (which has, among other things, a huge supply of provisions, including whiskey, on board).

Despite what looks like a dire situation, the next day food is still being offered by the Sioux: *"a large fire was made on which a Dog was Cooked, & in the center about 400 wt of*

Buffalow meat which they gave us ..." [J3:116] Another *Journal* entry for the day praises the meat as *"excellent Buffalo Beif."* In other words, it is not a shoddy present of tough, gristly meat.

Not only is there the meat gift, but that same day the Captains are invited to smoke the peace pipe. During this ceremony the principal chief *"took in one hand Some of the most Delicate parts of the Dog which was prepared for the feist & made a Sacrifise to the flag – & after pointing it to the heavins the 4 quarter of the Globe & the earth ... we were requested to take the meal ..."* This is a religious ceremony, much like asking grace before the banquet guests start eating. That the dog meat is offered toward the flag, the symbol of the United States, is equally significant. The Sioux chief is an excellent diplomat, and his compatriots are all involved in the event, from the cooks to his guests. It would be highly unlikely (and horrid diplomatic manners) for anything agressive to happen at this juncture.

Editor Biddle inserts Clark's statement: "[they] *then put before us the dog which they had been cooking, & Pemitigon* [pemmican] *& ground potatoe in Several platters."* He continues that the Sioux prefer raw dog as a culinary dish, and it is served at festivals. If this is the case, the dog they are now being served has likely been cooked as a goodwill gesture to white sensibilities. The Captain is not wild about dog himself, but remarks that the pemmican and potato are good. Later, he revises his opinion of the ground potato, *"little inferior,"* and clarifies that its preparation gives it the

Arrival of the Oto's for peaceful meeting and feast.

appearance of hominy. He is quite taken with a bighorn sheep (serving) spoon, which he says will hold two quarts.

The party proceeds on, Sioux lining the banks of the river and the Corps giving the two principal chiefs a blanket each, as well as a gift of a peck [2 dry gallons] of corn for each man from their provisions. The overall good will and reciprocity continue, despite more incidents of bullying and obstruction. As the trip upriver continues, another band of the Sioux appear and after being told what had transpired, *"they appeard ansioes* [anxious] *for us to eat with them"* J3:128 to show they are friendly.

Prairie Indian horn-bowl ladle.

Food appears to hold the key here. There's a lot of pushing and shoving going on, but everyone is still eating together and doing it politely. The ceremonial dinner is far more civilized than some medieval banquets at which swordplay erupts and blood spills into the soup. Seen in this light, perhaps things were not so bad as has been previously thought.

Adventures of the Youngest – LOST!

As the party moves upriver again, there are no villages as reference points, just endless geography waiting for explorers and cartographers. Without mapping aids travel was confusing and dangerous, as the *Journals* detail. Private George Shannon is the youngest of the party at nineteen years of age. On the frontier, experience is safety – knowing how geography provides clues to avoid being lost; knowing how to build snares to trap animals; knowing which plants can be eaten, which ones are medicine, and which are nerve toxins, poisonous. By virtue of his youth and therefore less experienced, Shannon is definitely at a disadvantage and the Captains' logs will consistently note looking after him in a brotherly fashion.

On August 26, 1804, Shannon goes out with Drouillard to round up some lost horses, probably after breakfast that morning. It is 10:00 AM, the two hunters have finished jerking the meat, and the elk skin has been fashioned into new tow ropes. Somehow, that night, Shannon goes missing and Drouillard returns to the flotilla, saying he can find neither man nor horses. Clark responds by sending two good hunters, Shields and Joseph Field, to track him.

Two days later the hunters return, reporting that Shannon has the horses, but he's up ahead and they can't catch him. *"This man not being a first rate Hunter, we deturmined to*

Send one man in pursute of him with Some Provisions." J3:20 Now, this is a kindly thing to do, even if it does highlight at least one of Shannon's shortcomings – not staying put. John Colter, later to become a famous mountain man, is sent out to find him.

Then, the problem disappears from the *Journals* for a few days. The Captains are busy attending to Indian affairs, their own progress, provisioning, etc. Imagine being in Shannon's boots – lost in Indian country with not a lot of ammunition. Will they give up on him and leave him to die alone? Are the Indians out here "bad" Indians who will scalp him for the fun of it? One of the lost horses gives out as does the small supply of bullets, which would have provided meat. Finally, buffalo come *"within 30 yards of his camp ..."* J3:65 These tremendous animals dwarf a human in size and scale. Just being up close to one of these immense creatures inspires fear: Will it charge? Gore me? Toss me in the air, or just trample me?

Finally, on September 11, seventeen days after going lost, an emaciated and half-dead young private is brought in. In the mistaken belief that the keelboat and pirogues had passed him, Shannon charged on ahead and *"pushed on as long as he Could."* The commander wryly observes, *"he Shot away what fiew Bullets he had with him, and in a plentifull Country like to have Starvd. he was [12] days without provision, Subsisting on Grapes ..."* J3:65 Then Clark gives Shannon a pat on the back for showing several positive bits of

R. L. Rickards - courtesy: Rickards Western Art

Shannon returns after being lost and alone for 17 days.

ingenuity: (1) he saved *"one horse for the last resorse,"* (2) *"when he became weak and fiable deturmined to lay by and waite for a tradeing boat, which is expected"* and finally, (3) there was the *"one Rabit, which he Killed by shooting a piece of hard Stick in place of a ball [bullet] ..."*

This story is interesting as a backdrop for what is to come. Hunters do become lost, and not infrequently. Always the Corps marches on, doing their duty. It also emphasizes the need for experience to enhance survival.

The Summer Menu

The food supply for the Corps is boundless, and life along the Missouri River valley is abundant. From the river the men catch fish, catfish in abundance, and fat beavers from the small tributaries. Birds are flying overhead; prairie larks and even the great pelican end up in the soup pot or over the flames. Turkeys strut. In the trees, fox squirrels bound, and badger and porcupine waddle through stream-freshened glades. Through the open grassy country the great herds of hoofed mammals thunder across the prairies: dainty prong-horns, three types of deer, the huge elk, and the immense buffalo – all running with the freedom born of minimal hunting and no fences. Chasing behind them is the predatory coyote. These animals form the backbone of the Corps diet. What they do not eat freshly cooked turns into "jerk" or jerky, and this dried meat can be pounded to a dust, then mixed with fat and berries to form pemmican.[a]

The balance of the food choices come from carbohydrates such as breadroot (prairie turnip), corn, groundnut, and hog peanut. These four carbohydrates are native choices, served to the visiting whites. Delicious, flavorful fruits are a joy for everyone, even the questionable buffaloberry, which metamorphoses into a *"Delightfull Tart."* [J3:136]

Buffaloberry Tarts

Buffaloberry tarts are certainly not a native specialty and sound far more French or American. To construct the pie is not difficult, although a person must have access to the berries. That is where the first and most difficult problem arises: picking them. It is a vicious, wickedly thorned bush that defies standard picking.[b] A second variety, a more northerly bush, doesn't have the thorns but grows a far more sour berry.

Constructing the tart requires two steps: the shell and the filling. Here follows a recipe that the Corps' mess cooks could have made with provisions at hand:[c]

THE SHELL: SHORT PASTRY

2½ C.	flour
½ tsp.	salt
1 C.	lard
4 T.	cold (river) water

Blend flour and salt. Chill lard (in river). Add to flour by cutting in with two. Keep cutting and slowly add cold water. Roll out to ¼" thick. Note: it's more crumbly texture than flaky. Shape for a 9" tart.

BUFFALOBERRY FILLING

6 C.	buffaloberries
1 C.	sugar
¼ tsp.	flour

Mix berries, sugar, and flour; and fill pie shell. Cover with a pastry top if you have enough dough. Bake tart at 375°F for 1 hour.

So impressed is Clark with the fruit compote growing on bushes before his very eyes that he effuses, *"here [near the Vermillion River] we got Great quantities of the best largest grapes I ever tasted, Some Blue Currents still on the bushes, and two kind of Plumbs, one the Common wild Plumb the other a large Yellow Plumb ... double the Size of the Common and Deliscously flavoured."* [J3:8]

---

[a] See a full discussion of "Pemmican" in *Food Preservation in 1800,* page 12.
[b] See also "Buffaloberry" in *Plant Foods,* page 241, for discussion on a way to pick the berries.

[c] The shell recipe generally follows a traditional short-pastry recipe such as listed in *The Old West Baking Book,* and the filling is from the author's experience. Modern adaptation of the shell would substitute ½ cup butter and ½ cup solid shortening for the lard, and ice water for "river water."

The winters are particularly frigid in Mandan territory. This Carl Bodmer painting depicts the extremes faced by the corps in the 1804–05 winter.

Karl Bodmer, collection of Mr. & Mrs. Paul Mellon

Winter with the Mandans

Fort Mandan: October, 1804 – April, 1805

"If we eat, you Shall eat; if we Starve, you must Starve also."

— CHIEF SHEHEKE (BIG WHITE)

THE GREAT PUSH TO REACH THE MANDANS before the winter of 1804–05 is fueled by the need to reach the last outpost truly known by the traders, as mapped, outlined, and re-told so many times in St. Louis. On October 27, 1804, the Corps reaches the five winter villages of the Mandans and Hidatsas. Snow flurries, very cold winds, and the specter of an arctic winter are hard on their heels. Hoping to end the season's travel as far upriver as possible, the Expedition pushes on and overshoots the areas that have the greatest potential for firewood and game hunting. Just as one criterion for Camp River Dubois was the availability of food, so it is here: *"... all the white men here informed us that wood was Sceres, as well as game above, we Deturmined to drop down a fiew miles near wood and game ..."* J3:215

It is not yet the end of what the Captains might consider the civilized world. Living in the area is a small cadre of white men – a British trader, Charles Mackenzie of the North West Company; Hugh Heney, an independent; and the Frenchmen Laroque, Jusseaume, and Charbonneau. Their advice is valued, the decision made. After his exploratory venture Clark returns to their temporary camp, which is vibrantly full of natives and his men – to whom he gives the evening dram of liquor. *"they Danced as is verry Comn. in the evening which pleased the Savages much."* J3:216 Things are going well.

A full week is devoted to Indian diplomacy before the Captains decide on the exact location for building their winter fort. Consideration is given to the traditional and unwelcome aggressions of the Sioux and Arikara, which continue to have a huge impact on the Mandan villages, especially regarding safe storage of the years' harvest. Starving the enemy

is a universal, time-honored tradition. In the cycle of raiding and retaliation, no one is exempt.

As far as the Commanders are concerned, there is psychological insurance with this tribe. From James Mackay – a trader and veritable font of reliable information they met in St. Louis – they understand these people "as well as all other nations that inhabit to their West, near the Rocky Mountains, are in general people as good as they are mild who lay great value on the friendship of the Whites."[133] Some of these venerable native cultures have been in the area for more than seven hundred years, and the sedentary Mandans have built themselves into a position of trade prominence through astute bargaining, much like other major crossroad cultures. Logically this hub of a huge trading network may have extra food they can barter for, or buy. It is also the farthest point they can reach before launching into the unknown wilderness the next spring. As with the winter layover near St. Louis, the Captains will spend the time getting the lay of the land ahead of them and keeping the troops provisioned.

Mandan Matriarchy

In contrast to the patriarchal societies of the Americans and French, matriarchy is common among the Mandans. The women run the agrarian trading economy, they build and own their large domed homes, and female relatives all look after one another's households, fields, and welfare. The men they marry will move into their homes, father their children, hunt for the clan, and look after the religious welfare of the village. Care should be taken in reading the *Journals* at this point, for the men writing them are looking at a very different culture through patriarchal eyes.

The Mandans have a strong matriarchial society.

It is uncommon for a woman to live in a man's house, an exception that is accorded to chiefs and to white traders, as with Toussant Charbonneau – the translator – and his wife Sacagawea. She is a teenage Shoshone from the west who was stolen as a girl by a Hidatsa raiding party into those Montana lands. Raised a Hidatsa, she has learned many of her mothering, survival, and plant-gathering skills from them, all of which will prove immensely useful to the Corps as they travel westward.

Wooing the Mandans

The initial contact begins with a rocky start. Both food and diplomacy turn cold – Clark is sick and *"... my indisposition prevented my eating which displeased them, untill a full explination took place, I returned to the boat and Sent 2 Carrots of Tobacco for them to Smoke, and proceeded on ..."* J3:204 Since food-gifts and buffalo-related activities are high on the Mandans' interaction scale, not eating violates one of their cultural rules. The Captains, for their part, hand out gifts and Chief's peace medals showing the native handclasp on one side and Jefferson, the Great White Father, on the other. The lesser chief's medals visually display Jefferson's

agrarian ideals: domesticated cattle and sheep, a woman peaceably weaving, a man sowing wheat.

Gift exchanges are mandatory. The Grand Chief of the Mandans, Black Cat, invites the Captains to his lodge for a speech and negotiations, informing them in advance of a personal goodwill gesture – bags of corn. Happily, Jefferson's message of peace is well received, particularly Lewis' promise, which Black Cat summarizes as meaning, *"they now Could hunt without fear & their women could work in the fields without looking every moment for the ememey ..."* As a goodwill token the Chief also gives back two beaver traps taken from some French trappers and still useful, as well as twelve bushels of corn, *"put before me by the womin of the Village ..."* J3:218 The Captains are no doubt pleased to be adding more corn to their provisions.

This "third-grade" medal, minted during Washington's second term and depicting the importance of farming in America, was carried by Lewis and Clark and given to lesser chiefs.

And no wonder the women are grateful to talk peace. The Mandans are traders, not warriors. They farm and their lives are, by many standards, prosperous and socially gratifying. But agriculture as a lifestyle makes a stationary target for hostile neighbors creating chaos, riding through fields, pillaging as they go. To the west, their immediate Hidatsa neighbors are farmers but maintain warrior raiding parties; and these two tribes bicker. The Arikara to the south are suspect, and the warlike Teton Sioux still farther south are highly dreaded and feared. Buffalo Bird Woman, a Hidatsa and one of our earliest native voices from this region, recalls, "The Sioux sometimes comes up against us in winter and raids our cached corn. One winter ... they came up and burned our lodges and stole all that was in our cached pits."[134] For now, the low-key group of men heading upriver look nonthreatening, are carrying European-style trade goods, and are therefore welcome. Since the usual company traders won't be coming through until spring, this is an extra opportunity that looks advantageous for all concerned.

The Allure of Trade

"White men's" goods fascinate the Indians. Trade goods coming up the Missouri are alluring, and the Captains are becoming quite accomplished at bringing out their best samples and giving them away. Lewis brings with him axes and

Howard Terping, 1989, from Greenwich Workshop, Inc., Trumbull, Connecticut tomahawks, and chopping firewood suddenly becomes easier. He loads up 2800 fish hooks, some brass kettles, and eleven dozen red-handled knives beloved by the men and currently available only through the British competitors. False tales of great give-aways precede the Corps and the would-be recipients in the village are curious and anxious to be included. Word travels out to the grassy prairies and the hunters return early. Maybe there will be guns.

Kitchen Goods Here!

Consider the simple matter of kitchen tools. A successful Mandan woman who is a corn trader with corn to spare might be pleased with a new metal cookpot because she does the cooking as well. The native kitchen is rather uncomplicated, as seen in this description dating from later in the 1800s: "They use large earthen pots of their own manufacture of a black clay which is plentiful near their villages. They make them of different sizes, from five gallons to one quart. In these vessels nothing of a greasy nature is cooked, every family being provided with a brass or copper kettle for the purpose of cooking flesh ... they assured us that any kind of flesh cooked in those earthen pots would cause them to split."[135]

Earlier, many families may not have had a brass or copper cookpot, so they are coveted tools.

Getting Settled

There is a final positive thread that will bind these two groups of people together for the five long months of winter. The Mandan nation believes that the whites are good and strong medicine; their presence is welcome. When there is no game and much hunger, white medicine will be incorporated in the religious Buffalo Medicine ceremony. But that is later in the winter.

Before building a fort can begin, a full week is devoted to crafting out a peaceful coexistence. Finally, on November 3, the men begin building Fort Mandan. It is fairly spacious and has more than just fireplaces for heating and cooking, for on November 19, *"our Perogue of Hunters arrive with 32 Deer, 12 Elk & a Buffalow, all of this meat we had hung up in a Smoke house, a timeley supply –"* Their smokehouse is essential for preserving meat.

Dining with the Chiefs

Surprisingly, there is little mention of foods that are served at the chiefs' lodges (the emphasis being placed on diplomatic smoking of the peace pipe), but this may be due to the very simplicity of the Mandan meal. However, from notes written by George Catlin, a touring artist who visited the Mandan

Gary P. Miller, courtesy of Gary's Gallery, Bismarck, North Dakota

Fort Mandan was constructed just inland on the east bank of the Missouri near today's Bismark. The keelboat and pirogues were pulled partially onshore and secured for the winter freeze.

about thirty years after Lewis and Clark, we know what the lodges looked like and how the diners comported themselves.

The floors of these dwellings ... so hardened by use, and swept so clean ... have almost a polish, and would scarcely soil the white linen. Under a sky light, is a fire-place ... [and] over the fire-place, and suspended from the apex of diverging props or poles, is the pot or kettle, filled with buffalo meat. Around it are the family, reclining in all the most picturesque attitudes and groups, resting on their buffalo robes and beautiful rushes of mats.[136]

Karl Bodmer, from the Beinke collection of Yale University

Mandan earth-house interior.

It almost sounds like a cold-weather Rome. As an artist who knows his colors, Catlin's verbal descriptions paint these people – surprisingly – as very lightly toned, many having hazel, gray, or blue eyes. But then, many Mandan women have married French fur traders over the years.

Native men value their appearance. Bear grease appears in the *Journals*; not only is it a food, it is also a cosmetic. Mandan men use it for a body and hair oil, making them shine and glow, with the marvelous side benefit of repelling mosquitoes. Males augment their good looks with a hot sauna, a quick slap of bear grease for pomade on their hair, dress, and then they are ready for a ceremonial dinner.[137] As a group they are gregarious to the extreme, good-natured, and indeed, mild. Perhaps the brawling, fighting, un-regimented young privates will learn thing or two from them.[138]

Well-dressed Mandan

Karl Bodmer, from the Beinke collection of Yale University

A Bitter Winter

The winter of 1804–05 is cruel almost beyond comprehension, the frigid weather forcing huddled bodies to withstand bitter, biting temperatures from minus 30°F down to minus 70°F [-39°C to -64°C]. These are thermometer readings and don't account for wind chill. Everyone is prepared, food is set aside. But such harsh conditions play havoc with the body, demanding more and more fuel just to stay alive, let alone support the exertions that accompany hunting. The animals, especially the game that provides much-needed protein and fats, become thinner and thinner and then starve.

The bleakness is most eloquently reflected in a simple *Journal* entry: *"17th December Monday 1804 ... the thermometer fell to 74° below the freesing pointe"* [minus 42°F, or -46°C].

Clark records their early privations. At Fort Mandan, December 7, 1804: *"We were informed by a Chief that great numbers of Buffalow were on the hills near us Cap Lewis with a party went out & Killed 11 three in view of our fort, The weather is so excesive Cold & wolves plenty, we only saved 5 of them ..."*

Soon the competition along the food chain is in earnest. *"Capt Lewis went out 9th & Stayed all night out Killed 9 buffalow – maney of the Buffalow Killed were So meager that they not fit for use – Collected by the ade of Some horses the best of the meat in fact all we could Save from wolves ..."* J3:254 In the usual pattern of feeding, birds also follow after the wolves, cleaning a skeleton down to the bones.

Ever opportunistic like the hungry wolves, the young privates aren't fussy about how they get their meat. *"one Cow was killed on the ice after drawing her out of a vacancey in the ice in which She had fallen, and Butchered her at the fort ..."* J3:254 Think of trying to pull a 400-pound animal up several feet, especially when lack of traction on the slippery ice has the buffalo's weight pulling you toward or, worse yet, into the icy river. Not an easy job, made worse since the buffalo is still alive.

Hunting Hazards

On December 7, there is a laconic note: *"Several Men badly frost bit. — The Themormeter Stood this morning at 44d. below Breizing [freezing]"* The next day, Clark finds himself *"a little fatigued haveing run after the Buffalow all day in Snow many Places 10 inches Deep"* and reports that *"two men hurt their hips verry much in Slipping down ..."* J3:253-5

The physical injuries that come with hunting are downright dangerous: frostbite and the possibility of freezing to death. Shannon gets frostbitten feet and can't walk back to

George Catlin, collection of the Smithsonian

Winter buffalo hunting is fatiguing and downright dangerous.

camp. York, answering nature's call, has his private part frost-bit. Lewis stays out on the night of December 9 and awakens to a temperature that is minus 10°F. His co-Captain shrugs it off. *"Capt Lewis had a Cold Disagreeable night ... with one Small Blankett."* J3:255-6 On another of their joint ventures with the Mandans, one of the chiefs must be guided back to camp by his men – he's snowblind.

Being warm is the key. Hunting is suspended and the frostbitten men continue to improve. On December 12 at minus 38°F, it is again decided that hunting will be post-poned – it's just too cold. Acclimation to these extremes is just a pipe dream; the human body can adapt only so far.

Since the keelboat came upriver fully loaded, the crew of the flotilla has been eating their rations of carbohydrates to supplement the meats being brought in. With passing time, the Expedition needs to replenish some of the corn supplies – more for their winter fare and certainly some for the road. The Mandan women are the key to these food supplies, for they are keepers of the agricultural "Three Sisters" culture. But even greater than nurturing a garden economy is a total cosmology, a religious system that is closely comparable to deep and ancient beliefs proclaimed on the other side of the globe in Asia.

Mandans were agricultural, but used simple hoe and rake implements. Crops included the "Three Sisters": corn, squash, and beans.

The Native Cosmology and Food

Central to natives in America is the primary belief in a Great Spirit that manifests itself throughout the cosmos. All the natural world is imbued with energy manifestations, differ-ent qualities and benefits that make themselves apparent if one is aware. They are intermeshing and form the Great Cir-cle of Life. Humans, plants, animals – all have their own communities, and interactions exist among these communi-ties as well. The hunters who ride after the buffalo or deer view these animals as participants in the Great Circle who are there to help people. In explaining this, Joseph Bruchak, an eloquent native writer, simply says that native men "un-derstand that the deer which the people hunt only give up their bodies and survive in spirit, as long as the people treat them respectfully and hunt in the proper way."139

Likewise, the women who plant want peace and serenity for their land, knowing that their garden is a nursery of young things that must be cared for and nourished. Buffalo Bird Woman reflects this particular harmony: "We cared for our corn in those days as we would care for a child; for we Indian people loved our gardens, just as a mother loves her children; and we thought that our growing corn liked to hear us sing just as children like to hear their mother sing to them."140

Hospitality (and Survival)

Cordially, these white strangers are welcomed onto Mandan lands. Is this welcome unusual? Other past examples show this welcome to be a constant, demonstrating a broad sense of hospitality. Just a few months earlier, on August 30, five Yankton Sioux chiefs and their escort of 70 warriors parad-ed into a Mandan camp. A feast was set out for them. Even earlier, the legendary Canadian explorer David Thompson who explored the American Northwest from 1784–1812, dropped down south, escorted by 300 warriors. Hoping to save his village from the embarrassment of having to serve a decent meal for an army of that size at literally a moment's notice, the chief thanked the guide for bringing the honored guest and suggested the escort could now comfortably re-turn home knowing that their job was well done. No deal. They hadn't come this far to be turned away hungry – what kind of hospitality was this? Imagine having 300 hungry men drop in for dinner! They stayed and were served.

In fact, the ethos of sharing is such that the Mandans think of satisfying that primal need, hunger, without the hungry one even having to ask. The artist George Catlin in the 1830s further observed: "The pot is always boiling over the fire, and anyone who is hungry (either of the household or from any other part of the village) has a right to order it taken off, and to fall to eating as he pleases. I very much doubt whether the civilized world have in their institutions any system which can properly be called more humane and charitable. Every man, woman or child in Indian communi-ties is allowed to enter anyone's lodge, and even that of a chief of the nation, and eat when they are hungry ..."141

The Gardening Cycle:
Sunflowers and The Three Sisters

Nature's own rhythms govern those who live off the land. As soon as the ice breaks up on the Missouri and the ground can be worked, the first into the ground is a fence of sunflower seeds, separating each family's fields, planted in April. It is "Sunflower Planting Moon." Several varieties are planted, each family choosing the type(s) they like best – black, white, red, or striped. Not only are the seeds harvested and eaten raw or parched, but the roots are gathered in the fall as well. These root are known today as "Sunchokes" or "Jerusalem artichokes." This is the last crop harvested in the fall.

What the Expedition's men may never learn, even as they are beginning tentative friendships and seeking to understand the culture of the Mandans and Hidatsas, is the central dominant role of three linked vegetables. Across the Americas, the Corn-Beans-Squash sisters are a sacred circle unto themselves. Listen to Chief Louis Farmer, of the Onondoga:

They're not just plants – we call them the Three Sisters. We plant them together ... they want to be together with each other, just as we Indians want to be together with each other. As long as the Three Sisters are with us we know we will never starve. The Creator sends them to us each year. We celebrate them now. We thank Him for the gift He gives us today and every day.[142]

Considered the primary staple of native diet, these vegetables are eaten fresh in the summer and reconstituted from a dried state in winter.[a] In May, the Mandan women see the wild gooseberry bushes leafing out and know it is time to plant. First they sing sacred songs blessing the earth, the seeds, the benefits that will come to them. Then the corn seeds are planted into mounds. Next, the squash go into their mounds in early June, followed immediately by the beans, which are scattered between the mounds, in alternating fashion.

The scientific explanation for this grand trilogy works from the ground up to the mouth. The seeds form their own ecosystem, a companion-planting. The beans are nitrogen fixing and create a beneficial soil condition for the other two sisters. The native story called "Bean Woman" paints a vivid picture of the Bean sister being supported by the sturdy upright frame of her Corn sister. The Squash sister's dark green, shady leaves keep weeds from growing under them (lack of sunlight) and, umbrella-like, deflect the rain so that it puddles in place rather than running off. This combination promotes not only healthy soil but sturdy plants that attract beneficial insects, thus keeping the pests at bay.[143]

A second crop of corn is planted when the June berries come ripe, providing an extended season for fresh corn.

Crop rotation isn't necessary because the plants aren't grown as a monoculture, but the practice of letting the land lie fallow is followed. Weeds are hoed down and left in place, another way of improving soil with a free compost.

By early August, 1804, the Corps is meeting the Oto Indians upriver near what is now the lower border of Nebraska, and the privates are happily picking a variety of berries that are coming ripe. The village women see that the corn is coming ripe, too, and set young girls to guarding the crops from the marauding birds and boys. Even a wandering horse might stop for a browse. So, two little girls, maybe ten or twelve years old, sing songs and wait to shoo pests away. Older women will stop by to sing, or perhaps even eat with the girls. The job is so vital that the fields are guarded dawn to dusk until the crop is harvested; even cooking is done there. The innate poetry in the natives' lives is expressed in this way: "The first corn was ready to be eaten green early in the harvest moon, when the blossoms of the prairie golden rod are all in full, bright yellow ..."[144]

Buffalo Bird Woman describes how they knew the corn was good, "The blossoms on the top of the stalk were turned brown, the silk on the end of the ear was dry, and the husks on the ear were of a dark green color." This gardening wisdom still holds true.

As the Corps is laboring up the Mississippi in the hot days of late September, native families begin preparing for the harvest. Men ride to the prairies and bring in meat for the husking feasts. Women in the family go through the garden, happy with picking the corn – today's meal, winter's stew. Piles of corn accumulate in the middle of the fields.

Word is sent out that there will be a husking party and all the young men are invited. Just as the southern plantations had husking bees to work the crop, so do the natives. It is a labor-intensive time; all hands needed to process fields and fields of ripened corn. The quicker the harvest, the less chance of damage or loss. Meals are meat – sometimes dried and then boiled in a kettle with the corn; or more lavishly, a side of fresh buffalo is roasted near the corn pile. It is a social occasion and a time of unusual camaraderie between the sexes, whispering and flirting, meaningful glances.

The final step is drying the corn. It is dried on the cob, strung on braided strings to air dry, and finally stored in caches; or it is dried, hulled, and stored loose. Sometimes the kernels are parched (heat dried) before going into the cache. Nothing is wasted, not even the unusual corn smut, called *Mapë'di* or, in Mexican, *cuiclacoche*, a grayish fungus that comes into vogue every so often and is adored by

---

[a] *Buffalo Bird Woman's Garden* is an oral history related in 1917 to Gilbert Wilson by Buffalo Bird Woman of the Hidatsa tribe. It is a classic in discussing the "old ways" in Great Plains gardening methods by the Native Americans.

Mandan corn is drying in braided strings.

Gilbert Wilson photo, 1909

Caches

When all the harvest is in, it will be stored in caches, an underground storage area Lewis likens to a root cellar. This cache (in French meaning "hidden") is the secret weapon of the women, hiding their corn from ever hungry insects, rodents, and marauding enemies. Shaped like a bell, the top "neck" is a little more than two feet across. A ladder in the neck drops down into a rounded sort of cave. The size of a small cache is described: "when standing on the floor within, my eyes just cleared the level of the ground above, so that I could look around."[146] Larger and deeper ones could hold greater amounts.

The caches are exceptionally organized, with logic behind each placement. The contents are protected by layering willow twigs on the earthen floor, followed by bundles of dried grass, and finally topped with a protective layer of skins. Strings of braided corn are placed around the rim of the cache, next to the walls. The stem ends of vegetables are placed to the outside, being the least likely to be injured if wet. Then loose shelled corn is laid down inside that, with dried squash (most subject to rot if dampened) placed at the very middle of these insulating layers. Before closing the cache, a further layer of dried grass and skin finishes the protective layering. Finally an access cover made of split timber is laid into the hole (strong enough to withstand the

gourmets.[b] The Mandans half-boil the cob, then dry it, and finally break the fungus pieces off and mix them with corn, which "tasted good, not sweet, and not sour."[145]

Corncobs find another use as a seasoning ingredient, used in place of alkali salts found in local springs. At sunset during a time of low wind, a manageable pile of corncobs is torched and then watched until it ceases to be a fire threat. In the morning the ash has a thick layer or crust upon it. This is gathered up by one of the women and rolled into perhaps a half dozen balls that are then carefully stored in the lodge to be used as a seasoning in boiling corn.

On October 30, the Corps receives a gift of corn and corn bread made from parched meal, fat etc. *"which eats verry well"* [J9:92] Ordway, in another entry, describes the bread as being made in round balls. [J9:106] The wives are strutting their culinary stuff.

[b] A fine recipe for this is found in Diane Kennedy's *Essential Cuisines of Mexico,* page 227, and features onions, garlic, squash, corn, corn smut, and chiles.

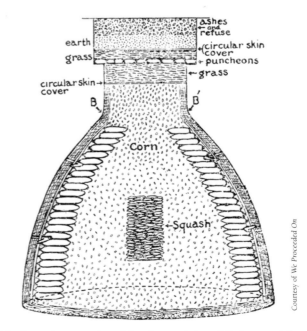

Courtesy of *We Proceeded On*

Mandan caches were about 5 feet deep and about 5 feet across at the bottom, narrowing to an 18-inch access neck.

Caches are organized to protect the contents. Willow twigs and grass line the floor and walls; whole corn is layered around the outside—stems out—while loose corn and softer crops are in the center.

weight of a horse standing directly on the mouth of the cache), and then more layers of grasses are packed tight, a second cover of buffalo hide is added, and then dirt and ashes are spread on top as a final camouflage.

At the Mandan villages, the caches are dug in the summer camp, the permanent location. It is not far from the winter camp, which is lower down and nestled in riverside bluffs, protected from the prevailing weather. In the late fall dried corn, squash, and beans are carried down to the winter camp, and if supplies run short, a woman could always return to her family's summer house and get more. It is possible that not all the villagers left the summer camp, hoping for protection from raids behind its wooden palisades.[147]

The caches' importance cannot be overstated and their usefulness does not escape Pierre Cruzatte, who takes with him the knowledge of how to build one. Lewis, too, stores the idea away. Later the Corps will dig a number of caches as they are forced to ditch weight and bulk for their journey over the Rockies.

Defining Roles

Several *Journal* entries find Clark either astonished or offended by the issue of men "loading" the women and children with goods, like pack animals. *"the Big White principal Chief of the lower Village of the Mandans Came Down, he packd about 100 W. of fine meet on his Squar for us."* J3:233 Ordway remarks, *"the Savages came in large crouds the Squaws laded with corn & Beans."* J9:105

The men are involved with religious ceremonies, protection of the tribe, negotiating treaties, and hunting. Native writer Joseph Bruchak remarks, "when [white men] saw Native men 'lying around while their wives worked' those men were not slackers, they were recuperating from the rigors of hunting and respecting the fact that the women did not wish to be interfered with in the work which they knew best."[148] This puts quite a different light on the entire interplay between job functions as seen by outsiders from a different culture.

Chief Little Crow's Wife's Present

The winter dish Clark describes could be either a cornmeal mush or a brothy vegetable stew depending on which type of corn was used and whether it was ground meal or kernels. In either case the chief's wife rises to the occasion by dressing up the two primary ingredients with a third contrasting ingredient (squash) and then outdoes herself by extravagantly adding a fruit.

MANDAN WINTER STEW

"a Kettle of boild Simnins, beens, Corn & Choke Cherris" J3:261

The corn would probably have been a varietal favored for this type of dish: hard white. Nine different types of corn are listed as being grown in the area, including a hard variety called Flint (one that is not particularly affected by drought or lower temperatures), sweet or gummy corn for eating off the cob, and a flour corn. Each has qualities that recommend it for specific purposes: winter storing, fresh eating, ease of preparing. While little recognition is given to native civilizations as being accomplished agriculturists, the Mandans and Hidatsa "understood how to keep their [corn] stocks pure by keeping varieties separate, and each family grew only one or two varieties. They also used a considerable appreciation of the principles of scientific selection in selecting the best, ripest, and most uniform ears for seed purposes."[149]

The second main vegetable crop is squash. Clark uses *"simnins,"* a changed form of *simlin* or *simnel,* referring to what Southerners call as "summer squash." Apparently he is a little off. By botanical description it seems to be a winter squash or edible pumpkin, with a hard rind, as opposed to a summer squash with a soft surface that spoils easily. The native practice is not to allow the developing squash to grow old or tough. They are harvested every four days – young, thin-skinned, and with a minimal amount of seed growth, certainly an advantage in simple one-pot cookery. Cooking time is reduced by using a young vegetable, and the seeds are crunchily edible. Only seed squash were allowed to age to full ripeness. The chief's wife probably preserves her squash as Buffalo Bird Woman details it. "When the strings of squash were thought to be thoroughly dried, they were ready for storing. A portion was packed in parfleche (bags)[c], to be taken to the winter lodge, or to be used for food on journeys."[150] The squash in the stew probably arrived this way.

The beans, chosen from a colorful array of black, red, white, spotted, and shield-figured beans, might have been white, a favorite. Finally an added luxury, fruit, which had been air-dried and stored in far less quantity than farmed produce, makes it more special, the "treat" it's reported to be. Before bringing this dish to the fort, Little Crow's wife would have spent quite a bit of time preparing her winter stew.

Diplomatic Events with Food Involved

From October, 1804, to March, 1805, there are many dinner discussions – what will the territory beyond this place look like? Is game available? Are there friendly tribes ahead? Is food always available? Subtleties and intuition are the vanguards of diplomacy. Both Captains are masters of observation, each in his own way, and what characterizes these two remarkable leaders is an ability to come out of situations with their troops alive and proceeding on. The time spent with the hospitable Mandans offers the Corps a full variety of situations in which they gain expertise in co-existing with a native tribe. It is the best experience, especially with cheerful friends who are well-stocked for the winter and generous beyond expectation.

For this Plains tribe, corn is the cement which glues relations together. When the first village of Mandans promises to make peace with the Arikaras, they give eleven bushels of corn to Lewis as a sign of their good faith. On January 16, 1805, Chief Little Crow comes to the fort, hoping to get approval for a war plan against the Shoshone – actually a horse raid. He brings corn, hopefully a subtle inducement. Clark, of course, disapproves of the war plan, and spends the rest of the visit persuading the chief to maintain peace.

Gilbert Wilson photo, 1909

Mandan squash is sliced and the slices air dried on long sticks.

---

[c] The term "parfleche" is a French Canadian term (pronounced parflesh) meaning a bag or pouch made from rawhide with the hair removed by soaking it in water and lye.

Natives from the villages on the south bank cross the frozen Missouri to visit Fort Mandan.

Karl Bodmer, Mih-Tutta-Hang-Kusch, Joslyn Art Museum, Omaha, Nebraka

from their packets of Indian goods. It is difficult to measure whether the gift giving is of equal value, but no one seems displeased:

♦ On November 3: Little Raven, and his woman loaded with 60 pounds of dried buffalo and a pot of meal, come visiting.

♦ On November 10: Chief "The Coal" brings in an entire side of buffalo.

♦ On November 12: Chief Big White, not to be outdone, brings in 100 pounds of fine meat.

These gifts appear to be establishing the stature of the donor and his high rank. The chiefs apparently have discretionary powers over giving away meat, while vegetable gifts are more likely to come from women. The Captains hand out axes, a one-time-only gift, and they distribute small trinkets. Representing the Great White Father, they have already established their rank. And, they represent promises of goods yet to come.

Hospitality with Food Implied

Fort Mandan is an open house. Chiefs, their families and clansmen come visiting. Three curious chiefs from the second Mandan village come and pay their respects and stay all of a snowy November day. Black Cat and The Coal, highly regarded chiefs, pay a social call and are invited to stay overnight. In all of these visits it is a certainty that they would be offered food as an expected, accepted part of hospitality.

Gifts of Food as an Initiative in Fostering Friendship

Several women appear on October 28, at the river encampment, bringing gifts of corn in many guises: soft corn, boiled hominy, regular dried corn. Such open-handed generosity, a welcome to their new neighbors, brings out an instant reciprocity. A glazed pot is given by Lewis in return. The Mandan pot sent back to Jefferson is plain, as glazing is unknown to this northern tribe. Lewis' gift, with its shiny surface, is no doubt quite special.

November, 1804, is a big month for chiefs bringing ample and impressive gifts and the Captains reciprocating

Food Shared in Friendship

The easy give and take between individuals is notable. On November 20, 1804, three Mandan chiefs appear and settle in for a hot dinner of fresh meat. On this occasion and on February 8, the guests eat meat, a great treat since their villages have run out and are on vegetarian fare. Other visitors appear several weeks later, and one brings some squash along. One of the interpreters (Drouillard?) is given some meat – and this gift, not directed at the Captains, shows it is a personal token rather than a political one. Clark sends some stewed fruit and tea to one of Charbonneau's sick wives (he has two) on January 20, 1805. Little Crow's wife spends a few hours cooking up a special stew for the Captains. On one occasion Big White of the lower Mandan village dines at the fort and presents a fine thank-you to the Captains – *"a Scetch of the Country as far as the high mountains, & on the South Side of the River Rejone [Yellowstone] ..."* J3:269 It is an important present, this map of Montana, and includes the Yellowstone River and the entire Missouri basin to the Rockies.

At least once a month, chiefs such as Black Cat or The

Coal, sometimes alone, sometimes together, or with family (wives or sons), come to visit and are invited to stay overnight; presumably they dine with one or both of the Captains. Black Cat, when visiting, regularly brings a little meat. After one such day's visit on February 25, with Hidatsa visitors, *"Black mockerson Chief of the little Village of Big Bellies, the Chief of the Shoe Inds and a number of others,"* one of the chiefs asks to stay overnight with his two wives, as do two boys, one the son of Mandan chief Black Cat. Clark happily writes that *"The Day has been exceedingly pleasent ..."*

Bad Table Manners

Usually, eating in a group favors relaxation, letting down one's guard. But history records poisonings, and the poor minion taster whose life is always at risk. Disputes have caused men to leap to the tabletop fighting, and a host of other bad banquet manners. On March 16, 1805, Clark writes about a trivial episode, which takes place at either the fort or in one of the Mandan villages, that could have become a major event. Peace is broken at the table: *"one Indian much displeased with whitehouse for Strikeing his hand when eating with a Spoon for behaveing badly."* This certainly is the worst kind of diplomacy; but the Captains simply brush it aside.

A Collision Course: Community versus Technology

A standard part of the Captain's "Impress the Indians Show" is firing the airgun and demonstrating the corn mill. There is no doubt it could be likened to displays at a county fair: *"had the mill erected shewed the savages its operation."* [J3:221] In a splendid gesture, the Captains present one of the very latest, high-tech, steel corn mills from the East, *"which was verry pleasing to them."* Jefferson, intrigued with all things mechanical, deems this to be the proud successor to the mortar and pestle, and so it is.

Technology and communal values are about to meet, much like two continental plates on a collision course. Almost universally, natives are eager to get metal and metal products. The hunter/warriors want quick and reliable guns instead of bows and arrows. The women covet metal gardening tools instead of the traditional digging sticks, bent twigs lashed into rakes, and antler-horn hoes. Mandan eyes see the metal, not the intended function. Steel (the corn

R. L. Rickards - courtesy: Rickards Western Art

The Corps and the Mandans hunt buffalo together.

mill) and sheet iron (which Lewis will shortly salvage from the keelboat in the form of the defunct stove) are precious.

White eyes, prizing the result and totally accustomed to metal tools of all sorts, would see things differently, as did Alexander Henry the Younger, who several years later writes disapprovingly of the natives as "foolish fellows." [151] By Alexander's visit, the Incredible Home Grain Processor has been dismantled and broken up, now being used for other purposes. Metal arrows, barbs, and buffalo hide scrapers replace earlier obsidian models; wives and daughters are now pleased with durable and familiar tools. The largest unbreakable piece of the original mill is refitted with a wooden handle and becomes a handy, handsome tool for pounding marrow bones to obtain the grease. Rather than changing the age-old method of grinding corn, the community benefits more by dismantling the tool and sharing the metal. When the Corps runs out of trade goods, Lewis commissions the blacksmiths to cut up a broken stove and begin bartering pieces of metal for foodstuffs.

Hunting with the Warriors

For tribal hunters on the prairie, security comes in many ways: alliances, strength in numbers, keen perception, caution, a determinedness, a bravado, all honed against the extreme of dying. Boys are raised this way. And this is much the way in any wilderness, so the troops of the Corps fit right in, allying themselves with the Mandans, hunting together.

It is a fair, cold day, December 7, 1804, the morning temperature standing at minus 1°F. Clark writes, *"the Big White Grand Chief of the 1s Village, Came and informed us that a large Drove of Buffalow was near and his people was wating for us to join them in a Chase Capt. Lewis took 15 men & went out joined the Indians, who were at the time he got up, Killing the Buffalows on Horseback with arrows which they done with great dexterity ..."*

While the Corps and the Indians hunt together, each group takes home what they kill. The meat is not openly shared, at least not out on the prairie. Lewis' group shoots 14 buffalo, about an animal per man, but bringing the meat home is the problem. They apparently butcher the animals where shot, returning with *"<u>five</u> of which we got back to the fort by the assistance of a horse in addition to what the men Packed on their backs ..."*

The animals left behind are not wasted, for *"those we did not get in was taken by the indians under a Custon which is established amongst them 'i'e. any person Seeing a buffalow lying without an arrow Sticking in him, or Some purticular mark takes possession ..."*

The Buffalo Dance ritual is believed to bring the herds near.

On December 17, the Corps receives word from the chiefs that buffalo are nearby and they will come by in the morning to go hunting. Whether it is machismo, fear of losing face, or a belief they'd acclimated, seven men are sent out. Somewhat later, the entire party – whites and natives alike – returns. Shivering is probably too mild a word with the temperature at minus 42°F.

The growing scarcity of game is a serious concern by early January, 1805. On January 3, eight hunters are sent out for buffalo and return with a hare and a wolf, skimpy rations at best. While the Corps has barrels of provisions, the Captains are far happier saving them for the unknown parts of the trip, hence a strict adherence to local goods.

Buffalo Dance

When an invitation arrives on January 5 for a Buffalo Dance (or a Medicine Dance), the Mandans are eager for the white men to attend. The purpose of this ritual ceremony is to *"cause the buffalow to Come near So that They may kill thim."*

What is unexpected, however, are the native beliefs that form the core, the enabling part of the rite. Just as the Great Spirit must send the buffalo, so the seekers must do their part to insure success in the venture. And who knows better about great deeds of the hunt than the old hunters themselves? The elders, the very old, *"who verry often can Scercely walk"* are repositories of such knowledge. During this ceremony each young hunter seeks to obtain all the power he can from this source. He does this by picking one of the wisest elders, and his wife then sleeps with the chosen elder; the woman thus receiving his wisdom and great skill through their intimate interaction. The wife then passes on that skill and knowledge to her husband by her relations with him. The Captains are surprised when one of their Corps [unnamed] is seen as a great hunter and warrior and is chosen instead of an elder for four of the women to absorb his skill and knowledge.

Despite such optimistic activities, on January 7 the mess cooks still serve deer and wolf. Whether it is a result of the dance or not, on the bitterly cold January 9 buffalo cows appear and the warriors go hunting, as does Clark with three or four men. It is a happy day with meat for the stomachs.

Celebrating the Holidays – Christmas, 1804

Ice-shimmering hours and days interweave as the fort is completed and friendships fostered. Just as life begins to settle into a routine, the first Christmas away from Western civilization arrives. Christmas, to the Corps, isn't much of a religious event, and one of the most intriguing insights into

Lewis' character emerges. Although he is a Freemason and churches abound in Virginia, where he grew up, he is totally silent. He writes nothing. Nor does Clark. In fact, all the *Journal* entries record only events of the day, summoning up no religious musings, but instead reflecting the "duty" of reporting. So, Christmas serves as a useful ploy for putting out the "Closed" sign. The young men withdraw and guard their white American privacy: *"the Savages did not Trouble us as we had requested them not to come as it was a Great medician day with us."* J9:106 But the Captains have a little surprise in store for their men, a Christmas Eve treat of food goods. Glimpsing through Joseph Whitehouse's diary entry for Monday 24 December, 1804, *"Some Snow fell this morning. about 10 oC cleared off a fair day. we finished our fortifycation. in the evening our Captains contributed to the party Some flour pepper dryed apples &c. to celebrate the Chrisstmas."* J11:113 Unexpected rations are always a happy present.

A traditional ceremony marks the next day's early beginning, as the young studs can't wait to get their guns going. Under a cloudy sky, Clark writes, *"I was awakened before Day by a discharge of 3 platoons [meaning volleys, several men firing in unison] from the Party and the french, the men merrily Disposed, I give them all a little Taffia and permitted 3 Cannon fired, at raising Our flag, Some men went out to hunt & the Others to Dancing and Continued untill 9 oClock P. M, when the frolick ended &c."* J3:261

Christmas 1804 at Fort Mandan is marked by drinking, dancing, and high celebration – the Expedition is still in its early stages and energies are high.

R. L. Rickards - courtesy: Rickards Western Art

RECONSTRUCTING CHRISTMAS AT FORT MANDAN

7 AM	Volley of three platoons (individual gunfire), glass of taffee (brandy), three cannons fired. Raising of the flag, a second glass of brandy. Some men go out to hunt, others begin dancing.
10 AM	A glass of brandy, others commence dancing.
1 PM	Cannon fire, announcing the best to eat that could be had.
2 PM	Firing of cannon: official start to dancing.
8–9 PM	Dancing, frolicking – and finishing, according to Ordway, "in peace and quietness."

Detail-oriented Gass gets us into the minutia of the day. *Captain Clark then presented to each man a glass of brandy, and we hoisted the American flag in the garrison, and its first waving in fort Mandan was celebrated with another glass. – The men then cleared out one of the rooms and commenced dancing. At 10 o'clock we had another glass of brandy, and at 1 a gun was fired as a signal for dinner. At half past 2 another gun was fired, as a notice to assemble at the dance, which was continued in a jovial manner till 8 at night; and without the presence of any females, except three squaws, wives to our interpreter, who took no other part than the amusement of looking on.* J10:68

January 1, 1805 – New Year's Day

"on the N E bank of the Missouries 1600 miles up Tuesday"

While the traditional firing of the swivel guns propels New Year's Day from its dawn beginnings, Clark's outlook is somewhat subdued; Indian relations have been strained. This is not a good position to be in, let alone to start a new year. He sends sixteen men to the first village to soothe hurt feelings with a little music and dancing. Then at 11 AM, he and an interpreter and two men, *"walked up to the village (my views were to alay Some little miss understanding which had taken place thro jelloucy and mortification as to our treatment towards them [)]"* J3:267 *"I went into the lodges of all the men of note except two, whome I heard had made Some expresseions not favourable towards us, in Comparing us with the trabers from the north ..."* The chiefs, however, are more embroiled in mediating a dispute involving 150 Gros Ventres who have come down to force the return of a young girl stolen by the Hidatsa.

With this going on, the American slight is relatively minor. Fortunately, all goes well and Clark orders York to dance for the Indians, *"which amused the Croud verry much, and Some what astonished them, that So large a man Should be active &c. &."* But York isn't the only act; Gass writes that, *"a frenchman danced on his head."* This small circus act is rewarded by food, and *"they then brought victules from different lodges & different kinds of diet ..."* [J9:107] By the time Clark returns in the evening *"the party except 6 returned, with 3 robes, an 13 Strings of Corn which the indians had given them."* – about 65 feet of food, 715 ears, ready to cook[d] – both valuable gifts. Moreover, the highly respected chief *"Black Cat with his family visited us to day and brought a little meet ..."* [J3:266] Good relations are restored.

Sergeant Ordway writes:

> cloudy but moderate. we fired a Swivel & drank a Glass. about 9 o.C. 15 of the party went up to the 1st village of Mandans to dance as it had been their request. carried with us a fiddle & a Tambereen & a Sounden horn. as we arrived at the entrence of the vil. we fired one round then the music played. loaded again. then marched to the center of the vil, fired again. then commenced dancing. a frenchman danced on his head and all danced round him for a Short time then went in to a lodge & danced a while, which pleased them verry much ... [J9:107]

Gass seconds the observation:

> Two shot were fired from this swivel, followed by a round of small arms, to welcome the New year. Captain Lewis then gave each a glass of good old whiskey; and a short time after another was given by Captain Clarke. ... The day was warm and pleasant. Captain Lewis in the afternoon issued another glass of whiskey ... [J10:68]

Since Clark, York, the interpreters and their wives have all gone over to the villages, Lewis issues whiskey to the men who remain at the fort. Clark's concerns over Indian diplomacy are woes he keeps to himself. As for the young studs, the Corps is ready for fun and celebrating. If they don't have fireworks, they have shots in the air. They are dance crazy and in fine fettle, and the Indians obviously enjoy the partying as much as the young men.

Sidestepping Jefferson's Orders

By the end of January, the Captains are facing a serious dilemma: they are out of corn. The Mandans are feeling pinched as

---

[d] Buffalo Bird Woman says her family wove about 55 ears of corn onto one string – Gilbert Wilson, *Buffalo Bird Woman's Garden.*

Fort Mandan blacksmiths work to convert spare metal into war axes and Indian hatchets in exchange for corn in February 1805.

R. L. Rickards - courtesy: Rickards Western Art

well, and the plentitude of November has dried up. The Corps has blacksmiths who can manufacture war hatchets, and customers who will swap corn in an instant for those exactingly wrought battle tools. But Jefferson has expressly forbidden anything that will resemble breaking the peace. It's not a difficult decision. The Captains order up a flaming pit of timber to produce coals sufficient *"to mend the indians hatchets, & make them war axes, the only means by which we precure Corn from them."* [J3:281] Food moves to top priority, above Presidential diplomacy. It is, after all, very cold. Disagreeable. And ice on the Missouri is three feet thick.

Lewis writes on February 6, 1805: *"the blacksmith's have proved a happy resoce to us in our present situation as I believe it would have been difficult to have devised any other method to have procured corn from the natives. the Indians are extravegantly fond of sheet iron of which they form arrow-points and manufacter into instruments for scraping and dressing their buffaloe robes ..."* And so the smithies – Shields, Bratton, and Willard – dismember the sheet iron "callaboos" (the previously mentioned unusable galley stove from the keelboat) and cut it into four-inch squares, trading each small scrap for an extravagant seven to eight gallons of corn. [J3:288] Lewis' relief at finding a method of obtaining corn shows the sharpening realization of fueling necessities and the need to keep food supplies always on hand, ready. In his last "miscellany" report home to the President, Lewis writes, *"we by the aide of our Black smiths precured Corn Sufficient for the party dureing the winter and about 70 or 90 bushels to Carry with us."* J3:48

PRIVATION RULES

✦ Buffalo become meager before elk, elk before deer.

✦ Females carry more fat than males, bulls or bucks are often unusable.

Winter Fasting

The fresh meat supply, which is exhausted the first week of February, leads Clark to conclude that the game has moved away. He determines to pursue it, following the frozen river south until they can replenish their supplies. On February 3, 1805, he sets out on foot with sixteen men, three horses, and two sleighs. It is a ten-day, sixty-mile outing, with temperatures ranging from 18°F below to 18°F above zero. Unlike the men at the fort, but like the rest of the hungry animals that winter, they suffer. *"Killed nothing, & nothing to eat ..."* J3:293 The stalwart hunters comb frozen fields, wade through snow, and bring in as much meat as they can kill. Nine days later, the *Journal* entry reads, *"forty Deer, 3 buffaloe bulls, & sixteen Elk, most of them were so meager that they were unfit for uce ..."* J3:292

Clark and his troops finish combing the high jutting points of the riverbank for game and begin a steady sweep upriver. When the eagerly expected horses do not arrive from the fort, and their moccasins begin wearing out, there is a rising level of concern. Warily, at two different locations, they fell thick saplings and construct a shanty to protect the meat from predators. The cold, burdened hunters are carrying the heavy bloody carcasses into camp over their shoulders, dropping the animals to be butchered on the ground, and finally loading the finished meat pieces into the closed pen for safekeeping. Protecting the meat long enough to get it home is no easy chore. Even as the hunters finish the kill (man being at the top of the food chain), it is time for every opportunist to move in. The men fight off wolves, magpies, and ravens. Everything is hungry.

On the trip down from Fort Mandan the horses are able to walk on ice, but they slip when pulling the heavily laden meat sleighs and cannot move them upriver. Charbonneau and an engagé return to the fort on February 10 with the bad news, reporting they have left two men guarding the horses and *"the best of the meat"* at some distance downriver. Al-though there has been no sign of raiding parties, this is a dangerous situation, portending loss of men, horses, and the much-valued meat for the men at the fort. Lewis apparently judges the distance to be too far for that day and orders two men and two small sleighs to leave early the next morning. The meat will be pulled home, two men to a sleigh, four men total. The other two will stay off the ice and bring the horses back across the prairie.

On the February 12, Lewis pulls the smithies off battle axe construction and has them begin shoeing horses, the shoes calculated to add traction and reduce the cold on the horses hooves. Three more sleighs are prepared for hauling in the rest of the meat.

Downriver, Clark's anxiety rises to new levels. His *Journal* entry on February 14 tersely records the event: *"Sent 4 men with the Horses Shod & 2 Slays down for the meat I had left, 22 miles below those men were rushed on by 106 Sioux who rob[b]ed them of 2 of their horses – & they returned."* There is mortal danger lurking in the woods. The four men – Drouillard, Frazer, Goodrich, and Newman – have taken serious opposition to being robbed and/or killed, and fight back. They resent having their knives and a tomahawk taken, but the standoff ends with a mild loss of two horses and two knives, and nobody injured or dead.

Finally, with enough meat gathered, the benumbed party returns to home-base, exhausted. On February 14, a still tired Captain records, *"I returned last night from a hunting party much fatigued, having walked 30 miles on the ice and through wood land Points in which the Snow was nearly Knee Deep."*

The Sioux attack infuriates Lewis, who sets out in a coldly determined rage with a party of men, a Mandan chief, and four warriors. But the affair of the horses and knives is a mere indignity compared to what comes next. The Mandans return the next day (February 16), with the chief nearly snowblind, telling of the Sioux continuing downriver, discovering one of the meat pens, and heedlessly burning it to the ground. All that meat is gone. All the pain, time, and effort wasted, totally. Animals sacrificed for nothing. The Teton Sioux warriors leave the burnt meat pen as an insolent, jeering reminder of their continuing aggression. The miracle is that they had seen Clark, but did not attack. In a supposed sleight of hand, they leave behind some corn at a campfire, hoping to redirect the blame onto their sometime allies, the Arikaras. They ruin their case by accidentally leaving some moccasins behind.

And so, after ten days of miserable exposure and hunting, sending the meat back (which stalled out on the river and didn't get quickly to his hungry men), having a huge meat supply maliciously destroyed, on February 18 Clark is reduced to writing, *"our Store of Meat is out to day."* The only good news is the demand for blacksmithing, and corn is rolling in as the smithies turn out battle axe after battle axe.

Lewis' party of twenty-four returns three days later on February 21. Clark is happy: *"a Delightfull Day."* Not only is it a nice day – 6°F above zero – but he has reason to be pleased. *"Capt Lewis returned with 2 Slays loaded with meat, after finding that <they> could not overtake the Sious war party … deturmined to proceed on to the lower Deposit, which he found had not been observed by Soux he hunted two day Killed 36 Deer & 14 Elk, Several of them So meager, that they were unfit for use, the meet which he killed and that in the lower Deposit amounting to about 3000 wt was brought up on two Slays, one Drawn by 16 men had about 2400 wt on it …"* The supplementary log at the end of the month lists 100 pounds more meat for a total of 3100 pounds. The bulk of the meat supply is promptly dealt with, "hanging up meat" in the smokehouse.

In a report to Jefferson, Lewis sums up their winter as having a *"sufficiency"* except for the bitter temperatures. *"… we found it imprackable to precure … a Sufficiency of Meat without*

The 3,000 pounds of meat from the successful February 1805 hunt is brought back to the fort by two horse sleds.

R. L. Rickards - courtesy: Rickards Western Art

the riesque of friesing maney of our men, who frequently, were Slightly frosted." J3:486

Spring Rain

The very next day (February 22) actually heralds the slightest beginning of spring: it rains, briefly. Then it's back to snow. But the Captains have not missed the tiny signal beacon and send their men to exhume their imbedded boats from the frozen river. The upriver Hidatsa chief Black Moccasin and a number of other Hidatsa apparently rethink their view of white men being bad medicine. They and their wives, loaded with meat, come visiting, intent on catching the Captains before they might escape in an early spring. One wants a battle axe made for his son, and an influential party of Chief, wives, and several sons ask to stay overnight.

Meanwhile, Indian hostilities and new alliances are stewing like a bubbling pot. The bad news reaching them is that a collection of Sioux bands – the upper *Tetons*, the *Sisetoons*, and a band of *Yankton of the North* intend to wage war *"against the nations of this quarter, & Kill everry white man they See —"* J3:304 The good news for the Corps and the Mandans is that the Teton Sioux, in trying to divert blame onto their Arikara allies, have provoked a diplomatic break. *"Mr. Gravilin further informs that the Party which Robed us of the 2 horses laterly were all Sieoux 100 in number, they Called at the Ricaras on their return, the Ricares being displeased at their Conduct would not give them any thing to eate, that being the greatest insult they could peaceably offer them, and upbraded them."* J3:305 Diplomacy on the western frontier is directly tied to food.

But what is the Corps doing with 3100 pounds of meat? They are preparing it for the trip, slicing it as thin as possible, hanging it in the smokehouse to become jerky. Some of it they eat fresh, refrigeration not being a problem at this time of year. The smithies continue arming the locals with battle axes in exchange for corn.

The work on river transport is in earnest now, and on March 11 the Captains determine to build another two canoes for the explicit purpose of *"transport[ing] our Provisions &c."* This implies a substantial amount of food. Later, canoes are discarded as provisions run out.

Yet More Corn

While this small drama is going on, the work effort is directed toward corn. For two days (March 14 and 15) some of the men are *"Shelling Corn,"* *"Hulling*

Corn," and putting parched meal out to dry in the sun. Ord-way's log makes the process look less onerous: only two men are involved in the hulling. But there is some confusion about what these terms mean. Shelling corn means to pop the dry kernels of corn off the cob. Parching corn, the pounding of dried corn and then heating it in a heavy pot, is a mechanical way to super-dry the starch and separate the hulls off the kernel – it's known that they were parching corn at the end of their stay. Ordway also records the shelling of corn on March 25.[e]

The Nearly Forgotten Food Disease: Pellagra

While corn is nutritious, it also has a potentially debilitating effect in the form of pellagra. This disease is actually two nutritional deficiencies of both protein and niacin caused by an over- consumption of unprocessed corn. The natives of the western hemisphere prevented pellagra by using lye from wood ash as a soaking agent. Another way of forestalling pellagra is food combining. Beans are a direct compliment to corn, and their niacin, lysine, and tryptophan are readily available.

Ice Floe Jumping

The finale of a winter's culinary history is a gymnastic spectacle which leaves no doubt about the natives' athleticism. On March 28, Clark remarks on an Indian preference in buffalo meat: *"but few Indians visit us to day they are watching to catch the floating Buffalow which brake through the ice in Crossing, those people are fond of those animals ta[i]nted and Catch great numbers every Spring."* The next day he adds, *"I observed extrodanary dexterity of the Indians in jumping from one Cake of ice to another, for the purpose of Catching the buffalow as they float down maney of the Cakes of ice which they pass over are not two feet Square."*

The Indians' agility is formidable, but the drive, the risk, is also amazing. What is so delicious, so enticing, to prompt this act of craziness? Clark's simple observation leads to sev-eral ideas. First, if the Mandan/Hidatsa snag great numbers of these carcasses, it is a major protein source. Winter is bad for the buffalo, they would be thin and tough. In some of our best restaurants, the aspect of decomposition is referred to as "aging" and is associated with "tenderizing".[f]

Packing Up, Ready to Go

Winter is fading in fits and starts, and the Corps is eager to head out for the unseen Pacific. The men are finishing up their provisioning and wrapping the gear for travel. Clark details, *"18th of March 1805 ... I pack up all the merchindize into 8 packs equally devided So as to have Something of every thing in each Canoe & perogue ..."* a cautious thing to do considering the potential for drenching or capsizing. The pirogues are reconditioned and the cottonwood canoes are completed and moved one and a half miles from the construction site down to the shores of the river. Ice jams and floes continue to be a hazard to navigation. Finally the flotilla of two pirogues and six canoes is assembled.

The keelboat is loaded and dispatched downriver, packed with Indian trappings, animal and plant specimens, and much more. Among the plant specimens are *"... a species of Cress, taken at St. Louis May 10, 1804. It is common in the open growns on the Mississippi bottoms, appears in the uncultivated parts of the lots gardens and orchards, the seeds come to maturity by the 10th of May in most instances."* [J3:451] May 27 of the previous year was also a healthy day in terms of menu vegetables: *"... near the mouth of the Gasconade ... a species of cress which grows very abundantly along the river beach in many places; my men make use of it and find it a very pleasant wholsome sallad. – "* and also *"... a species of rape or kail, it grows on the beach of the river, when young my men used it a boiled green and found healthy and pleasant."* [J3:452-3]

They send back a specimen of wild ginger that was not used for cooking, although it was used as a stomach stimulant and *"frequently used in sperits with bitter herbs* [an aperitif ?]." [J3:454] Another specimen was taken June 3 above the Osage River. It is the ground plum or buffalo bean and Lewis compares its appearance to indigo but cites it in the following way, *"the Indians frequently use the fruit of this plant to alay their thirst as they pass through these extensive dry praries."* He apparently tried it himself, although the plant was not yet fully ripe. *"the pulp is crisp & clear and tasts very much like the hull of a gardin pee.— when ripe the fruit is of a fine red colour and sweet flavor."*

---

[e] But how else do you take the hulls (the bran) off corn? Harold McGee, a food scientist, addresses the process in *On Food & Cooking*, page 243. He points out that boiling corn kernels in a 5% lime solution for about an hour, then rinsing, draining, and grinding the corn will loosen or soften the bran to the point that it will separate. Welcome the corn mill; this is labor intensive activity. The second advantage of this process is that it chemically converts the locked-in essential elements in corn (lysine, tryptophan, niacin, protein) into forms that are most easily used by the human body. Today we can pick up lye-treated corn at the market: hominy (large pieces) and masa (pounded) being most familiar.

---

[f] In a conversation in Great Falls, June 28, 2002, the Lewis and Clark Honor Guard suggested that this meat was reduced to a "meat pudding."

Collected August 12 is a fruit that does not seem to have aroused much interest, *"one of our hunters brought us a bough of the purple courant, which is frequently cultivated in the Atlantic states; the fruit was ripe; I presume it is a native of North America— here it grows generally in the praries but is not very abundant."*

The only culinary artifact sent back is an unglazed Mandan cooking pot.

Reviewing the Winter Menu

So, what is the Menu du Corps for this winter of 1804–05? Corn. Lots of it – on strings, in pots, rolls, wife loads, son loads, bushels, and *"considerable quantities."* It comes on the cob, as shelled corn, or parch meal. There is yellow corn, soft corn, flint corn, hominy. It is cooked as cornbread, corn balls, combined with other vegetables, and sometimes has fat or fruit added. There are about 100 bushels, plus 50–60 pounds that a woman might carry, 30 pounds that a young son might carry, and approximately 715 ears sent home on the strings. The carbohydrate part of the diet is decidedly corn-heavy.

The protein side of the menu is far more varied – 3 antelope, 2 beaver, a hare, 3 wolves. They kill 87 deer and 49 elk. Buffalo, the largest protein source, comes dried (60 pounds), fresh (100 pounds), by the horse load (7), and by *"brought back"* count (14). More are killed but are declared unfit (8) and some are left for the natives. One of the most perplexing questions in tracking the Corps of Discovery is the amount of food they actually eat. There are "kill" versus "brought-back" versus "eaten" figures. Broad guesses are in order and the number of servings, a restaurant concept, is nonexistent. What occurs is family style, the entire body of men and Sacagawea sharing what there is. The men drink their antifreeze: gills of whiskey, and drinks of *"tafia."*

Meals change with the circumstances. There are visitors: French, British, and American traders drop in. Natives regularly come and go; some are invited to stay, particularly if it is politically expedient. The hunters go out and don't return for a day, or sometimes many days. Often, the Corps splits in half, and once even into four parts – the groups each fending for themselves and eating different things. Perhaps one or more of the party is sick and unable to eat. Tracking this,

Elk hunting provides the second-largest weight of food consumed at Fort Mandan over the 1804–05 winter (bison were first).

E.P. Haddon, Bureau of Sport Fisheries and Wildlife, U.S. Dept. Of the Interior ex post facto and two hundred years later, is an exercise in inferential logic.

As they leave in the spring of 1805, Whitehouse casts a backward glance at the first Mandan village. It's a town of 300 lodges with a large number of inhabitants, many of whom *"live to a very old age, numbers being 100 Years old."* So much for the need to swear off red meat. He observes:

... the Soil is very rich, producing Indian Corn, pumpkins, Squashes & beans in abundance ... [there are] large fields, which they cultivate and which produces plentifully, They have likewise Gardens, which they plant & have several kinds of Garden Vegetables in it, such as Lettuce, Mustard &c they have likewise growing in their Gardens, Gooseberrys, which is superior in Size, to any in the United States & Currants of different kinds.

He observes the same agricultural practices at the second Mandan village. From this brief glimpse, it is apparent that the Corps spent their five months dining on austere winter fare. They had seen very, very little of the variety that constitutes the yearly native diet.

With their stay at its end, relations are much improved with the Hidatsa, and might even be termed convivial. Their friendship with the Mandans, with whom they have spent many meals, many moons, is sealed. April 6, 1805, is their last night at Fort Mandan.

Karl Bodmer, Joslyn Art Museum, Omaha, Nebraska

Although painted almost thirty years later, artist Carl Bodmer captures the essence of the vast herds of bison along the Missouri seen by Lewis and Clark.

Feasting on the North Plains

April – July, 1805

Treat the earth well.
It was not given to you by your parents, it is loaned to you by your children.
We do not inherit the earth from our ancestors, we borrow it.

— NATIVE PROVERB

ND SO THE ABUNDANCE OF SPRING lays across the land and in the air above. To the men canoeing in this lushness, these sights and sounds and smells are balm to the soul. The *Journals* record the wonder of this natural bounty.

Lewis: *"we saw a great number of brant passing up the river ..."* J4:14

this creek ... passes ... through beatifull, level, and fertile plains ..." J4:16

Clark: *"flowers in the praries to day ..."* and *"Great numbers of Gees feeding ..."* J4:17

Ordway: *"handsome bottoms plains hills & vallies &.c. we Saw flocks of Goats ... and Gangs of buffaloe ..."* J9:131

Gass: *"We saw a great many buffaloe and elk on the banks. ... in a few minutes killed 2 buffaloe."* J10:80

Overhead the honking V-shaped wings of geese are passing, calling to each other, and there are the sounds of swishing buffalo tails keeping the buzzing flies at bay. The warm smell of the soil intermingles with fragrant bushes, grasses, and flowers issuing up from the newly reborn land. Spring is as heady and exuberant as the party itself.

This fresh season brings new variety to the menu – the end of meager meat and unvarying pots of corn meal mush. They are living mostly off the land with some of their previously reserved provisions, the carbohydrates. The precious barreled meats will be saved for emergency rations.

So, what does their diet include this April, 1805? The *Journals* provide two contradictory conclusions: (1) it is bountiful, plentiful, and satisfying or (2) it is still hard going. Lewis sums up both views most succinctly, *"we sent out four hunters who soon added 3 Elk 4 gees and 2 deer to our stock of provisions. the party caught six beaver today which were large and in fine order. the Buffaloe, Elk and deer are poor at this season, and of cours not very palitable, however our good health and apetites make up every necessary deficiency, and we eat very heartily of them."* J4:55 In other words, to hungry men food tastes good!

This spring the menu is replete with natural abundance: meat items are high on the list, followed by poultry entrees. Ordway presents a puzzle, a biologic anomaly, on April 30 – describing an immense *"70 or 80 pound"* goose which *"had large young ones in it,"* instead of eggs. The meager fish list has *"small fish,"* *"several fish,"* and *"a quantity"* of small catfish.

With a certain amount of indifference, several other dinner items get tucked into the list: Ordway making an obligatory note of a gill of spirits being doled out, and mentioning onions. The Captains have far fewer items but some of them are very different from what the troops are eating. So far, onions are the only vegetable mentioned. Lewis also adds Jerusalem artichokes, sagebrush (which reminds him of a variety of herbs rolled into one plant), previously wetted biscuit cooked along with meat, and marrow-bones, an elitist treat. Clark spots wild onions or garlic, he isn't sure which, and both Captains make a terse observation on the beverage of the day, *"unfit drinking water."*

Ordway records the greatest variety, from eggs to liquor, and it's almost a sure bet that Silas Goodrich, the Corps' fisherman, is not far away considering the amount of fish caught. Clark's version is fairly pedestrian, and Lewis' emphasis on marrow-bones, tongue, and buffalo calf (veal) is

THE PLAINS PANTRY

Sergeant Ordway, a good detail man, records the largest variety of foods. Here's what he saw going over the campfire from April 9–27, 1805:

- 35 beaver, 1 listing of beaver tail (no doubt given to the Captains)
- 10 deer
- 1 white-tailed deer
- 1 deer liver (eaten by Lewis only)
- 8 elk
- 5 buffalo and "several" noted two different times
- 5 buffalo calves or veal and "several"
- 2 buffalo tongues
- 3 antelope
- 1 white rabbit
- 1 muskrat
- 1 otter
- 1 grizzly bear

For poultry, the men devour:

- 15 geese
- 13 goose eggs and "several nests [worth of eggs]"
- 2 bald eagles
- 1 white swan

Michael Haynes

Sgt. Ordway is one of the most observant and detailed of the enlisted journalists.

more elitist, perhaps the gourmet speaking?

This brief sketch gives an idea of the substantial choices of food to be found on the Plains. However, this is still early spring, and the grasses have just begun to emerge from the newly thawed land – a nutritious fresh spring browse but not yet enough for lean animals to flesh-out after a difficult winter. The full abundance of summer is still several months ahead. The geese, eggs, plump beaver, and fish are probably in better shape than the mammals, with the exception of the buffalo calves. Being milk-fed, they are plump and pleasing, and best yet – easy to catch. The Captains record different fruits in bloom, but it is too early in the season for those to be plucked and popped into the mouth. Again, as the Mandan winter, the Corps is off-season. But it is this great abundance of meats, this apparent plentitude which will, in just a few short months, lead the Captains into some decisions which may be questionable.

Onward Up the Missouri

Breaking the party into at least two parts is a common mode of operation. One captain (they seem to alternate as the mood strikes) goes ahead on land, often accompanied by one of the hunters. The rest of the party comes along in the canoes and pirogues, sailing upwind against the current if the weather is willing. Otherwise they are paddling and rowing upstream, building up a tremendous caloric debt.

Lewis specifies this on Thursday, April 11, 1805. *"Set out at an early hour; I proceeded with the party and Capt Clark with George Drewyer walked on shore in order to procure some fresh meat if possible. we proceeded on abot five miles, and halted for breakfast, when Capt Clark and Drewyer joined us; the latter had killed, and brought with him a deer which was at this moment excepable as we had had no fresh meat for several days."* [It appears that Lewis is forgetting the beaver tails given to them the day before by three trappers. J9:128-9] Being quite loquacious that day, Lewis continues – elaborating on the hunting conditions. *"the country from fort Mandan to this place is so constantly hunted by the Minetaries (Hidatsa) that there is but little game we halted at two P.M. and made a comfortable dinner on a venison stake and beavers tales with the bisquit which got wet on the 8th ..."* Nothing is wasted.

Ordway records dinner at 2 PM, and elaborates further on the meal composition. There are two beaver, a deer, and three geese killed the night before; and since poultry grows bacteria faster than any other food, those geese must have gone straight onto the spit. They wouldn't have been carried along waiting for a better picnic site some other day.

Lewis likes red meat and succulent, moist beaver tail

On April 6, 1805, the Corps leaves Fort Mandan in the two pirogues and newly made dugout canoes heading up the Missouri, and the keelboat is dispatched downriver back to St. Louis.

R. L. Rickards - courtesy: Rickards Western Art

better than goose, but geese form the bulk of the days' catch. Jefferson's gourmet Captain commandeers his favorite pieces, and this is not unusual. Privilege goes with rank and the most powerful individuals pick and choose as a matter of course. Beaver tail and steak are the Captain's Choice.

Since there is too little red meat, an immediate adjustment is called for, and the next day Lewis corrects the situation by sending out a party of ten men to hunt in hopes of improving the odds. Furthermore, on April 12, his keen eye picks up on a singular detail of beaver behavior that is important to the party as a whole: *"the beaver being seen in the day, is a proof that they have been but little hunted, as they always keep themselves closly concealed during the day where they are so [hunted]."* It would be easy to speculate that there are no Indians in the vicinity but for the second day in a row he complains that earlier parties of Hidatsa have scared the game away. This observation infers that the Hidatsa do not relish beaver.

The Captains' conclusion is to think of the familiar Hidatsa, and not jump to alarm-status thinking of other hostile tribes. It takes a scattering of metal barrel hoops to convince them that the previous Indian presence they are sensing is not the security of the friendly teetotaling Hidatsa, but Assiniboine. Lewis raises the flag of concern: *"as they are a vicious illy disposed nation we think it best to be on our*

guard." J4:136 Clark, having encountered two recently deserted large encampments, writes, *"no other nation on the river above the Sioux make use of Spiritous licquer."*

Meat is never the sole ingredient on the menu if vegetables are available. Although the arduous job of canoeing upstream affords little enough time for gathering fresh roots and greens, sometimes those nutritious wild things are scarce even when sought. On April 12, the men are delighted to find fields of small onions near that nights' encampment and cook them up, finding them quite *"agreeable."*

While beaver, geese, and eagles are being turned into supper, the availability of hearty game improves only as grasses and other browse mature. *"the Game is getting pleantyier every day."* J9:133 But even at the end of April the condition of the animals, and therefore their menu selections, is still not particularly desirable. *"Saw a buffaloe Swim the river close before us but would not Shoot him for he was not fat."*

While the spiritual outlook on hunting for the natives is not the same for the Americans, every shooting member of the Corps declines to overhunt or kill for pleasure. Their inclination is to take only what is needed and kill only what looks sufficient. Sometimes, though, they are forced into the position of leaving behind carcasses ... *"very poor,"* *"meagre,"* *"unfit for use."*

A Few Bear Stories

While the men marvel at the huge throngs of hoofed animals that are docile, curious, or unimpressed with the party, the terrible and awesome grizzly gets everyone's attention and

Karl Bodmer, collection of the James Jerome Hill reference library

Beaver hunting adds to the Corps' tasty meat supply.

respect. This eventually will include a humbled Lewis who had earlier derided the Indians' fear of the monster bear. Although recently re-designated as *Ursa arctos horribilis*, its earlier scientific name, *Ursa horribilis horribilis*, clearly designated a double warning as explicit as the universal skull and crossbones.

By late spring, just past the confluence of the Yellowstone River, the grizzly are becoming more numerous, and the men are becoming more acutely aware of the danger. In a grand tribute to faith in European technological superiority, Lewis writes on April 29, 1805, *"the Indians may well fear this anamal equiped as they generally are with their bows and arrows or indifferent fuzees, but in the hands of skillfull riflemen they are by no means as formidable or dangerous as they have been represented."* J4:85 Lewis believes it is simply a matter of having the right gun, a new, modern rifle rather than an outdated and technically inferior fuzee.

The same day Clark writes that Lewis and another man killed a yellow bear (a color variation of the grizzly) and wounded another. Lewis finds this easy. But the bear is a juvenile male, not yet fully grown and weighs a mere 300 pounds or so. They haul the meat onboard. In a dazzling show of arrogance, they disbelieve native hunters who have gone against this living nightmare time and again, and who rightfully wear bear claw necklaces as a sign of extreme bravery. This attitude lasts exactly seven days. *"Capt. Clark and Drewyer killed the largest brown bear this evening which we have yet seen. it was a most tremendious looking anamal, and extreemly hard to kill notwithstanding he had five balls through his lungs and five others in various parts."* J4:113 What the Captain still doesn't recognize is the aggressive and confrontational nature of the beast, for this particular bear retreated and did not attack. In what modern sensibilities might find a disturbing and oddly sad episode, the bear made *"the most horrendous roaring from the moment he was shot ... and it was at least twenty minutes before he died ... "*

Having taken out the enemy, they measure him – over 8½ feet tall, 500 to 600 pounds (the Captains disagreed), and almost 4 feet around at the neck. A healthy specimen, the bear is divided among the messes and the fat rendered down and stored in kegs for future use. Lewis, always alert to the small details, notes that the fat is *"as hard as hogs lard when cool, much more so than that of the black bear."* J4:113 When considering the prospects of making candles and choosing which container for storage, the hardness of various fats becomes important.

Two particular traits of the grizzly are important in the context of geography. While the black bear originally is a forest creature and relatively timid, the grizzly is a Plains predator. As a species it is fast on its feet and broadly omnivorous – a serious competitor to man in the food chain. The *Journal* entry for May 5, 1805 notes that the bear's stomach contains both fish and flesh, and that roots and *"almost every species of wild fruit"* comprised the rest of the diet.

Overnight contemplation of the situation has its results. The next day, May 6, Lewis has had enough excitement, and the thrill of the bear is overshadowed by a serious and very real concern for the safety of his troops. *"I find that the curiossity of our party is pretty well satisfyed with rispect to this anamal ..."* But he worries that some of the young macho men are still undeterred, for they still *"seem keen for action with the bear ..."* J4:118

Even if they aren't out intentionally provoking the bears, the human presence is still pervasive. On May 14 another solitary walker shoots a grizzly, and this time the backup hunters are in for a full terror shootout which comes close to being a massacre, with the Corps on the wrong side. Six of the hunters in the rear canoes come upon the wounded bear about 300 paces from the river, and thinking that this should be relatively easy, hop out to kill the animal. By now they are more savvy and a bit more cautious. They sneak up on the bear, then four men shoot and the other two hold their fire as a precaution. The monster scrambles to its feet and charges, roaring in their faces and in hot pursuit. The two men who had held their fire until now shoot directly at him, one a feeble hit, the other bullet breaking his shoulder. *"... this however only retarded his motion for a moment only, the men unable to reload their guns took to flight, the bear pursued and had very nearly overtaken them before they reached the river; two of the party betook themselves to a canoe and the others seperated,"* reloading and firing from their hiding spots in the willows. Hit again and again, the wily old bear charges in the direction of the gunfire and chases down his tormenters, two of whom jump off a twenty-foot cliff into the river. *"... so enraged was this anamal that he plunged into the river only a few feet behind the second man ... "* It is only a final shot in the head that stops this *Horribilis*. When his body is dragged to shore, it is found to have eight (Whitehouse says nine) balls in it with four major hits: two through the lungs, one through the shoulder bone, and one through the head. Whitehouse records a telling description, *"his feet was nine Inches across the ball and 13 in length his nales was Seven Inches long ... "* This was a gargantuan brute! Lewis is both relieved and appalled at the near miss from *"ruinous injury."*

Awestruck, terrified, and finally relieved, the men have now come full circle from cockiness to respect to downright fear. Clark, with impressive coolness, notes that *"indeed he had like to have defeated the whole party."* From this adventure they gain more experience, one bearskin, and enough rendered fat for several gallons of oil. The Corps has finally learned what the Indians preach: always go in a party of six to ten men; pray a lot; be prepared to die.

It's Big!

The astonishing report of a seventy or eighty pound goose that Ordway mentions on April 30, 1805, is just one more episode marking the Corps' fascination with "Big!" that carries straight on throughout the Expedition. The *Journals* note the immense blue catfish, the tremendous grizzly, and the huge buck elk, which in all likelihood would have towered head and antlers over the average engagé. It doesn't take long to realize that the West is on a grander, larger scale than the East, and the results are awe-inspiring.

Hard Weather

Even early spring is grandly and hugely ferocious, and hugely miserable. Ice freezes in the kettles to a depth of a quarter-inch overnight, winds *"blow with astonishing violence,"* flukey and cold – basically out of the north. Lewis notes that it has been seven and a half months since he has seen rain (as opposed to snow) and at the end of the month, *"Vegetation has progressed but little since the 18th in short the change is scarcely perceptible."* [J4:95] Winter is ending hard. On April 27, Clark notes that the morning temperature is 32°F, square at the freezing point. Nearly a month later, one northwesterly is so bad that *"we found ourselves so invelloped with clouds of dust and sand ... we could neither cook, eat, nor sleep ..."* [J4:176] They are obliged to pack up camp and flee into the lee of some cliffs for protection.

Geographic Variability

Geographical range for both plants and animals is one of the variables noted over and over throughout the *Journals*. The land from the Dakotas to the Rockies is prairie country. Tall grasses wave their tasseled tops in the winds and turn from spring green to gold, and this browse beckons both animals and birds – which are followed in turn by the predators. More abundant vegetation clings, twines, and jostles for space along the river valleys and shorelines. There are outbreaks of forested areas. Edible migratory birds such as brant or geese fly in, and there is food in abundance.

Eventually the prairies meld into the territory where the great river tributory systems converge at Three Forks – the Madison, the Jefferson, and the Gallatin – forming the mighty Missouri. Marshy areas give way to the first hillocks of the Rockies, and the native grasses become thin and sparse, barely able to support life – be it Indian, animal, or the Corps. The indigenous species found within these changing ecosystems have adapted, and in many cases are only minutely different in form (for example: varieties of currants) or in range (white versus black-tailed deer). Some differences will go unnoticed until decades later when a firmer grasp on biology prompts regulations hitherto unknown. In the late 1800s, Yellowstone National Park will actually forbid the mixing of plains and mountain buffalo, two sub-species, within the park.

But botanical and biological sciences are in their infancy in 1800. Linnaeus has finalized his ultimately elegant system of species classification. Animal taxonomy is in the future. Armed only with the most rudimentary knowledge, but vast practical experience, the Corps marches on – hunting, eating, and making observations that will be sorted out over the next two hundred years. During this segment of the trip the hunters begin bringing in mule or black-tailed deer. The primary deer until this point, ranging far west from their first observed home in Virginia, has been the eastern white-tailed deer. On May 10, Lewis sees a new mixture of the two species, with the astute observation that *"from the appearance of the Mule deer and the bighorned anamals we believe ourselves fast approaching a hilly or mountainous country; we have rarely found the mule deer in any except a rough country."*

The plains of Montana are also an admixture of zones for the currant, which Sacagawea recognizes and points out to Clark.[a] To even her keen eye, a currant is a currant and therefore good to eat, although botanists note that the species she grew up recognizing is locally specific to the Rockies and she mistakenly believes the ones she is seeing to be the same. [J4:90n3] *"the Squar found & brought me a bush Something like the Current, which She Said bore a delicious froot and that great quantites grew on the Rocky Mountains ... the froot when ripe is yellow and hangs in bunches like <graps> Cheries, Some of those berries yet remained on the bushes."* [J4:89] Identification is made more difficult because, again, the Corps is off season and are seeing dried fruit from the previous year and it is too early for this year's crop. But in just this hundred or so miles, there are six different types of currants: the buffalo, the garden, the golden, the squaw, the swamp, and the wild black. The fruit colors range from red to

---

[a] They could be seeing: the buffalo currant, the golden currant, and the wild black currant. Sacagawea is in a zone where they coexist, and she mistakes her native golden currant for the actual buffalo currant.

orange, yellow, and then purple to black. So close are they in structure and appearance that springtime identification often hinges on the comparative lengths of the blooming flowers, a difficult chore indeed, if these subspecies don't grow in immediate proximity.

Furthermore, Lewis is confused. On July 25, he is describing *"a red as well as a yellow species of gooseberry"* while Clark simultaneously is making note of *"Mountain Currents."* Both men are probably referring to the squaw or western red currant. J4:429n6 Are they happy with the supposedly delicious fruit of Sacagawea's memory? Neither is impressed with the desirability or flavor of the fruit, Lewis calling it an *"indifferent fruit"* J4:427 and Clark describing it as *"inferior in taste."* J4:429 The only good thing that comes of their discovery is that Lewis decides to ship the seeds back as part of his collection of native plants.

Geese or brant are another family that fall from the flyways into the dinner pot, and Ken Walcheck, researcher and ornithologist, notes that waterfowl experts now count eleven subspecies of Canada goose, ranging from those which feed in the tall grass prairies to those which feed in the short grass prairies – one of these subspecies is most likely the birds that appear on May 5. Lewis, ever meticulous, notes that they look like the common or Canadian goose, have the same color and number of tail feathers, but are thicker in *"their neck head and beak ... a third smaller, and their note more like that of the brant or a young goose which has not perfectly acquired his notes ..."* Given his inexperience in the West, the scientifically minded Captain comes very close to a perfect identification. Another treat for the men is gathering eggs. Goose eggs are a consistent part of the Corps' diet for about a month, after which hatching or onward travel changes the scene. How the eggs are used are used is a matter of speculation, but they are popular.

Sacagawea's Gleanings

Although game is abundant, edible vegetation is not too prominent on this mostly carnivorous expedition. Sacagawea's gleanings bring some balance to the Captains' diets – there is no direct evidence that she gathered extras to be distributed among the other messes. Considering the value of this woman's gathering efforts, it would be as an enhancement to health rather than a significant substitute for the huge volume of food being served. However, there is now evidence of increased nutritional superiority of eating "the wild things" versus cultivated crops.[152]

Lewis mentions *"wild Licquorice ... found on the sides of these hills, in great abundance"* J4:125 which Sacagawea gathers

as food, along with another Plains staple called breadroot. For winter storage this vegetable would be dried and then threaded into a necklace of sorts.

PLANT AND FOOD NAMING

Various names are given to foods depending on the region of the speaker. Breadroot is also: pomme blanche (French), white apple (English translation of pomme blanche), prairie apple, prairie turnip, scurf-pea. Another example is Sage grouse, which becomes: sage hen, cock of the plains, cock of the prairie, prairie cock, mountain cock, white booted turkey, and heath cock.[153]

Three Bad Days

May 14–16, 1805, are three particularly hair-raising days. An enraged grizzly begins the run of bad luck on the first day, and a sudden, violent windstorm blows in the next day. The white pirogue, which has been under sail, nearly sinks and Charbonneau, at the helm, panics. Cruzatte, the one-eyed boatman, threatens to shoot him if he doesn't control the tiller, Sacagawea is feverishly trying to save items floating by while holding onto baby Pomp, and the Captains are shooting off their guns to alert the crew to the danger. It is total chaos. Ferociously high waves crash into the tiny vessel. Only after men cut down the sail does the pirogue right itself, and only after taking in water to within an inch of the gunnels.

The men who can't swim are praying fervently. Cruzatte, the happy fiddler, roars orders to man the kitchen kettles and bail. Others row toward shore. Eventually they get the sinking vessel to the bank. From the food perspective it is not disastrous. Some gunpowder disappears, but the provisions dry and they merely lose *"a few culinary articles which fell overboard and sunk."* J4:156 Lewis, who is frantic and almost jumps into the cold, swift river before his sensibilities return, finally – and calmly – notes the loss of *"some gardin seeds"* destined for Jefferson. The episode is so traumatic that the Captains *"thought it a proper occasion to console ourselves and cheer the sperits of our men and accordingly took a drink of grog and gave each man a gill of sperits."* J4:153

If bad luck comes in threes, the third is a close encounter with another high-up competitor on the food chain, a *"panther."* Although they are not being hunted directly, the cat is quite near their camp and happily devouring a deer. Probably it would not have been a menace, but if it is hungry or annoyed by their proximity, who knows? The hunters shoot

Charbonneau almost capsizes the pirogue on May 15, 1805.

R. L. Rickards - courtesy: Rickards Western Art

it, apparently without a qualm, preventing trouble before it could get started. This is the first of three panthers eventually shot. Score: two killed, one wounded and escaped.

Days of Plenty

The Corps has been feasting through the northern Plains. The meats – antelope, beaver, bear, buffalo calf, buffalo, common and mule deer, elk, game birds, wolf – all smell delicious roasting over the campfire. Now, deer are fat, beaver plentiful. Each Captain walks the shore regularly providing game, in addition to what the hunters and trappers are providing. Nature's bounty is all around; there is no lack of abundance; not one voice is declaring hunger. This interlude is important in setting the stage for what provisions will be cached just a week or so in the future as they prepare to portage the Great Falls.

The only lack is pure clear water. What they have tastes salty or alkaline, but they drink it anyway. They pass Milk River, chastely white from the alluvial sediment found in its waters. The Corps trudges past Big Dry River and innumerable dry creeks. Lewis wistfully pens, *"I have not seen a bould fountain of pure water except one since I left the Mandans; there [NB: are] a number of small ones but all without exception are impregnated with the salts which abound in this country, and with which I believe the Missoury itself considerably impregnated ..."* J4:171

Ordway believes the Missouri is not as muddy as lower down, but it still has the same color. Apparently intrigued with the issue of water, he records on May 22, *"Many of the creeks which appear to have no water near their mouths have Streams of running water high up which rise & waste in the Sand or gravel the water of these creeks are so much impregnated with the Salt Substance that it cannot be drank with pleasantness."* Four days later, he again notes the land and its nonexistent water: *"this country may with propriety be called the Deserts of North america for I do not conceive any part of it can ever be Setled as it is deficient of or in water except this River ..."*J9:155 He may have been wrong about settlements, but much of Montana is today considered a high desert with only twelve to fourteen inches of rain annually.

Uncharacteristically, Goodrich is not catching fish. *"we have caught but few fish since we left the Mandans, they do not bite freely, what we took were the white cat of 2 to 5 lbs. I presume that fish are scarce in this part of the river."* J4:180 If fish don't thrive in the river, at Teapot Creek there is a turnabout, *"all the wild anamals appear fond of this water."* Lewis himself tries the water, pronounces it *"unfit for use"* and in an experiment notes it to be, *"moderately pergative, but painfull to the intestens in it's opperation."* J4:183

Changing Ecosystems

There are signs, however, that the geography is changing. Trees are giving way to scrub pine and cedar, *"nine tenths of the country being wholy destitute of timber of any kind, covered with a short grass, arromatic herbs [sage] and the prickley pear."* J4:170 On May 21, Lewis further notes that the *"... praire hen are now less abundant on the river than they were below ..."* and wonders whether they've changed habitats. Game is not so abundant. Clark, out on an evening walk, discovers gumbo, a tremendously sticky alluvial till soil created during the last Ice Age. This name probably stems from the thick and elastic soup of the same name. He properly notes that it has little or no vegetation, which doesn't bode well for fruits or vegetables in their diet.

By the end of May they have traversed about one-third of present-day Montana. For the first time the Rockies are in sight. Lewis' philosophy?

while I viewed these mountains I felt a secret pleasure in finding myself so near the head of the heretofore conceived boundless Missouri; but when I reflected on the difficulties which this snowey barrier would most probably throw in my way to the Pacific, and the sufferings and hardships of myself and party in them, it in some measure counterballanced the joy I had felt in the first moments in which I gazed on them; but as I have always held it a crime to anticipate evils I will believe it a good comfortable road untill I am compelled to beleive differently. J4:201

Although the game continues to be present, a wee hint of scarcity begins to creep into the diaries. Clark writes on May 23: *"Saw but five Buffalow a number of Elk & Deer & 5 bear & 2 Antilopes to day."* This is certainly a decrease from the vast herds, the thousands of animals, they encountered previously. On May 24, Lewis notes, *"game is becoming more scarce, particularly beaver, of which we have seen but few for several days the beaver appears to keep pace with the timber as it declines in quantity they also become more scarce."* Since beaver and buffalo calves are the Corps' dinner of choice, these two reports are unsettling. The Captains change strategies and leave behind two canoes and six men to *"dress the Cow and bring on the meat,"* meaning they can no longer afford to eat on the spot and proceed without saving the remaining meat. Moreover, Lewis is upset by the prospect of diminishing game, *"buffalow are now scarce and I begin to fear our harvest of white puddings are at an end."* J4:195

Boudin Blanc or White Pudding

Lewis' lamentation revolves around the most complicated preparation of buffalo cooked on the trip, a handmade sausage. Charbonneau's *boudin blanc* (white pudding) is distinctly French in origin, the name itself showing that a white meat is the favored choice. Veal might be used in an area where dairy cows produce a surplus of male calves. Pork, "the other white meat," is currently used for this sausage. Instead of white meat, the Expedition adapts and relies on what the hunters bring in. The sausage is not white, but a deep brown – for buffalo is, after all, a deep-red, lean meat.

The *Journal* entry of Thursday, May 9, 1805 by Lewis gives us a sense of the mouth watering expectation which precedes dinner on these nights:

> *Capt C. killed 2 bucks and 2 buffaloe, I also killed one buffaloe which proved to be the best meat, it was in tolerable order; we saved the best of the meat, and from the cow I killed we saved the necessary materials for making what our wrighthand cook Charbono calls the <u>boudin blanc</u>, and immediately set him about preparing them for supper; this white pudding we all esteem one of the greatest delacies of the forrest, it may not be amiss therefore to give it a place.*

The cuts of meat used are the most tender (beneath the shoulder blade and the filets), adding to the sausage's delicacy. The suet adds moisture and flavor to the lean buffalo meat, and flour serves as a binder. Using the gut as a sausage skin is an ancient technique and it contributes to the flavor of the finished *boudin* (permeated as it is with salts and minerals) as does the *"good coat of fat"* on the intestine wall.

Here follows Lewis' description of this favorite entree:

BOUDIN BLANC
CHARBONO'S HIGHLY ESTEENED SAUSAGE, OR WHITE PUDDING J4:131

About 6 feet of the lower extremity of the large gut of the Buffaloe is the first mosel that the cook makes love to, this he holds fast at one end with the right hand, while with the forefinger and thumb of the left he gently compresses it, and discharges what he says is <u>not good to eat</u>, but of which in the squel we get a moderate portion; the mustle lying underneath the shoulder blade next to the back, and fillets are next saught, these are needed up very fine with a pood portion of kidney suit [suet]; to this composition is then added a just proportion of pepper and salt and a small quantity of flour; thus far advanced, our skilfull opporater C–o seizes his receptacle, which has never once touched the water, for that would intirely distroy the regular order of the whole procedure; you will not forget that the side you now see is that covered with a good coat of fat provided the anamal be in good order; the operator sceizes the recepticle I say, and tying it fast at on end turns it inwards and begins now with repeated evolutions of the hand and arm, and a brisk motion of the finger and thumb to put in what he says is <u>bon pour manger</u> [good to eat]; thus by stuffing and compressing he soon distends the receptacle to the utmost limmits of it's power of expansion, and in the course of it's longtudinal progress it drives from the other end of the receptacle a must larger portion of the [blank] than was prevously discharged by the finger and thumb of the left hand in a former part of the operation; thus when the sides of the recepticle are skilfully exchanged the outer for the iner, and all is compleatly filled with something good to eat, it is tyed at the other end, but not any cut off, for that would make the pattern too scant; it is then baptised in the missouri with two dips and a flirt, and bobbed into the kettle; from whence after it be well boiled it is taken and fryed with bears oil untill it becomes brown, when it is ready to esswage the pangs of a keen appetite or such as travelers in the wilderness are seldom at a loss for.

Boudin blanc frying in oil over a campfire at a
re-creation demonstration event in 2001.

Courtesy: C.H. Holland

BOUDIN BLANC –
LEWIS AND CLARK HONOR GUARD

As a modern interpretation, the following recipe was
showcased at a Lewis and Clark Trail Heritage Foundation
annual meeting:

Soak: 12 ft. of 2-3" sausage casing overnight in warm water

Cut: 2 lbs. of suet cut fine, or ground
(The aim is for about 10-15% fat, no more.)

Dice: 5 lbs. of beaver meat – if available
20 lbs. of buffalo roast or hump
⅔ whole tongue
a handful of liver – if available

In a gigantic bowl, mix finely diced meats together by hand.

Throw in a handful of freshly ground pepper, ½ palm of salt
(4-6T.), and 1-1½ Cups flour. You can add fresh wild
onions or ¼ of a red onion (a little sweeter than the
wild variety).

Mix thoroughly, until the meat is coated (it may feel a little
"slimy").

Stuff sausages, tying off the casing for each sausage.

Boil until done; then fry 'til brown.

Serves approximately 50 people.

Lewis loves his *boudin blanc* and is obviously loathe to
give it up, but the change of terrain is responsible.

Clark, Bratton, and Drouillard kill two bighorn sheep –
the first mentioned. These animals are denizens of rocky,
craggy places, the opposite of the prairie home of the buffalo. Surprisingly, food connoisseur Lewis has nothing to say
about the bighorn meat, but Clark does. *"The flesh of this animal is dark and I think inferior to the flesh of the Common
Deer, and Superior to the antelope of the Missouri."* J4:198

Meat is becoming more scarce as is firewood, but at least
the men have learned their lesson about grizzlies. Lewis
writes, *"One of the party saw a very large bear today but being
some distance from the river and no timber to conceal him he
did not think it proper to fire on him."* J4:212

Wolves are around, and contrary to the popular image,
they are well-fed, *"... fat and exteemly jentle."* J4:217 Clark kills
one with his espontoon and, knowing the men's propensity
to eat almost anything that moves, the meat is probably
eaten,[b] although it is not noted at the time.

Bad weather and another upcoming shortage of wood
prompts them to put in for the night of May 29. The Corps'
sleep is interrupted in the wee hours by a buffalo bull running wildly through the camp, chased by barking Seaman,
and it's a wonder no one is trampled to death. They've had a
long day and it's time to call it a night, the second time. The
Captains deem it worthy of a drink and dispense a half issue
of spirits, *"several of them were considerably effected by it;
such is the effects of abstaining for some time from the uce of
sperituous liquors; they were all very merry."* J4:217 The next
morning several of the canoes are left behind as their crews
process the buffalo.

The area around the confluence of the Marias River with
the Missouri, just forty-two miles below the Great Falls, is a
Plains habitat. For all the lamentations about disappearing
game, it is now back into abundance. On June 3 Lewis
writes, *"the country in every direction around us was one vast
plain in which innumerable herds of Buffalow were seen attended by their shepperds the wolves; the solatary antelope which
now had their young were distributed over it's face; some herds
of Elk were also seen ..."* J4:247 Drouillard is earning his keep,
bringing in deer for breakfast and more for dinner, but
prairie hen leaves the menu. The men are suffering from cut
and abused feet and their pain finally causes complaining.
To improve spirits the Captains dole out alcohol, the great
soother.

---

[b] For more detail, see *Meats,* page 218.

A bull buffalo rampaging through camp awakens the Corps in the early hours on May 30th.

R. L. Rickards - courtesy: Rickards Western Art

From the Marias to the Great Falls

On June 4, the party splits up three ways: Lewis takes seven men to explore the Marias River, Clark takes six men and sets out to explore the Teton River, and the main party remains stationary. Clark's party fares well, on June 5 killing three grizzlies which are approaching their camp, and then two deer, *"verry fat."* They arrive back in camp, *"much fatigued"* after two days of hard hiking over difficult terrain. The main party waiting back at camp has, in the meanwhile, killed elk and buffalo.

Lewis' group is far less fortunate and very hungry, *"as we had not killed or eat anything today we each killed a burrowing squirrel as we passed them in order to make shure of our suppers."* These little animals have been alternatively identified as either prairie dogs, or Richardson's ground squirrels; whichever, they are *"roasted by way of experiment and found the flesh well flavored and tender; some of them were very fat."* J4:259 At the end of the day they find the large game again and take five elk and a mule deer.

An empty Indian lodge shelters them on the night of the June 7, and a contemplative Lewis reflects, *"we had reserved and brought with us a good supply of the best peices; we roasted and eat a hearty supper of our venison not having taisted a mosel before during the day; I now laid myself down on some willow boughs to a comfortable nights rest, and felt indeed as if I was fully repaid for the toil and pain of the day, so much will*

a good shelter, a dry bed and comfortable supper revive the sperits of the waryed, wet and hungry traveler." J4:263 They are gone four days instead of two, the main party worries about their safety, and eventually Lewis' group returns exhausted – a liquor ration is dispensed to all hands.

Pushing ahead, Lewis and four men continue scouting to determine which river is the Missouri, their choice to follow through the Rockies. On June 10, feeling *"somewhat unwell with the disentary,"* the tough Captain proceeds on and, not unsurprisingly, becomes even more unwell. Thrown back on his own resources since they have no medicine, he brews up a chokecherry decoction and settles in, for *"... before the meal was prepared I was taken with such violent pain in the intestens that I was unable to partake of the feast of [elk] marrowbones ... finding myself unable to march I determined to ... remain all night."* J4:278

This is unremarkable, but what follows is quite exceptional. Lewis, cerebral creature that he is, may be violently sick (as in this case) or badly wounded (as on the return trip), but his mind doesn't turn off or blank out. He remarks that his pain *"still increased and towards evening was attended with a high fever"* but he's caught up in minutely describing two species of fish that Goodrich has brought in, the sauger and goldeye. He notes the type of bait used (grasshopper or deer spleen) and the eating qualities of both, preferring the goldeye to the sauger. By the next day Lewis is feeling much better, marches twenty-seven miles, and amuses himself by fishing – landing more sauger, which *"bit most freely."* J4:280

As the Corps approaches the Great Falls with the question finally resolved as to which river was truly the Missouri, their culinary world sparkles with gourmet dishes. Lewis, carried away with gustatory glad tidings exults, *"my fare is*

William Jacob Hays 1860

Lewis is fascinated by the large fields of prairie dogs - or as he calls them: *"Barking Squirrels"* or *"Burrowing Squirrels."*

The sight of the Great Falls of the Missouri on June 13, 1805, quickly convinces Lewis that the pirogues can not be portaged and have to be left behind. Therefore, supplies have to be reduced, with caches built to hold the excess until the return trip.

Charles Fritz, used by permission

really sumptous this evening; buffaloe's humps, tongues and marrowbones, fine trout [cooked in] parched meal pepper and salt, and a good appetite; the last is not considered the least of the luxuries." The gorgeous cutthroat trout, now named for William Clark [*Salmo clarkii*] are an angler's delight. Indeed, on that June 13, life is beautiful. All the men behold the glory of nature's abundance, *"vast flocks of geese which feed at pleasure in the delightfull pasture on either border"* and *"a herd of at least a thousand buffaloe."* These views graphically portray an America that has ceased to exist.

The Need for Caches

At the Marias River, the Captains decide to lighten the cargo load. The idea of a cache, that simple but elegant hole that held the Mandans' dried vegetables, now comes into play as Lewis contemplates the difficulty of paddling upriver. He decides to abandon the big red pirogue until they return. A quick survey of their goods convinces the Captains that extra weight and redundant materials can be held in safekeeping until their return trip. On June 10, 1805, a serious amount of food and some of the important beaver traps go into this cache – Lewis' list includes:

1 Keg of flour - 70 lbs. net
2 Kegs of parched meal - 140 lbs. net
2 Kegs of Pork - 140 lbs. net
1 Keg of salt - 20 lbs.
some tin cups

Whitehouse's list written the next day includes a Dutch oven [c] and a corn mill. J11:193

With the load now lightened, the Corps proceeds up the south fork, which the Captains determine to be the main river. Lewis, in an advance exploration, encounters the Great Falls only three days later.

The thundering, pounding roar of the Great Falls is all the Captains need to hear before deciding that the upriver trip is about to change dramatically. The other pirogue must be stored along with more supplies. Another cache is needed at Lower Portage Camp, and Cruzatte is appointed to supervise, being *"well acquainted [with] this business and therefore left the management of it intirely to him."* J4:269

The French river man has apparently learned the process well, for his cache (by Lewis' description) sounds just about like that of Buffalo Bird Woman. Clark reports that it takes seven men one day to build the cellar.

Five Good Reasons to Stash Food

◆ For months the Corps has been surrounded by Plains abundance. There seems to be plenty of food.
◆ Continuing to carry extra weight and gear over the Rockies is undesirable.
◆ The Captains believe that they are now approaching Shoshone lands and probably expect a hospitable welcome similar to those previously accorded them. A welcome feast or two, some food gifts.
◆ Geography, as visualized in 1800, is based on symmetry. If there are deer in Virginia and then the Appalachian mountains, symmetry would say that if the Rockies are before them, there should be deer awaiting them on the Pacific Coast.[d]
◆ A short trek over the Rockies, perhaps eight days, is

[c] This is the first, and only, mention of a Dutch oven, an interesting confirmation that items for which there are no purchase orders or receipts actually went along – further confirmation of the recent archeological campsite evidence for a three-legged cooking object.

[d] A belief promoted by John Mitchell (1711–1768), a distinguished and highly regarded scientist in many fields, and taken as fact by Jefferson.

expected. The contemporary belief is that the mountains are a single range, a deceptive and dangerous fallacy the Captains discover to their deep regret.[e]

On June 22, the Lower Camp cache is loaded with more foodstuffs: "... *2 Kegs of Pork, ½ a Keg 4* [f] *of flour.*" [J4:334] The weight here would be 140 pounds of pork and 70 pounds of flour.

Foodstuffs Cached below the Great Falls

Between the Marias River and the Lower Portage caches, the provisions stored are: 280 pounds of pork, 140 pounds of flour, and 140 pounds of corn. Total weight of edibles cached: 560 pounds of ingredients plus 20 pounds of salt. Lewis has just succeeded in eliminating over a quarter of a ton of weight and the volume of eight unwieldy containers. Each man now has about twenty less pounds to carry. Food, should they need it, is ready for the return trip. But it really doesn't matter to the men that they are taking hundreds of pounds of pork off the menu that day, for all the diarists agree with Whitehouse who marvels, "*we Saw great numbers of buffalow on the plains in every direction. the plain appear to be black with them.*" [J11:212]

Just Add Water

The weight of the supplies cached – 580 pounds – is a baseline measure, far less than the consumable yield. In other words, during the cooking process certain ingredients, particularly preserved or dried foods, will often gain weight and in the end produce more food per volume or weight than the original ingredients indicate. Measure a dry raisin in its shriveled state, and then plump it in water. Re-measuring after soaking will reflect the absorbed or added weight as well as an increased volume. This principle also works when adding water to dry ingredients such as corn or flour. When stewed, items like meat or preserved pork have an increased number of portions as a result of adding water to the meat as part of the cooking process. The resultant broth is an extra, filling part of the dish.

Pork – Pork, be it brined or salted, needs to be washed thoroughly to eliminate the salt residue and then cooked in enough water to take the pucker out of the end result. The amount of water to be used varies, but stew instructions usually read, "cover ingredients with water." This would probably be about a pound of meat to a pound (2 cups) of water – a ratio of 1:1.

Corn – Both the corn and flour would be mixed with water, in proportion to the dish being served. The parched corn is tempting in a combination cooked up with the preserved pork, for it would absorb and reduce some of the saltiness, thus enhancing the end product. It can also be a porridge by itself. A *Native American Gardening* recipe makes hominy grits with a 5:1 ratio (cups of water to cups of corn.)[154] Instructions from both *Indian Recipes*[155] and *Enduring Harvests* [156] make a corn gruel with a 3:1 ratio.

Flour – Analysis of the flour is more difficult as there is little mention of how it is used. Lewis made suet dumplings, and there is a possibility of flat breads, with a sticky dough, baked on embers or some nominal pancakes, perhaps leavened with goose eggs, and baked on a hot, flat rock. The amount of water would vary from 1:2 to 1:1.

Since some of the flour thickens the game soups into hearty stews, what are the cooking practices of the time for proportions? True to the British, or even more broadly, European customs, *The Virginia House-wife* emphasizes the importance of dredging the meat in flour before putting it on to brown, then boil.[157] No additional weight needs to be added for this use of flour because the water has already been accounted for with the meat.

What Did They *Really* Leave Behind?

Looking again at the potential meal weight of the food which was cached, totals show:

280 lbs. pork + 280 lbs. water = 560 lbs. pork stew
140 lbs. corn + 420 lbs. water = 560 lbs. corn meal mush
120 lbs. flour + 120 lbs. water = 240 lbs. dough
plus 20 lbs. of flour for thickening and dredging.

This gives approximately 1380 pounds of prepared food. If this amount is allocated at a 5 pounds of food per person per day, it yields enough for each member of a 34-person party to survive well for about eight days, or quite meagerly for a month.

Not everything is being cached, for there is "*a second alotment of baggage consisting of Parched meal, Pork ... bisquit, portable soupe*" [J4:334] as well as hunting/weaponry needs, tools, and trade goods to go on.

The caches then are a reasonable strategy to reduce supplies on the outbound trip and save them for future use on the way home. They are hidden, and thus secure. June 26

---

[e] Canadian explorer Alexander Mackenzie wrote that he had crossed in this amount of time. Lacking other information, the report was taken at face value. What was not expected were the difficult passes, the extent of the mountain ranges, and getting lost – especially with a guide.

[f] As it is unlikely that a half-full container would be cached, and because flour was initially packed in half-barrel sized containers (not "kegs"), it is more likely that Lewis meant a full half-barrel of flour.

buzzes into existence on the whining of mosquito wings. Charbonneau is rendering tallow and by the end of the day has processed three whole kegs of buffalo grease, 210 pounds. Lewis, in gourmet benevolence, *"made each man a large suet dumpling by way of a treat,"*g this to float in his buffalo-jerky stew.

Preparing to Portage

Even before the caches are built, decisions follow in logical order.

◆ Clark determines that the least painful route ends in grizzly terrain. Hunting grizzly for oil takes second seat to the very primary need of eliminating a fearsome adversary.

◆ Second, Lewis decides that as much meat as possible should be butchered and dried immediately so that the portaging efforts are not diluted by time spent hunting, transporting meat, and cooking it. *"my object is if possible while we have now but little to do, to lay in a large stock of dryed meat at this end of the portage to subsist the party while engaged in the transportation of our baggage &c to that end, that they may not be taken from this duty when once commenced in order to surch for the necessary subsistence."* J4:317

R. L. Rickards - courtesy: Rickards Western Art

The heavy dugout canoes and all on-going supplies have to be portaged up 500 feet and overland 18 miles around the five falls.

> ### THE DAILY GRIND:
>
> 5 AM   start – work until noon, 7 hours.
>
> 12 PM   dinner stop – the only respite is at the small Willow Run, about seven miles on the route which *"afford[s] plenty of fine water and a little wood."* J4:329 Red ripe currants grow here but Lewis reports men are too tired to pick berries. They are issued buffalo jerky; more than 600 pounds of dried meat is ready for consumption at Lower Portage Camp and Goodrich has provided several dozen dried (probably smoked) trout. J4:299
>
> 5 PM   or much later – The men reach one of the camps, always exhausted. Lewis is sometimes cooking at the upper camp, Charbonneau is cooking at the lower camp.

---

g See recipe in *Cooking Techniques*, page 61.

18 Miles and Too Tired to Eat – June 22 to July 2 , 1805

The back-breaking portage burns calories at a prolific rate for several wretched weeks. The Corps settles into a routine that is horrendous during the day and amazingly full of vitality at night. The tough, dirty, muscular young men struggle along a buffalo-rutted treadmill, going back and forth from one camp to the other, day after backbreaking day. They are pounded by weather vicious enough to kill them, eat dry, tough meat that demands laborious chewing, and suffer agonizing thirst. When they arrive back at lower portage camp, they immediately begin hauling canoes and goods up the dusty, steep canyon trail to the top of the plateau to get an early start for the next day's work. Finally, there's the reprieve of night. It's amazing how the end of a fourteen- to sixteen-hour day of exhausting labor can be transformed – by refueling over good grub and a little rest – into a miracle of joking, singing, and even more activity, those who *"were able to shake a foot amused themselves in dancing on the green to the music of the violin which Cruzatte plays extreemly well."* J4:332

What if you gave a dinner and no one came?

June 28 – Lewis plays host for a dinner with absentee guests: *"expecting the party this evening I prepared a supper for them but they did not arrive."* The weather has been 75°F accompanied by seven-inch hailstones and freezing rains. Are the men safe? Why haven't they shown up? Eventually the exhausted crew arrives later in the evening, and dines on fresh leftovers.

Clark has been struggling with logistical difficulties. The cottonwood wagons, trucks, or carriages (they are called all three) are falling apart under the strain of pulling such great weights on a rutted, demolished "road." Precious pork, flour, and ammunition are left behind for the time being. All these unexpected glitches mean that the troops are so delayed as to force them into spending a cold, star-studded night on the plateau, causing them to miss out on a nice, hot supper. Clark sees that his men are given fresh buffalo for their miseries and treats them to a dram of consolation. Always looking out for the troops.

The issue of cooking at the lower portage camp is more time-consuming than it had been earlier in the spring, for the issue of wood is pressing. Clark blames poor soil for lack of trees, noting *"the wood which we burn is drift wood which is broken to pieces in passing the falls, not one large tree longer than about 8 to 10 feet to be found drifted below the falls."* J4:332 Many trips just carrying wood will occupy quite a bit of time.

Sacagawea no doubt busies herself between baby and berry bushes. On June 25, Clark describes, *"great quantities of Choke Cheries, Goose burres, red & yellow berries, & Red & Purple Currents on the edges of water Courses in bottoms & damp places ..."* Influenced by living with Indians and being married to two of them, Charbonneau probably knows a few ways to incorporate these ripe berries into his cooking, or perhaps York takes over. Here there are no menus or descriptions of everyday food preparations, but a few guesses might be in order. Perhaps cornmeal is cooked up with a touch of sugar, then mixed with handfuls of fruit. How about "fritters" enriched with the pale blue and black speckled eggs of the large brown curloo which Clark notes laying around in nests on the ground? Perhaps they put by some newly-made pemmican. Maybe the berries went into a meat stew to make a complimentary dish of savory venison with a sweet-tart berry sauce.

Dealing with the Griz

The weather continues in a ferocious fashion on June 27 with *"violent Thunder, Lightning and hail &c."* and Lewis continues in his role as cook *"to keep all hands employed."* The smells of a good meal entice a nearby grizzly into poaching, leaving the men nervous and Seaman in a frenzy of barking. Lewis and Drouillard are occupied on July 1 with the continuing saga of rendering oil, and they put up another hun-

dred pounds (for future use in caulking the iron boat). The bear predations continue and the now-displeased Captain decides to convert the rest of them into tallow as well. The next day another grizzly goes into the rendering pot.

July 4, 1805 – Great Falls of the Missouri

Two years after the party at Monticello, with the Corps approximately 2600 miles away from their starting point, the Fourth dawns *"a beautiful clear pleasant warm morning,"* according to Ordway. The Corps has finished the grueling portage around the Great Falls, and the Sergeant reports, *"one of the hunters went on bear Island a Short time and killed an Elk and a beaver. we Saved the Skins and Some of the meat. we finished putting the Iron boat together ... it being the 4th of Independence we drank the last of our ardent Spirits except a little reserved for Sickness. the fiddle put in order and the party amused themselves dancing all the evening untill about 10 oClock in a Sivel and jovil manner."* Easy-going Clark enjoys the celebration and calls the amusement *"all lively and Chearful"*

Lewis, however, is overtaken by a more complicated mood; he is brooding but optimistic. *"we all beleive that we are now about to enter on the most perilous and difficult part of our voyage, yet I see no one repining; all appear ready to met those difficulties which await us with resolution and becoming fortitude."* The hazardous and arduous journey ahead does not deter the Corps from celebrating the nation's twenty-ninth birthday. *"our work being at an end this evening, we gave the men a drink of sperits, it being the last of our stock, and some of them appeared a little sensible of it's effects the fiddle was pleyed and they danced very merrily untill 9 in the evening when a heavy shower of rain put an end to that part of the amusement tho' they continued their mirth with songs and festive jokes and were extreemly merry untill late at night. we had a very comfortable dinner, of bacon, beans, suit [suet] dumplings & buffaloe beaf &c. in short we had no just cause to covet the sumptuous feasts of our countrymen on this day."*

Liquor, that beloved joy-maker, rewards the backbreaking work of the portage and reinforces the men's threadlike connection with the *"U. States of America."* It is the last big party with alcohol, and that almost-sacred Independence Day justifies its consumption, the final swan song of the empty keg. While drinking may still affect the privates, gone are the hostile, fighting outbreaks like those at Wood River. The team camaraderie surges into an approximation of the best of times back home, the Corps now being the family unit.

Alas, No More Boudin Blanc

As the Corps readies itself for the next leg of the trip, the messes need a bigger supply of pemmican, and again Lewis sends the hunters out for buffalo. This time it is with sadness in his heart and hunger in his belly, for the winter tribes told him that the Great Falls are the end of buffalo territory. *"... this I much regret for I know when we leave the buffaloe that we shal sometimes be under the necessity of fasting occasionally. and at all events the white puddings will be irretreivably lost and Sharbono out of imployment."* J4:354

The Hidatsa are correct, for the hunters came back with just one buffalo and a mere two antelopes. Clark actually orders a retrograde trip back to the area that had been so dense with the enormous beasts: *"4 men in 2 canoes to the falls to kill Buffalow, for their skins & meat."* J4:364 The great herbivores had no particular intent in staying put, and the hunters *"reported that the buffaloe had gone further down the river."* Whatever the case, the yearning of the men to get going is heightened by hordes of mosquitoes, biting gnats, and a sense that the summer season is being wasted at camp. The Captains are still for hunting, heavy loads of meat being brought in and dried – 200 pounds of fresh meat in just one day on July 12.

Hunting continues with a vengeance on July 13, for Lewis is ever mindful of the good advice given him by the Indians. *"meat now forms our food prinsipally as we reserve our flour parched meal and corn as much as possible for the rocky mountains which we are shortly to enter, and where from the indian account game is not very abundant."* J4:379

Fasting – First Signs?

Perhaps the days of fasting are approaching before the Captains fully realize. While the hunters still bring in adequate meat, Clark already noted on the 8th: *"the emense herds of buffalow which was near us a fiew days ago, has proceeded on down the river, we Can See but a fiew Bulls on the plains."* J4:368 Gone are the prairie hens. The buffalo are dispersing, seemingly the elk, too. As some fowl and game reduce, new items come to replace them. One new item is otter, those sleek little riverine animals who adore playing and eating fish – two on July 11 and two more on July 12, for *"the otter are now plenty since the water has become sufficiently clear for them to take fish."* J4:376

Certainly the land had provided for their great appetites during the trek across the Great Plains. But, now what?

From Great Falls to Three Forks – July 15–27, 1805

The eight canoes that pull out above the Great Falls are loaded – about five men to the vessel and bearing *"a considerable stock of dryed meat and grease."* All aboard are delighted to be underway. As usual, the solution for too many people

per canoe is for someone to walk with Lewis along the banks. Two elk miraculously appear and the party stops and dines on the spot. Skins, marrow bones, and more of the meat are loaded onboard. Twice in two days, contrary to Hidatsa wisdom: *"many herds of buffaloe were feeding in this valley."* J4:382

New varieties of edible vegetation appear, some of which Sacagawea knows. There are wild sunflowers, a native staple. Lewis recognizes *"the lambsquarter, wild coucumber, sand rush and narrow dock ... also common here."* J4:383 Three of the four are edibles, the fourth (sand rush) is used for scrubbing pots and pans. Clark notices stinging nettle, another potent food. J4:385 It is not clear if they eat any of these, so great is their hurry.

Green Stuff Sausage

There are still more surprises, for the gourmet officer decides to try a new treat, a native dish. *"here for the first time I ate of the small guts of the buffaloe cooked over a blazing fire in the Indian stile without any preparation of washing or other clensing and found them very good."* J4:386

This might be shocking to current sensibilities, but upon reflection the concept is less repugnant than it sounds.
✦ Indians eat this food without aversion.
✦ The animal is herbivorous and thus has very little grease or proteins – maybe a grasshopper or two – clogging up the drainpipe of a salad disposal system.
✦ It is well documented from Capt. Cook in Tahiti onward that vegetarian mammals have a far cleaner, purer taste than protein eaters.

Thus, a roasted buffalo gut might be arranged like a spinach sausage, the liner providing the luscious fats and flavoring of oils, and the stuffing being nutritious green stuff. Lewis, the sophisticated palate trained at Jefferson's table, finds it *"very good."* It is unlikely that the man who critiques slimy, insipid gooseberries and dislikes bitterroot will suddenly have a lapse of judgment regarding this "sausage." Certainly the native predecessors judge it as a fine bill of fare, too.

More Gourmet Reviews

Mid-July is full summer fare and the last of the plains is a golden carpet of sunflowers. Lewis remembers his culinary lessons from the Missouri River tribes and describes a few of their foods well, adding that he favors one that most nearly resembles a high-density protein bar, the Sunflower Rawdough Cookie.[h] Then he turns his attention to the berries,

[h] See recipe in *Plant Foods*, page 243.

the golden or yellow currant being his favorite. Meanwhile, the canoes ascend this upstream portion of the Missouri, and Lewis literally has his instruments hand-carried while the boats pass by Tower Rock, a difficult passage, but with no damage to the load of food.

Herds of bighorn sheep appear and disappear just as swiftly, and there is very little other game. The long-sought Shoshone Indians are nowhere to be found, and the Captains begin to worry that his technique for contacting the Indians will not work, fretting that *"the daily discharge of our guns, which was necessary in procuring subsistence for the party, should allarm and cause them to retreat to the mountains and conceal themselves ..."* J4:398 The only good thing noted is finally water in rivulets, *"... exceedingly cold pure and fine."* J4:399

Gates of the Mountains

Ahead of the explorers is the transition zone called the Gates of the Mountains. The heat is excessive, confined as it is in this mountain valley. Streams run free and clear, and the mammals are now either sure-footed mountain denizens or riverine stock like the ever-present beaver or playful otter. Transition zones embody surprises, and Lewis stumbles upon a gang of elk – promptly dispatching two of the large beasts. Clark, who has gone ahead with a small party seeking the Shoshone, hunts carefully: *"as we had no provision Concluded to kill Some."* J4:405 The meat is the positive part of the surprise, the lack of firewood a negative. Barbeque is done over a smoky buffalo-chip fire. But what has happened to those hundreds of pounds of dried meat? The hungry troops are eating voraciously. Sacagawea, reminding them of further scarcities, points out pine trees that have been deformed by natives, probably her own tribe, who eat the soft bark and collect sap as part of a starvation/scavenger diet. J4:403

Mosquitoes, prickly pear cactus, and other travails are taking their toll. Clark kills two elk and leaves them to be picked up, but one disappears and the other becomes a predator's leftovers – the remainder is merely skin and part of the flesh. The men are now towing and poling upriver in cold water and walking on broken rock. When they spot some swans that are still in molt, there is no question of what to eat. Two swans become supper, as do a number of geese that Seaman retrieves. Clark makes a cryptic note about catching *"a young curlooe which was nearly feathered."* J4:412 Most likely it goes into the pot like the young featherless geese.

The caloric output is creeping up while intake declines. The canoes are being moved at a rate of fifteen-plus miles a day. There is no wood – it has run out; and without a smoking fire to scare them off, the mosquitoes could carry off an undefended sleeper who might have forgotten his precious mosquito bier, that simple piece of gauze or cotton. Lewis praises these biers, declaring, *"it would be impossible for them [the men] to exist under the fatiegues which they daily encounter without their natural rest ..."* J4:412 Having forgotten his own cover a while back, the Captain knows of what he speaks.

Trout reappear. Berries are overwhelmingly abundant and delicious. On a small island Lewis and his party discover musket-ball–sized onions and rave about them like starving men finding manna. *"I called this beautifull and fertile island after this plant Onion Island."* J4:416 A considerable quantity of seed is gathered for shipment back East.

However, not all is well – on July 22, Clark notes: *"having nothing to eat but venison and Currnts, I find my Self much weaker ..."* J4:418 On the same day, Lewis – staid as he is – acts with a stunning display of spontaneity, or is it hunger? He shoots an otter, and in some quirk of nature it sinks to the bottom of the river, where he spots it, a good eight feet down. Without hesitation, he jumps in and brings dinner to the surface, immediately halting the company. What is he wearing? Probably, a buckskin war-shirt, cotton shirt, and leather or cloth britches. Strip off the shirts, the pants will dry soon enough. But think of this menu item, Otter with Sauteed Onions. Still more shocking is the effort of aristocratic Lewis learning to pole a canoe, which he does to encourage his men.

Even with a modicum of deer or antelope adorning the spit at night, Lewis still yearns for buffalo. He sighs, *"from the appearance of bones and excrement of old date the buffaloe sometime straggle into this valley; but there is no fresh sighn of them and I begin think that our harrvest of white puddings is at an end, at least until our return to the buffaloe country."* J4:423

Clark's advance party spots a wild Indian horse, but nothing results. The hunt for game goes on, grizzly now almost elusive. Lewis forbids the men to shoot at the young geese anymore *"as it waists a considerable quantity of amunition and delays our progress."* J4:426

The Extraordinary Salvation

On July 26, Clark on blistered and bruised feet takes two men from his advance camp on a twelve-mile side trip to the top of a mountain. Clark gives in to the effects of heat exhaustion, drinks cold water, and suddenly feels terrible. He marches on, returning to camp; finding dinner cooked, he feels *"so unwell that he had no inclination to eat."* J4:431 After dinner they continue marching and Charbonneau, who can't swim, is pulled into the river and is in danger of being swept away. Clark, for all of his debilitating symptoms, jumps into the frigid, rushing waters and saves the Frenchman's life. Going back to the Philadelphia test of health and ability to eat, Clark fails to pass the eating part of the test and decides to camp until he feels better. They kill two grizzly as some sort of bonus, but bears and men are both in poor condition, which says something of the local nutrients at the height of the summer growing season. J4:433

The Corps' main party is now working at the utmost physical exertion, *"the current still so rapid that the men are in a continual state of their utmost exertion ... and they begin to weaken fast from this continueal state of violent exertion."* J4:433 They are existing primarily on a diet of deer and berries, supplemented with otter, and on one day even a two-pound muskrat. Lewis, tense and under considerable pressure to find the Shoshone, worries, *"if we do not find them or some other nation who have horses I fear the successfull issue of our voyage will be very doubtfull or at all events much more difficult ... we are now several hundred miles within the bosom of this wild and mountainous country, where game may rationally be expected shortly to become scarce and subsistence precarious ..."* J4:437 But Lewis was not chosen by Jefferson for his pessimism. He continues, *"if any Indians can subsist in the form of a nation in these mountains with the means they have of acquiring food we can also subsist."* J4:437 With this sort of philosophy, it is small wonder that the Expedition succeeds.

The Captains view "These Terrible Mountains" from the summit of Lolo Pass on September 13, 1805; but the worst is still to come as food runs out and the meeting with the Nez Perce is still a week away.

R. L. Rickards · courtesy: Rickards Western Art

Fasting Over the Rockies

August – September, 1805

From this mountain I can observe
high rugged mountains in every direction as far as I can See
— CLARK, SEPTEMBER 15, 1805

I**N LATE JULY** 1805, in what will become western Montana, Clark's body succumbs to indisposition, and his recuperation gives the men time to restock the pantry with huge amounts of deer, which are pleasingly fat, and Lewis judges to be *"very fine."* The hunters no longer find those long-eared mule deer; there is a species shift to the western white-tailed deer. From feasting on venison to fasting takes only two days, and on July 31 there is an unsuccessful party-wide hunt to kill an elusive grizzly *"but he had escaped in some manner unperceived but how we could not discover."* The situation grows worse – *"nothing killed today and our fresh meat is out."* J5:17 The hungry young privates have been stuffing themselves when fresh game is brought in, and this is actually a rather irksome issue with Lewis. He is at a loss as to why the men gorge. He is more restrained and considers himself far more insightful. For the present, the Corps will experience a seesaw of plenty and privation, feasting and fasting.

The Seesaw of Plenty and Privation

On August 1, Whitehouse writes, *"it being Captain Clarkes birth day; he ordered some flour to be served out to to the party"* A second entry adds, *"which with the mountain Sheep made us an excellent meal ..."* J11:249-50

The party resumes its march, and it is Lewis' turn to feel unwell. Heat and dysentery (plus his purgative medical treatment) leave him fatigued, almost exhausted ... until he spots elk. *"I felt my sperits much revived ... at the sight of a herd of Elk, of which Drewyer and myself soon killed a couple."* The situation is seemingly fairly dire and definitely urgent,

for the hungry Captain orders two of the troops to go back for the meat while he and another man gather enough wood to start the fire. This demands a barbeque on the spot, because the pot for boiling is probably in the canoe. Dinner is cooked as quickly as possible. *"we made a comfortable meal on the Elk and left the ballance of the meat ... on the bank of the river for Capt. Clark and party. this supply will no doubt acceptable to them, as they had had no fresh meat when I left them for near two days except one beaver, Game being very scarce and shy ..."* The frustration of it is that *"we had seen a few deer and antelopes but had not been fortunate enough to kill any of them."* J5:26

Lewis becomes slightly fixated on how he's going to build a fire now that there are no buffalo-chips to burn; *"the mountains are extreemly bare of timber"* and *"a scant proportion of timber"* haunt his thoughts. And well it should, for suddenly there is a plethora of food to cook: the blue grouse (new on the menu), a bighorn, more deer. The food obviously had a salubrious effect, the Captain is satisfied, and *"after dinner we resumed our march and my pack felt much lighter than it had done about 2 hours before."* J5:27 The Corps is operating high on the list of primal needs here, and there's nothing better than hot food for an empty stomach. Just knowing food is available improves the disposition.

And it isn't all meat. Service berries are *"now ripe and in full perfection, we feasted suptuously on our wild fruit particularly the yellow courant and the deep purple servicebury which I found to be excellent,"* and unable to stop, the writer continues praising *"the superior excellence of it's flavor and size."* J5:31 But the pickers needed to be wary – the grizzlies are now beginning their process of stuffing themselves to prepare for winter. Despite several attempts, the bears still prove elusive and none are taken.

The caloric needs of the men with the canoes are being pushed to extremes beyond the Three Forks of the Missouri. The Jefferson's current is so strong that *"it required the utmost exertion of the men to get on, nor could they resist this current by any other means than that of the cord and pole."* J5:33 The daytime heat is sweltering. By August 3, Lewis and his men are above *"the Big Hole River"* J5:39n4 and have come some twenty-three miles, while Clark and the canoes make only thirteen miles – the low water requiring them to *"double man the canoes and drag them over stone and gravel."* Such exertions require heavy fuel, and it is deer for breakfast, deer for dinner. Trout is mentioned, as is a new fish – the northern sucker. It will show up on the menu in a few weeks.

This timberless land produces greater animal abundance than the Hidatsa had believed, the Beaverhead area still having sufficient water for vegetation, a powerful magnet for browsers. Clark spots some *"Deer Elk & antelopes & Bear in the bottoms."* There are *"great numbers of Beaver Otter &c. Some fish trout & and bottle nose. Birds as usial. Geese young Ducks & Curlows ..."* This is not an area devoid of resources, although their elusiveness is a different issue. The thorny buffaloberry also comes ripe.

More worrisome is the issue of finding the Shoshone. This urgent need propels Lewis and his interpreter, Drouillard, to go ahead of the canoe party, while Charbonneau – now derailed by a bad foot – walks ahead with Sergeant Gass. These two are given Lewis' and Drouillard's packs, which hold the meat rations, and are told to go ahead at their leisure to a point seven miles ahead. At the end of the day, a now-injured Drouillard and tired Lewis are forced to backtrack three miles in the dark through thickets of prickly pear cactus and pulpy-leafed thorn (greasewood) to reach Charbonneau and Gass, who apparently have eaten a fair amount of the meat. *"they had a small quantity of meat left which Drewyer and myself eat it being the first we had taisted today. we had traveled about 25 miles."* J5:45 Originally Charbonneau wanted to have his own private rations on the trip, an issue faced back at Fort Mandan and indicating a certain need to control the food supply. Tough Sergeant Gass is more likely to be egalitarian when sharing food among the troops, but Lewis' words are perhaps an intimation of displeasure with the final allocations.

The canoe party is faring no better, and the men are at the end of their ropes, literally. They are in *"great pain as the men had become very languid from working in the water and*

On the upper Jefferson River. The water becomes so shallow and rocky that the men are forced to tow the canoes with ropes.

R. L. Rickards - courtesy: Rickards Western Art

many of their feet swolen and so painfull that they could scarcely walk ... The men were so much fortiegued today that they wished much that navigation was at an end that they might go by land." J5:46 This is pure physical and psychological burnout, and Clark has no gills of whiskey to alleviate their pain or refresh them, since it ran out on July 4.

By August 6, three weeks after leaving White Bear Islands, Lewis records *"our stores were now so much exhausted that we found we could proceed with one canoe less."* This move has its advantages: *"we had now more ha[n]ds to spear for the chase; game being scarce it requires more hunters to supply us. we therefore dispatched four this morning."* J5:58

Lewis is meanwhile becoming quite desperate to find the missing tribe, and now goes out vowing to search until he does. *"it is my resolution to find them or some others, who have horses if it should cause me a trip of one month. for without horses we shall be obliged to leave a great part of our stores, of which, it appears to me that we have a stock already sufficiently small for the length of the voyage before us."* J5:59 The ugly and unwanted specter of starvation is already rearing its ugly head, even though it is still summer and game's aplenty.

The days continue with dawn marches and an 8 AM breakfast. Lewis is up and roasting two fine geese when Shannon appears after being missing for three days. On yet another day the main crew has one deer for all of them, but finds another carcass Lewis left hung on poles, waiting for them for a full three days. In restaurant parlance, it is hung and aged meat. After three days, this meat probably needed a good scrubbing in the river to cleanse it of the first layer of bacteria, and twenty-first-century food-safety inspectors wouldn't pass it. If the earlier quartermastering formula holds true (four deer to satisfy the Corps), then the party is now down to half-rations. Instead of nine pounds of meat per day, they are down to about approximately four and a half pounds – fasting is approaching.

On Sunday, August 11, Lewis' advance party spots a Shoshone warrior who promptly disappears. This leaves Lewis with the problem of how to demonstrate good will from a very long distance, and putting out an array of trade goods to indicate that they are both white and friendly should do the trick. Unfortunately it doesn't work. Lewis then decides eating is a good solution as it is nonthreatening and clearly indicates relaxation. *"I therefore halted in an elivated situation near the creek had a fire kindled of willow brush cooked and took breakfast,"* but breakfast and the peace signs are washed out by a heavy rain and hail. Bedraggled but still trailing the Indians, they come across horse tracks and an area where women have been digging roots.

The canoe party is similarly drenched and an understanding Clark boosts morale by starting the day with a warm breakfast rather than a cold pull in the stream. But this doesn't mean that everything is sweetness and light; there is a bit of desperation in the air. *"the men killed a beaver with a seting pole and tommahawked several Otter. the hunters killed three deer and an Antelope."* J5:71 Clark is facing discontent and he cajoles his men, but his sunny disposition is fading the next day as he grumbles, *"nothing to eate but venison."* He offers no treats to the men, no carbohydrates to raise the blood sugar.

Sacagawea's Elusive Tribe

The food situation is probably not much better for the Indian women and children who have been out digging roots, probably camas, for their winter supplies. Little, if any, animal protein is in sight, and what the Captains don't know is that the Shoshone have just taken a terrible beating from marauding Atsinas or Blackfeet sweeping down from the north. They are jittery and skittish to the extreme. As soon as the women finish the root harvest, the whole tribe is ready to leave on their annual buffalo hunt with their Flathead allies. Lewis, ever curious, tries to find specimens of what the women are digging but has no such luck: *"I could not discover the root"* but he sees that they have really *"toarn up the ground."*

On August 12, his small party eats the last of their venison, holding a *"small peice of pork in reserve."* J5:74 They spot a new type of bird, a sage grouse, but it flies away without becoming food in the pot. The hungry searchers resort to the last of their pork they have with them, using it instead of the elusive poultry and saving the *"little flour and parched meal"* they have with them. Ever inquisitive, Meriwether samples the Hudson gooseberry, another new item, and finds it a culinary horror. The only good thing is the water, for their three-thousand-mile journey has brought them to the clear and sparkling start of the mighty Missouri, whose headwaters spring from under *"the base of a low mountain or hill."*

The Headwaters

It is a moment of celebration in the Lemhi Pass, for *"two miles below McNeal had exultingly stood with a foot on each side of this little rivulet and thanked his god that he had lived to bestride the mighty & heretofore deemed endless Missouri."* Lewis, too, rejoices, *"thus far I had accomplished one of those great objects on which my mind has been unalterably fixed for many years, judge then of the pleasure I felt in allying my thirst with this pure and ice cold water ..."* Descending a little less than a mile down a steep slope, the elated commander drinks from a *"handsome bold running Creek of cold Clear*

The first Shoshone seen is a young man on horseback. Lewis shouts what he thinks to be "friend," *Tababone,* but the man flees.

R. L. Rickards - courtesy: Rickards Western Art

water," J5:74 of a different headwaters. This blue cascade runs west to the Columbia, and then on to the rolling Pacific.[a] As they cross the Continental Divide, this is a transcendent moment on the trip, a bright and shining glimmer to be remembered as the days become increasingly stark.

The Shoshone Disadvantage

While their Mandan hosts of the previous winter were primarily sedentary and agricultural, with their buffalo hunters returning to established villages, these Northern Shoshone live nomadically. Sacagawea's band had spun off from a more southerly group of hunter/gatherers, migrating from Nevada and Utah north into Idaho and Montana somewhere around the 1500s.

The Shoshone hunter/warriors have horses, but they lack guns. Unlike the more northerly Blackfeet and Atsinas, who can procure armaments from Canadian traders, Spanish policy restricts selling weaponry to any natives. Those living under Spanish jurisdiction are intentionally unarmed and disadvantaged; the precious guns can only be stolen and traded out. The Shoshones arrival on the Montana plains prompts enmity from the highly armed locals, for land, resources, and food supplies are now at stake. Even the distant Hidatsa raiders take every opportunity to get into the fracas, which is how Sacagawea came to live with them and consequently accompany the Corps.

Bitter territorial warfare is common, and fighting of this sort is often based on protecting the totality of natural resources: plant and animal foods and their by-products used in daily life (horns, hides, etc.). Trees mean wood for the fire pit, tepee poles, travois poles. The limited supply of obsidian is harvested for making arrowheads, spearheads, and hide scrapers. The locals don't want to share their weapons materiels; they want to control them. Hot springs serve as amenities or function as a medical treatment center. Whatever is there, it is used, and sharing territory, especially in a region of harsh winters, is counterproductive. Tribal enmity ceases by declaring a temporary status of "brothers-for-the-day," but only when the value of trading overcomes the need to dominate or exclude strangers. For now, the Shoshone are living a tenuous, stressful life.

With tribal competition at high levels, and lacking firepower, the vulnerable Shoshone are thrust into a less-than-hospitable niche of sparse resources on the Continental

Contact is finally made with the Shoshone on August 13, 1805. This painting idealizes that meeting.

Divide near the Montana/Idaho border. Part of the time they live in a tradition of gathering and fishing which provides a minimal diet, but by late summer they risk all in search of the rich, satisfying meals of buffalo. On a daily basis it is a marginal existence. North in the Bitterroots, the Salish live in much the same way. Forming a natural alliance, these two tribes meet and hunt buffalo together in the Three Rivers Valley, their greater numbers forming a common protection against the dangerously-near Blackfeet. It is in these hot days of mid-August, with high grass and fat buffalo, that the Indians rendezvous. The camas has bloomed and sent its strength back into the bulb; women and children are finishing the last of the harvest. Departure is imminent. However, to the great joy of Lewis, the much anticipated contact with the Shoshone finally occurs on Tuesday, August 13. He doesn't realize how lucky he is to have found them still there.

No Diplomatic Feasts among the Poor

In the scheme of foods, feasts, and diplomacy, this initial meeting is a hard let-down. The four whites are thirsty and have no food to offer as good will. Chief Cameahwait indicates that he has no food either, just berry bars, and Lewis is given the best they have. *"by this time it was late in the evening and we had not taisted any food since the evening before ... [they] gave us some cakes of serviceberries and Choke cherries which had been dried in the sun; of these I made a hearty meal ..."* Despite their poverty, the native tradition of giving food is in

---

[a] In actuality it is the beginning of a tributary of the Snake River, which eventually flows into the Columbia. The Columbia itself originates much farther north.

J.K. Ralston - courtesy: Jefferson National Expansion Memorial/NPS

place and functioning. The philosophy earlier espoused by Mandan Chief Sheheke still holds: "If we have food you will eat, if we don't then you will starve." It's that simple.

Going down to the creek for some water, the Chief gives the commander a quick geography lesson on waterways, leaving Lewis downcast at best. "*the river* [the Salmon] [J5:86n18] *was confined between inaccessible mountains, was very rapid and rocky insomuch that it was impossible for us to pass either by land or water down this river to the great lake where the white men lived as he had been informed.*" [J5:81] Since Cameahwait has not traveled to the west, he refers Lewis to a visiting old man who knows the route. The food picture is even bleaker than the upcoming geography: "*in order to get to his relations the first seven days we should be obliged to climb over steep and rocky mountains where we could find no game to kill nor anything but roots ... the next part of the rout was about 10 days through a dry and parched sandy desert in which no food* [is available] *at this season for either man or horse, and in which we must suffer if not perish for the want of water.*" Should they manage to surmount those obstacles, they will reach the Snake, a navigable river, which "*afforded neither Salmon nor timber.*" [J5:89] For his informational efforts, Lewis gives the man a knife, another treasure from the diminishing white-man's trove.

However dispiriting the news, today Lewis is the optimist. He sees horses, which to him mean salvation. He is invited into a wicker lodge where another Shoshone "*gave me a small morsel of the flesh of an antelope boiled, and a peice of a fresh salmon roasted; both of which I eat with very good relish. this was the first salmon I had seen and perfectly convinced me that we were on the waters of the Pacific Ocean.*" [J5:83]

Too Elusive Game

While the Captain is waiting for the rest of his party to arrive before beginning trade negotiations, he amuses himself by watching the inefficiency of Cameahwait's men trying to hunt pronghorn antelope on horseback with bow and arrow. Forty or fifty horsemen working in teams might harry the fleet pronghorn for miles and still return with frothing horses and nothing more than two or three animals to feed the entire tribe. The disadvantages of the bow and arrow are glaring. Drouillard, McNeal, and Shields get off no better shots and everyone is vegetarian. Lewis gives a partial flour and berry recipe with: "*a little paist with the flour and added some berries to it which I found very pallateable,*" but he fails to give cooking instructions. He doesn't bring tallow along, so they are not beignets. Is it is boiled up like a dumping, or perhaps baked on a hot rock?

This is actually cleared up the next day when Lewis awakens,

> *hungary as a wolf. I had eat nothing yesterday except one scant meal of the flour and berries except the dryed cakes of berries which did not appear to satisfy my appetite as they appeared to do those of my Indian friends. I found on enquiry of McNeal that we had only about two pounds of flour remaining. this I directed him to divide into two equal parts and to cook the one half this morning in a kind of pudding with the burries as he had done yesterday and reserve the ballance for the evening. on this new fashoned pudding four of us breakfasted, giving a pretty good allowance also to the Chief who declared it the best thing he had taisted for a long time. he took a little of the flour in his hand, taisted and examined very scrutinously and asked me if we made it of roots. I explained to him the manner in which it grew.* [J5:96-7]

Skittish Natives

But the commander is not doing well, despite his best efforts to satisfy the Shoshone suspicions of his good will. They are convinced that their enemies are right behind these front men, and it is all Lewis can do to get them to believe that there are more white men coming with provisions and merchandise. Food is the imperative, the critical factor. At length he appeals to their bravery – to go look – persuading a small number of men to ride out with the Captain and his men as they begin to retrace their path back to the river. Another small group of native men join in. Finally, an hour or so away, the rest of the men from the village and a number of women appear. It is becoming a traveling parade, a reluctant gambling pilgrimage to die by "devil enemies" or live off white-man's manna. Drouillard is sent out for meat but returns unsuccessful, game being scarce. Lewis falls back on what is left, "*I now cooked and among six of us eat the remaining pound of flour stired in a little boiling water,*" [J5:97] a meal something akin to wallpaper paste.[b]

All-Out Hunting!

On August 16, Lewis is hungry and crabby. He is tired of having no food and the diplomatic restraints placed on him in the face of tribal suspicion. He decides to send Drouillard and Shields out ahead as no one, white or native, has any food left and hunger breeds ill will. "*I informed the Ceif of my*

---

[b] During World War II, starving Russians actually pulled down their wallpaper to scrape the paste off the back – flour is good when you're hungry; it can be filling.

William Henry Jackson, collection of the American Antiquarian Society

The poverty of the Lemhi Shoshone is appalling to Lewis, who, while forced to negotiate for food and horses, is nonetheless empathetic to their condition.

view in this measure, and requested that he would keep his young men with us lest by their hooping and noise they should allarm the game and we should get nothing to eat ..." His request is totally ignored. The braves are gone down both sides of the valley in a flash, a pincers of observation, like two sides of a binocular being folded up tight against each other. It is not a long wait, for the two extraordinary hunters are back in animal country. The exultant Captain is a bit smug in his next entry, "we were all agreeably disappointed [c] on the arrival of the young man to learn that he had come to inform us one of the whitemen had killed a deer."

What follows leaves the small group of white men totally flabbergasted, for never have they seen such a sad testimonial to the extremes of hunger. The braves ride off in a frenzy of horsewhipping toward the incoming hunters, fearing that they "should loose a part of the feast." The deer carcass is left on the ground in plain view. "they dismounted and ran in tumbling over each other like a parcel of famished dogs each seizing and tearing away a part of the intestens which had been previously thrown out by Drewyer who killed it; the seen [scene] was such when I arrived that had I not have had a pretty keen appetite myself I am confident I should not have taisted any part of the venison shortly. each one had a peice of some

discription and all eating most ravenously. some were eating the kidneys the melt [spleen] and liver and the blood runing from the corners of their mouths, others were in a similar situation with the paunch and guts but the exuding substance in this case ... was of a different discription."

Lewis, the cosmopolitan gourmet who has dined on Presidential china with silver utensils carefully arranged on an ironed linen tablecloth, is obviously discomforted. But he continues his careful observations, recording the face of starvation in early America: "one of the last who attracted my attention particularly had been fortunate in his allotment or reather active in the division, he had provided himself with about nine feet of the small guts one end of which he was chewing on while with his hands he was squezzing the contents out at the other."

"Pity and Compassion"

This genteel planter, the President's secretary, the Army Captain, the commander of the Corps of Discovery finds feelings he has never experienced before. "I really did not untill now think that human nature ever presented itself in a shape so nearly allyed to the brute creation. I viewed these poor starved divils with pity and compassion." Lewis' orderly mind quickly returns:

I directed McNeal to skin the deer and reserved a quarter, the ballance I gave the Chief to be divided among his people; they devoured the whole of it nearly without cooking. I now boar obliquely to the left in order to interscept the creek where there was some brush to make a fire, and arrived at this stream where Drewyer had killed a second deer; here nearly the same seene was encored. a fire being kindled we cooked and eat and gave the ballance of the two deer to the Indians who eat the whole of them even to the soft parts of the hoofs. Drewyer joined us at breakfast with a third deer. of this I reserved a quarter and gave the ballance to the Indians. they all appeared now to have filled themselves and were in a good humour.

Perhaps this is noblesse oblige, or perhaps it is diplomacy. However, Lewis is doing as much as anyone can do, and doing it well.[d] But assuaging hunger pangs is not always a panacea. Suddenly the Shoshone became anxious and

---

[c] Here is one of Lewis' literary quirks: when things turn from the expected "bad" to a happy "good," he regularly writes that he is "agreeably disappointed."

[d] It is worth considering that the issue is most probably their lack of manners and indiscrete eating – which can be excused in the face of starvation, and in a very different culture – and not the food they are consuming. Two hundred years later people still eat raw beef, not warm but chilled, under the discrete name of carpaccio and it is selling at a posh restaurant for $12.50 for less than two ounces of meat, with garnish. If the meat were venison rather than beef, the price would rise substantially!

suspicious again. Dinner is a divided antelope. With thirty-five people, this is going to be a small appetizer-sized meal. Everyone is wondering, and perhaps not too kindly, where the ephemeral white men are.

And where are they? Struggling upriver. Lewis' group departed on the August 11. Back on the river there is enough food but the crew needs all the fuel they can get. Working incredibly hard, they achieve only five miles by Clark's estimation.

The Corps is now in a close struggle for its very existence. On August 13, the men are working in 52°F rainy weather, almost naked (because their deerskins have worn out) and pulling canoes in frigid mountain water for three-quarters of the waking day. The two miles they have come by water is barely a half-mile by land. It is a wonder they haven't succumbed to hypothermia. What sort of fuel is keeping the home fires burning? They have a small deer and *"a number of fine trout."* Dry willow, a skimpy firewood, is what they have for cooking and warmth. And there isn't much of that – *"we had great difficulty in procuring a sufficient quantity of wood to cook with."* J10:125

Rattlesnakes!

Rattlesnake Cliffs, an imposing and picturesque bit of geology, is named for the reptiles found there – a potential food opportunity, although no one on the Expedition really wished to go that way. The explorers named places for their most salient features, and here they are – faced with rattlesnakes. Lewis writes: *"Capt Clark was very near being bitten twice today by rattlesnakes, the Indian woman also narrowly escaped."* J5:98 "It tastes like chicken!"[e] may describe the flavor, but the issue of the snakes is twofold: (1) who wants to fiddle around with poisonous snakes and collect them for dinner? and (2) the effort involved. While throwing a few dead, beheaded snakes into a canoe is no big deal, snake would be last on the list for quantity of protein versus time and effort involved. Not only must the snake be skinned and gutted, but it is like cooking a six-foot-long turkey neck which has to be picked. For little return, it's not worth it. No one's that hungry.

Rattlesnake

---

[e] Description from a group of Boy Scout leaders.

Ordway describes the general diet during this time: deer, pronghorn, trout, duck, red and yellow currants, *"the black goose berry verry Sower,"* and a pail full of berries gathered by Clark, Charbonneau, and Sacagawea: *"the largest and best I ever Saw,"* which are distributed at the noon dinner break. The quantity of meats is as meager as the fuel. The wood situation by August 16 has become so difficult that *"we gathered Small willow Sticks only to boil our venison."* Again, here is the trick of using water to add bulk to the meal. Any extra flour might have been thrown in to make a stew, but at least soup is more filling than several slices of meat. Clearly the menu is down to about five items with no frills added. The immense difficulty of travel during August 11–17, 1805, is evident from the reduced miles gained, declining to a low of four miles a day. When the remaining Corps members stagger into view, Lewis writes, *"all appeared to be transported with joy."* J5:109

Camp Fortunate

Reuniting the Corps at Camp Fortunate resolves the suspicions plaguing the Shoshones, and the Captains stage one of their diplomatic events under the shade of a billowing canvas, followed by the usual and more-than-welcome feast. A debt of gratitude is certainly owed to the skillful hunters who provide the four deer and a pronghorn, particularly considering the placating quality of the food. However, the arrival of the Corps is a jarring note that throws Sacagawea's tribe off their delicately-balanced dance with nature. Lewis, intensely focused on haggling for horses, has no cognizance that the Lemhi Shoshone are starving in the forlorn hills, waiting to leave for their annual hunt. The commander is oblivious.

The first round of horse-swapping begins. Gifts are exchanged, and Lewis doles out *"a plentifull meal of lyed corn which was the first they had ever eaten in their lives. they were much pleased with it."* J5:112 This depletes the Corps' inventory and gives primary evidence that food from the central plains is not grown in the western part of the plains and the mountains. The culinary gold is fortified by an abundance of meat brought in by the hunters.

Lewis begins his barter, wanting a few horses for Clark and one to help carry the baggage and – in particular – the meat up from the lower hunting grounds. For three horses, *"in very good order"* he trades *"an uniform coat, a pair of leggings, a few handkerchiefs, three knives and some other small articles the whole of which did not cost more than about 20$ in the U'States ..."* and *"the Indians seemed quite as well pleased with their bargain as I was."* J5:117 The pleasure with the knives can be well understood, for Ordway writes, *"they have no knives* *tommahawks nor no weapons of war except their bows and arrows."*J9:205

A New Bartering Pattern

An important pattern begins here and should be closely watched as the forerunner to later transactions, particularly with the Clatsops. The troops are allowed to bargain for themselves. Food purchasing becomes a new job skill, like hunting. This particular brand of bargaining becomes so efficient at the coast that certain men are dispatched as the Corps' hagglers, regularly doing business. And, as with any enterprise requiring experience and talent, some have it and some don't.

As Clark goes to reconnoiter the Salmon River, the entire tribe accompanies him while four native hosts remain behind. Two lesser chiefs, Jumping Fish (a friend of Sacagawea's), and another woman stay while Lewis' group occupies itself with airing the provisions and baggage, and then begins to bunch them into horse loads for the overland journey. At this point it is not so much the wrapping of the provisions that is of concern but the lashings: *"I had the raw hides put in the water in order to cut them in throngs proper for lashing the packages and forming the necessary geer for pack horses, a business which I fortunately had not to learn on this occasion."* This very brief, sigh-of-relief comment is actually quite humorous but reflects the difficulty inherent in really securing goods onto pack animals. Tales of the Old West abound with lost items falling off horses, donkeys, and mules. God forbid losing the portable soup!

Lewis' Birthday – August 18, 1805

This Sunday is not a particularly exciting day nor even a social one. Clark has gone ahead, their desperate prospects for the Rockies loom large even as their food supply is visibly diminishing, and it is Lewis' thirty-first birthday. There is no birthday cake, no well-wishing from family and friends, no adoring woman at his side. In short, it is a painful day for the young commander. *"I reflected that I had as yet done but little, very little indeed, to further the happiness of the human race, or to advance the information of the succeeding generation."* He resolves to *"live for mankind, as I have heretofore lived for myself."* J5:118

Short Rations Even Before the Bitterroot Mountains

Tracking food at this point requires a split. Clark's party is eating fish and berries with their newly acquired native family. Lewis is quartermastering for himself, eighteen privates, Drouillard, and four Shoshone – a total of twenty-four people; many mouths to feed. The hunters bring in a mere pittance, barely enough to keep the home fires burning. The weight of food consumed appears to be just over a pound per person, trout weighing somewhere in that vicinity and the beaver adding a bit more. This is a considerable decrease from the Plains feasting.

LATE AUGUST, 1805, FOOD ENTRIES INCLUDE:

19th - a beaver, large number of trout, Northern sucker.

20th - a beaver, several dozen trout; Ordway says the Indians eat the beaver.

21st - no proteins brought in; Lewis issues pork and corn.

22nd - a fawn, and "Indian plunder."

"Indian Plunder"

From a group of Indians (tribe unknown) Drouillard confiscates *"about a bushel of dried service berries some checherry cakes and about a bushel of roots of three different kinds dried and prepared for use ..."* J5:142 as retaliation for a young man attempting to steal his gun on August 22. But Drouillard doesn't keep the booty. He hands the food over to Lewis, who gives it to the hungry Shoshones and they cook up the roots immediately. Lewis' descriptions provide us with enough detail to identify these roots: bitterroot, western spring beauty, and edible valeriana. These are packed for traveling, *"foalded in as many parchment hides of buffaloe"* and carried in bags woven from silk grass.

Thinking back to the community distribution of food among the Mandans, Sacagawea's native tribe differs greatly from this model. While the Shoshones are generous with their salmon, when it comes to meat, it is a different story.

Western Spring Beauty is one of the three roots described by Lewis.

On August 23, Lewis is amusing himself, watching the native hunters pursuing a mule deer buck – *it was really entertaining.*" Then he snaps to, aware of a difference.

I observed that there was but little division or distribution of the meat they had taken among themselves. some families had a large stock and others none. this is not customary among the nations of Indians with whom I have hitherto been acquainted I asked Cameahwait the reason why the hunters did not divide the meat among themselves; he said that meat was so scarce with them that the men who killed it reserved it for themselves and their own families." J5:149 What follows is a further expression of the commander's pity and compassion. When the hunters come in with game that afternoon *"I distributed three of the deer among those families who appeared to have nothing to eat.*

An Unsatisfactory Situation

Chief Cameahwait is torn between leading his famished tribe to food and remaining encamped to please the whites who promise to open the way for American trade, which will include precious guns – those metallic beacons of hope for successful hunts, for tribal safety. Lewis restates their position:

they told me that to avoid their enemies who were eternally harrassing them that they were obliged to remain in the interor of these mountains at least two thirds of the year where the[y] suffered as we then saw great heardships for the want of food sometimes living for weeks without meat and only a little fish roots and berries. but this added Cameahwait, with his ferce eyes and lank jaws grown meager for the want of food, would not be the case if we had guns, we could then live in the country of buffaloe and eat as our enimies do and not be compelled to hide ourselves in these mountains and live on roots and berries as the bear do. we do not fear our enimies when placed on an equal footing with them. J5:91

Lewis is caught in an equally delicate position. He knows the Corps' success depends on the Shoshone remaining long enough to provide horses and guides over the Rockies. To keep them from leaving, he needs – indeed is forced – to provide food for an entire tribe, *"some fifty Shoshoni men along with unnumbered women and children,"*[158] seriously depleting his own supplies for his troops. Indeed, feeding more than a hundred people on a daily basis (50 native men, 30 Corps, plus unnumbered women and children, at least 20 and likely many more) is a huge undertaking.

Lewis acts calm but is, in fact, fretting. He takes a broad view and commissions the hunters to go out earlier, go farther afield. Local supplies are very short. Then he gripes in his log about making it possible *"to obtain some meet for ourselves as well as the Indians who appeared to depend on us for food and our store of provision is growing too low to indulge them with much more corn or flour."* Later he goes one step further and *"I reminded the chief of the low state of our stores of provision and advised him to send his young men to hunt ..."* J5:148 It is an incompatible and unsatisfactory situation all around.

Both Captains have met with the Chief, promising better living through an American presence, and now guns. Furthermore, Lewis is forced into a political decision that calls for breaking out more food from the dwindling supplies the Corps needs to make it over the mountains. Ordway writes on August 22, *"we being out of fresh meat and have but a little pork or flower [flour] we joined and made a fish drag of willows and caught 520 fine pan fish. 2 kinds of Trout & a kind resembling Suckers. we divided them with the Indians, gave them a meal of boiled corn & beans which was a great thing among them ..."* J9:208 They are fast approaching the dire straights of the very tribe they are nurturing. Meanwhile, both the Shoshone and the Corps are not stationary; they are all traveling on a *"verry Steep and rocky mountain."* J5:146

During these ten, unendurably long days of negotiations, it is important to see the world through native eyes. Hungry bellies long for big slabs of roast buffalo. They're anxious to put by their supplies of dried meat. This is a critical time for the tribe, supplying their needs for an upcoming winter and meeting with their allies. Besides, buffalo hunting is hard – still done the "old" way with bow and arrow, no guaranteed easy shots fired from a rifle – and they need the support of their Salish (Flathead) friends.

Lewis, at cross-purposes with the tribe, needs the Shoshone right now. He needs them more than they need him. Held in the thrall of this gripping drama for days they can't afford to lose, Cameahwait finally sends his young warriors out to gather up the rest of the tribe and begin their trek to the buffalo hunt while he remains behind. On the other hand, the Shoshone need the Americans in the long run. Lewis counters with a trump of not sending traders or guns. The Chief is forced into a defensive position and the haggling for horses continues. By this time the starving natives are wily traders. They extract their fee for hunger pangs in tremendous prices for their horses, most of which are the cast-offs and the least-wanted of the herd.

Over Lolo

August 23 is the last day the entire Shoshone tribe accompanies the Corps. Sloshing in the cold rain through the afternoon produces a definite need for food, and Clark sends two men to *"Fish Creek"* to buy provisions. The dried salmon that comes back will be the first of many meals as a staple protein. Indeed, it will continue to be on the menu throughout their stay on the Pacific side of the Rockies for the next ten months.

For the hungry diners, fresh salmon are gigged, and surprisingly deer and bear are still in the area, one remorseful comment reading, *"one man Shot two bear this evining unfortunately we Could git neither of them."* To the relief of all concerned, the Indians happily depart for their fall encampment with other Shoshones and the Salish, leaving Old Toby as chief guide for the Corps.

Fasting

The next three weeks are a blur of struggling through the most inhospitable terrain imaginable with horses slipping and falling down impossibly steep slopes; snow, sleet, and freezing temperatures; and a food supply that finally gives out. The specter of starvation arrives and taps each and every person on the shoulder. Food is not even mentioned on September 2. The next day the total kill is five pheasants, cooked with a little corn. The following day, the 4th, they dine on one deer.

That afternoon the Corps encounters a very large party of Salish, *"33 Lodges of 80 men 400 Total and at least 500 horses."* Here in the Bitterroot River valley, the natives have never seen white men, but make a spontaneous evaluation of the strangers who have entered their territory and decide to welcome them rather than fight.[f] And so, the reception is pleasant and the Corps overnights with them. The usual ceremonial meal of chiefs and captains does not take place – there is little to eat, no grand feasting in the halls of diplomacy. The Salish generously share some berries, and the next day *"the women brought us a few berries & roots to eat."* J5:188

Those Important Horses

For carrying what is left of the provisions and the baggage,

In the Bitterroot Valley on September 4, 1805, the Corps meet the Salish. Eleven new horses were obtained, but no food.

eleven new horses are added in exchange for seven worn-out ones and some trade goods. But the next *Journal* entry makes it more than clear that the horses are loaded with few of the dry ingredients or carbohydrates that previously filled the crevices of the men's stomachs. *"nothing to eat but berries, our flour out, and but little Corn ..."* J5:189

The importance of horses now becomes paramount. As pack animals, they save the men from even greater hardships. And they are the only mode by which the hunters can roam, or bring back heavy loads of game if fortune smiles. A third benefit will appear in the next few weeks – they will appear on the menu. The pack train includes at least three nursing colts. Food. Protein. Salvation.

Just after acquiring the Salish horses the Captains put a guard on them, fearing they will bolt and return home or that they will be stolen. This is a new worry. Furthermore, the Corps encounters *"2 horses left by the Indians Those horses were as wild a[s] Elk."* Why didn't they just shoot the abandoned beasts and eat them? Apparently this thought didn't cross the hunters minds.

Back on the trail, trouble is haunting the band of hunters. Whether the horse involved is one of the fresh supply is unclear but *"One of our hunters Came up this morning without his horse, in the course of the night the horse broke loose and Cleared out ..."* J5:190 Another hunter is left behind, as they later discover, because he bagged an elk, *"packed his*

---

[f] Salish oral history explains four reasons for the welcome: (1) since cutting hair was a sign of mourning, the Corps' short hair was taken for a sign of a defeated war party with many losses; (2) their pale skin made them look ill and hungry; (3) they didn't carry blankets and their clothing looked torn and pitiful; and (4) being Black and strong, York was taken as the only successful warrior of the group.[159]

R. L. Rickards - courtesy: Rickards Western Art

As the party begins the two-week journey across the Bitterroot range, the Shoshone and Salish horses become a critical asset.

horses" (note, more than one) and can't catch up. But there is a surprise here, not noted in the daily record but appearing in the assiduously kept geographic log, an odd place to find a menu entry. *"2 deer 2 crains & 2 pheasants killed to day."* [J5:194] The sleek steel-blue sandhill crane, which winters as far south as Arizona, has become a new entry on "poultry specials of the day." There is also a new stream, christened *"Tin Cup Creek."*

Whipsaw between Plenty and Privation

The backlog of hunger, the need and greed to catch up and replace lost calories, emerges in the September 9 entry: Two hunters bring in an elk (200 pounds of meat) and a buck (about 80 pounds); Drouillard kills a deer (60–70 pounds); and one prairie fowl (about 8 pounds) is shot by Lewis – this is the day's take. Altogether, 34 people [g] consume almost all of 350+ pounds, over 10 pounds per person. According to Lewis, breakfast is *"a scant proportion of meat,"* but again they are saved by the hunters, for three geese are brought in and Drouillard arrives with two more deer. On September 9, a happy Sgt. Gass records *"we have plenty of provisions at present."* [J10:140] Four hunters are working the food problem and doing well. If there ever was a question about why hunters are paid more, this would be the time to discuss the wages.

[g] 32 Corps members plus 2 guides.

What Time's Breakfast?

The earlier regimen of eating after several hours of travel has changed radically and is unstable. On July 17, there is enough food that Gass reports, *"we took an eairly breakfast and set out."* By September 9 there is no morning breakfast, *"at 12 we halted … we breakfasted on a scant proportion of meat which we had reserved from the hunt of yesterday."* It's a late brunch. As the days progress the Captains can't even offer jerky for breakfast, and so breakfast disappears. Even staying put waiting for breakfast sounds unappealing – the weather has already turned cold by August 21, with *"the ice 1/4 of an inch thick on the water,"* and now there are snow flurries, cold rain, continuous rain. Moving to keep warm sounds better than staying still.

The Cross-Rockies Highway

While making this traverse, Lewis comes to an admirable but discouraging conclusion: the *"handsome stream"* of *"very clear water"* that they are enjoying (obviously for drinking purposes as well as aesthetic ones) has *"no sammon in it I believe that there must be a considerable fall in it below."* [J5:192] This means no food, and that there is a considerably steep downhill route ahead. That day the Corps travels nineteen miles at a high altitude.

The Corps is now traveling along the traditional native trail across the Bitterroots, complete with an old encampment and even the accommodations of a sweat lodge. In fact, it is a well-used highway, for they encounter several angry warriors hiking east in hot pursuit of two Shoshone who have stolen some horses from them. Clearly it's a cross–Continental Divide route, one the Captains know about. Remember Lewis' belief that if tribes with their women and children can pass through, so could the Expedition. Like any modern road, it has two-way traffic. Lewis and Clark happen to be going west.

Several days later, Sgt. Gass adds a note on food supplies, *"Having travelled 2 miles we reached the mountains which are very steep; but the road over them pretty good, as it is much travelled by the natives, who come cross to the Flathead river to gather cherries and berries."* [J10:141, h]

Lewis doesn't specify how many hunters he has out, but he gives explicit instructions for *"two of them to procede down the river as far as it's junction … and return this evening."* [J5:196] Of the two, only one returns *"accompanyed by three men of*

[h] Today Flathead Lake is one of the best cherry-growing areas in the Northwest.

The route across the Bitterroot range from "Traveler's Rest" on the Bitterroot River on September 11 to the Nez Perce village on a tributary of the Clearwater River on September 22 is probably the most harrowing of the entire Expedition – food is gone, the weather bitter, and the route difficult.

the Flathead nation whom he had met in his excursion up *travellers rest* Creek." J5:196 This may be a case of mistaken identity: Many scholars believe the men to be Nez Perce, which would make more geographic sense. However, by the simple gesture of offering hospitality to strangers, *"we gave them some boiled venison, of which the[y] eat sparingly,"* the party is in for a surprise windfall. One of the men will stay on and guide them to his relations on the plain below the mountains. His relations, he reports, have seen white men at what inland natives call "the stinking lake," the Pacific Ocean.

The Spectre of Starvation

Fear now preoccupies the Corps, beginning as it had some two weeks earlier when, on August 27, Clark heard rumblings. *"my party hourly Complaining of their retched Situation and doubts of Starveing in a Countery where no game of any kind except a fiew fish can be found ..."*

The Hidatsa had warned of no game. But the Corps had unexpectedly found some, at first. The Shoshone warned of no food on the mountain crossing. So far the commanders have not been misled by even a hint of duplicity. But Ordway

pens a contrary view: *"they tell us that their is no timber on the head waters for canoes. they also tell us that their is no game, but we do not believe them."* J9:205 Is the Sergeant's statement a reflection on the poor hunting skills displayed by the bow and arrow hunters, and that with their best hunters armed with guns, the Corps would have game? The probability of absolutely no game doesn't seem to cross his mind.

Their new guide again restates the warning that there is no game. Despite Ordway's optimism, contrary evidence will fly in the face of his beliefs. But Clark isn't discounting the stranger's advice. He is ever-cautious, always planning ahead for provisions, *"as the guide report that no game is to be found on our rout for a long ways ... despatched all our hunters in different directions, to hunt the Deer which is the only large game to be found ..."* J5:197 Clark even adds a bit of leadership strategy, *"we have Selected 4 of the best hunters to go in advance to hunt for the party. This arrangement has been made long sinc[e] ..."* J5:199

The Indian who so generously offers to help them is adorned with a piece of hair-bow ribbon and rewarded with a ring fish hook. The hunters, including Colter, later bring in *"4 deer a Beaver & 3 Grouse which was divided."* Ordway adds a fawn and *"several ducks and geese."* Assuming that the geese are now full grown, a substantial amount has been added to the meal.

The Captains Remain with their Troops

Clark's September 11 entry in his well-used, elk-skin journal makes abundantly clear the crisis now looming. No longer do the Captains count themselves among the hunters, even though both are quite good at it; only the best shots are allowed out. Extreme accuracy with the rifle is necessary so that every animal is killed and none flee from the warning clap of a missed shot. Despite these precautions, *"nothing killed this evening."* The elk and bear that were present at lower altitudes have reached the limits of their natural range. But no one is going back. While meat is missing, nature's abundance yields fruit. Whitehouse revels, *"We found the Wild or Choke Cherries plenty at this place."* [J11:311] The one deer taken on September 13 is not enough for the thirty-some-odd poor souls who are burning their bodies to the extreme. By the next day, the situation is near catastrophic. The horses have no forage and pose yet another eating problem if the party is to move forward. Gass flat out declares that, *"without a miracle it was impossible to feed 30 hungry men and upwards, besides some Indians."* Even the serviceberries that had been ripe at lower elevations are still abundant but disagreeably green at higher altitudes. Lives now teeter on the brink of starvation.

Mental Confusion?

Clark's methodical descriptions, keeping the daily events separate from his mapping notations, begin to mingle. On September 12, in his cartographic notes, he comments *"no water"* and *"Killed 3 [words illegible] this morning."* His thinking doesn't appear to be clear. Is he metabolically out of order from malnutrition, altitude, or both? After almost two weeks into the excruciating crossing, supper this day is followed by a steep descent on *"a verry bad trail rough and rockey"* down a rugged mountain slope, about the third or fourth of the day. Blessedly, at the bottom is a creek to satisfy their thirst. Stress in the form of extreme fatigue, hunger, and caloric deficit begin showing up in the *Journals;* the reader is literally left to guess what is going on. Compare three reports for September 12, 1805:

    Clark: *"our hunters Killed only one Pheasent this afternoon."* [J5:202]

    Ordway: *"our hunters had killed this day 4 deer and a pheasant"* [J9:222]

    Gass: *"our hunters has killed this day 4 Deer and a fessent"* [J11:311]

In his survey log, Clark records killing three things, but his usual clear writing is illegible. Later that day he puts the Corps on starvation rations, while Gass agrees with the senior Sergeant and copies Ordway's description, adding his own variant spelling. Lewis is not writing, and Whitehouse's stomach hasn't led pen to paper.

Horse Business

Famine is also stalking the horses, which plod on or slip and plummet in their dangerous and laborious work, with *"Scarcely any feed."* [J9:222] Perhaps this prompts a general rebellion in the equine troops, for the morning of September 13 *"Lewis and one of the guides lost their horses"* as Clark tells it, and the Virginia Captain and four men remain behind to search for them. Also missing, reports Ordway, is a canny little colt. Perhaps this is a case of "dinner to go" or more accurately, gone, because no more is heard of it. Whatever the case, the horses elude the first group searching for them and it is left to two of the hunters, who have finished their morning job by killing a deer, to go back for a second try.

This day is not any better for catching game than it is for corralling horses. The one deer serves the entire party for two meals that day, a short two pounds per person. Lewis' runaway is finally shepherded in by the hunters the next day.

R. L. Rickards - courtesy: Rickards Western Art

The route over the Bitterroots is fatiguing and treacherous.

What Do Starving Men *Really* Do to Sustain Life?

Approaching the critical period of starvation, what do the *Journals* actually reveal about food supplies and provisions? Lewis elaborates on the inventory on September 18:

> we suffered for water this day passing one rivulet only; we wer fortunate in finding water in a steep raviene about 1/2 maile from our camp. this morning we finished the remainder of our last coult. we dined & suped on a skant proportion of portable soupe, a few canesters of which, a little bears oil and about 20 lbs. of candles form our stock of provision ...

Nothing is more pathetic than listening to voices facing starvation, and there is little the Captains can do. Whitehouse, September 20: *"we eat a fiew peas & a little greece which was the verry last kind of eatables of any kind we had except a little portable Soup."* J11:323 Will they drink bear grease? Eat candles? These items are no surprise, for Lewis lists them among the potential provisions that will save his party. Gass' miracle comes in two forms: the first being portable soup, the emergency ration so carefully commissioned, preserved, and stored in canisters long ago in distant Philadelphia; and the second is the decision to eat horseflesh.

Portable Soup – UGH!

The 193 pounds of bouillon in tin canisters has traveled, at great cost in energy, all the way across the country; its weight is equivalent to toting a good-sized man along. Lewis' heroic endeavor at foresight is a start, but a feeble one. Some of the men balk, *"they did not relish this soup."* J10:142 Why didn't they? Soup, that ancient form of nourishment that prevails right through Colonial times, is certainly an acceptable meal, nothing unusual about it. So, what's wrong? The soup the troops are drinking is not a chunky, tasty concoction usually associated with soups; but rather it is equivalent of highly concentrated bouillon – a gelatinous or dried bar of what is basically beef stock. Two definitions clarify what the soup would ideally taste like. A bouillon is a "consommé with pronounced beef flavor," and consommé is defined as a "clear, strong, sparkling broth clarified." [i]

The taste of the broth is probably what bothers the men the most. A contemporary cooking of *p.Soup* shows that it is quite flavorful before being dried. However, during the final cooking and the drying, the protein structure changes, and not for the better. Think of eating freshly cooked chicken for dinner, putting the leftovers in the refrigerator overnight, and then reheating them the next day. Does it taste the same? No. The "sparkling" part of the taste is dulled. The scientific explanation of this phenomena is that the proteins are subject to *denaturation*, an alteration in the molecular structure by means, in this case, of heat. As the beef protein is boiled and then dried, the bonds break down and become scrambled. This alteration is what sends the taste buds recoiling.[160]

No instructions show how far down Francois Billet reduced the stock, but Ordway's September 16, 1805, *Journal* entry inadvertently gives a very small clue about the consistency of the soup base: *"about one oClock finding no water we halted and melted Some snow and eat or drank a little more Soup ..."* Perhaps the soup base is in a gelatinous form. If that is so, there are a few possibilities to consider.

A gelatinous soup cylinder would be elastic, rubbery. To reconstitute: bring water to a boil, and then stir in the gelatin until it dissolves, and reheat to serving temperature. The unforeseen problem with this direction is the consideration of altitude and the physics of boiling.[161] At altitude, water doesn't boil at 212°F, it boils at a lower temperature. [j] At Lolo Pass (5233 feet) the boiling point would be 202°F or less, depending on any low pressure from bad weather. Although the water boils, as it is not as hot, foods take longer to cook. The exhausted men are not in a position to spend hours scavenging for wood. Furthermore there is no water, only snow, and that is yet another temperature barrier to overcome. Imagine a moderately heated, lumpy, glue-tasting soup. Worse yet, will this thin bouillon soup satisfy ravenous men? The answer is an emphatic no! If the men are expending nearly 5000 calories per day, it would take 22 cups of soup per day just to satisfy just one man.[k]

Not surprisingly, the *p.Soup* is a topic which the Captains prefer to ignore. There are no diary entries for Lewis on September 14 through 17; he first notes using the soup on

---

[i] More tasty is consomme properly enhanced by the addition of lean chopped meat, egg whites, and aromates, as described by Bernard Clayton in *The Complete Book of Soups and Stews,* page 421.

[j] The rule is that for every 1000 feet above sea level, the boiling point is reduced about 2°F from the sea-level boiling point. And low-pressure bad weather (storms, snow, and rain) also lowers the boiling point of water.
[k] Dr. Ken Walcheck, a Lewis and Clark researcher, has worked with the Nutrition Coordinating Center (NCC) of the University of Minnesota, delving into the nutritional aspects of the soup. He found that each ration (125g of gel per serving) would provide 231 Calories, 36g. protein, 8.5g. fat, and no carbohydrates. Additional data can be found in his article in *We Proceeded On* (August 2003).

September 18. Clark ignores the soup entirely. An unfavorable review of portable soup is given by Sgt. Ordway on September 16: *"nothing to eat except a little portable soup which kept us verry weak."* It may be hunger-induced lethargy, or depletion of energy from altitude sickness, or a temporary slight mental aberration which leads Whitehouse on Sep-

MORE ON *P. SOUP* – HOW MUCH?

Despite disliking it, the Corps actually drinks a good portion of the soup. There is uniform agreement that Lewis had 193 pounds of portable soup prepared. And if all 32 empty purchased canisters were then needed, that gives him 32 six-pound canisters of soup. The only references to its use are in September 1805 in the Bitterroots as serious emergency rations and later two minor uses on the return trip for "medicinal purposes." If, from May 1804 through September 1805, the *Journal* entries in September are indeed the only usage, with none of it left in caches (as per the detailed *Journal* inventories of the caches), how is it then that Lewis, in his September 18, 1805, *Journal* entry notes that *"... portable soup, a few canesters of which ..."* is all that was left? Where did it go?

Portable soup is first used on September 14, 1805, in the Bitterroots and then twice a day continuously through September 19 per diaries of both Ordway and Whitehouse . This yields about 12 meals of 35 servings each, approximately 420 servings of *"p.Soup"* utilized. Using Walchecks's recent nutritional analysis of portable soups and a generous ¾-cup of soup-concentrate per serving to get a bare-survival 360 calories, we get about 155 pounds of soup used, which leaves about 38 pounds of soup on September 19, or about 6 canisters worth.

Lewis writes on the September 18, *"... suped on a skant proportion of portable soupe, a few canesters of which, a little bears oil and 20 lbs. of candles form our stock of provisions ..."* Considering that they have likely been consuming the portable soup at about 4 canisters a day, only 6 left would indeed be a worrisome few – less than two days from starvation.

tember 15 to quite surprisingly and rather simplistically say, *"we melted what we wanted to drink and made or mixd a little portable Soup with Snow water and lay down contented."* [J11:317]

The *"Kilt Colt"*

When the hunters return with Lewis' horse, again on September 14, they bring with them two or three spruce grouse, enough for a mouthful or two per person, which prompts the straightforward statement about needing a miracle. Sergeant Ordway's journal shows him to be the eloquent and forceful spokesman for the entire Corps declaring, *"we being hungry for meat as the Soup did not satisfy we killed a fat colt which eat verry well."* [J9:223] Gass notes that they roasted it and it made a far more satisfactory meal ... the coals were probably built up from heating snow for soup. Whitehouse adds, *"hunger made us all think that it eat delecious."* As a matter of form, they name the left-hand fork of the creek *"Kilt Colt Creek."* Gass notes that breakfast the morning of September 15 is leftover colt; Clark mentions it for dinner.

This horror of an overly steep, snow-slick rocky trail is downright dangerous. Horses fall backwards, roll down slopes studded with rocks, *"which hurt them very much."* and sometimes it takes eight to ten men to push a horse back up the hill. It is surprising that there is the inexplicable hesitation to put the injured horses out of their misery and roast them up instead of surviving on portable soup. Instead, the men proceed to *"lay down without anything else to Satisfy our hunger."* Clark mentions two more grouse brought in, but that is a mere nothing. September 16 is a day of darkening disaster – a gloomy snowstorm: *"In the night and during the day the snow fell about 10 inches deep."* [J10:143] A second colt goes the way of the first.

Did They *Really* Eat Candles?

Lewis' reference to the *Portable Soup* and the *Bears Oil* as edible items are credible, but then he lists *"... 20 lbs. of candles ..."* as provisions. How can this be? Just as bear grease is a high-calorie fat, so are tallow candles. They are a fine source of nutrition if needed. The Corps would have shared them, melting them in the soup.[1]

But did they really eat the candles? While some historians have suggested that they did, two recent studies indicate that they did not: Historian Bob Moore draws his conclusion from *Journal* analysis, while other research draws the same

---

[1] One park ranger's little daughter with a taste for fat actually ate some straight and thought they were fine.

conclusion by accounting for all remaining candles. Thus, while that entry lists *'Candles'* as a possible "last ditch" provision – the Corps never used them for food. However appealing a rugged tradition like "eating candles," the facts say they probably stopped after the bear grease.[m]

Could it be Worse?

A brief overview of the Corp's physical conditions might be instructive:

- ◆ Over-exertion, bodily fatigue:
  "very fatigueing" [J11:322] – Whitehouse
- ◆ Malnutrition/Starvation – caloric burnout:
  "we all being hungry and nothing to eat" – Ordway.
  "Exceedingly hungry." – Whitehouse
- ◆ Dehydration:
  No water in *"this horrible mountainous desert."* [J10:145] – Gass
- ◆ Verging on Hypothermia:
  "The snow fell so thick, and the day was so dark, that a person could not see to a distance of 200 yards." [J10:143] – Gass
  "I have been wet and as cold in every part as I ever was in my life, indeed I was at one time fearfull my feet would freeze" [J5:209] – Clark
- ◆ Altitude sickness: probably present, but unrecognized in 1800s.

Hunting, Down off the Mountain

The extremity of the situation is bleak if not black. Lewis writes on September 18, *"there is nothing upon earth exept ourselves and a few small pheasants, small grey Squirrels and a blue bird of the vultur kind"* – obviously not enough to keep body and soul together. The presence of bear and deer scat and the howling of wolves tells the savvy outdoorsmen that game is becoming available again, but the party is still at too high an elevation. With this hopeful idea, Clark optimistically sets out for *"Some leavel Country"* on September 18 with a party of six hunters (including crack-shots John Shield and Reubin Field), [J5:214n2] determined to make haste and kill enough food to send back, hoping to nourish and revive their starving men. *"The want of provisions together with the dificuely of passing those emence mountains dampened the Spirits of the party which induced us to resort to Some plan of reviving ther Sperits."*

While Clark is delighted to do something eminently speedy and useful, Ordway is balefully eying the scenery, *"the Mountains continue as fer as our eyes could extend. they extend much further than we expected."* The caloric burn rate is right at the limit when Whitehouse pens, *"we descended down the mountn. which was verry Steep descent, for about three miles. then assended another as bad as any we have ever been up before. it made the Sweat run off our horses & ourselves."* [J11:322] That day the sorry plight of *"but verry little water"* passes, the Expedition finally freeing itself from what Gass calls *"this horrible mountainous desert."* [J10:145] At least the burble of a running stream coursing over its rocky bed is back again, benefitting both men and horses. The physical agony is still present, however, *"most of the party is weak and feeble Suffering with hunger. our horses feet are gitting Sore and fall away in these mountains,"* [J11:322] but hope is still alive that they are close to the end of the Rocky Mountain trail.

On September 19, totally without food except portable soup, the emaciated men are obliged to hike down a two-hundred-foot slope not only to rescue a horse that has fallen, but more importantly the two precious boxes of ammunition it is carrying. The morale of the troops goes up as they spot level ground that Lewis reports as *"a large tract of Prairie country ... widening as it appeared to extend to the W. through that plain the Indian informed us that* [is] *the Columbia river, in which we were in surch run."* Sick with dysentery, irritated by skin problems, they down their portable soup.

By the morning of the September 20 things are appreciably better, even with the horses having taken off again and running the inevitable morning roundup. Two miles into the trek the Corps comes upon the horsemeat hung up by Clark's hunters the day before, and not even the tempting thought of flame-broiled meat detains them from going straight down the mountain. General rejoicing ensues, Whitehouse remarking that they *"dined Sumptiously"* and Lewis expansively noting, *"we obtained as much as served our*

---

[m] May 1999, WPO published a definitive article by Bob Moore, "The Making of a Myth," in which he concludes, mostly from the absence of *Journal* notations about consumption, that they did not eat the candles. More recent analysis corroborates Moore's conclusion by another route. Clark's May 1804 loading inventory lists 120 pounds of candles. Measurement from candle molds available in collections from that period – about 10" long, slightly tapered, about a 1" diameter at the base – weigh 5+ candles to the pound – a total, therefore, of about 610 candles. Data from Colonial Williamsburg includes notes of George Washington's 1790s measurements reporting such tallow candles burn about 5 hours. If the Captains burnt one candle each evening to write their journals, there would be about 610 days worth of candles. There is no *Journal* reference to the Corps making candles at Mandan – in April 1805 there should have been about 280 candles left. On September 19 there would be about 115 candles left (22 pounds), just about what Lewis reported. If they continued burning candles at the one-per-night rate, the candles would have run out around January 14, 1806. In fact they ran out on January 13 – an almost perfect correlation.

culinary purposes and suped on our beef ..." making "*a hearty meal on our horse beef much to the comfort of our hungry stomachs.*" He also discovers and samples "*a growth which resembles the choke cherry bears a black bury with a single stone of a sweetish taste, it rises to a hight of 8 or 10 feet and grows in thick clumps.*" It actually does more than resemble the chokecherry; it is one.

A Nez Perce Welcome – Invasion of Aliens; Salvation by a Grandmother

The issue of hunting is moot, for there is no sign of game. On September 20, Clark and his men drop down another fifteen miles and are welcomed into Nez Perce country by one native man who invites them to his village where their arrival balloons into a great, happy, interested confusion, the little party being the first whites ever to enter the territory. Gracious hosts, the band showers their guests with "*roots dried roots made in bread, roots boiled, one Sammon, Berries of red haws some dried.*" After days of weak, thin bouillon, this is a sudden and wonderful profusion and variety of foods.

This welcome seems almost too cordial, considering the Corps are strangers in a strange land. There is seemingly none of the wariness or shyness that usually accompanies a first encounter of this sort. The reception from the Teton Sioux (hostility), from the Hidatsa (who initially considered the white men bad medicine, due to Mandan deception), and from the Shoshone (flight, reluctance) all might be considered normal. No formal diplomatic speeches by the Captains preceded the food gifts, so it isn't a result of protocol. Why, then, this celebration, this abundance of edibles showered on men who must have looked like the refuse of humanity?[n]

The Nez Perce had dreamed prophetic dreams and were responding to this invasion of aliens who look uncouth and are hungry, as well. Food is calming, so is a friendly welcome, and the Nez Perce are looking out for their own best interests as they should have. They are gracious and hospitable. But even then, the fate of the sickly Expedition is still in jeopardy until an ancient one, a woman named Watkuweis, pleads on their behalf. Another one of the

R. L. Rickards - courtesy: Rickards Western Art

The Nez Perce village is a welcome relief from the cold, hungry mountains. But the new foods – dried fish and camas – have their own ill effects on most of the Corps, debilitating them for 12 days.

"stolen ones," she had been treated kindly as a child by whites in Canada. No doubt she had been fed and sustained, and this memory of a full stomach lead to kind remembrances. In a society that treasures the advice of the elderly, she is listened to and respected. She dies the next day, but amazingly and miraculously the Corps is saved. This entire recounting of the Nez Perce's oral history is quite prescient; some might term it eerie.

New on the Menu: Dried Salmon, Camas Root

Ever mindful of their provisioning obligations, Clark's party moves on in about an hour, escorted to the next camp by a man of rank who indicates there are fish to be had there. One hundred men plus women and children crowd into a parade that flows around the white men and carries them on. Clark sends four men out to hunt and is taken aback and unhappily surprised to find that the advertised salmon isn't fresh but dried, and there is no river nearby. The little party is again offered food and this time it is a new culinary item: the camas root, a significant carbohydrate staple for the region. The Corps has arrived at the fertile Wieppe (We-eye-p) Valley in Idaho, a major breadbasket region and home to this abundant member of the lily family.

Tribes from as far as the Pacific Northwest and Shoshone from the east traveled great distances to harvest this crop and apparently this was very much a social occasion. [J5:224n14]

---

[n] Jim Magera is a white man adopted by the Nez Perce as a blood brother. His long experience as a U.S. Park Service ranger and interest in local history made him all the more interested in one particular oral history which he heard passed down from the elders to the upcoming generations. "The Nez Perce had dreams of people coming from the east who had hair on their faces, smelled bad and ate horses and dogs, something they would never do. Furthermore, it was clear they were incompetent woodsmen because they were taking all the wrong trails and passing up food." (WPO, News Update. Vol. 24, No. 2 [5/98])

For gatherers, securing and preparing food for winter storage is good reason to rejoice, their efforts resulting in at least partial insurance of making it through another winter. The sociability, festivities, courting – all seem to go hand-in-hand with the event.

Blue Camas

Despite the foreignness of the food, the hunters' bodies are crying out for it, lots of it, and variety. They down a *"Small piece of Buffalow meat, Some dried Salmon beries & roots in different States, Some round and much like an onion ... of this they make bread & Supe they also gave us the bread made of this root all of which we eate hartily, I gave them a fiew Small articles as preasents."* [J5:222] The buffalo has been carried back across the Rockies, the salmon has been air-dried and is probably laden with all sorts of new bacteria, and the camas produces a gaseous compound which accumulates in proportion to the amount of root eaten. Except the buffalo, the hunters are used to none of these. Clark morosely scrawls, *"I find myself verry unwell all the evening from eateing the fish & roots too freely."*

"Verry Sick"

The next morning, September 21, the hunters go out again, this time in all directions, and again return with nothing. The Nez Perce are not eating salmon just for the delight of it; fish appears to be the sole protein supply available. No doubt disappointed in the hunting and faced with this commissary issue, Clark, the man raised on inland meats and still suffering from last night's meal, buys enough fish, roots, and berries to load up one horse. He then sends Reubin Field and a native back to meet the Corps. The price for this food is *"what fiew things I chaned to have in my Pockets ..."*

The conclusion to send food back to his starving compatriots is obviously correct, but does Clark have certain misgivings about what he is sending back? His body, accustomed to cold mountainous temperatures, is now debilitated by *"weather verry worm"* in this lower elevation and a stomach in turmoil. *"I am verry Sick to day and puke which relive me."*

Reubin Field and his native guide reach the party in one day, the Expedition coming down and the supplies going up. Since Clark's hunting party departed, the thirty people have eaten part of the horse previously mentioned, *"a prarie woolf [coyote] which together with the ballance of our horse beef and some crawfish which we obtained in the creek enables us to make one more hearty meal, not knowing where the next was to be found."* [J5:226] They are into serious scavenging. Even Lewis' meticulous powers of description are failing him, for he doesn't record the *"duck and two or three pheasants"* that Gass does. [J10:146] The usually stoic Captain admits, *"I find myself growing weak for the want of food and most of the men complain of a similar deficiency and have fallen off very much."*

The symptoms Lewis observes – dysentery and irruptions (breaking out of the skin) – are due to malnutrition and a weakened immune system. There is also the possibility of scurvy.

Refreshments Are Served – September 22, 1805

With a rescue packet at hand (a later entry by Clark specifies three salmon, and mostly roots) the commander orders an immediate halt, *"for the purpose of taking some refreshment."* This language smacks of Eastern gentrification in the worst way, and implies something more like iced mint tea and a dessert table set with cakes and cookies rather than a crude meal set before starving men. But he is indeed reviving his men, making them stronger and more energetic – qualities implicit in the word "refresh." *"I divided the fish roots and buries, and was happy to find a sufficiency to satisfy compleatly all our appetites."* He also credits *"Field ... who killed a crow."* If eating crow is something to be avoided, the Corps doesn't know it. As might be expected, the men's stomachs have shrunk considerably (along with their muscle mass) during the period of starvation and this small amount of food is completely satisfying to them.

They have narrowly escaped starvation and death.

Running the Western Rivers
September – November, 1805

*You can't measure the importance of salmon in terms of pounds and dollars and cents.
[To] catch those fish is irreplaceable and part of a lifestyle that few people understand.*

— JAIME PINKHAM (NEZ PERCE)

Angry River by John F. Clymer, 1978, courtesy Clymer Museum of Art

The swift waters of the Columbia negotiated by the Corps in November/December 1805.

THE FOOD SENT BACK UP THE TRAIL by Clark from the Nez Perce village has revived the main body of the Corps – they eat and proceed on, an elated group now fed. Their feelings are amplified by Lewis, exulting, *"the pleasure I now felt in having tryumphed over the rocky Mountains and descending once more to a level and fertile country where there was every rational hope of finding a comfortable subsistence for myself and party can be more readily conceived than expressed, nor was the flattering prospect of the final success of the expedition less pleasing."* J5:229

What Kind of Welcome?

On this warm Sunday morning of September 22, the Corps arrives at the Nez Perce village that welcomed and fed Clark, and according to Lewis: *"most of the women fled to the neighboring woods on horseback with their children."* J5:229 Lewis writes that it is hardly the greeting they expect, and his observation seems paranoid or strange to say the least. By comparison, the other journalists see warmth and hospitality in their welcome. Sgt. Ordway almost effusively describes the scene as: *"they appeared very glad to see us ran meeting us*

163

with *Some root bread which they gave us to eat.*" [J9:228] Gass and Whitehouse agree.

Clark Commanding

Clark, now the leading diplomat, is ahead and giving out medals, trinkets, and good will. One of the Chief's five wives had, like Sacagawea, been captured by the Hidatsa, seen white men, and apparently holds positive feelings towards whites, for *"those people were glad to see us."* [J5:226] A dried salmon is a welcoming present.

Still looking to provision the main party, Clark dispatches the hunters. Shields comes in with three deer and is heading for the village when Clark commandeers a chunk of meat and a fresh horse and heads back for the Expedition. The meat may have been a good choice but the horse isn't; it throws him three times and leaves him battered and suffering from a sore hip, after which he changes and rides a colt. Arriving at the first village, Clark's group finds the main party has gone onto the second village, where they are *"Encamped, much fatigued & hungery, much rejoiced to find something to eate of which They appeared to partake plentifully. I cautioned them of the Consequences of eateing too much &c."* [J5:230]

If there is even a question about eating to appease the hunger or abstaining to remain well, it comes and goes in a flash. The malnourished men, finding themselves amidst plenty and provided for by a pleasant, hospitable people, eat. And eat. The gorging syndrome kicks in. They most likely overeat in compensation for the starvation they have experienced.

So begins more than two weeks of unmitigated gastric distress probably unparalleled in the annals of indigestion. Several factors are at work, all combining with hideous effects. First, the men are in terrible condition, *"fatigued and reduced,"* and their immune systems are no doubt compromised. Add that to the following:

- The inability of the digestive system to process solids after shutting down (while starving).
- Possible dysentery from drinking bear fat (nutritious, but an unintentional laxative) in the soup.
- A change of diet from red meats to fish, and the reintroduction of carbohydrates – Sgt. Gass' explanation of their illness as well as that of Ordway's and Whitehouse's.
- The introduction of new bacteria from the fish.[a]
- Gaseous camas.

---

[a] It doesn't affect the natives since their systems are used to the bacteria. They have accommodated them since childhood.

- Different drinking water. Gass notes: *"The water* [the North Fork of the Clearwater] *also is soft and warm, and perhaps causes our indisposition more than any thing else."* [J10:148]
- A change of climate (Ordway, Whitehouse).

Physically their bodies have suffered from starvation and dehydration. Their immune systems are weakened, and their bodies are in rebellion against any sort of food, especially anything carrying bacteria that need to be purged from the system. The primary symptom for both maladies is dysentery; and the men are so weak that they are unable to even stay upright. *"Capt Lewis Scercely able to ride on a jentle horse ... Several men So unwell that they were Compelled to lie on the Side of the road for Some time others obliged to be put on horses."* [J5:232-33] Consider the outward effects of this debilitation in an age when toilets and toilet paper have not yet been invented; it is not a pretty picture. And the Nez Perce, like all curious humans, become gawkers, *"The planes* [plains] *appeared covered with Spectators viewing the White men and the articles which we had, our party weacke and much reduced in flesh as well as Strength ..."* [J5:230]

The list of miseries is so distressing and Lewis himself so sick, that he ceases writing. In fact, his silence goes on much longer than the illnesses themselves, lasting an astonishing two months, until November 29. This is a repeating pattern: when things go terribly off, Lewis clams up and becomes silent; a great debt is owed to faithful Clark who learned the art of consistent journal-keeping and correspondence from his sisters.

What of this Sickness?

Clark first notes his own queasiness on September 20. The next day, he miserably scrawls, *"I am verry Sick to day and puke which relive me."* September 22 is no better, *"Two hunters left here ... verry Sick,"* although they manage to kill two deer. The job of hunting becomes even more important, and they intend to bring in food that will suit the abused stomachs. The hunters don't have time to be sick.

Sunny, red-headed Clark offers the only bright hope, Gass relays, *"He thinks we will be able to take to the water again at that place"* some eighteen miles distant, *"where he left 5 hunters as there was some game about the river in that quarter."* [J10:147] Whitehouse notes that, in addition to the salmon and roots, they are given red and black haws, berries from two distinct hawthorn varieties. This literate private, seeing berries now, is the very man who looked back wistfully at the gardens when the Corps left the Mandan and Hidatsa villages. And if the troops are suffering from scurvy, the vitamin C in these berries should help. Medicinally a hawthorn tea may help strengthen damaged connective tissues, but even more importantly the berries "eaten in moderate amounts ... relieve diarrhea."[162] Their native hosts, directly or indirectly, are contributing to their recovery.

From Gifts to Trading

On September 23, Clark writes, *"Capt. Lewis & 2 men verry Sick this evening."* As diplomats they are expected to eat with the chief, and do, *"broiled dried Salmon."* The cooking should have killed off the bacteria, unless it is just passed over the coals for a quick re-heat. The party stays in the first village to procure provisions of roots, camas bread, red haws, and fish, for which they trade small items. Then, proceeding on to the second village, they trade for more. Clearly the point has been reached when hospitality gives out and practicality calls for a shift to commissary status. Trading is a well-practiced skill along these far-reaching paths of commerce, and keen-eyed Ordway spots a true American or European luxury, *"Some of them have fine copper kittles."*[J9:228] Whitehouse reports seeing, *"knives &c. which they tell us that they got from the traders to the west, which must have Come from the western ocean."*[J11:329]

The Indian trading routes are well established, and goods travel great distances with amazing speed, so much so that the Captains are surprised to find that some of their gifts/ manufactures are keeping pace with them in travel time. Great centers of native commerce are under the control of power brokers (the Teton Sioux on the lower Missouri, the Mandan in North Dakota, the Blackfeet in northern Montana). While Spanish guns, horses, and equestrian gear are smuggled and sold at high prices by southern tribes to central tribes, seashells make their way eastward from the coast. In fact, shells are hair decorations for the Shoshone people. This vast emporium of commerce extends across the continent.

The shipping trade is also well established at this point, all part of the great jostling for empire and power. European-style goods are sold by American, British, and Russian ships that ply the cold but lucrative waters of the north, making merchant calls on their way along the coastline. From these primitive, windblown trading ports the prized manufactures move inland, no doubt gaining value each mile away from the sea. No wonder the Corps is surprised to find familiar copper kettles gracing native fire pits. But it's a sign that the Pacific is not far away.

On September 24, Sergeant Ordway complains about the lack of water on the plain. The hunters, obviously not as incapacitated as many of the others, bring in *"4 deer and two*

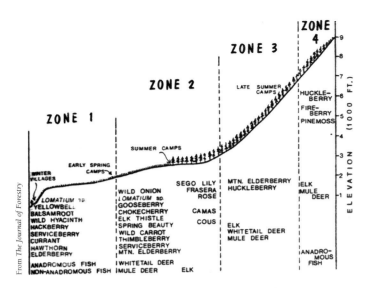

From *The Journal of Forestry*

The Nez Perce had a complex and well-developed existence. They migrated from winters in low river valleys to late summer in high mountain hunting camps; each zone with its own foods and season.

Sammon which they killed." Gass reports that the valley is filled with serviceberry bushes, and the *Journals* note that both serviceberries and chokecherries become ripe and abundant on September 2 and 3 on the east side of the Rockies that year. However, by this late date, it is past the ripening time and the berries are likely gone.

The violence of their maladies is particularly acute this day. Whitehouse says it comes from *"eating too hearty of the bread & Salmon that we got from the Indians."*[J11:332]

Eating Camas – Over-consumption is a Risk [b]

With this desperate indisposition felling the men like flies, what is known about these exceptionally nourishing roots that sustain the native populations and stupefy the explorers? Camas, despite its later discomforts, is initially a pleasurable dining experience. Shaped much like an onion or a medium-sized oval potato, and sweated (steam-roasted) in a meter-deep hole, the roots are then served as a vegetable Ordway describes as *"Sweet and good to the taste,"*[J9:228] a description Whitehouse also uses. Gass elaborates on a second preparation for the roots, *"a kind of bread which is good and nourishing, and tastes like that sometimes made of pumpkins."*[J10:146]

A member of the Lily family, the beautiful purple-blue

[b] See further discussion of camas and its preparation in *Plant Foods*, page 237.

flowers rise in the spring and glow in sunlit valleys like Van Gogh's fields of iris. Camas is a staple for many western tribes, quite high in fructose (which gives the sweet taste noted) and can be eaten raw, roasted, or boiled. The bulb's strong chemistry can also cause gas and/or indigestion. Despite the heat and steaming which diminishes the pungency of the bulbs, the Corps is much reduced by gas pains and dysentery. A warning in an ethnobotany text warns that over-consumption can cause diarrhea and vomiting.[163] This in itself is enough to cause problems for the novice eater, let alone compounding it with all the other factors.

Finally, on September 25, on a small branch leading to the Columbia River, they are able to fish. That night, after a hot day and traveling just four miles, one of the privates gigs six fresh salmon and *"two of them were roasted"* for dinner. At least there are no bacteria lurking here, and they are a nourishing source of protein and healthy oils. Lewis continues *"verry sick,"* and *"most of the Party Complaining."* Clark observes that Benjamin Rush's "thunderbolts" haven't effected a cure and switches medicines, trying Salts and Tartar emetic. Are the remaining four fish roasted and carried along? Probably not, since the days are hot and bacteria breed quickly. Clark heeds this cautionary wisdom and buys fresh fish at every opportunity.

Is it the Water?

The mineral balance and bacterial assemblage found in every different source of water is well known among seasoned travelers and is often a source of trouble. Even the cleanest of waters can be wildly different from what the men's bodies are accustomed to, tolerate quite well, and may prompt a memory-set to which the body chemistry clings in some enigmatic fashion. Given a change in water sources, maybe the water is suspect. Previously, their source came from the eastern Rockies, flowing along its fore-ordained course to the Missouri and ultimately the Mississippi, terminating in the Gulf of Mexico. They drank this water for 3000 miles or more. Now they are drinking westward flowing streams headed for the Columbia and eventually the Pacific. Some mineral change, and therefore bodily reaction, might not be all that surprising.

Water pollution may be a factor here as well, although certainly later than the first outbreak of illness. By the end of the summer water levels are at their lowest, and contamination rates are at their highest. In this environment, bacterial concentration results from lower water flow not flushing the contaminants out, and higher air and water temperatures that promote bacterial growth.

Later, on October 10, there is a water report that is quite vivid. Gass, suffering from malarial fever, manages to describe the incoming confluence of the Snake as: *"goslin-green colour."* Clark sees it as *"greenish blue, the north as clear as cristial."* In other words, the water is not turgid or muddy, littered with bloated bodies or any other visual pollution. If water is possibly the culprit, the cause must be microscopic.

Cooling at the River

Dragging themselves off the hot plain on September 26, the men go down to a cooler, timbered area near the Clearwater with enough trees to begin construction of new canoes. It will be a long stay of twelve days, owing to the weakened state of the men and the difficulties in canoe building. At *"Canoe Camp"* Clark purchases fresh salmon for those who can eat and administers *"Salts, Pils Galip* [Jalap, a homeopathic powder used to incite vomiting], *and Tarter emetic &c."* J5:234 The doughty Captain is feeling unwell himself and the medical curatives of blood-letting and purgatives are not working.

September 27 marks a turning point. Those who are able among the weakened and almost useless men begin work, going out in five teams to procure *"five pitch pines for five canoes."* The exertion is too much for several of the men and they return, sick again, to camp. Hunters return sick and without meat. John Colter – later famous for his mountain-man exploits and his naked run from the Blackfeet – is sent out to retrieve missing horses and returns with only one horse and half a deer, having shared the other half with the natives. Meat is only used for *"nourishment for the Sick."* At least the venison is a food to which their stomachs are accustomed, and following the procedures that accompanied previous bouts of illness, the meat will be turned into soup, insuring a heat-sanitized supply of water as well. The Captains are vitally involved with Dr. Rush's Philadelphia cautionary that eating and wellness are inextricably connected.

Complaining Equals Health, Too

By September 28, Clark writes, *"Our men nearly all Complaining of ther bowels, a heaviness at the Stomach & Lax, Some of those taken first are getting better ..."* He still has trouble on his hands, but the digestive problems seem to be running their course. This is further substantiated by new and heartfelt objections to the Indian food, *"men complaining of their diat of fish & roots."* Days before, in their extreme illness, they didn't have the energy to complain. The hunters bring in nothing this day, Gass writing, *"Game is very scarce, and our hunters unable to kill any meat. We are therefore obliged to live on fish and roots, that we procure from the natives; and which do not appear a suitable diet for us. Salt is also scarce without which fish is but poor and insipid."* Salt is another need of the body, essential in maintaining a mineral balance when overheated and sweating. Lack of this vital element could be another factor in the men's out-of-order bodies.

The Nez Perce come by selling salmon and the Captains buy a few. Looking at the descriptions of the fish purchased, they are all fresh – no more dried stuff. But devastated gastro-intestinal systems play havoc with the body's desire to eat, and no one is eating much. Somewhere, someone decides that paying the Nez Perce to fish for them is a waste of trade goods and valuable beads, and the men fix up gigging poles to fish for themselves.

Overheated and Sick

September can be one of the hottest months of the year. Heat itself throws many people into a lethargy, thus slowing the metabolism and offering odd bacteria a chance to grow prolifically without being thrown out by a more active system or being burnt up by a high fever. A brief look at the data gives some credence to this idea.

NINE DAYS OF SICK CALL

Date	Temp	Sick Roll
9/24	*hot*	Lewis; 8-9 men
9/25	*hot*	Lewis; 3 parts of party sick
9/26	*verry hot*	Lewis; several men
9/27	*verry hot*	Lewis; nearly all men sick
9/28	*verry worm & sultry*	several men sick
9/29	*(weather changing)*	Lewis; 5-6 men *"sick as usial"*
9/30	*cool*	2 *"verry sick;"* all others at work
10/1	*cool*	Lewis much improved
10/2	*a fair morning*	Only Clark mentions any sick men

Will This Never End?

The Corps absolutely believes that they need to go back to their old diet – fresh deer, fresh fish, and a lessened amount of camas. It seems to be contributing to their recovery. Passing of time also is allowing their bodies to recuperate from nearly starving to death.

On September 29, *"men Conte* [continue] *Sickly"* although some are beginning work. *"Cap Lewis verry Sick, and*

most of the men complaning very much of ther bowels & Stomach." At noon that day a load of meat comes in, no doubt to everyone's great relief; Collins or Colter (Clark mistakenly cites both, which is not possible for one deer) and Drouillard bring in a total of three deer. The Indian fish-hawkers must have come by earlier, for the party purchased some fresh salmon – something they wouldn't have done had they known meat was on its way.

The turning point is September 30, the day is cool and there are only two men still very sick. For the first time in almost two weeks, the sergeants all agree in their diary entries. One of the two hunters who stayed out overnight brings in a deer and a pheasant. For their depleted appetites, this is probably adequate.

There is a cool wind blowing in from the northeast on October 1, and canoe making is underway. Lewis is better. Appetites must be picking up, for the deer and poultry are gone, and Clark is lamenting that there is *"nothin to eate except a little dried fish which they men complain of as working of them as as much as a dost of Salts."* The men are square-on with their lamentations, for being that sick is surely something to be avoided. Apparently there is no option this day.

Sickness versus Starvation

Now the Corps is caught in a quandary: they are thoroughly afraid of Indian food, but on October 2, that's all there is to eat. Starving is just as grim. Clark dispatches the hunters, who bring in one lone coyote, and he, himself, is equally unsuccessful. As insurance, he dispatches Frazer, Goodrich, and one of the Indians back to the first village to buy provisions, *"... with Six of our horses and Some marchandize to trade."*

Coyote

This will be a big shopping trip but a long three days before supplies arrive at camp. Again the Captains are sending competent bargainers instead of doing the trading themselves.

That night, Clark stoically writes, *"we have nothing to eate but roots, which give the men violent pains in their bowels after eating much of them."* Ordway and Whitehouse must have been sitting together composing their entries for the day, because they read quite similarly, *"the party are so weak* and unwell living without meat that our officers thought proper with the oppinion of the party to kill a good horse which was done and we eat the meat as earnest as though it had been the best meat in the world." Whitehouse compares it to *"fat beef"* and goes on to note that in the evening they purchased some fresh Salmon and root bread from the Indians. Clark writes that the horse is used to *"make Suep for the Sick men."* Always soup for the sick.

Good News!

By October 4, the sickness is generally abating, and a new food comes onto the menu, one which will last until they re-cross the Rockies: dog. *"Some of the men eat a fat dog ... roasted."* The next day the canoes are being readied for launch, and the thirty-eight horses are branded and put into the care and safekeeping of three Nez Perce men. The traders, *"loaded with commass [camas] roots and Some more in loaves and a considerable quantity of dryed Sammon [salmon] &c."* More fishing gigs have been made to assure a supply of fresh fish, the canoes are on the river and Whitehouse proclaims,*"Our Men that had been sick for some time past, had nearly all got their healths, & are fit to do their duty again."* It has been a tough start for the second half of their westward trip.

Running the Clearwater

And it is just as well that the young men are fit for their duties, for ahead lie dangerous rapids requiring brute strength to navigate, and leaking canoes to be hauled out, unloaded, and re-caulked. The vicious rapids are *"So bad that we take water over the canoes by the waves,"* Whitehouse writes, in what must have been a horror for the non-swimmers. J11:340 Even their oh-so-carefully wrapped goods are soaked, and they spend unplanned hours in drying, so fearful are they of losing the small amount of provisions and merchandise they have left.

Dog Equals Food

Two Nez Perce chiefs, Twisted Hair and Tetoharsky, join the Corps as Salish translators, replacing the Shoshone guides, Old Toby and his son, who have returned home; so the dinner count remains the same. Meanwhile, the unwavering Clark, sticking with his notion of diet, *"tried to purchase a fat horse for us to eat but the Natives did not bring him as they promised. in the evening we purchased a considerable quantity of Sammon, a little bears oil or grease, Some root bread 2 dogs &c."* J11:344 Gass cheerfully records, *"some Frenchmen, who prefer dog-flesh to fish; ... here got two or three dogs from the Indians."* J10:152 The next day, October 10, the reluctant Cap-

tain Clark admits, *"all the Party have greatly the advantage of me, in as much as they all relish the flesh of the dogs, Several of which we purchased of the nativs for to add to our Store of fish and roots &c. &c."* Of course the best part of this is the vision of the Indian dogs bracing themselves with paws on the bows of canoes and yipping at the waves rolling over them like nautical bowsprits.

Theft: Two Viewpoints

Of a more serious nature is theft, a new phenomena cropping up. In the earlier halcyon days of the Expedition when the Corps is sympathetically embraced by the Mandans and accepted at last by the Hidatsa, there are few conflicts. The Shoshone continue the pattern of supportiveness, despite their urgent need to leave for the annual buffalo hunt. One of the first instances of theft is when Drouillard's gun was almost stolen.

Having crossed the Rockies and emerging starved on the other side, the Nez Perce appear as salvation to the Corps, amenable hosts and providers, feeding them generously for a number of days. But two ominous events occur at the interface of the two cultures meeting, just as the Corps emerges from the last range of the Rockies.

Horses, of course, are of prime importance as transportation, and the loss of even one is enough to send someone back looking for it. The animals have a difficult time finding enough grass for grazing and often wander off – the privates are often on one- or two-hour searches before they round them all up. But just as the mountains tail off, the horses become more than troublesome. Even though the forage is closer, they keep disappearing. On September 22, among the Nez Perce, Whitehouse reports, *"The Men overtook us; who had found the lost horse and clothing, but on their way to us lost both the horses ... they had found the horse & port mantaus ... then they lost boath of the horses. they expect they were Stole by Some of the natives. So they brought the portmantaus &c. on their backs."*

That same day Clark pens, *"Those Indians Stole out of R.F. [Reubin Field's] Shot pouch his knife wipers Compas & Steel, which we Could not precure from them, we attempted to have Some talk with those people but Could not for the want of an Interpreter thro' which we Could Speake, we were Compelled to converse alltogether by Signs ..."*

These two incidents – one suspicion, the other fact – are probably the beginning of an uneasiness and wariness that is heightened and accentuated during the upcoming winter on the coast.

The troubling issue continues, Clark noting a curious

dichotomy on October 8. The *"people appeared disposed to give us every assistance in their power dureing our distress"* yet *"every thing wet ... had everything opened, and two Sentinals put over them to keep off the Indians, who are enclined to theave haveing Stole Several Small articles ..."* J5:251 The final indignity comes when Clark leaves his spoon, of all things, unguarded – and it is stolen. The next day, October 9, it reappears. Theft is apparently endemic, because the chief had told Clark not to bother paying Old Toby as *"his nation would take his things from him before he passed their camps ..."*

While stealing is a cardinal sin among Christians, this pilfering is viewed very differently by the natives of the Columbia plateau during this period. Theft is seen in socialistic terms as a redistribution of wealth from the donor (the Expedition) to those who helped them with information, portaging, provisioning, etc. – a "proper payment" even if it isn't authorized.[164] This leaves the natives happy and the Corps with a declining supply of trade goods and therefore unhappy. Even more interestingly, this redistribution is apparently designed to "normalize" relations, to balance wealth so that all may share more equitably. Perhaps this is the Northwest Coast version of the Mandans breaking up the corn mill so that all can share.

Just Fiddle On
Despite the thefts, for the first time in weeks the two fiddlers, Cruzatte and Gibson, break out their instruments. The Corps is on the road again and feeling fine, eating nice fat dog and fresh salmon, surrounded by pleasant, helpful Nez Perce. All this is surely cause for a grand celebration. On October 3, the cold night air sparkles with good will, alive with the happy sounds of men singing, lilting tunes accompanied by the thready voice of the fiddle, and foot-stompin' dancing.

However a truly bizarre event is about to occur, one seriously shocking to the whites, which Whitehouse describes in detail as the *"crazey fit by our fire"*:

> one of their women ... She Set to Singing Indian and gave all around hir Some roots, and all She offered had to take from hir. one of our men refused to take them from hir. She then was angry and hove them in the fire, and took a Sharp flint from hir husband and cut hir arms in Sundry places So that the blood gushed out. She wiped up the blood and eat it. then tore off Some beeds and peaces of copper &c which hung about hir and gave out to them that were round hir a little to each one. Still kept hir Singing and makeing a hishing noise. She then ran around went to the water Some of her kindred went

after hir and brought hir back. She then fell in to a fit and continued Stiff and Speechless Some time they pored water on hir face untill She came too. Capt. Clark gave hir Some Small things which pleased hir ... J11:344

What does all this amount to? Food is being given as a gift. The Corps is in the middle of a diplomatic situation, even if it is not formalized. Things are going well until one of the men refuses her present, probably associating roots with indigestion. Bad manners. Diplomatic faux pas. Next the woman goes crazy and inflicts self-damage, finally falling senseless and immobilized. In this different culture and time, there are different means of handling the psychic unknown. The woman's relatives respond lovingly, and her culture would see this behavior not as an abnormality but as being prompted by a "guardian spirit."[165] Clark offers more trinkets as appeasement. As at the Mandan dinner months earlier, here is another instance of one of the men not having his guest behavior completely in order. The commanding officer makes amends, and all is forgiven.

Thrills and Terrors
The joining of the Clearwater and Snake Rivers spells an end to the rock-studded shallows as the sheer volume of water increases greatly. With the physical burden of tugging and hauling eliminated, wild drenching rides in the rapids become more common. The paddlers are now engrossed in staying upright, off the rocks, and alive. River-running is a class-five whitewater event with no rules or amenities. *"One of our Canoes run fast on a Rock, & broke a hole in her side ..."* J11:346 The boatmen steer the canoes through wild rapids, past lethal "suck holes," and haul-in just short of horrendous waterfalls. Ordway's description on October 13 is terse and succinct. *"towards evening we passed through a place in the River where it was all confined in a narrow channel of about 15 yards wide for about 2 miles and ran like a mill race."*[c] Whitehouse, in a fascinating comparison, points out that Indians on horseback cannot keep up with the canoes. Non-swimmers portage the goods along sheer cliffs, and there's always adrenalin running.

With thrills and terrors now forming the backdrop of their journey to the sea, what of these new salmon cultures? The rocky tributaries teeming with salmon are clearly a culinary and economic gold mine for the locals. Ordway feels compelled to write about it all, noting that not all fish are

---
[c] The old mills were situated where the greatest force of water would turn the wheels at a fast speed, thus allowing for speedy grinding of the grain. A narrow slot focuses the power of the water, increasing its velocity, and shoots it through like a thoroughbred at a race.

taken at the *"large fisherys"* he sees; *"they have pleanty of Small canoes for the purpose of fishing."* J9:236 They're on a busy river with lots of traffic. Clark, from a rich family himself, remarks that the natives have considerable wealth, citing a chief *"who as the Indian Say has more horses than he can Count."* Hindered by a diminished supply of trade goods, the Captain buys for all tastes – fish and dogs. Clearly the caloric needs of the outfit have not decreased; Whitehouse notes two stops to buy provisions. It is always the same supplies, no variety.

A Desolate Territory

October 10 is a day without much reassurance. The earlier Shoshone warnings of no animals or fuel on the Columbian plain are holding true. Gass is awed by the forbidding nature of the canyons: rocky hills, river shores that are *"very stony."* Ordway observes; *"no wood only a fiew willows in Some places."* Dinner that day is no doubt cooked over the barest amount of fuel. Nor is the land naturally abundant or teeming with flora and fauna; only the rivers hold that honor. Looking ahead, much the same is coming: shortages of firewood, diets of salmon/dog/roots. In a gustatory sense, this is like going from the five-star steakhouse (the buffalo days) to the no-star fish-to-go.

A New Pattern: Take-out Breakfast

The next morning, October 11, they stop at 8:00 AM to buy the morning's groceries: *"7 dogs & fish roots &c to eat."* J5:261 This is another early breakfast stop. Since there are no leftover stews from the night before, their shortage drives a different breakfast behavior.

Ordway and Whitehouse are struck by the snippets of civilization found at one of the fishing villages, *"Saw among them Some peace of fish net which they must have come from white people. a tea kittle made of copper Seen also &c."* J11:348 It must have been truly astounding to see an expensive tea kettle being used by "savages."

Trouble is ahead. On October 14, two canoes run up on the rocks and shortly thereafter a third gets stuck on a rock midway through a waterfall. Ordway's canoe breeches upon a rock and sinks, losing a goodly portion of the cargo and leaving four men stranded on the rock mid-rapids. The men are working furiously in wet and dangerous conditions to save the canoes, their cargo, and friends; eventually all are retrieved from their precarious perch.

Coming ashore on an island to stabilize themselves, dry their goods, and work on a canoe, the party finds a buried cache of fish, which they are careful not to touch. They do,

however, ask the chiefs if they can take some wood from an Indian house and use it, which they do. Gone downriver are food and hunting items: a small brass kettle and bowl, two spoons, one bag of root bread, and one shot pouch and powder horn. J11:352 One tomahawk is missing, a vital firewood-chopper/animal-hacker. The total cargo of camas is ruined and beyond salvage. One mess will be short a brass kettle, and two privates will be carving wooden spoons or trading for horn spoons. Some gunpowder is soaked, there is leaking around the lid of the lead canister, but Clark hopes it can be salvaged. Their packing holds in one respect: the ammunition canisters are tied down and don't wash away.

Healthy Appetites

The healthy and vigorous young athletes are in full appetite. On October 10, they buy thirteen or fourteen dogs. These animals are rather a thin build, medium stature and are not fed dog-food, so they might weigh a skinny thirty pounds each. If one-third of the animal is usable meat, that yields just over four pounds of meat per person – half the peak rate at the Great Falls portage.

The salmon are left for anyone who wants some, and Clark crabbily announces *"our diet extremely bad haveing nothing but roots and dried fish to eat."* He has forgotten the bread and berries, but he also buys dried cherries, possibly

October 14 on the Clearwater River, a canoe gets stuck on a rock at a rapids necessitating ropes to extract it, as depicted in this 1954 oil painting *The Rapids.*

Harold Von Schmidt, courtesy Montana Historical Society

harvested near Flathead Lake. In the vicinity are some hackberry bushes, which bear sweet fruit resembling cherries, but the Indians have already harvested them. He might have known these bushes at home – they range from Canada to Tennessee – where they can be rather large, but these are very few and they grow low to the ground due to the arid conditions on the plain. In actuality he is eyeing them as firewood.

The continuing problem on the food scene is the lack of firewood. Two days later, Gass writes of an unpleasant vista, *"The country on both sides is high dry prairie plains without a stick of timber. There is no wood of any kind to be seen except a few small willows along the shore; so that it is with difficulty we can get enough to cook with."* J10:153 Even the Nez Perce are forced into ingenuity by this scarcity. Ordway writes that, *"they raft all their wood down the River a long distance and they put it up on Scaffels and take great care of it."* J9:238

Bird Watching

Keen-eyed Gass is on the lookout: *"We saw some ducks and a few geese, but did not kill any of them. There is no four-footed game of any kind near this part of the river, that we could discover; and we saw no birds of any kind, but a few hawks, eagles and crows. At noon we halted, cooked and eat some fish and then proceeded on."* J10:154 If birds are seen, they are hunted. The good news is that *duck du jour* goes on the menu. Clark smilingly recovers his good nature, for *"here we dined, and for the first time in three weeks past I had a good dinner of Blue wing Teel."* J5:271

By October 15, 1805, frost is on the ground. Game birds are back on the menu, and stolen firewood is cooking them. *"Labiesh killed 2 gees & 2 ducks of the large kind."* Clark goes on to note, *"Killed 2 teel this evening."* Again, Ordway and Whitehouse disagree with Clark's number; they add one more goose, which makes for more generous servings. The firewood situation has become so acute that the men filch wood off one of the innumerable scaffolds they have observed. Clark writes apologetically, *"here we were obliged for the first time to take the property of the Indians without the consent or approbation of the owner. the night was cold ..."*

The run down the Clearwater and then the Snake has proved an arduous 200 miles, demanding full concentration and great bravery. The Corps is succeeding on the military trek as well as the gastronomic one. They have recovered from their violent indispositions, adjusted to a vastly different native diet, and added new items to the menu that will be served for the next many months. And while they have lost items to the river, they have not been overly inconve-

nienced by the voids. The availability of poultry and dog make meals more filling and palatable, and the Nez Perce and later the Palouse supply them with provisions. Living has greatly improved since Lolo Pass.

Down the Mighty Columbia

Friday, October 16, 1805, is another milestone day. The Corps paddles into the major confluence of the Snake and Columbia rivers and is now positioned for a straight shot down the Columbia River to their winter headquarters.

That evening, *"the Chief brought down all his men Singing and dancing as they Came, formed a ring and danced for Some time around us."* J5:277 This Chief is Cutssahnem, accompanied by two hundred visiting Wanapam compatriots from upstream on the Columbia. Obviously, the visitors are in control of the evening, but what a way to welcome foreigners!

The earlier food wealth of the Expedition has long since been exhausted. With the game animals gone, the Corps has no chance to shoot dinner nor is there a plentitude of corn. It is another humbling display of neediness, even greater than with the Shoshone. They are literally empty-handed in the provisions department; they have no food to offer, no stomach-soothing, goodwill-engendering feast to sponsor. Only a local resident with a trading network behind him would have food for two hundred, and that would require several days preparation.

Cutssahnem doesn't bring food, and while Clark hands out smokes and medals, some attempt at communication is made with hand-signs. But this time there is no well-worn "Great White Chief in Washington" speech: the translation chain has broken down. With that oratory abandoned, there a no place for the ritual banquet. Music and tobacco will have to suffice. Diplomacy is getting loose around the edges.

Food Gifts, Food Sales

But there are food gifts from the natives. Fresh salmon and *"about 20 lb. of verry fat dried horse meat"* are goodwill gestures. J5:278 Horsemeat may not normally be on the menu, but it appears to make fine jerky in place of elk, which aren't available in this environment. Twisted Hair and Tetoharsky, the two Nez Perce chiefs in advance position, have parlayed brilliantly with their Shahaptian-speaking neighbors. The Yakamas, the visiting Wanapams and those other Wallula and Umatilla people have listened and know about the ragged explorers. Word spreads quickly, and advance warning must have gone out about the foreigners' vile predilections for fresh horseflesh and dog – which becomes available for sale as the group travels through.

Natives fishing on the Columbia use stick dip-nets and spear-fishing from both the shore and platforms extending over the river.

Clark reports, "Scaffols of fish drying at every lodge."

Clear and Crouded with Salmon in maney places," *"emence numbers of dead Salmon I can't account for."* The troops marvel at the native way of life: *"great numbers of Indians appeared to be on this Island,[d] and emence quantities of fish Scaffold,"* and *"2 Lodges of Indians Drying fish, ... nine large Lodges of Indians Dring fish on Scaffolds ..."* J5:298 Utilizing the arid air, drying is done not with smoking, but simply by draping the fish over sticks.

Over My Dead Body
While the tribes are flush with this good harvest, the army men are leery. Wasn't it just a couple weeks ago that they were sicker'n dogs because of that fish? Unlike the natives, they can't account for the dead and dying salmon. After all, aren't the symptoms of wasting away, flesh decomposition, and death something horrible? They don't realize this is part of the circle of life, a certainty after the great migration from the sea ending in the fish's ultimate gift of new life – eggs and their fertilization. Their ravaged bodies are not up to fish market expectations. Gass complains that they *"are very plenty but poor and dying, and therefore not fit for provisions."* J10:157 If nothing else, these eaters have learned to be very careful, discriminating and cautious about fish. As outdoorsmen it would not take them more than a year to tune in to the cycle of life on the Columbia River, but for now it is foreign, inexplicable, and probably dangerous.

Now, Silas Goodrich alone is counted as the Expedition's fisherman, and he is accustomed to inland streams and rivers, so this is a whole new arena. Sending Goodrich fishing here would be like sending one coyote out to catch thirty generations of rabbits. The scale is staggering. As Clark takes salmon off the menu, the men look harder at the plains

Everywhere native men are fishing, and still more villagers come to view these voyagers. As the Captains are discovering, the Pacific Northwest appears to be as crowded as the eastern seaboard. Moreover, the natives are equally willing to deal. They even wait patiently, willing to retrieve capsized goods if the crazy white men defy the deadly whitewater and die in their lunatic endeavor. The next day, October 17, is off to a bad start when it is discovered that one of the jovial visitors from the night before has made off with a large axe, a highly valuable tool for fire-making, fort-building, and canoe-making.

The Magnitude of Fishing
It is totally overwhelming – the river itself, the stupendous spectacle of the migrating salmon, the vastness of the harvesting being done by the natives. The magnitude of these fishing operations is awe-inspiring. The town where "Two Rivers Meet" is a center for trade, a gathering area for consolidation of goods and shipment out. It's cosmopolitan, judging from the number of tribes visiting or living in proximity. And Clark is bowled over. *"Scaffols of fish drying at every lodge," "piles of Salmon lying," "This river is remarkably*

---

[d] Likely Rabbit Island, now underwater in a reservoir – Lake Wallula.

Paul Kane, collection of the Royal Ontario Museum, Toronto

Paul Kane, collection of the

and discover them becoming more bountiful. The golden grassy plains are yielding *"a great many hares and a number of fowls, between the size of a pheasant and a turkey, called heath hens or grous. We killed a great many of these fowls which are very good eating."* J5:278 They are probably sage grouse, J10:157n2 *"a large fowl which I have only Seen on this river."* J5:287 From this entry, the sage grouse appears to be more than welcome. It's big like a turkey, up to two-and-a-half feet long with a three-and-a-half-foot wing-span.

Horse is another protein possibility. Whitehouse comments on the vast number of horses held by the Indians J11:359 yet there is no offer of horseflesh for dinner. The tribes of the Columbian Plain are obviously as skeptical of eating horse, or offering one as food, as are their fellow Shahaptian-speaking neighbors, the Nez Perce.

Elk and Deer Again

But good news is at hand, literally. The locals, through sign language, indicate that elk and deer territory is downriver. The meat-loving canoeists are elated. Clark, himself, has seen natives wearing *"robes of Deer, Goat & Beaver."* J5:286 What a welcome revelation. And they are approaching the Pacific. They are encouraged by the strange admixture of trade goods they see: bright blue beads, shiny brass pots, sailor's clothing. Foreign traders must have called at some nearby port; perhaps they will be lucky enough to sail home. Perhaps the Corps can buy food and even trade goods. The one drawback of this European influence is that the paltry amount of trade goods they are carrying is worth far less; their merchandise is not unique or new. But these negative ideas are not those of the Captains or the Corps. The evidence of game and the proximity to the sea spell fulfillment, both for success at reaching the long-awaited journey's end and for a more immediate prospect of a continually filled stomach.

What's in the Shopping Cart?

Wednesday, October 17, and Thursday, October 18, are prime examples of how four journalists can have completely different perceptions. At the Forks of the Columbia, the other journalists stay in camp. On the other hand, Clark writes two separate entries for October 17. In the first entry he says they purchase dogs, but not fish; an Indian woman gives him a dried salmon; he kills a sage grouse. J5:285-6 In the second entry he notes that he buys dogs but omits mentioning a gift of the dried salmon; tallies in the sage grouse; and then says that he travels upstream on a little exploratory trip (a little half-day trip) where he eats boiled salmon *"which was delicious,"* offered by a man who is working in a lodge where women are processing fish. He is given several fish, and reciprocates by giving pieces of ribbon. On his return, he says *"I shot a large Prairie Cock (sage grouse) Several Grouse, Ducks and fish."* Shooting fish? Clark's afternoon shopping cart is therefore:

- ◆ boiled salmon (eaten at the lodge).
- ◆ fish: several bought (fresh or dried), one gigged.
- ◆ several grouse, and then *"another."*
- ◆ ducks and fish.

On the October 18, Sergeant Gass doesn't mention food, nor does Ordway. Whitehouse says *"Some of the party killed Several more haith hens."* Clark also reports on the sage grouse, "the men killed Six of them" and then reports, *"we purchased forty dogs for which we gave articles of little value, Such as bells, thimbles, knitting pins, brass wire & a few beeds."* J5:296

Now, for these two days, how do the journalists line up?

	Dogs	Sage Grouse
Clark	*some* (Wed.) *+40* (Thu.)	*some +6*
Gass	*A number*	*A great many*
Ordway	*several more*	*several*
Whitehouse	*26* (Wed. only)	*Several +3 +several*

Between Clark and Whitehouse there could be up to 66 dogs purchased – that's a sizable pack of curs. Obviously this barking, whining, jumping pack cannot be carried in the canoes, nor can they be carried as fresh meat which can rot, nor can they be eaten in just two days. It is all quite problematic and the *Journals* are strangely silent on the solution.

Misunderstanding the Chief

Later, diplomatic contacts begin as *"our old Chiefs* [Twisted Hair and Tetoharsky] *informed us that the large camp above 'was the Camp of the 1st Chief of the all* <u>tribes</u> *in this quarter,' and that he had called to us to land and Stay all night with him, that he had plenty of wood for us &.' "* Somehow the message is misunderstood and the Corps fends for itself, not taking advantage of this fine offer of firewood. *"we were compelled to Use drid willows for fuel for the purpose of cooking ..."* J5:300 Late that October 18 night, about twenty men come down to visit, and *"the chief ... brought a basket of mashed berries ..."* It is certainly a fine, and appreciated, gift.

The next day, thirty-three miles downriver, the men spot natives *"drying fish and Prickley pare (to Burn in winter)"* J5:301 If cactus is fuel, it becomes apparent that a gift of firewood, the real thing, is a sign of great hospitality as yet more Indians bring this scarce item, the same as offered by the Great Chief the night before. The Shahaptian-speaking tribes living in this area are a loose collection of Yakamas, Wanapams (who came to sing at their camp), Walla Wallas or Walulas, Palouses, and Umatillas.

Pounded Salmon

The first supplies of *"pounded"* salmon come in on Saturday, October 19. The men are too inexperienced to know this is rated as a gastronomic delicacy on the Pacific coast, and is indeed a highly valuable trading item. Whitehouse is so pleased with this preparation and its ultimate form in little tidbits that he writes of its virtue, saying, *"the Natives came to See us in their canoes. brought us Some fish which had been roasted and pounded up fine and made up in balls, which eat verry well."* [J11:360] Nowhere before has there been this much praise for salmon, especially in its dried form. And, while the process undoubtedly removes some of the oil, it is surprising that just pounding and rolling the fish would account for such a taste change.

However, in addition to the pounding, beargrass and cedar-ribbed baskets are used for storing the pounded salmon. It's likely that the fish absorbs some faint hints of flavor from the beargrass and/or the cedar, and this "extra" is what distinguishes pounded fish from the plain dried salmon.[e] Also, Chinook tribal tradition has pounded salmon being prepared like pemmican, with tallow and berries. This, too, would yield a different and more pleasing flavor.[f]

Nature's Own Cleansing Cycle

Geographically, the Corps is moving downriver and seeing the distant, rugged Cascades for the first time, and the Nez Perce chiefs announce the end to their sphere of influence. Drying salmon continues as a pink curtain across their horizons. Meanwhile, the cawing of scavenger birds – crows and ravens – accompanies the soaring swoops of the great bellied pelican, pointing to nature's own cleansing of overabundance. What the native fishermen can't process goes back into food chain, into the cycle of life.

A Supernatural Event

What follows is one of the more astonishing stories in the shooting history of the Expedition. On the 19th, the boatmen are struggling to get the canoes through a series of risky

Not all the fish appear in edible condition; they are dying all along the river – a natural consequence of their upstream battles.

Boneville Power Administration

rapids and swift currents that dash past a treacherous high rock. Clark goes below and is sitting on another rock. It is an agonizingly slow process, over two hours, during which *"the men were obliged to get into the water and haul the canoes over Sholes ..."* It is interesting, or possibly boring, this waiting for the exertions in the cold water to be finished. Clark is wiling away his time; seeing a crane fly over, he shoots and bags it for dinner, along with duck. There is nothing extraordinary here.

As the last of the canoes come through the rapids, Clark goes on ahead in a smaller canoe, only to find hitherto teeming villages now seemingly abandoned in an instant. The soldiers walk into lodges filled with despondent natives awaiting death, *"Some hanging down their heads, Some Crying and others in great agitation ..."* [J5:303] This new and amazing phenomena, something bewildering, can only be explained in metaphysical terms. The locals somehow now believe that the white men *"came from the clouds &c &c and were not men ..."* [J5:305] This spontaneous and visceral belief is truly a challenge for the Captains. Clark's explanation in retrospect fills in the story from the Umatilla's point of view.[g] *"These shots (having never heard a gun), a few light clouds passing, the fall of the birds and our immediately landing and coming towards them convinced them we were from above."*

The epidemic of fear soon passes, allayed into goodwill by Sacagawea's presence with little Pomp, a time for smokes, and

---

[e] Contemporary cooks use this historic style to produce "planked salmon." The plank is made of cedar, which imparts its flavor to the cooking fish.

[f] Pounded salmon was discussed at the *Confluence of Cultures* conference, May 2003 in Missoula, MT, by Pat Cole of the Chinook tribe where she indicated it was a long-standing process used by her people.

[g] This explanation is not in the *Journals* – rather, it is believed that Clark gave this view directly to his editor, Nicholas Biddle, after the return of the Expedition, as it is in the Biddle edition as if it were *Journal* text.[166]

an exchange of small amounts of their scarce, precious trade goods for fish and berries. Perhaps these pale creatures are not Sky Gods coming to destroy the tribe. The Corps canoes on. Observing these Spirit Beings giving gifts and taking earthly food helps quell some of the natives' doubts. Further on, when the group stops on an island a vast number, some *"100 Indians Came from the different Lodges, and a number of them brought wood which they gave us ..."* J5:306 Are these curious, dark-eyed earthlings coming in a huge protective group to look at spirit beings, and bringing their most valuable gift (wood) as a supplication? Has the frightening rumor spread downriver faster than the speeding canoe convoy?

Food and the wood to cook it on (with the resultant warm, comforting fire at night) puts the ragged travelers solidly back on an earthly plane. Thanks to Clark's fine aim, the two Captains dine sumptuously this night, indulging in *"a Crain & 2 ducks"* which York or Charbonneau probably cooks up. Around the other mess fires their men are working their way through the newly discovered pounded salmon and presumably more of the dog supply. To enhance the re-emerging hospitality, Cruzatte and Gibson fiddle up a musical storm to please their visitors and the officers *"gave to the principal man a String of wompon treated them kindly for which they appeared greatfull."* J5:306

Shipping Supplies

On the mercantile side, while stopping for some fishy supplies and *"other provisions,"* Gass astutely observes *"some articles which shewed that white people had been here or not far distant during the summer."* J10:159 But no one is trading tea, biscuits, or flour. Everything is relatively indestructible hardware. The ribbons distributed earlier are one of the few luxury, or decorative, goods other than beads. It is easy to imagine upgrading from common, everyday cookware to an improved quality as a surplus of money becomes available, so the savvy salmon traders of the Columbia barter their salmon and relegate their utilitarian but nondescript pots to the shelf in favor of beautiful shiny copperware. Each is hand-hammered and every tap of the mallet leaves a wonderful indentation that, when finished, produces a sculpture, almost a three-dimensional glowing globe, not quite drawn together at the top. Surely it appeals to their aesthetic sense as well as the practical, and these copper kettles are quite popular.

In an Ecological Nanosecond

On this chilly, clear frosty Friday morning of October 20, the men *"brackfast on Dog's flesh."* They shrug off the usual lack

of firewood and move out. The entourage accompanying them is about 350 sightseers. Later that morning they find that native lodges are loaded with another winter provision: *"we Saw in the last Lodges acorns of the white oake* h *which the Inds. inform they precure above the falls."* J5:309

Seabirds – pelicans and cormorants – are sighted. Sixteen miles downstream they haul in to purchase *"a fiew indifferent fish and Some berries."* Within an ecological nanosecond the Eastern hunter, Clark, is shooting Pacific seabirds: *"Killed 2 large speckle guls"* which are not positively identified, but Clark appears to be acquainted with the species. Four *"Small ducks the flavour of which much resembles the Canvis back,"* join the dinner plans. The hunters bring in nine ducks and a goose. More rapids ensue, the now-ordinary fish lodges are passed. The quality of fuel is actually declining further yet, *"only a fiew Small Sticks, & green willow &c."* J11:361 This is a meager and smoky fire.

Fueling Problems

Early the next day the explorers set out, again shivering and working against the cold. *"we Could not Cook brakfast before we embarked as usial for the want of wood or Something to burn."* This marks a change in routine, a contrast to the early daylight and departure time of the summer months when they stopped for breakfast only after two to three hours of travel. It is approaching winter, it is cold, and they need food, warm food, to fuel and perk them up after a cold night. Without a campfire they literally need to raise their bodily temperatures, and they do this through activity, becoming smooth-running machines. As they proceed, Clark sees five lodges where they stop to purchase wood for boiling dogs and fish. Despite his earlier comments of a *"verry Cold morning,"* after forty-two miles of paddling J5:315 Capt. Clark writes, *"fortunately for us the night was worm."* Life improves as the day goes on. But the dense, protein-rich foods available to them are those they can't hunt (dog and fish) and the botanic bounty of greens and berries is disappearing with the season. Gone is self-sufficiency; once again they are buyers in a sellers' market.

Gone, too, are the gifts of wood. They buy at a high price. And for the first time, the Corps buys a complete take-out breakfast: *"a fiew pounded rotes* [NB: roots] *fish and Acorns of the white oake, those Acorns they make use of as food*

---

h The only white oak found in Washington is the Oregon white, or Garry oak, (*Quercus garryana* Dougl.ex.Hook) which occurs mainly west of the Cascades, but extends up the Columbia gorge to about twenty miles above The Dalles.

[NB: raw and roasted], and inform us they precure them of the nativs who live near the falls below ..." J5:317 The roots are probably the staple, wapato. Gass describes the final product: "Here we got some bread, made of a small white root, which grows in this part of the country." J10:159

High Water + Camas Bread = Homemade Beer

As the party discovers, the village below is reached by a path, for at this point the rapids are so dangerous that the commanders put ashore anyone who cannot swim. The grueling task of getting the canoes through the "verry dangerous" rock-studded whitewater consumes the entire day, and they make thirty-two miles, coming to rest at an Indian encampment, where they buy wood.

The party had apparently purchased camas bread weeks before, at one of the upper Nez Perce villages, for the uneaten dregs were stashed by John Collins. Thoroughly wet from the drenchings in the whitewater, they soured and fermented, and on October 21 the private presents the party with "Some verry good beer." This appears to be a one-time occurrence and the camas is quashed, perhaps discouraged by the Captains, who don't want nutritious food converted into alcohol. It is the last mention of alcohol until the Expedition is nearing white civilization in the fall of 1806.

New Foods

Several new and welcome vegetables hit the menu. On October 21, wapato or arrowhead comes from the bakery in the form of cake or bread, which the men enjoy. The next day, Shahaptian natives introduce filberts, and a strictly local cranberry. Gass writes: "some call them cranberries, whether the real kind or not I am not certain." J10:161 He remarks that the cranberry seems similar to ones he knows but it is a new scientific discovery, probably the American cranberrybush, a viburnum. The filbert is totally new, another scientific find (Corylus Cornota var. californica); although commonly confused with its previously known relative, the hazelnut.

There is even more welcome news from the locals: great quantities of the pounded fish are "Sold to the whites people who visit the mouth of this river." J5:325 Regrettably, the men are also beginning to view the constant presence of the natives as a threat, and the old Nez Perce chiefs have overhead whispers of an attempt to kill them. J5:326 Violence really isn't necessary; simply withholding food and fuel would have done the job. Even more surprisingly, the Indians become reluctant to sell their salmon, which, Captain William shrugs off, "compells us to make use of dogs for food." This inconvenience really isn't troublesome, since the men have come to enjoy the flavor.

Preparing the Food: Native Ways

Much of the food that the Corps is eating is prepared in styles new to their palates. In fact, part of the changed flavors and textures come from the the cooking itself (the pit) and the modes used in preparation and preservation (pounded, then pressed salmon). On September 20, 1805, Clark gives a very explicit and technical description of how Nez Perce pit roasting is done, and it is reminiscent of the technique used in a traditional Hawaiian pig roast.

... dig a large hole 3 feet deep Cover the bottom with Split wood on the top of which they lay Small Stones of about 3 or 4 Inches thick, a Second layer of Splited

---

POUNDED SALMON

Clark describes the following process for preparing pounded salmon while on the upper Columbia: October 22d, Tuesday, 1805

... I observe great numbers of Stacks of pounded Salmon <butifully> neetly preserved in the following manner, i e after Suffiently Dried it is pounded between two Stones fine, and put into a speces of basket neetly made of grass and rushes of better than two feet long and one foot Diamiter, which basket is lined with the Skin of Salmon Stretched and dried for the purpose, in theis it is pressed down as hard as possible, when full they Secure the open part with the fish Skins across which they fasten tho' the loops of the basket that part very Securely, and then on a Dry Situation they Set those baskets the Corded part up, their common Custom is to Set 7 as close as they can Stand and 5 on top of them, and secure them with mats which is raped around them and made fast with cords and Covered also with mats, those 12 baskets of from 90 to 100 w. each <basket> form a Stack. thus preserved those fish may be kept Sound and Sweet Several years, as those people inform me, Great quantities as they inform us are Sold to the whites people who visit the mouth of this river as well as to the nativs below.

wood & Set the whole on fire which heats the Stones, after the fire is extinguished they lay grass & mud mixed on the Stones, on that dry grass which Supports the Pash-Shi-co [camas] root a thin Coat of the Same grass is laid on the top, a Small fire is kept when necessary in the Center of the kile &c. [The "kile" most likely is a "kiln," meaning a furnace or oven used in baking or steaming.]

In storing salmon-trout and other types of smaller trout, the Chinookian/Shahaptians use a technique similar to that of the Mandans: earth burial (caching). According to Clark, *"the mode of buring those fish is in holes of various Sizes, lined with straw on which they lay fish Skins in which they inclose the fish which is laid verry close, and then Covered with earth of about 12 or 15 inches thick."* J5:331

The Horror of The Dalles and The Great Falls of the Columbia

A mere issue of food is almost meaningless in the face of what lies ahead, which calls for every ounce of courage and strength the boatmen have. The red-headed Kentuckian walks the trail overlooking the chasm and evaluates what ac-tion to take. Horrified, on October 24 he pens, *"the water was agitated in a most Shocking manner boils Swell & whorl pools"* then later, *"I deturmined to pass through this place notwithstanding the horrid appearance ... whorling in every direction (which from the top of the rock did not appear as bad as when I was in it;[)] however we passed Safe to the astonishment of all the Inds ..."* J5:333 This should have produced total ex-haustion, but the excitement of conquest animates Cruzatte and the other boatmen, who have gotten themselves and the boats through what is probably the worst water adventure of the trip. That night they dance for the natives, feet falling in time with the rollicking strains of the violin. It is a good night.

Clark, too, is jacked up by adrenalin. He writes and writes, about sending the non-swimmers by pathway carry-ing their precious guns, paper, and the critical ammunition. About construction, in which he remarks with elation that the local houses are the first native wooden housing he's seen since leaving Illinois. He points out that at least half of each house is reserved for storing a small supply of berries and pounded fish, a good practice that means less searching for food in the harsh winter weather. He is awed by the sheer

Courtesy of *We Proceeded On*, collection of the Oregon Historical Society

The major falls on the Columbia are a canoeing challenge. Not wanting to take the time, and in some cases having no reasonable land route, portage is bypassed in favor of just running the rapids and the falls. Mirac-ulously, all attempts succeed.

quantity of fish being preserved: *"I counted 107 Stacks"* and *"10,000 w. of neet fish."* [J5:335] The next day is almost a repeat, complete with canoes sinking, being refloated, and sinking again. But then they are through.

With the horror of The Dalles behind them, the men once again turn their attention to food. Fortune smiles upon the happy conquerors. They make a large purchase of *"16 common bags of pounded Sammon Some white bread cramberies &c,"* Whitehouse records, continuing, *"we Saw a war party of Indians, with horses. they had deer & bear meat with them ... our Capts. gave him [the chief] a meddle, then he gave our Capts. Some bears oil and a freah Sammon."* In a second entry for that day, the Kentuckian adds, *"he gave us Some meat of which he had but little ..."* Clark must have been inspired by the sight of deer meat, for that afternoon he sends hunters out to look for any sign of game. Drouillard returns with a small deer. The Captain has meanwhile shot a very fat goose, and he smugly remarks that he, and presumably his mess, *"Suped hartily on venison & goose."* No other sergeants report this for dinner; they must have been eating pounded salmon and dog.

Diplomatic Moves

However inconceivable it may seem, so far removed from the White House and later the formalities first observed in the Mandan villages, a modified diplomatic ritual is now in place. The local Chinook host gives a little food as a sign of friendship, the Captains give a medal in return, and then they smoke the pipe. The scene is not as elaborate as the posh events staged along the Missouri, but it is quite within the tradition.

On the following day, October 26, the same ritual will be repeated as two great chiefs and fifteen men come over in a huge canoe. The exchange list of the day is a little more interesting than the previous token gifts:

GIFT EXCHANGE

Indians give:	Corps gives:
Dressed elk skin	A medal to each chief
Some deer meat	A red silk handkerchief to each chief
2 cakes of white bread made of white root	A knife to the first chief
	An arm band, paint, a comb to the chief's son
	A ribbon tied with a tin gorget
	2 venison "hams"

In a second *Journal* entry for that Saturday, Clark makes a rather confessional statement about their gift-giving, *"as we thought it necessary at this time to treat those people verry friendly & ingratiate our Selves with them, to insure us a kind & friendly reception on our return, we gave Small presents to Several, and half a Deer to them to eat."* Cruzatte breaks out his fiddle, and guests sit by a warm fire watching York dance, enjoying the party. Building a fire to host the chiefs is no problem, an interesting transition from previous days when no fuel except willow was available. The hunters report pine and white oak in the vicinity; the firewood crisis has eased.

The importance of the chiefs must have prompted the quantity of gifts, but the ability to give food back marks the Corps' independence from the grips of a barren wasteland and the ever-present salmon along the river. Once again, guns are cracked out for hunting, and their owners are inspired. *"our hunters killed five Deer, 4 verry large gray Squirrels, a goose & Pheasant, one man giged a Salmon trout which we had fried in a little Bears oil which a Chief gave us yesterday and I think the finest fish I ever tasted."* Clark's optimism is up, and he continues listing more welcome signs, *"Saw great numbers of white Crains,"* and *"our hunters Saw Elk & bear signs to day in the white oake woods ..."* Whitehouse has slightly different information: *"they Saw a great nomber of deer in the timbered land. we saw a great no. of geese and ducks."* [J11:372]

Enough to Drive You Crazy

If the prospect of an enlarged menu is looking good, a few other things aren't. The disappointing and perhaps hazardous news is, *"maney of our Stores entirely Spoiled by being repeetedly wet."* Another distracting nuisance is the tiny, itchy, biting fleas from the salmon camps (most likely human body lice [J5:344n6]). They are making everyone a little crazy, and there are no spare clothes to change into while the first set is washed and dried.[i] So, *"they Strip off their Clothes and kill the flees, dureing which time they remain neckid."* [J5:343]

Having been deprived of hunting for such a long period, some of the men go out again on October 27. Again the *Journal* entries are inconsistent, but the Captain tallies what appears to be the days' total: four deer, a sage grouse, and a squirrel. This is all fine, except that the overnight chiefs and

---

i   Military historian Bob Moore, in *Tailor Made, Trail Worn*, page 244, notes that during intense water activities and while washing clothes, the men were not completely naked as the *Journals* might suggest, but wore a modest but minimal breechclout [breechcloth].

a few of their men stay on and are then joined by seven other members of the tribe, smoking and eating. Whitehouse appears not too pleased with this unwelcome distribution of food, *"we Set the Savages across the River which had been with us all day eating our venison."* J11:374

A New Language
Having passed through The Dalles, the Corps is entering the territory of a different linguistic group, the Chinook. The Wishrams and the Wascos both speak this language and live on opposite sides of the river. The falls at The Dalles created a convenient demarcation for two distinct subcultures. Continuing downriver on October 28, they are into new linguistics and must rely completely on their sign-talker, Drouillard.

Again, Lewis complains of pilfering. What he does not understand is the 'give-away' custom of the river people. When natives pass through another nation's territory, the travelers give gifts to the host people as a token of appreciation for a safe passage. This is done by laying out the gifts on the riverbank. Therefore, as the Corps laid out their water-sodden supplies and tools to dry, the Chinooks assumed that the items were gifts and could not understand the whitemen's ire when they took them.[167]

Shopping for breakfast with the native merchants is the first order of business – the messes opt for a healthy meal of dog balanced with wapato bread and dried berries. One Indian they meet dresses his hair in queue and wears a European-style round hat. This headgear apparently is a trade from another Indian farther downriver. Clark sees others *"have a musket, a Sword, and Several Brass Tea kittles which they appear to be verry fond of ..."* The European influence is becoming highly visible and is being incorporated into the local culture.

Eco-Zone Change & New Dishes for the Menu
In just four days – from October 24 to 28 – the ecological zone changes, or perhaps it is the gathering or trading pattern of the natives that changes. Whatever the cause, berries are the tip-off. Bearberries first appear upriver, cranberries downriver. Bearberries prefer dry, well-drained soil – preferably in pine woodlands, while cranberries – like their eastern cousins – prefer a boggy, marshy terrain.[168]

To the carnivorous crew, the robes worn by the Wasco natives indicate what local game is available: wolf, deer, elk, wild cat or lynx, fox, mountain sheep, and otter [a misnomer: Clark is actually referring to the harbor seal].

After making a large purchase of twelve dogs, four sacks

of fish, and some *"ascid"* berries, the canoe party paddles off. There is little of significance for the next several days; they eat duck, squirrel, venison, nuts, berries, and fish.

Then, on October 30, the party spots a few of the largest birds on the American continent, the California condor – wingspan nine and a half feet. These huge birds are quite far from their current range, but apparently they inhabited Washington and Oregon two hundred years ago. At a loss for names, the explorers search their memories and apply the only possible name they can relate to, calling them *"turkey buzzards."* Reubin Field kills their first specimen on November 18, and despite the amount of meat that could have been eaten, it is not. Historically the label "buzzard" carries with it the notion of scavenger, an eater of dead and rotting meat, and an unpleasant, disagreeable association with flies and maggots. Human culinary tradition dictates that the buzzard is never delivered to the cookpot, nor brought to table. It is one of the untouchables.

If this bird is a reject, others are not. The men are spotting an abundance of wild fowl: tundra swans, geese, duck, sandhill cranes, loon – and all of these birds might have come to rest on the cookfire spit.

New Fuel, Strawberry Farms
The *Journals* record that the Captains have again taken to camping on islands, and this little bit of isolation without company gives them a chance to wander about and make some botanic observations. The poverty of the high Columbian plain has changed to an abundance in the wet mountains, which grow spruce, pine, cedar, oak, and cottonwood. While camping on the October 30, Clark notes a new tree, a new fuel. Ash. And it *"makes a tolerable fire,"* he laconically jots.

The last day of October brings another surprise, Strawberry Island. Despite the change of season as winter is setting in, the coastal weather is mild enough that the tender strawberry plants have not yet been decimated. Clark is strolling. *"I walked thro this Island which I found to verry rich, open & covered with Strawberry vines, and has greatly the appearance of having at Some period been Cultivated."* To those who have never lived in wild places, or dug their hands into Mother Earth for years on end, this statement may be questionable. How could he tell? But these explorers have keen eyes for the wild versus the cultivated, and their families farm. Anyone who pays attention to the natural world, or whose family eats off the land, knows what to look for.

As Clark views the island, it is fairly large; he estimates it to be about three miles long and one mile across. It is easy to imagine the indigenous women sitting on this fine spot in the middle of the river, chatting and carefully picking the fragile berries in the summer sunshine. Their children might pick a while, but like all restless young, they would soon be whooping and chasing, entertaining themselves regardless of the tedious work absorbing their elders.

The fertility of the washed-down, sandy mountainous grit is apparently quite hospitable to native plants taking hold, as well as to Clark's notion of cultivation, for he observes that *"The natives has dug roots in Some parts of this Isld."* Most likely it is the wapato or arrowroot, which thrives in a wet situation; and the geologic composition of the island is favorable and fortuitous.

Cold at the Lower Elevation

By now, mornings are raw – November has arrived and on November 1, Gass reveals a bit about the men's view of the weather when he remarks, *"we could not go into the water, without uneasiness on account of the cold."* Yet the uncomfortably cold water does not deter a hungry native man who they encounter at another waterfall along their way. Just the day before, Clark wrote, *"one of the men Shot a goose above this Great Shute, which was floating into the Shute when an Indian observed it, plunged into the water & Swam to the Goose and brought in on Shore, at the head of the Suck."* Editor Nicholas Biddle notes, *"great danger, rapids bad, a descent*

The Columbia plank-house is new to the Captains who admire its design and effectiveness in the climate.

Paul Kane, collection of the Stark Museum, Orange, Texas

close by him (150 feet off) of all Columbia river, current dashed among rocks if he had got in the Suck – lost."

The Corps has known near-starvation, and Clark pityingly observes this man's hunger, *"as this Indian richly earned the goose I Suffered him to keep it which he about half picked and Spited it up with the guts in it to roste."* J5:363 To risk everything over a goose – gambling with the morbid prospect of a smashing end to your life, and then leaving feathers and annoying pin feathers on, with guts inside, in the haste to cook it, is to be desperately hungry. This one goose means little to the Expedition, and compassion is one of Clark's greater virtues.

The Food Business

But the red-headed Captain is not totally happy with the buying process. The merchants are not appealing and while their health is good, Clark finds their appearance appalling. He notes, *"Sweled legs, large about the knees, – owing to the position in which they Set on their hams ..."* J5:367 and is uncomfortable with their hygiene, *"They are durty in the extreme both in their Coockery and in their houses."* Five or six families live in one house and the fish is stored under their beds, which are raised like the upper level of a bunk bed. Nuts, roots, and berries are stored between the bed and the outside wall. From the native point of view, it is logical to keep your food where you can get at it, and it's protected.

If trading is the key, the Corps can still eat. Seduced by trade beads, the natives *"will part with the last mouthfull"* to obtain them. J5:371 Food has become foremost in the Corps concerns. After near-starvation, the dietary change from meat to fish, and the debilitating gastro-intestinal ailments in late-September, the party wants nothing better than an elk or deer. However, it's still the wrong terrain and they're not available.

The End is in Sight

By the time they sight the Pacific Ocean on November 7, 1805, it is almost winter. Berries have ripened and are already gathered. The hoofed animals they enjoy eating are living off fading grasses; soon they will begin to deplete their body fat. On the other hand, plentiful salmon runs have come in – along the length of the Colombia tons of fish are dried, preserved, and awaiting the trade in pounded fish. There will be an upswing in fish bartering as winter sets in, as there will be for the vegetable root, wapato. Clark notes on October 22, 1805: *"Captain Lewis joined me haveing delayed on the way to examine a root of which the nativs had been digging great quantities in the bottoms of this River."*

"Ocian in View, O! the Joy!" – November 7, 1805 – Clark.

So, how to express the importance of food on the trip within the context of the trip? The Captains resort to the simple expediency of *naming* and in so doing, weave the warp of food against the weft of geography. Since the United States Board of Place Names has not yet been invented, the men are free to attach whatever title they wish to any feature they deem worthy. A short inspection reveals:

Influences on the Choices of Place Names

◆ Animals or foods make excellent choices.
◆ Manufactured items are allowable.
◆ Adjectives or themes expressing disappointment are acceptable.
◆ Renaming is allowable if the theme of the day changes.

Animals they encounter leave them simply astounded – and many names reflect this awe. Buffalo River, Goose River, Grouse Island, Turkey Island, Fish Creek, Porcupine River. The imprint of the fauna on their minds calls to their inner being. What did that place look like? Maybe it smells, as does another natural feature, Sulphur Springs. And so, the men develop a heightened image, a remembrance of special places. If they remember now, they can go back.

Themes of difficulty or disappointment are also expressed in the same fashion, not just by the Corps but also by the French who named their villages "short of bread," "misery," and a host of other evocative nicknames. This entire naming process, and the remembrance it brings, infuses much of the trip with memories of how they got there, how they felt: *"Traveler's Rest;" "Camp Disappointment;" "Friendly Village."* Finally, when talking about name changes, there is a little quip about "good humored island becomes bad humored island when the day goes bad."[169]

Later, Clark's *"Butter Island"* provides a similarly sardonic view of provisioning shortages, directed at himself, *"I call this Island Butter Island, as at this place we mad use of the last of our*

At this point there is certainly no feasting, but starvation has stepped aside.

Food and Geography

In the eighteen months since leaving "civilization" at St. Charles, the Corps has feasted and fasted, been frozen and sweltered, found routes expected and became lost or disappointed. The hunters go out on a daily basis, an important function for their collective well-being. Trying to determine the correct direction in a densely vegetated wilderness is a singularly difficult task which engages both the hunters and the entire Corps. And somewhere along the line, food and geography intersect.

Food is one of the constants on the men's minds: They want and hope to eat on a regular basis. As part of their job, the journalists record the kills, and sometimes they mention what foods comprise a meal. The Captains always mention what the native hosts serve for dinner. Running out of food is also part of the drama, and it brings forth a fretful reminder of what has been lost, something that probably will not be regained until they are safely back to civilization.

R. L. Rickards - courtesy: Richards Western Art

EXAMPLES OF PLACE NAMES

Animals
Buffalo River
Grouse Island
Fish Creek
Porcupine River

Foods
Butter Island
Hungry Creek
No Preserves Island
No Water Creek

Equipment
Long Knife Creek
Gun Brook
Tin Cup Creek
Fishhook Rapids
Bakers Oven Island

Activities
Traveler's Rest
Kilt Colt Creek
Canoe Camp

People
Friendly Village
Jefferson, Madison, Gallatin Rivers
Shields River

Important Virtues
Wisdom River
Philosophy River

butter." J2:395 Similarly, Clark describes "*no preserve Island*" as the "*place* [where] *we used the last of our preserves.*" J3:49 Other negatively named features are "*no water creek,*" "*big dry river,*" and "*Hungry Creek.*"

"*Kilt Colt Creek*" J5:204 represents the ultimate of a desolate and rugged mountain wilderness in which the Corps is literally close to dying. Fasting becomes simple starvation, and it is this young, unweaned colt that saves them, at least for the moment. Emerging alive after coming through that horrifically rough, jumbled, rocky, and frozen terrain of the Bitterroot Range is the ultimate tribute to the men's ability to survive. But the name calls to memory that first little colt, that source of life-giving food, which receives Clark's tribute. Today, that place name remains unchanged, unlike many other less meaningful ones.

Such emotional highs/lows often define the *Journals*, but when it comes to naming, manufactured items also have their history: their manufacture, their use, perhaps even their loss. Just listen to the names from the past ... "*Knife River,*" "*Teapot Creek,*" *Tin Cup Creek.*" There are "*Bakers Oven Islands,*" "*Long Knife Creek,*" and "*Gun Brook.*" At one point, earlier along the Midwestern rivers, there is the "*Mill Island*" and "*Tavern Creek.*" These are reminders of something that has come before – places named, sometimes even before Lewis and Clark, places from our collective past.

Wintering on the Pacific Coast

Fort Clatsop: December, 1805 – March, 1806

sent out the men to hunt and examin the country...the wood was so thick that it was almost impenetrable, and... there was but little appearance of game ...

— LEWIS, DECEMBER 1, 1805

This reconstruction of Fort Clatsop near the Oregon coast is on the site of the Corps' 1805–06 winter quarters.

JUST THREE YEARS EARLIER, Meriwether Lewis had been dining on a regular basis with the President of the United States, eating what were probably the most sophisticated meals then being served in America. Now here he is, in the Pacific Northwest, looking every inch the ragged traveler. Gone from everything but memory are his sleek fitted pants, starched shirt, and handsomely ornate jacket. On his feet are *"mockersins"* instead of hose and buckled leather shoes.

Lewis, on September 22, 1805, expresses *"the pleasure I now felt in having tryumphed over the rocky Mountains ..."* He then goes silent for more than two months. Something seems to have broken his spirit for writing, perhaps the defeat of his hopes for finding that *"comfortable subsistance."*

Or is it the breakdown of his Easterner's vision of how easy it would be to reach the Pacific? Whatever it is, even eating becomes a picky, worrisome chore. After weeks of eating dried salmon – laced with pungent new forms of bacteria – his keen palate rises again; he takes up his pen and his eloquence returns, describing the new foods he is now encountering. What will they eat? What will comprise the Pacific provisions? On November 29, 1805, he records that *"the hunters they killed 4 deer 2 brant a goos and seven ducks."*

Necessary: Good Hunting Territory

The issue of how they are going to feed themselves over the winter becomes preeminent. On November 24, Clark writes that they must look for *"a convenient Situation to precure the Wild animals of the forest which must be our dependance for Subsisting this Winter, we have every reason to believe that the nativs have not provision Suffient for our Consumption, and if they had, their price's are So high that it would take ten times as much to purchase their <u>roots</u> & <u>Dried fish</u> as we have in our possesion ..."* J6:85 The choice begins to boil down to the type of animal they want to eat – elk being favored over deer for several particularly strong reasons. The men are now nearly naked and elk skin makes better clothing. Moreover, these animals are larger and easier to kill. Following the deer would take the party back upriver (to a colder location), away from the seacoast where they are determined to make salt and hail any passing merchant vessel. It is interesting to note that Sacagawea expresses her preference *"in favour of a place where there is plenty of Potas"* (probably Wa-patos). J6:84 To aggravate the situation further, there is a shortage of firewood and it is raining so heavily that the men probably couldn't bring back dry wood even if they could find it.

Canoes or Coffins?

On the northern shore of the Columbia, the Corps' wooden canoes might easily have become wooden coffins. Every element of nature has turned hostile and violent, impassively directed not just at the hungry travelers, but at everything around. Horrible squalls blow down trees, deluges and torrents of rain chill the men to the bone, for all the protective fabrics they've brought with them have rotted. Bedding is sodden; nothing remains dry. One of the canoes is thrown up like a pick-up-stick and is smashed in the storm, developing a two-foot-long crack. Even the animals which might have offered consolation in the form of hot soup have fled. A stoic's dinner review reveals, *"we Sent out the most of the men to drive the point for deer ... we Could find no deer ... the Swan & gees wild and Cannot be approached, and the wind to high to go either back or forward* [to places they expected to find elk], *and we have nothing to eate but a little Pounded fish which we purchasd. at the Great falls, This is our present Situation,! truly disagreeable."* J6:91

Feasting and Fasting

What the men are experiencing is their old foe, hunger, and they are involuntarily fasting. Their bodies are craving extra calories due to the cold, and there is no succor. These dreadful times are reminiscent of their suffering in the Bitterroots.

On November 29, 1805, while the main crew remains stationary, Lewis and five of the better hunters – *"drewyer R.Fields, Shannon, Colter & labiesh"* – set out to reconnoiter the area, hoping to find reliable hunting grounds for the winter. The happy shock of returning successfully with *"4 deer 2 brant a goos and seven ducks,"* jogs Lewis out of his literary lethargy. His scouting group takes one deer and moves into an abandoned native hunting lodge, which shelters the bedraggled party. The remainder of the game goes back to the main camp. In the meantime, the mess cooks for the main party are serving out *"dried pounded fish ... boiled in a little Salt water,"* and the salt water cookery makes the men sick.

While elk or deer may top the preference list, fowlers are also sent out. From his vantage point that same day, Clark notes the presence of the California condor, *"grey and bald eagle's, large tailed Hawks, ravens & crows in abundance."* Lewis, in a different locale, is seeing the same plentitude: *"a great abundance of fowls, brant, large geese, white brant sandhill Cranes, common blue crains, cormarants, haulks, ravens, crows, gulls and a great variety of ducks, the canvas back, duck-inmallard, black and white diver, brown duck – &c &c – ."* The abundance of gamebirds seems to be something of a surprise, summoning up memories of avian stews and roasts that the meat-eating, fish-devouring troops may have missed since their happy experiences with the plump, tasty grouse of the Plains. Indeed, on November 30, Clark's fowling squad brings back *"<u>three</u> Hawks, which we found fat and delicious"* and *"3 black Ducks,"* or coots, which are not really ducks at all. However lip-smacking these are, they are only tidbits, little appetizers when compared to the totality of food needed.

A Meager Provisions List

These are bleak times. By the time Fort Clatsop is finished in late December, the Corps is already settling into homebase, complete with a gray and dreary routine. The inventory

After selecting the winter site just inland on the south side of the Columbia, the first task is to build the winter fort. It is completed in three weeks, just before Christmas, despite daily rain.

R. L. Rickards - courtesy: Rickards Western Art

pedition began with a set of six nesting kettles. They document at least one floating away. There was a small black tin saucepan: not noted here. Do they still have a corn mill; it appears not (gave one away, cached one, but what of the third one?). The rivers (and perhaps the natives) seem to have caused disappearances that are un-logged, forgotten in the midst of too many drenchings, too many wild river rides. Most items listed on the *"Camp Equipage"* list are irreplaceably lost. They still have flints, because they continue to cook and the rifles work. And, despite the listing of only one kettle, they clearly had several more operating at the Salt Works.

Missing in the Fog, Missing in the Bog

A gnawing, haunting concern for missing men is a constant theme throughout the trip, but even more so when the Corps reaches the coast and small parties go out in the fog, through bogs, tangling with dense thickets. Before they have settled in and gotten their bearings, Lewis and his party of five are gone for six days, November 29 through December 5, and Clark begins fretting. Hunters and meat bearers wander without compasses and have no sun to help them navigate. One of Clark's major operational concerns for the hunters and saltmakers is to assure they have a beaten path to find their way back to the fort. Lost men would be an emotional and military complexity they don't need.

The going is rough. Rain and sleet fall – the cold air is soggy, clammy, and piercingly wet. On the north shore of the Columbia on December 16, storm winds reach hurricane strength: *"The winds violent Trees falling in every derection, whorl winds, with gusts of rain Hail & Thunder, this kind of weather lasted all day, Certainly one of the worst days that ever was!"* [J6:126] This is in the midst of a meat-gathering foray, and sturdy, stable Clark certainly is not given to dithering. Another time, Lewis and his party find that retrieving the game is almost impossible due to wind, weather, difficult terrain, and distance. Burden bearers from Clark's detachment are sent out and what happens? *"they found the Elk after being lost in the woods for one Day and part of another, the most of the meat was Spoiled, the distance was So great and uncertain and the way bad, they brought only the Skins."*

Clark compiles on December 7 also itemizes the minuscule number of items left in the provisions category. It corroborates what they already know; they have almost nothing. *"Salt ... Kittle ... Sugar ... Coffee ... Bread ... Pork"*

Bread & Pork? The last two items raise some questions for any reader. Back in the Bitterroots these items were clearly gone (*"... portable soup, a few canesters of which, and a little bears oil and 20lbs. Of candles form our stock of provision ..."*), and there have been no references to any new acquisitions. The bread is likely wapato-cake "bread" obtained from the Clatsops. The pork is more troublesome – there are no references to wild pig (and it is not clear that any existed in the territory). This may be another writing "glitch" that has been seen before – Clark is thinking preserved meat (elk, deer, etc.) and instead writes his favorite: "pork."

The Long-Gone Equipage – Harkening back to the original equipage lists compiled both in Philadelphia and St. Louis, there are some implications that shouldn't be overlooked. Almost nothing is left – not the Indian goods, not the basic comforts of canvas and clothing, nor the tons of provisions. Even some of the basic cooking tools are gone, which means that the cooks are improvising a lot. The Ex-

R. L. Rickards - courtesy: Rickards Western Art

The terrain and climate decrease the hunters' success.

Even as they settle in, the inclement weather can be blamed for less-efficient hunting: Wounded game escapes and becomes lost in the snow or the rain. There is suffering all around, needless waste, frustration instead of food. Even the efforts of the careful hunters are defeated, *"landed to take bracfast on 2 Deer which had been killed & hung up, one of which we found the other had been taken off by [s]ome wild animal probably Panthors ..."* [J6:114] The day's events sometimes provide a bad tale told over dried fish – *"our Standing friend,"* [J6:104] or a parsimonious root dinner.

A recent analysis of historic weather patterns leads one atmospheric science researcher to conclude that the terrible weather in the winter of 1805–06 was a rain-dumping La Niña in the Northwest.[a]

Down to Salt Camp

Of the five items listed by Clark for provisions upon arrival at Fort Clatsop, it appears that the Corps has salt, but only a little left on December 7. Although they left St. Louis with 750 pounds of it, there is not enough to last until the Corps returns to Montana and reaches the cache at the Marias River, where they had left a keg of salt. [J4:275] Remembering back, they have a lusty taste for it and complain in its ab-

sence, as Gass writes on December 25. *"We have no kind of provisions but meat, and we are without salt to season that."* Or, *"Salt is scarce without which fish is but poor and insipid."* [J10:150] To that end the salt camp, a manufactory, is established in what is now Seaside, about sixteen miles south-west below the mouth of the Columbia. It is approximately fifteen miles by trail from the Fort.[170]

On December 28, 1805, *"J. Field, Wm Bratton, and George Gibson"* are sent to scout out *"a convenient place [to] form a Camp and Commence making Salt ..."* The location they choose is environmentally sound: it has fresh drinking water nearby, a good source of wood – which they will be burning continually – and a high concentration of salt in the water. As the fresh water of the Columbia meets the sea, the water turns brackish. This fresh-water dilution decreases as currents sweep past the outgoing river, dispersing fresh water into the sea as it travels down the coast. Just above Seaside, the land at the northerly side of the little inlet helps deflect the current seaward, and a small back-eddy caused by Tillamook Head to the south carries concentrated salts north. In other words, the saltmakers chose a perfect location.

One gallon of salt is brought home for the Captains' approval on January 5. Lewis opines that it is *"excellent, fine, strong, & white; <salt;> this was a great treat to myself and most of the party, having not had any since the 20th ..."* The Corps has been without salt for almost two weeks.

On January 25 the saltmakers report they have made a bushel of salt in three weeks, which was brought to the Fort on February 3. This amounts to two fluid-quarts a day, less than expected. Three weeks later, on February 19, Sergeant Ordway is sent with a party to close the salt camp and return with the equipment and remainder of salt, and at that point Lewis reports that their inventory is now 20 gallons of salt, 12 gallons of which he sets aside in two iron-bound kegs for the return trip. Assuming that some salt from the 9 gallons returned on January 5 and February 3 is used in camp, then the total salt camp production is about 3 bushels, just what Lewis listed as his requirement on February 3. This suggests that the salt makers became much more efficient in the last four weeks and produced 2 bushels, about three fluid-quarts per day, up by a whole quart a day from when they started. When the Corps leaves Fort Clatsop on March 23, they have apparently used about half the salt produced, just under two pounds per day.

But, this level of production does more than make salt; it also makes invalids. Salt water has to be hauled from the sea to the shore, lifted, and poured into the boiling pots. These, in turn, are lifted and poured again as the water goes from

[a] Dr. Terrence Nelson, University of California–Davis, in a short note to the author, expressed his belief from tree-ring and other data that there was a sizable El Niño in the winter 1804–05, followed closely by a large La Niña in the 1805–06 winter the Corps spent in Fort Clatsop.

one pot to the other, being condensed. It is back-breaking work. The saltmakers fare badly and are finally returned home, carried in the arms of their compatriots, to mend. Bratton is literally invalided for several months until the Captains try a serious and strenuous set of steam baths, quite enough to get his body's attention.

How Can They Use All that Salt?

Not only are the cooks salting the pots of stew, but making jerky in the wet, humid atmosphere is still a problem. Salting the meat while smoking it is a good solution, speeding the process along and protecting the meat from putrefaction. Whitehouse addresses this point early on, commenting that *"the want of it in preserving our Provisions for the Winter, would be an object well worth our attention."* [J11:398] Processing skins for future use would entail far more salt than is practicable, so this is not really a consideration.

R. L. Rickards - courtesy: Rickards Western Art

The saltmakers labor to produce three bushels of sea-salt in just over seven weeks by boiling and evaporating sea water.

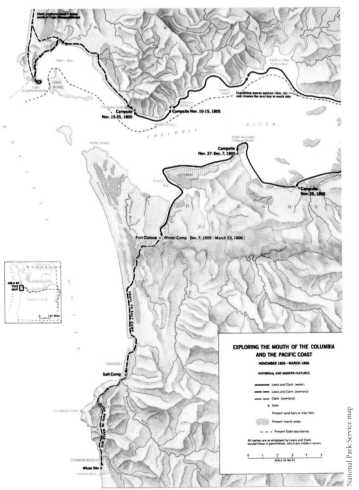

National Park Service map

The mouth of the Columbia and the fifteen-mile route to salt-camp.

Spoilage

There is a second, equally disturbing effect of the weather on the Expedition. The saturated air, the dripping moisture, creates a perfect humid breeding ground for bacteria. From a health perspective this isn't good; from a food perspective, it's nearly catastrophic. On December 14, 1805, Clark notes, *"all our last Supply of Elk has Spoiled in the repeeted rains which has been fallen ever Since our arrival at this place, and for a long time before."* The *Journals* are replete with harbingers of danger: words like *spoiled, tainted, unfit for uce, rotten.* The Captains address this issue head-on, using the time-honored smokehouse. The orders below show its importance.

For all of the times on the trail that the men had meat brought to them, now it is their job to help keep the smokehouse stocked. On January 1, 1806, Lewis issues a new set of standing orders; several commands relate directly to the food supply: *"No man is to be particularly exempt from the duty of bringing meat from the woods, nor none except the Cooks and Interpreters from that of mounting guard."*

The cooks, as always, are exempt from guard duty. Everyone gets to share in the unpleasant chore of carrying or hauling meat in from the fields, through bogs, fogs, and tangled morasses. Regarding the meat house, or smokehouse: *"It shall be the duty of the Sergt. of the guard to keep the kee of the Meat house, and to cause the guard to keep regular fires therein when the same may be necessary ..."*

The smokehouse is critical to the fort as a means of

preserving the meat that can rot too easily. Finally there is the issue of maintaining the Captains' fires, remembering that the Captains' mess will be cooking at one of those fires: *"Each of the old guard will every morning after being relieved furnish two loads of wood <each> for the commanding offercers fire."*

Provisions: Haggling and Niggling

Fort Clatsop is not isolated, and merchants from local tribes pass by – not with any regularity, but rather as another trading stop added onto their route. Trade among the locals is vigorous and involves the Clatsop, Chehalis, Clatskanie, and Tillamook to the south; Chinook, Wahkiakum, Cathlamet, and Cowlitz to the north. Reminiscent of other seafaring cultures that use waterways as trade routes (Venice, Italy, and Bangkok, Thailand, for example), the *"War ci a cum [Wahkiakum] Nation arrived ... they pass altogether by water."* J6:144 It should be noted that this group, including a young chief, gives the Captains a present of a half-bushel of roots, again affirming the value of food in good will and diplomacy.

But the Corps is becoming cynical and distrusts most of the overtures and interactions that occur that winter. These tribes, on the whole, are not seen as pleasant, reliable, trustworthy suppliers like the Mandans. They haggle, and the niggling over provisions is time-consuming and perhaps unpleasant. Clark, in growing aggravation, describes at various times the asking prices as being *"a high price,"* or even *"enormous prices."* Historian James Ronda suggests this nitpicking is a skill faintly admired by the whites accustomed to the tight Yankee sense of value; but on December 12, Clark notes, *"they [the Clatsop] are Close deelers, & Stickle for a verry little, never close a bargain except they think they have the advantage ..."* J6:123

However, *Journal* entries also call the Clatsops *"cheerful,"* *"very loquacious and inquisitive"* people who demonstrate *"extrodeanary friendship"* toward white men. Coboway, one of the local chiefs, makes somewhat regular visits to the fort, and is always pleasant; he and his people are viewed as *"mild inoffensive people."* However, Lewis, in particular, begins to lose his open view of the native people and is reverting, ever

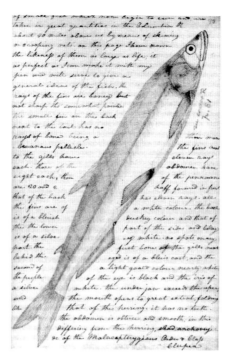

Lewis' eulachon sketch. J6:350

more strongly, to a hostile stance that characterizes much of the Eastern "white" population.

Fish Quest

And so the quest for food goes on. The Pacific Northwest protein supplies in winter vary, but not greatly. The cold, gray seas deliver up whale and seal, but fish are the mainstay. Seafood entrees include salmon, fresh "greenfish," sturgeon, and, beginning in late February, the little eulachon – a favorite of Lewis and indeed of all the men. Whitehouse is enthusiastic, calling it *"small fish, of a very excellent kind, resembling a herring, and about half the size."* J10:194

This eulachon, or "little candlefish," captivates the fussy gourmet Captain, who effuses that, *"the scales of this little fish are so small and thin that without minute inspection you would suppose they have none."* J6:344 Anyone familiar with the coarse, rough scales of larger fish can understand his excitement. He avidly continues, romancing the fish as surely as Shakespeare writing, "Shall I Compare Thee to a Summer Day?" *"... I find them best when cooked in Indian stile, which is by roasting a number of them together on a wooden spit without any previous preparation whatever."*

The ease of preparation here is an obvious plus. Consider them a self-basting food, something like chicken cooked on a vertical roaster. But there is more. Moist with natural oil, *"... they are so fat they require no additional sauce,"* and perhaps Lewis is thinking back to fish sauces he has eaten in the East. At the President's House, several of Jefferson's fish recipes feature either a savory anchovy sauce or a more gentle French preparation of melted butter mixed with chopped parsley and seasoned with pepper.[171] Unlike fish that need knives with special points to pry the bones out (a fine English invention), the eulachon is also easy to eat. *"I have heard the fresh anchovey much extolled but I hope I shall be pardoned for beleiving this quite as good. the bones are so soft and fine at they form no obstruction in eating this fish."* Lewis crowns his description with, *"... I think them superior to any fish I ever tasted, even more delicate and lussious than the white fish of the lakes which have heretofore formed my standart of excellence among the fishes."* [172]

Pit roasting is used when cooking sturgeon: layering hot

stones, the fish, then substituting *"boughs"* for the grass/mud mixture, and finally using mats to cover the whole opening. Water is then poured over the pit, steaming the large chunks of sturgeon. The difference of the unknown boughs adds a special distinctive layering of flavors. It cooks rapidly (one hour by Clark's estimation), and *"the Sturgeon thus Cooked is much better than either boiled or roasted. in their usial way of boiting [boiling] of other fish in baskets with hot Stones is not so good."* J6:380

Canine Cuisine

Fish is a normal food item for the Clatsops and other coastal natives to sell; but also one of the less common tastes is dog. The Columbian basin and Pacific coastline environments prompt the inclusion of dog on the menu, a meat first introduced a year earlier when several Missouri River tribes served dog feasts to the Captains as part of their native diplomacy.[b] But dog is not a staple in either of those native diets, nor on the normal American table.

The entrees are described as *"small ... party coloured; black white brown and brindle"* with long heads and pointy noses. Their ears are upright like wolves. However, *"the natives do not eat them nor appear to make any other use of them but in hunting the Elk ..."* J6:318 Rationally we might believe that the natives would find eating their hunting dogs incomprehensible, but they are not emotionally attached to these curs. Giving your favorite dog up to the ceremonial stew-pot is a mark of honor, showing that you have given your best. And dogs can be either items for sale (money in) or sometimes even recompense (money out). *"This morning we were visited by a Clatsop man who brought with him three dogs as a remuneration for the Elk which himself and Nation had Stolen from us Some little time Sence ..."* While the humans are comfortable with the exchange, the sparky little dogs seem to have innate misgivings. Perhaps doggy whines and howls carry on the wind, for *"the dogs took the alarm and ran off."* J6:300

On the other hand, the young army men are imbued with the Anglo-American view of canines as pets, as well as hunting companions; definitely mans' best friend. Seaman, the beloved Newfoundland, is almost a person. He certainly doesn't belong to the dog species anymore than do his friends, the privates. After all, aren't dogs are on the menu and being eaten on a regular basis? His master Lewis, the sophisticated eater, writes:

Our party from necessaty having been obliged to subsist some lenth of time on dogs have now become extreemly fond of their flesh; it is worthy of remark that while we lived principally on the flesh of this anamal we were much more healthy strong and more flesshey than we had been since we left Buffaloe country. for my own part, I have become so perfectly reconciled to the dog that I think it an agreeable food and would prefer it vastly to lean Venison or Elk. J6:162

The American explorers are not the first to dine on dog, not by a long shot. In 1769 the naturalist Joseph Banks, accompanying Captain Cook on a scientific expedition in the Pacific, found dog to be part of the Tahitian diet. "Few were there of the nicest of us but allowed as South Sea dog was next to an English lamb." This is quite a tribute. He went on to note that the Tahitian dogs were extremely tasty since they were fed a vegetarian diet.[173]

Christmas, 1805

Christmas at Fort Clatsop is a time when the Corps is thrown back upon itself as a true island in a sea of natives who have never had French, Spanish, or British traders pass through and stay long enough to impart the importance of European religious traditions; a year ago with the upper Missouri tribes accustomed to the French and British, there had been a bonhomie, a mutual accommodation of customs. Despite a gift of black root [c] from the Clatsops, the men apparently feel isolated among these people and retreat behind the walls of the fort. Sacagawea, the only Indian who understands their ways, participates in the spirit of the day as roundly as (or perhaps more so) the men. Again, Clark makes careful accounting of the day:

at day light this morning we we[re] awoke by the discharge of the fire arm of all our party & a Selute, Shoute and a Song which the whole party joined in under our windows, after which they retired to their rooms were Chearfull all the morning – after brackfast we divided our Tobacco which amounted to 12 carrots one half of which we gave to the men of the party who used tobacco, and to those who doe not use it we make a present of a handkerchief, The Indians leave us in the evening all the party Snugly fixed in their huts – I recved a presnt of Capt L. of a fleece hosrie Shirt Draws and Socks – , a pr. mockersons of Whitehouse a Small Indian basket of Gutherich [Goodrich], two Dozen white weazils

---

[b] The Yankton Sioux on August 29, 1804, J3:22 and the Teton Sioux on September 26, 1804, J3:116-9 served dog as a token of honor to their guests.

[c] Fire-blackened edible thistle, see page 244.

tails of the Indian woman, & Some black root of the Indians before their departure – Drewyer informs me that he Saw a Snake pass across the parth to day. The day proved Showerey wet and disagreeable.

we would have Spent this day the nativity of Christ in feasting, had we any thing either to raise our Sperits or even gratify our appetites, our Diner consisted of pore Elk, So much Spoiled that we eate it thro' mear necessity, Some Spoiled pounded fish and a fiew roots. J6:137

Ordway echos Clark, adding other details,

we all moved in to our new Fort, which our officers name Fort Clotsop after the name of the Clotsop nation of Indians who live nearest to us. ... we have no ardent Spirits, but are all in good health which we esteem more than all the ardent Spirits in the world. we still have nothing to eat but poore Elk meat and no Salt to Season that with but Still keep in good Spirits as we expect this to be the last winter that we will have to pass in this way. J9:106

Finally, Whitehouse records:

We found our huts comfortable, except smoking a little ... [we] are mostly in good health, A blessing, which we esteem more, than all the luxuries this life can afford, and the party are all thankful to the Supreme Being, for his goodness towards us. – hoping he will preserve us in the same, & enable us to return to the United States again in safety. J11:406

Christmas as magnified in the twenty-first century did not exist for the Corps – it was impeccably simple. The men appear to be a-religious, lacking even a small church service or any biblical references. In three Christmases, only Private Whitehouse actually addresses the issue of a Supreme Being. Lewis, raised in the East where churches abound and himself a Freemason, maintains a stony silence. The last Christmas on the road is brief and unadorned, not much more complicated than first-century ones celebrating Jesus' birth.

However, the records for all the journalists seem to echo memories of raucous Christmases past: Guns and liquor are paired. Holiday began at dawn with shots, perhaps to waken the holiday gods. Gunfire certainly rouses the Captains on every notable day worth celebrating. Nothing on the calendar of events passes by without a round of shots, either in volley or individually.

Better food would have been welcome, but the men stoically make the best of what they have. Certainly rotting elk without salt leaves them among the needy, the poorest supplicants with an almost-empty larder. Yet they are supported by their absolute faith that they will return home within a reasonable time and that better food is just across the Rockies. They give testimony and gratitude for good health.

Are there presents? Surprisingly, yes! And these Christmas gifts display the soft, loving sentiments carried in their hearts. Even Sacagawea – a woman who has adapted to this new world – embraces this spirit. The Captains give their troops surprise gifts of tobacco and silk handkerchiefs. Lest these seem stingy, think of living through an unprecedented winter of snow and rain. Wouldn't a wonderfully soft silk hanky to be used, or traded with the natives, be a treat? And tobacco is unexpected, thought to be long gone. Probably destined as Indian trade goods, what a measure of giving from the Captains to treat their men to something so precious and not hold it in reserve. There are moccasins, stitched by hand from Whitehouse for Clark, and the humble Indian basket bought with foresight from fisherman Goodrich.

And how did Sacagawea hide a collection of white weasel tails for Clark? She probably carried them from her Shoshone home in the Bitterroots, a lot of foresight. Even visiting Clatsops remember the day is important to their visitors and leave behind gifts of black roots – food, nourishment. The men greet the day with cheer, a song, and goodwill. The respect, esteem, and love behind all these events measures their humanity. Who could say that this was not Christmas at its best?

New Year's Day, 1806

While New Year's with the Mandans had a great air of bonhommie to it, the Clatsop New Year is more somber. The troops are not entranced with the locals and the exhilaration of the outward-bound trek has subsided into "waiting it out." The climate is doggedly dreary, relieved only by, *"sun visible for a few minutes about 11 a m."* J6:259 This brief solar glimpse comes on one of the just six days when the sun shines at all this winter.

Both Captains chronicle the usual festive day drill, and Whitehouse spells it out quite explicitly, *"At day break, the Men at the fort fired several Guns, as a salute to our Commanding officers; & in honor of the day."* J11:409

For once, Clark is ominously matter-of-fact and all-business, anxious to get the men onto the operating rules for the just-completed fort. He seems relatively unmoved by the specialness of the day. Sergeant Ordway notes *"a pleasant morning. 2 hunters went out a hunting ... in the evening the two hunters returned & had killed two large buck Elk."* J9:263-4 Two large elk, and no one notes that they are meager or poor. So, things are actually going rather well; there is a large quantity of fresh, unspoiled meat for the stewpot and more than enough for jerky. This is definitely good news. Lewis writes,

> our repast of this day tho' better than that of Christ-mass, consisted principally in the anticipation of the 1st day of January 1807, when in the bosom of our friends we hope to participate in the mirth and hilarity of the day, and when with the zest given by the recollection of the present, we shall completely, both mentally and cor-porally, enjoy the repast which the hand of civilization has prepared for us. at present we were content with eat-ing our boiled Elk and wappetoe, and solacing our thirst with our only beverage pure water.

Remembering some of their complaints about water quality along the trek, maybe this pure water is an unrecog-nized blessing. Later in the entry, Lewis gives a better de-scription of dinner: *"the hunters presented Capt. Clark and myself each a marrow-bone and tonge, <each> on which we suped."* [J6:151-2] The men honor their leaders with the best food they can get.

Despite Lewis' happy dreams of food prepared by the *"hand of civilization,"* and supping on marrow and tongue, the hunters away from camp are far less fortunate. They don't celebrate with shots, nor do they have elk and root stew. Hoping to bag game for the troops back at the fort, the two or three buckskin-clad men (Reubin Field, Collins, and perhaps Potts) are driven to dine on a raven *"which they eat on new years day to Satisfy their hunger."* [J9:264]

The other journalists record more mundane details of the day. There is a tiny trading parade of Clatsops, and the di-arists gawk as shamelessly as any spectators might for the native physiological adaptation to cold climes is not only

When a whale is beached, the Tillamooks claim ownership and immediately carve off all edible portions.

Courtesy: Richard Schlect

remarkable, but odd to American eyes. Whitehouse declares them to be *"entirely naked, excepting a breech Cloth which they wore & Skins thrown over their Shoulders."* [J11:409] Ordway, too, is astounded by their lack of dress and hardiness, *"they go bare leged all winter and bare footed Some kind of little Robe over their Shoulders &C. the women have Short peticoats made of Some kind of grass Some of which are twisted like twine, and are nearly naked otherways   the general part of them are verry poor and ask a large price for any thing they have to part with."* [J9:264] The Clatsops have brought some roots and berries, for which they ask a metal file. The price is too high, there is no deal, but they are allowed to stay overnight.

For the first time on the Expedition, there is no fiddling, dancing, frolicking, or jesting. The liquor, which may have prompted much of the hilarity, is gone. Family and friends are conspicuous in their absence. It's a bleak beginning to a new year, but one which will finish with huge success.

A Gift from the Sea, or Begging for Blubber

If the dogs are prized for their fattiness, so is the whale. These great mammals have been hunted by many maritime cultures, including the Japanese, Eskimo, and North Americans on many coasts. During the winter of 1805–06, the northwestern natives in Oregon demonstrate their easy, laidback approach to this mammoth food source: patience. Whales occasionally beach, or simply die and wash up to the coastline. Clark believes that the violent storms they are experiencing could cause any sea life to be hurled from the sea against the coastal rocks, to die there and be washed to the nearest beach. Whichever way it happens, it is a New Year's treat which washes ashore. The Tillamook tribe immediately claims ownership.[d]

From Clark's measurements it is safe to assume that it is a blue whale, largest of all living mammals.[J6:185n5] Excitement about the serendipitous booty stirs the more distant tribes into unplanned and hasty trips south to get in on the spoils. The Corps, newcomers and out of the loop, are among the last to know by the time rumors reach Fort Clatsop. The carcass is being cut up and carried off almost before the men know of its existence. On January 3, Lewis indulges in some second-hand reporting: the blubber or fat, *"the Indi-*

ans eat and esteeme it excellent food." On January 5, two men return from Salt Camp and bring with them the true coin of the realm, a piece of blubber:

> ... it was white & not unlike the fat of Poark, tho' the texture was more spongey and somewhat coarser. I had part of it cooked and found it very pallitable and tender, it resembled the beaver or the dog in flavour. it may appear somewhat extraordinary tho' it is a fact that the flesh of the beaver and dog possess a very great affinity in the point of flavour.

By the time the Corps sets out to see the huge mammal, they are almost too late. The meat is gone. They settle for fresh blubber and boiled-down blubber (train oil). By January 9, these provisions have all been eaten. *"the whale blubber which we have used very sparingly is now exhausted. on this food I do not feel strong, but enjoy the most perfect health ..."*

If anything, it is worth noting that the men are not enamored with the maritime diet. They have grown up on an inland diet and would prefer to frequent a steak house. Some parts of the native diet are not even remotely considered as food by the Corps. The playful harbor seals bobbing by – faintly comical with their big brown eyes and whiskered snouts – probably amuse the young men. Lewis ignores the subject of their edibility entirely. Clark fills us in, *"the flesh of this animal is highly prised by the nativs who Swinge the hair off and then roste the flesh on Sticks before the fire."* [J6:342]

What to Feed an Elk

Like a good animal-husbandry expert, Lewis is aware of what makes a good steak. It all starts with the feed. On Tuesday, February 4, 1806, he begins the daily *Journal* entry with the following:

> the Elk are in much better order in the point near the praries than they are in the woody country arround us or up the Netul. in the praries they feed on grass and rushes, considerable quantities of which are yet green and succulet. in the woody country their food is huckle berry bushes, fern, and an evergreen shrub which resembles the lorel in some measure ... [J6:276]

Lewis even compares deer with elk, noting the differences: *"the deer are poor and their flesh by no means as good as that of the Elk which is also poor but appears to be geting better than some weeks past."* [J6:325] The black-tailed deer *"are very seldom found in good order, or fat, even in the season which the common deer are so, and their flesh is inferior to any species of deer which I have ever seen."* [J6:328]

---

[d] Our contemporary images of canoe-paddling, seagoing whale hunters – tribes specializing in that vigorous, dangerous occupation – derive from the more northerly tribes in Washington. The practice of whale hunting is not found in the vicinity where the Corps overwinters.

Fatty Delights

Although game is not abundant, the hunting is sufficient, and on February 7 Lewis is truly enjoying himself, quite unabashed in his pleasure: *"this evening we had what I call an excellent supper it consisted of a marrowbone a piece and a brisket of boiled Elk that had the appearance of a little fat on it. This for Fort Clatsop is living in high stile."* It is apparent that the allure of fat seduces almost everyone. The high fat content of marrow, the hint of fat in the normally lean elk, brings more flavor and a roundness in the mouth, a richness – high style indeed! Clark, generally a less sophisticated but an equally enthusiastic eater, is enamored of their current take, for the next day, February 8, he effuses, *"we have both Dined and Suped on Elks tongues and marrowbones. a great Luxury for Fort Clatsop."*

Seldom in today's food writing will you find such delight in fat. Today it's a sin; yesterday, a positive blessing. Two months before, when Joseph Field bagged an elk during the long streak of eating dried fish, he came back not with meat, but marrow bones. What a write-up is given to those bones, the unmistakable choice of a first-class, bound-to-please butcher. And even after eating the marrow, the bones are not pitched but thriftily saved and reworked. Surprisingly, it is not a case of wringing the turnip dry. *"after eateing the marrow out of two Shank bones of an Elk, the Squar choped the bones fine boiled them and extracted a pint of Grease, which is Superior to the tallow of the animal."* J6:107 It doesn't matter what the source, fat is fat. On February 14, Lewis happily writes: *"Drewyer visited his traps today and caught a very fine fat beaver on which we feasted this evening."* It goes to show

Wooden trencher.

that Drouillard never intended to cache his traps, that he carried them throughout the entire journey.

Food Diplomacy with the Coastal Tribes

Feasting is not just a fine meal at the fort. As they've learned traveling across the whole of the West, food figures high in local hospitality and diplomacy. On February 20, *"This forenoon we were visited by Tah-cum a principal Chief of the Chinnooks and 25 men of his nation. we had never seen this chief before ..."* Despite the regular lack of food and scanty supplies, the Corps lays out their full hospitality. *"as he came on a friendly visit we gave himself and party some thing to eat ..."* J6:330 and then they fall back upon the time-honored custom of smoking and conferring a small medal upon the chief.

While the Corps subsists primarily on protein for long spells at a time, the native diet does not follow that same prescription. No tribe living in a coastal area with abundant rivers, lush forests, and a sea coast eats just fish. Sacred wisdom dictates that gathering and using indigenous plants is part of a varied and healthy diet, and the vast botanical world offers not only an array of foods, but a veritable medicine box of curatives as well. This medical aspect of the plant kingdom is yet another complex body of knowledge, one well worth looking into, but not included in the scope of this book. Lewis confines himself to sampling the vegetable offerings, tasting the native cuisine of the Pacific Northwest and giving accurate and vivid commentary on both their botanic features and cooking styles.

On December 9, 1805, Clark and party are out exploring by canoe and chance upon a village where a young Clatsop chief invites them to dinner. The dinner symbolizes the best in hospitality and diplomacy, for they are given *"new mats to Set on,"* and the table setting is *"a neet wooden trencher, with a Cockle Shell to eate with."* For their enjoyment the men are given *"fish, Lickorish, & black roots, on Small neet mats"*, and cranberries and bearberries are served in horn bowls. The chief's wife serves course after course, finishing with a bearberry soup, and an old woman *"presented a bowl made of light colored horn [filled with] a kind of Surup made of Dried berries [salal berries] ... I thought was pleasent."* This is quite an elegant meal for unexpected company. Of manners, Clark says,-*"those people appeared much neeter in their diat than Indians are Commonly, and frequently wash theer faces and hands."* As an after-dinner treat, he goes outside and shoots a goose, *"which astonished those people verry much, they plunged into the Creek and brought the brant on Shore – "* It is a good show.

What of the Potlatches?

If food is indicative of a greater political and diplomatic well-being, how do we understand that winter of 1805–06? Perhaps the best way to start is by understanding the nature of the coastal potlatches, a series of feasts given within clans, villages, and tribes, each chief striving to achieve fame and status through the generous use of food and entertainment. In other words, a grand party.

As spring arrives, each tribe, with all its different bands, begins their yearly cycle of gathering and hunting. By the time the fall rains and storms drive them home to their winter residences, they have hopefully accumulated food in abundance. So much, in fact, that they can then begin a round of lavish parties designed to impress everyone invited with their largesse and the implied power behind such wealth. There should be so much food that a perfect ending to such a three- to four-day feast might be literally throwing extra food back into the sea.

An account of a burial potlach gives quite explicit details. After the funeral, the mourners fast, "but eat the next day: hair seal, berries preserved in oil, eulachon grease, dried fish, and with feasting the festival ends. [Often] the guests eat so much that they vomit for the host tries his hospitality by making his guests sick, and then it is to his honor afterwards that all got sick. And those who vomit and get sick are made extra presents of blankets. All guests bring [with] them spoons and dishes, and they carry away all the food their dishes hold." [174]

These potlatches are see-and-be-seen events from start to finish, and not to be invited is a diplomatic fall from grace. Never are the Captains or the Corps invited to one of these grand events. Since this would be an ideal place to woo a military commander, a representative of the Great White Father back in Washington, an enterprising American merchant agent, how can this omission be explained? What has changed so radically from the magnificent welcome afforded to the Corps by the Mandans until they reach the Clatsops? They are the same men, and their objectives and ideals have remained fairly constant. Several factors loom, and they are not trivial nor is their impact minor.

First, there is the communication issue. The diplomatic exhortations delivered by Lewis as they progressed up the Missouri have died a quiet death as language and translation-chains finally fail. Equally important is the concept of food and banquets as a primary symbol of status. When the Corps emerged from St. Louis they had uniforms and a tremendous amount of trade goods. In other

The northwest coastal tribe potlatches are major community events.

words, they looked (and were) rich and prosperous. Their commanders spoke for a Great White Chief who held unimaginably great territories, and pursuant to his orders, they were armed with powerful new weapons never before seen, weapons such as the blasting airgun and the impressive swivel gun. By the time they have struggled over the Rockies, they are mere shadows of their former illustrious selves. Their power has vanished in hunger, in defeated certainties, in a conflict with nature far exceeding the scope or range of any tribes living along the trail. In an ironic twist of fate, the two Captains, once among the wealthier men in the country, are now penurious, and their gestures no longer seem to "brighten the chain of friendship." In short, the Corps is marginalized, and there are no potlatches in store for them.

Homesickness at the End of the Continent

The white men are existing on the edge of a vibrant trade network. Upriver, The Dalles is, as Lewis says, *"the great mart for all the country."* Trade goods flow up and down the river, merchants in great prowed canoes hawk pounded salmon, roots, blubber. But during the four months the Corps spends at Fort Clatsop there is nothing but loneliness, isolation, and a great overwhelming urge to return home. The three isolated saltmakers struggle, almost alone, down the coast, afflicted with yet even greater isolation and sickness. The Captains are engrossed with their record-keeping, listing progressively more indigenous plants and animals, eating the same.

The passing months are simply a test of endurance, and living through this winter and going home is their strongest motivation. While the Captains are exposed to a whole buffet of new foods, nothing will give better solace to everyone than a home-cooked meal eaten in the company of a happy and laughing group of family and friends. The men are ready to pull out.

And while there are few culinary high points throughout that long winter, at least the troops have not been starving. As they prepare to leave on March 23, Ordway pens, "[we] *have lived as well as we had any right to expect, and we can Say that we were never one day without 3 meals of Some kind a day, either Elk meat or roots.*" J9:280

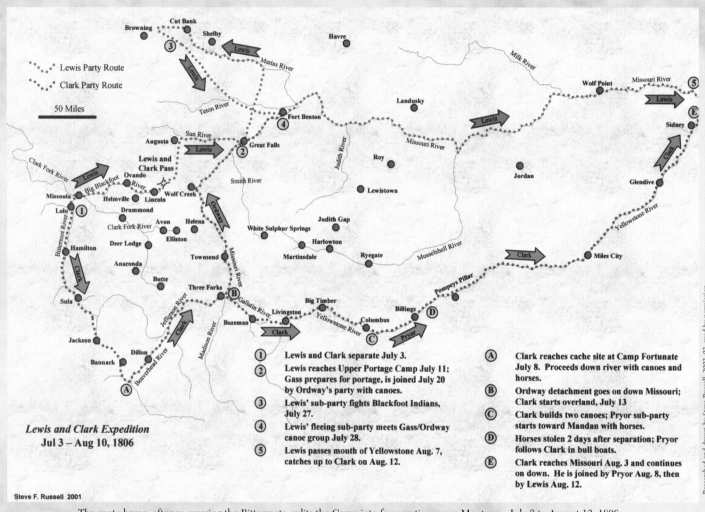

Lewis and Clark Expedition
Jul 3 – Aug 10, 1806

Lewis Party Route
Clark Party Route

50 Miles

Steve F. Russell 2001

① Lewis and Clark separate July 3.

② Lewis reaches Upper Portage Camp July 11; Gass prepares for portage, is joined July 20 by Ordway's party with canoes.

③ Lewis' sub-party fights Blackfoot Indians, July 27.

④ Lewis' fleeing sub-party meets Gass/Ordway canoe group July 28.

⑤ Lewis passes mouth of Yellowstone Aug. 7, catches up to Clark on Aug. 12.

Ⓐ Clark reaches cache site at Camp Fortunate July 8. Proceeds down river with canoes and horses.

Ⓑ Ordway detachment goes on down Missouri; Clark starts overland, July 13

Ⓒ Clark builds two canoes; Pryor sub-party starts toward Mandan with horses.

Ⓓ Horses stolen 2 days after separation; Pryor follows Clark in bull boats.

Ⓔ Clark reaches Missouri Aug. 3 and continues on down. He is joined by Pryor Aug. 8, then by Lewis Aug. 12.

Researched and drawn by Steve Russell, 2003–03, sued by permission

The route home, after re-crossing the Bitterroots, splits the Corps into four parties across Montana – July 3 to August 12, 1806.

Hurrying Home
April – September, 1806

I take my leave of the view of the tremendious chain of Rocky Mountains
white with Snow, in view of which I have been Since the 1st of May last.

— CLARK, JULY 27, 1806

T HERE IS NOTHING SO ENTICING to homesick people as returning home. Trees and familiar landscapes call; the sights of familiar birds and features strike a ringing chord in the heart. Humans want to be with family, friends, and loved ones, or walk into a beloved house and smell baking cakes redolent of cinnamon, or sizzling bacon frying. Imagine the anticipation of these men who have been

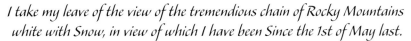

The re-crossing of the Bitterroots in June 1806 is far easier than the outbound trip, but it still involves a slow, snowy crossing.

gone so long from even the most remote signs of familiar civilization.

The first five weeks of the return trip are generally tedious and uneventful as the party hauls their canoes and supplies up or around each of the rapids, cascades, and falls on the Columbia. However, there were no significant new foods or native social encounters. Trading canoes for horses, on April 28 the Corp heads overland to the Clearwater, then along it up to the Nez Perce camp of Twisted Hair near today's Orofino, Idaho, arriving on May 8. Although the party moved a few miles (nearer today's Kamiah, Idaho), they were forced to wait yet another month for the mountainous walls of snow to melt and become passable. Finally, on June 10, 1806, Lewis is optimistic if not elated. *"at 11a.m. we set out with the party each man being well mounted and a light load on a second horse, beside which we have several supenemary [supernumerary] horses in case of accident or the want of provision ..."* Note, while "accident" is listed as number one priority; probably number two (feeding the troops) is the real reason for extras. Lewis has remembered the outbound trek and how horses saved the day. *"we therefore feel ourselves perfectly equiped for the mountains."* The first thing that happens is that they ford a deep creek and wet their roots and bread. But they are off. And although they lose another ten days waiting for snow melt just past Weippe, they cross the ridge on June 29 and return to Traveler's Rest in Montana on June 30.

July 4, 1806 – the Corp is Split
Once the drudgery of crossing the mountains is finished and

the party reaches familiar land points, little can deter the men from racing for home. On July 3, the Corps spends their last night all together for many weeks. The next day, the Expedition is on its way home, but has split up: Clark taking a party of twenty-two back toward Camp Fortunate, while Lewis with ten men and five Nez Perce use well-traveled native routes to return more directly to the Missouri.

Lewis, surprisingly, gives no mention to Independence Day which a year before had been worthy of great note. His Nez Perce guides are departing and, for him and his men, it is actually an occasion of sorrow. Gass records in a humanistic note that, *"as our guides intend to return ... we wish to give them a plentiful supply of provisions to carry them back over the mountains."* Lewis, unhappy with the days kill, laments his hunters' unsuccessful efforts but neglects to add what Gass does, *"We were, however, able to furnish them with two deer and a half, from those that were killed yesterday."* Sentimentally, Lewis continues, *"these affectionate people our guides betrayed every emmotion of unfeigned regret at seperating from us ..."* and they regretfully predict trouble from their hostile northern neighbors. At least the evening is fine, with no mosquitoes. Lewis happily records collecting a *"ground squirrel of a speceis which I had never before seen,"* and so another Fourth of July slips by.

Following advice of the Nez Perce guides, Lewis' party sets out from Travelers' Rest to the Missouri along the ancient Cokahlarishkit trail, the "Road to the Buffalo," arriving just above the Great Falls on July 11. Game abounds; *"there were not less than 10 thousand buffaloe within a circle of 2 miles arround that place."* Here Lewis assigns six of his group to wait for Ordway's party, which is bringing the canoes down from Camp Fortunate. They are to portage materials back down around the Falls, retrieve the supplies cached below the Falls, and then proceed down the Missouri to wait at the junction of the Marias River.

Meanwhile, Lewis takes Drouillard and the Field brothers to continue exploring the most northerly limits of Upper Louisiana (almost to Canada, as it turns out) looking for the headwaters of the Marias River. Although Lewis has his most capable men with him, the detour is a bad idea; it's Blackfoot territory and, a chance encounter leaves the four men fleeing for their lives after killing two warriors. On July 28, they rejoin the main party on the Missouri, consisting not only of the six men Lewis left to their tasks but now also including the ten-man Ordway party. Twenty mouths to feed.

The good news on their return is that, despite the loss of the red pirogue, the white pirogue is serviceable, and *"they had brought all things safe having sustained no loss ..."* On

opening the Marias cache, *"the gunpowder corn flour poark and salt had sustained but little injury, the parched meal was spoiled or nearly so."* During the next ten days, Lewis' main party travels more than 400 miles to reach the Yellowstone River confluence on August 7 – and meet Clark downriver five days later.

The loss of cornmeal is minor compared to a subsequent hunting disaster. On Monday, August 11, one-eyed Cruzatte hears Lewis rustling in the brush while they are hunting for dinner, mistakes Lewis' elk-skin garb for a meaty meal, and shoots him through the buttocks. Despite the severity of his wounds, Lewis enters a lengthy entry in his journal, concluding the next day with his last entry, *"however I must notice a singular Cherry* [the pin cherry]," and finishing 246 words later with the last he will write in the Expedition *Journals.*

Clark's Yellowstone River Party

This summer day of July 4, 1806, the men do not rise and waken the Captain with gunfire. Clark himself begins the day not with a swivel shot, but a command: *"I order three hunters to Set out early this morning to hunt & kill Some meat and by 7 a. m. we Collected our horses took braekfast and Set out ..."* It turns out to be a hard day. Indian footprints are found, and *"the last Creek or river which we pass'd was So deep and the water So rapid that Several of the horses were Sweped down Some distance and the Water run over Several*

Clark's journey down the Yellowstone in July 1806 is interrupted by a herd of buffalo so large that it blocks the river.

R. L. Rickards - courtesy: Rickards Western Art

others which wet Several articles." The good news for dinner is that "our hunters joined us with 2 deer in tolerable order." The jovial, irrepressible Clark surges on: "This being the day of the decleration of Independence of the United States and a Day commonly Scelebrated by my Country I had every disposition to Selebrate this day and therefore halted early and partook of a Sumptious Dinner of a fat Saddle of Venison and Mush of Cows (roots) ..." He has not forgotten.

Sgt. Ordway is more concerned with the affairs of everyday life, noting like Clark that "about 12 we Saw a large flock of Mountn. Sheep or big horn amimels. They run so near us that Some of the men fired at them. Shortly after we halted at a branch to dine." Finally he ups the food kill: "towards evening one of the hunters killed a deer ... one of the hunters killed a fat buck this evening." At least they aren't starving, and they are alive.

Clark's group returns to Camp Fortunate to pick up the canoes and travels down the Jefferson River to Three Forks, the headwaters of the Missouri. On July 13 a further split occurs: Ordway takes a party of ten with the six canoes down the Missouri to the Great Falls. Clark and the remaining group, including the Charbonneau family, follow Sacagawea's directions up the East Fork of the Gallatin River, crossing near what is now Bozeman Pass to arrive at the Yellowstone River on July 15.

Animals are again abundant, food plentiful. Hunting at this point changes in character to a certain extent because animals are being sought for clothing rather than meat. "I walked out and killed a Small Buck for his Skin which the party are in want of for Clothes." J8:226 The ragged travelers certainly would have settled for bighorn and pronghorn, which were also valued by the natives for clothing construction. J8:232

To some degree, souvenir collecting is underway, perhaps a few pelts thrown in for extra cash on the other end, and definitely specimens are being collected to go back east to Jefferson. Clark writes that he killed a couple of bighorns and, unable to get them, stops the party and goes back on foot to kill two more. J8:226 The immense, and heavy, gray horns from the illusive bighorn are so valuable that they are carried almost as a status item. After all, wasn't one found in the household of the Teton Sioux chief who used the horn as a serving spoon? Jefferson certainly would be interested. Even as late as August 28, Clark makes a last-ditch effort to bring back specimens of prairie dog and black-billed magpie, and sends the Field brothers out for skins and skeletons of mule deer and pronghorn antelope, knowing the inventory is incomplete. It seems as if the entire party is sent out in a hasty effort to redeem their collectors' integrity.

R. L. Rickards – courtesy: Rickards Western Art

Pryor's overland trip is cancelled the second day out by marauding Indians having stolen the horses before dawn.

It's the last chance to collect items from the West because huge distances are being traveled on a daily basis. On July 27, 1806, Clark's party is in central Montana, near the Bighorn River. His Journal entry records, "I take my leave of the view of the tremendious chain of Rocky Mountains white with Snow in view of which I have been Since the 1st of May last." J8:238 "By now the members of the Lewis and Clark Expedition just wanted to go home, as quickly and painlessly as possible. The purposefulness, the uncertainty, and the sense of wonder of the eastbound journey were gone now. There was nothing left to discover."[175] They traveled eighty miles that day. In fact, Clark believes that they are close enough to their friendly Mandan allies that he pens an order to Pryor on July 24, asking that four men (Pryor, Shannon, Hall, and Windsor) go ahead by horseback to the villages and look for any of their mercantile suppliers. He wants to trade the horses for: "Flints three or 4 Doz. Knives, a fiew pounds of Paint, some Pepper, Sugar & Coffee or Tea" and "2 small Kegs of Sperits" L1:313-4 This grocery-run, involving further separation, shows what the Expedition is lacking in the way of food and tools. It is a tell-tale sign that Clark is not asking for corn.

Unfortunately, Pryor's passage is complicated by marauding Indians who quietly steal their horses only two days out. The four men are forced to fend for themselves and "packed up their baggage on their backs." J8:284 The supreme issue of surviving and getting home now becomes uppermost – Shannon takes it upon himself to build a bull-boat from buffalo skin which *"will carry 6 or 8 Men and their loads."* Simultaneously *"Sergt. Pryor informs me that the Cause of his building two Canoes was for fear of ones meating with Some accedent in passing down the rochejhone* [Yellowstone] *a river entirely unknown to either of them by which means they might loose their guns and amunition and be left entirely destitute of the means of procurering food."* J8:284 Worrying now that they may, by some fluke of bad luck, be separated permanently the main party, and have to get to St. Louis as a foursome, these experienced men experience self-doubt, perhaps even panic. In an amazing turn of psychology, the men are no longer afraid of Indians, but of starving.

By mid-July the seasonal berries are ripe and an entry on the July 18 gives some indication of a break in the usual meat-only diet: *"yellow, purple, & black Currents ripe and abundant."* J8:265 Other than the more-than-usual torments by mosquitoes, and a tangle with an immense she-bear that comes after their canoes, they simply paddle on. They travel eighty-six miles on August 2. The next day, at the confluence of the Yellowstone, is devoted to food and maintenance:

> *a large Buck Elk which I had shot & had his flesh dried in the Sun for a Store down the river. had the Canoes unloaded and every article exposed to dry & Sun. Maney of our things were wet, and nearly all the Store of meat which had been killed above Spoiled. I ordered it to be thrown into the river. Several Skins are also Spoiled which is a loss, as they are our principal dependance for Clothes to last us to our homes &c.* J8:276

More adventures unroll. Not only are their horses are stolen, but on July 26 *"a Wolf bit Sergt. Pryor through his hand when asleep, and this animal was So vicious as to make an attempt to Seize Windsor, when Shannon fortunately Shot him."* J8:285 This is a more mature Shannon, one who takes charge, a change from his youthful enlistment year, a long two years ago. Fortunately, this straggling party catches up with Clark by August 8.

That same day Clark changes outlook – no longer are skins and horns for clothing or samples, but instead, *"My object is to precure as many Skins*

"Largest Buck [elk] I ever saw" – Clark, on the Yellowstone, July, 1806.

as possible for the purpose of purchaseing Corn and Beans of the Mandans." J8:285 They are beginning to have a hard time of it, and are in need of food. Certainly they would welcome the addition of carbohydrates to their diet, having survived as long as they have on protein. Clark pragmatically determines that, *"as we have now no article of Merchindize nor horses to purchase with, our only resort is Skins which those people were very fond the winter we were Stationed near them."* J8:285 Even though big game is easily available for the hunting, the Kentuckian demures, *"... the Elk appeared fat. I did not kill any of them as the distance to the river was too great for the men to Carry the meat."* J8:286

Clark's party reaches the confluence of the Yellowstone and Missouri on August 3 where they intend to wait for Lewis. However the *"Musquetors was So troublesom"* that Clark leaves a note on a stick for Lewis and moves down the Missouri several times over the next few days to find a better camp site. Despite his own comments on the unfavorable drying qualities of elk, on August 9, Clark is seduced by an enormous elk which he kills. *"this Elk was the largest Buck I ever Saw and the fattest animal which have been killed on the rout. I had the flesh and fat of this Elk brought to Camp and cut thin ready to dry. the hunters killed nothing this evening."* J8:286 Meanwhile, the men are happily digging *pomme blanche* or breadroot, for they are back into familiar territory where they recognize the native species and can pick plants without fear of poisoning themselves.

On August 11, the party meets two trappers – Dixon and Hancock– the first fresh white faces they have seen since the Corps left the Dakotas a year and a half before. The next morning Shannon, having once again forgotten his tomahawk, is sent back with Gibson to find it. At noon, Lewis' party arrives, having been told by Dixon and Hancock that Clark had just passed going downriver. A few hours later, Shannon and Gibson float into view in their bull-boat, bringing skins and the flesh of three elk they have just killed upriver, and the entire Corps is once again reunited. Knowing the rule of safety in numbers, and perhaps being lonesome themselves, the two trappers join the Expedition heading down to Mandan territory.

Return to the Mandan Villages

In only two more days the party reaches first the Minetares and then Black Cat's village, *"who appeared ... well pleased to See us ..."* J8:298 Clark repairs to one village to smoke a pipe and eat some squash with the chief. J8:303 There are gifts as well, *"The Maharha Chief brought us Some Corn, as did also the Chief of the little village of the Menetarras."* J8:302 This is a

August 1806, return to the Mandan villages.

R. L. Rickards - courtesy: Rickards Western Art

grand gesture of friendship, promising corn, for Clark is told it is in short supply. On August 16 *"Sent up Sergt. Pryor to the mandan village, for Some Corn which they offered to give us. he informed that they had more Corn collected for us than our Canoes Could Carry Six load of which he brought down. I thanked the Chief for his kindness and informed him that our Canoes would not Carry any more Corn than we had already brought down."* In another instance of hospitality, five days later, *"the Chief had prepd. a supper of boiled young Corn, beens & quashes of which he gave me in Wooden bowls."* J8:315

What a welcome reprieve this must have been. For the first time in a long time the men are being taken care of, rather than being one hundred percent responsible for themselves. The hunters might even have rested for a day. Up to the rim, their tin cups are loaded with yellow, flavorful, hunger-satisfying cornmeal mush. How long has it been since these men ate this familiar favorite? It must have been the last handful that went into the portable soup when they were starving in the Rockies.

Having reached the Mandans, the Corps begins to disperse. The first to leave is Colter, the epitome of a mountain man, gripped by the lure of the West and the distant tendrils of the fur trade. He fervently wants to return to the Yellowstone territory. Charbonneau, now back home, asks to be settled out and receives *"for his Services as an enterpreter the pric of a horse and Lodge purchased of him for public Service in all amounting to 500$ 33 1/3 cents."* J8:305 He and his wife Saca-

gawea, and their toddler, Pomp, remain with the Hidatsas.

The summertime weather this August is highly unstable – violent winds, rain, hot sun. Diplomatically the tribes are unstable, locked once again in seemingly hostile circumstances. The promises of peace left as quickly as the white presence. One Mandan chief, Sheheke, wishes *"to Visit the United States and his Great Father but was afraid of the Scioux who were yet at war with them ..."* J8:298 After reassurances for their safety, the decision is made to take a retinue to Washington. What this means is that the Corps has surpassed its original number of mouths to feed, but the native women who now travel with them fill the spot vacated by Sacagawea in knowledge of edible native plants.

Down the Missouri to St. Louis

Returning home is just not so simple as it seems: the Expedition's progress often is slow, not making huge headway – *"only 10 miles to day"* J8:310 and *"made 22 miles to day only."* J8:316 Downpours wet their goods and they are detained *"until 6 p m. and dryed our things which were much Spoiled."* J8:318 Before their departure in 1803, Jefferson included in a letter to Lewis, "Extracts from the Journal of M. Truteau, Agent for the Illinois trading company, residing at the village of the Ricara, up the Missouri. ... 'In the Missouri river ... The winds on it are so violent that the periogues are sometimes obliged to lie by one, two, three, or four days, and sometimes take as long time to descend as to ascend the river.' " L1:138

Again there is concern for adequate provisions. However, notwithstanding these delays, the Corps will arrive in St. Louis in just a month – a trip that took an entire six months going upriver just two years prior. Returning to civilization erases easy hunting. Unlike the abundance in Montana, game here is scarce, wary, and is pursued by Indians, white trappers, and traders. Obtaining meat becomes a sweaty, frustrating ordeal; and the party struggles with hunger as they head for St. Louis. The lower temperatures in the more northerly latitude of the Dakotas delay the summer season and *"there is great quantities of plumbs which are not yet ripe, [and] great quantities of Grapes, they are black tho' not thurerly ripe ..."* J8:324 The Corps may now travel sixty miles in a day, with the wind ahead. These conditions mean one thing: great caloric expenditures. The larder empties, and the hunters return unsuccessful.

Fruits are the best news, *"great quantities of Grapes and Choke Cheries,"* although a sniff of disdain is accorded to the variety of black currant, which is now considered inferior to those out West. J8:320 The party makes forty miles on

August 23. Deer is the only meat on the menu now. The gobbling sounds meeting their ears means the welcome appearance of wild turkey.

Returning to a place of known supplies is a useful strategy. Clark heads for *"Pleasant Camp"* where they had stayed on September 16 and 17, 1804, hoping its *"great abundance of Game."* J8:326 will feed the increased number of people. When some of the privates go out to collect fruit, so do *"the Squaws of the enterpreter Jessomme and the Mandan Chief"* who *"geathered more blumbs than the party Could eate in 2 days, those plumbs are of 3 Speces, the most of them large and well flavored."* J8:326 However, the forage in 1806 must not have been as sufficient as in 1804, for the hunters are finding lean game, despite the fact that it's summer and the grasses are up – *"Pore deer"* and no mule deer or antelope. The buffalo, too, are thin – a surprising condition for the majestic animals in mid-summer. Clark is more awed by their numbers than their decline from prime grade, *"from this eminance I had a view of a greater number of buffalow than I had ever Seen before at one time. I must have Seen near 20,000 of those animals feeding on this plain."* J8:328

Clark is sure that there must be something better out there. He joins the hunters *"with a view to kill Some fat meet. we had not proceeded far before Saw a large plumb orchd of the most deelicious plumbs, out of this orchard 2 large Buck Elks ran the hunters killed them. I Stoped the Canoes and brought in the flesh which was fat and fine. here the party Collected as many plumbs as they could eate ..."* J8:329

Did the elk swallow all those plum pits? Of course. And, in the cycle of life, the outer layer of the stones is softened up by the elks' gastric juices, making it easier for the growing kernel to burst through. As the pit is eliminated from the digestive tract, it hits the ground surrounded by a nourishing plop of fertilizer to give it a good start. Who knows how many of those plum trees in that large orchard had been propagated that way? And how long had those fat creatures been eating plums to appear in such magnificent condition?

By the end of August the Corps has eaten plenty of fruit. Turkeys reappear on the menu on September 2, an item of fascination to the Indians accompanying the party. The large and delicious fowl are *"very much admired being the first which they ever Saw."* J8:345 In this one comment are two separate territorial observations: (1) the turkeys inhabit a different ecological zone than the Mandans, and (2) the tribe limits its travel, not venturing too far south or east.

By September 2 the Corps is close enough to civilization that they are out rounding up cattle instead of wild game – escapee animals that never give a thought to returning home – free-roaming mavericks naturalized into the central grasslands. Since wild cattle are not as plump as the hay-fed model, the eight hunters pick selectively and *"killed two which was in very good order, had them butchered and each man took a load as much as he Could Carry and returned to the Canoes."* J8:344-5

Meeting Travelers Going Upriver

A volley of gunfire roars a salute to the Corps on September 3 as the men joyfully meet their first river merchant heading north from St. Louis, a Mr. James Aird in command of two bateaux, destined to trade with the Sioux. Quick as pronghorns jump, the canoes are tied alongside and the men leap onboard. The day is dedicated to catching up on two years of news. They discuss first the President's health, then Indian affairs, international politics as it concerns America and Britain, the famous duel in which Alexander Hamilton was killed (after their departure), the tragedy of Jean Pierre Chouteau's house burning down in St. Louis, that wonderful home where the Captains were guests. Why, civilization is nearly right around the bend!

Aird insists *"on our accepting a barrel of flour– we gave to this gentleman what Corn we Could Spear amounting to about 6 bushels ..."* The *Journals* record how this is a win-win trade, *"The flower was very acceptable to us. we have yet a little flour part of what we carried up from the Illinois as high as Maria's river and buried it there until our return ..."* J8:349 It is almost shocking to imagine that they are within nineteen days of St. Louis and by careful thrift still have some of the original flour to use. It has traveled more than 4200 miles through every water hazard imaginable, been buried for a year, and emerges dry and fine.

As a treat, the men are issued a cup of flour each. There is no mention whatsoever of what they do with it. Perhaps they make ashcakes. Ashcakes are an old dish, the result of Indians teaching the colonists a simple method of using cornmeal. The early cooks heated the cakes on the sooty hearth, hence the name ashcakes. This sort of treatment could also be done with flour and water:

ASH CAKES

Combine flour or cornmeal and water, making a thick dough. Pat into cakes and bake, without oil, in a frying pan (or a hot rock, or in the ashes) until hot, turning once.

Only fowl are noted on this portion of the river – pelicans and wild geese – but most likely the crew is still eating cow from two days earlier. Still swatting mosquitoes, the party is up at dawn, ready to roll. The hunters turn out to kill elk but fail: *"the Elk was wild and ran off much fritened."* [J8:351] Again, it is worth comparing this behavior to that of the placid game in Montana. Food supplies are by no means abundant; it is a time of scarcity.

Three days after encountering the trade bateaux of James Aird, another barge comes into sight plying its way upriver to the Yankton Sioux. The canoes pull alongside. The Captains want whiskey for the Corps but have no means of paying for it. Lewis, or perhaps it's Clark, proposes paying the barge's owner, their friend Auguste Chouteau, when they see him next in St. Louis. To the men goes *"a dram which is the first Spiritious licquor which had been tasted by any of them Since the 4th of July 1805."* This full-throttle jolt of taste from home is a call to action, *"Several of the party exchanged leather for linen Shirts and beaver for Corse hats."* [J8:351] Again, there are the ear-splitting salutes from the guns as a mark of respect, and the little flotilla paddles on. Dinner that night is two pelicans. Not only are there the vexations of sitting for days in a canoe, but they are famished, too. The atmosphere onboard plummets as the Indian families are weary of traveling and their children cry. This is not a triumphant hero's return.

Spirits rise when three elk are shot the next afternoon. They have *"the flesh brought in Cooked and Dined."* It is, in fact, *"a Sumptious Dinner."* [J8:353] Another forty-four miles of future Nebraska/Iowa has passed beneath their canoes.

The gathering evidence of civilization creates a burning desire to be home. On September 8, the crew *"Set out very early ..."* Not only are they rolling, they are inspired – *"all being anxious to get to the River Platt to day they ply'd their orers very well ..."* [J8:353] They make seventy-eight miles. *"Early the next day"* is 8 a.m. and they have already passed the mouth of the Platte. *"our party appears extreamly anxious to get on, and every day appears* [to] *produce new anxieties in them to get to their Country and friends."* [J8:354]

Every couple of days they run into yet another merchant coming up from St. Louis. This *"... man was extreemly friendly to us he offered us any thing he had, we axcepted of a bottle of whisky only which we gave to our party ..."* [J8:355] Although the game inventory is now adequate – *"we Saw Deer rackoons and turkies on the Shores to day ..."* [J8:355] the only thing killed is *"a racoon which the indians very much admired."* [J8:355] It probably makes only appetizer-sized portions.

The environment continues to change; Clark notes, *"the Climate is every day preceptably wormer and air more Sultery*

than I have experienced for a long time." [J8:354] What this means to the larder is the bad "P" word: putrefaction. *"... at 3 p. m we halted ... to kill Some meat that which we killed a fiew days past being all Spoiled."* [J8:356] Two deer are dinner. Meanwhile, some men absolutely yearning for positive signs of home take the nighttime howling of the wild coyotes to be the barking of domestic dogs. Heading-for-the-barn fever is running hot.

September 12 and 13 are once again a time of fasting – game is wary and supplies are ten days away downriver. Only one turkey is on the menu; deer are not bagged. A short visit as they come alongside the vessel of an old Army acquaintance, Robert McClellan, yields news, a little whiskey for breakfast, and they paddle on. It is not the substantial breakfast they hoped the hunters would provide. Suddenly Clark is indisposed, *"I felt my Self very unwell and derected a little Chocolate which Mr. McClellen [sic] gave us, prepared of which I drank about a pint and found great relief ..."* [J8:359] Was he terribly hungry and the sugary chocolate gave him a boost? It certainly is an unexpected luxury. Fortunately, by dinner the hunters have killed four deer, and their hunger is eased.

The next day, another windfall is blowing upriver – three large vessels headed for the upstream tribes. Clark happily records, *"those young men received us with great friendship and pressed on us Some whisky for our men, Bisquet, Pork and Onions, & part of their Stores."* [J8:360] Of course there is another round of inquiries about the *"state of our friends and Country,"* the local situation, politics, and two hours fly by. Of the thirty-seven deer that are counted on the riverbanks, five meager deer comprise dinner. But no matter if it is only fifty-three miles today, *"our party received a dram and Sung Songs untill 11oClock at night in the greatest harmoney."* [J8:360] It has been such a very, very long time since a blissful evening under the stars had occurred ... this celebration lends a bittersweet tinge to the approaching end of an almost unimaginable journey.

A rosy dawn welcomes September 15 as they pass the mouth of the Kansas River. Within a week of "home," the men's need for civilization so far outweighs any other considerations that they opt for speed over full stomachs. And this actually a positive, for deer are unusually meager, and cooking becomes a time-consuming impediment. By September 18 and 150 miles from home, Clark is in fine fettle despite logging, *"entirely out of provisions ..."* After dispensing the last of the biscuits, *"which amounted to nearly one buisket per man,"* one particular fruit begins to take on an important role and, despite low calories, fuels the party. It is a banana-like native of the Missouries, the "pawpaw." This fruit is not the papaya, sometimes nicknamed "pawpaw." Rather, it is an oversized berry native to Missouri and belongs to the custard apple family.[a] The men's morale is high, *"the party appear perfectly contented and tell us that they can live very well on the pappaws,"* and they stop just briefly to pick the meltingly sweet, luscious enticement. Forty-nine miles and one elk later, the army messes have their food for the day.

Now unaccustomed to the heat and humidity, Clark again comments unfavorably, saying the wind is their only saving grace. The country north of latitude 46° (North Dakota, Montana, and west to the Pacific) where they have been for two years is open and cool compared to what they are now experiencing in the sultry climes of Missouri. [J8:361] Probably this heat quells the appetite and makes the fruit even more appetizing and refreshing.

Two days later, on September 17, one of Lewis' Army friends, Captain John McClellen, is coming upriver and rejoices to find his old friend alive and well. In a quaint turn of phrase Clark records *"some civilities"* given by the Captain: *"Some Buisquit, Chocolate Sugar & whiskey, for which our party were in want and for which we made a return of a barrel of corn & much obliges to him."* [J8:363] The merchant-trader is open-handed, and the barter of corn enables the Corps to reciprocate rather than be beholden. McClellen confesses, *"we had been long Since given out by the people of the U S Generaly and almost forgotton ..."* but more agreeable is the news that *"the President of the U. States had yet hopes of us ..."* [J8:363]

Oh, Those Pawpaws

The next day, *"the men ply their oares & we descended with great velocity, only Came too once for the purpose of gathering pappows, our anxiety as also the wish of the party to proceed on as expeditiously as possible to <get to> the Illinois enduce us to continue on without halting to hunt. we Calculate on ariveing at the first Settlements on tomorrow evening which is 140 miles ..."* [J8:366] In fact they are on target and make seventy-two miles.

Mysteriously, an inexplicable malady appears, blinding and incapacitating some of the crew:

The pawpaw found in the lower Missouri River valley.

September 18:

    "J. Potts complains very much of one of his eyes which is burnt by the Sun ... Shannon also complains of his face & eyes ..."

September 19:

    "three of the party have their eyes inflamed and Sweled ... extreamly painfull"

So what is this sudden onslaught that immobilizes three previously healthy canoeists? On September 18, Clark (or Potts, the afflicted) attributes it to sunburn, *"from exposeing his face without a cover from the Sun."* [J8:365] This seems highly improbable, since they have been exposed to the sun and the elements for more than two years. Friday the mystery illness is worse:

    a very singular disorder ... that of the Sore eyes. three of the party have their eyes inflamed and Sweled in Such a manner as to render them extreamly painfull, particularly when exposed to the light, the eye ball is much inflaimed and the lid appears burnt with the Sun, the cause of this complaint of the eye I can't [account?] for. from it's Sudden appearance I am willing to believe it may be owing to the reflection of the Sun on the water [J8:366]

And so, on September 20, 1806, and almost home, this food mishap forces the Captains to once again readjust the flotilla. *"... three of the party was unabled to row from the State of their eyes, we found it necessary to leave one of our Crafts and divide the men into other Canoes, we left the two Canoes lashed together which I had made high up the River Rochejhone, those Canoes we Set a drift and little after day light we Set out ..."*

---

[a] Plant expert Calloway writes, "Fruit are produced in clusters and are oblong to banana-shaped, providing insight into the origin of one of [its] early names, 'Indiana banana.' The fruit may be eaten when it becomes soft although some prefer to wait until after the skin has darkened. Flesh is custard-like in texture with flavor resembling cherimoya or soursop. Flesh is typically orange ..." When evaluated, the nutritional quality of the pawpaw is far higher than other temperate fruits such as apple, peach, or grape. Janick, *New Crops*, pp.505–515.

THE PAWPAW MALADY

In 1979 Dr. "Frenchy" Chuinard, in *Only One Man Died,* guessed at infectious conjunctivitis. This doesn't seem terribly convincing. In 1987 Professor Ann Rogers found a far more likely culprit. She proposed an allergic food reaction to pawpaws, the only new item mentioned in the *Journals.*[176]

Fine eating is the positive side. The dark side in the nature of the pawpaw has been unraveled by botanists, and the medical symptoms dictate that this final "plant pox" is listed in *Poisonous Plants of the United States,* being something akin to poison oak or poison ivy. Its nastiness can cause dermatitis, "painful irritation and inflamation" and redness, swelling, and itching of the skin. The men are hell-bent for St. Louis and sweating profusely. They gobble down the juicy, thirst-relieving pawpaws as the only food they have. Since the men's tough, paddle-callused hands don't register the allergen, their fingers carrying the toxin are used for wiping their sweaty foreheads. The sweat and fruit juice mingle and drip down or are smeared across foreheads and eyes. Asimicin, a compound with active pesticidal properties, is the irritant acting on the three men whose systems are susceptible.[177]

La Charette is the first village encountered by the returning Corps on September 20, 1806, with St. Charles the next day, and St. Louis on September 23.

Lewis and Clark Return to St. Louis by Stanley Meltzoff

Cows and Toasts

September, 1806

To the hardy followers of Captains Lewis and Clark –
May they be rewarded by the esteem of their fellow citizens.

— A ST. LOUIS TOAST, SEPTEMBER 25, 1806

O N SEPTEMBER 20, 1806, a wonderful thing happens, a miracle in animal husbandry. *"... we Saw Some cows on the bank which was a joyfull Sight to the party and Caused a Shout to be raised for joy ..."* [J8:367]

The difference between the men's reaction to cows on September 2 and that on September 20 gives pause for thought. Perhaps the wild cows didn't act like domesticated cattle, and they certainly didn't elicit thoughts of home. But now, on the 20th, the shouts of joy springing from the men reflect a certain "appeal of a bovine landscape: familiar yet mysterious, a comforting frame of reference." [178] By today's urban standards, a cow is hardly worth cheering about – but to these men it means home is near. Astronauts recall tears in their eyes at returning to Mother Earth – the comparison is not unthinkable.

Some hours later the faint outline of little La Charette comes into view and *"the men raised a Shout and Sprung upon their ores and we soon landed opposit to the Village."* It is the beginning of the "tickertape parades."

> *our party requested to be permited to fire off their Guns which was alowed & they discharged 3 rounds with a harty Cheer, which was returned from five tradeing boats which lay opposit the village. we landed and were very politely received by two young Scotch men from Canada ... furnished us with Beef flower [flour], and Some pork for our men, and gave us a very agreeable supper. ... we purchased of a Citizen two gallons of Whiskey for our party for which we were obliged to give Eight dollars in Cash, an imposition on the part of the Citizen. every person, both French and americans Seem to express great*

pleasure at our return, and acknowledged them selves much astonished in Seeing us return. [J8:367]

Note Clark's indignation. Here they are, servants of the United States, who have been trading fishing hooks and buttons off their coats for food. Wouldn't any thinking man assume that they aren't carrying pockets filled with jingling coins? How are they expected to have the cash to pay for anything after living off the land for the previous two years? Surely payment with a beaver-skin pelt should be acceptable, but more to the point, why not a bit of generosity as exhibited by the previous traders they've met. *"An imposition,"* indeed.

The citizens of La Charette take the men into their warm and cheery homes overnight, and the soul-deep pleasure at returning is reinforced the next day as the residents of St. Charles turn out to welcome them home. No longer is the issue of distance so important. They have come only forty-eight miles, and *"rejoiced at the Sight of this hospital [hospitable] village ... we Saluted the Village by three rounds from our blunderbuts and the Small arms of the party, and landed near the lower part of the town. we were met by great numbers of the inhabitants, we found them excessively polite. we received invitations from Several of those Gentlemen ..."* [J8:369] The Captains receive five invitations, *"pressing on us to go to their houses,"* but they accept only two. *"Mr. Querie under took to Supply our party with provisions &c. ... the inhabitants of this village appear much delighted at our return and seem to vie with each other in their politeness to us all."* [J8:369] Such is the greeting for the lost who have been found. Moreover, the Captains are so at ease in their welcome that pouring rain the next morning is, for once, no cause for misery. They allow their men the luxury of remaining warm and dry indoors, proceeding on only after the sky clears.

The salutes and welcomes continue as the Corps and their Indian party canoe down to Coldwater Creek and the new Fort Bellefontaine, a military outpost established in 1805, after their departure. On the 22nd, Ordway writes that, *"the Company of Artillery who lay at this fort fired 17 Rounds with the field-peaces,"* and the almost-taken-for-dead privates are thrilled to discover that *"a number of these Soldiers are aqaintances of ours ..."* J9:366 Seventeen salutes! While the amazed artillery men welcome the explorers, Captain Clark marvels, *"at this place there is a publick Store kept in which I am informed the U.S have 60000$ worth of indian Goods."* J8:370 They have been isolated and poor a very long time.

The next day, the hospitality of hosting shifts to the Captains, who rise early and take Chief Sheheke to the store to outfit him in new clothing. They breakfast with their compatriot, Colonel Hunt, and then make the final triumphant leg of their journey into St. Louis where, *"we Suffered the*

George Catlin, 1832

Dressing the Chief. This Catlin drawing of another chief's visit to a European tailor twenty-five years later illustrates the impact on Chief Big White (Sheheke) of his visit to the white-man's world in 1806.

LEWIS' CHARLOTTE RUSSE

"Dissolve one ounce of isinglass[a] in a tumbler of water, add to it three tumblers of new milk and one large vanilla bean bruised; boil it slowly until reduced to one third; beat the yolk of 6 eggs with 8 ounces of fine sugar. Pour the infusion upon the eggs and sugar, stir it well and return it to the sauce pan, place it on the fire again, stiring it until it begins to thicken; as you are about to take it off the fire stir in the white of the eggs – sit it away to cool. When perfectly cool, have a hint of thick sweet creme beaten to a froth, add this to the mixture pour it into a form surrounded by ginger or sugar cake, set on ice or in some cold place where it must remain an [hour?] before you turn it out of the mold."

party to fire off their pieces as a Salute to the Town." J8:370 Sergeant Ordway views their arrival from the men's perspective: *"the people gathred on the Shore and Huzzared three cheers."* J9:366

For the young men of the Expedition, it is a grand day. Sergeant Ordway, so long the articulate spokesmen for his young, unmarried men, in finishing his journal touchingly reveals what is deepest in their hearts. *"we unloaded the canoes and carried the baggage all up to a Store house in Town. drew out the canoes then the party all considerably much rejoiced that we have the Expedition Completed and now we look for boarding in Town and wait for our Settlement and then we entend to return to our native homes to See our parents once more as we have been So long from them – finis."* J9:366

St. Louis, for both Lewis and Clark, is almost like returning home – they are intimates of many of the families and have abiding social relationships to renew. They are drawn immediately into the broad circle of the Family Chouteau, dining and staying with scion Pierre Chouteau. Longing for his own family and friends, Clark writes to all of them immediately; Lewis, apparently writing for the first time since his gunshot wound in North Dakota, dispatches

[a] 'Isinglass' is a gelatinous semitransparent substance obtained by cleaning and drying the air bladders of the sturgeon, cod, hake, and other fishes; it is used in the clarification of wines and beers and as a stiffening for jellies. www.slider.com/enc/27000/isinglass.htm. Today, gelatin is the preferred choice. Note: the "isinglass" referenced is not the mica sheets used for stove windows, nor the clear, flexible sheets used for buggy windows, as in the *Oklahoma* song.

a lengthy letter to President Jefferson. The two friends hie themselves off to a store and purchase new clothing, sending the clothes they buy to a tailor.

If riverbanks overflowing with cheering citizens are the equivalent of a Wall Street tickertape parade, the welcome continues in St. Louis. The stellar elite gather for a joyous celebratory dinner and ball on September 25, 1806. No daily entry in the *Journals* covers the event, for the Expedition is over. Missing, too, is a reporter's account in St. Louis, for the city did not have a newspaper until 1808. One hundred and eighty-seven years later, in a rare moment of serendipity, Professor James Ronda discovered an account of the ball in a Frankfort, Kentucky, *Western World* newspaper, dated October 11, 1806.[179] It was published about two weeks after the event, and its account and the following toasts are stunningly detailed.

Unfortunately, no mention is made of the specific foods served. One delicious dessert which might have been served is the St. Louis favorite, detailed several years earlier in Lewis' personal diary: Charlotte Russe.[180]

This gala night of accolades, so quickly planned, is hosted by politician and businessman William Christy, *"my old acquaintance,"* Clark calls him. The festivities are held at Christy's Inn, allowing the grateful citizens "to fully evince their joy at this event." A "splendid dinner" is accompanied by eighteen separate, and heartfelt, toasts. The article notes:

> "The respectable number of persons who attended both the dinner and ball, given on the occasion, together with the unanimity which prevailed throughout the company, cannot but be esteemed an honorable testimony of the respect entertained for those characters who are willing to encounter fatigue and hunger for the benefit of their fellow citizens: but what is not due to those who penetrate the gloom of unexplored regions, to expel the mists of ignorance which envelope science, and overshadow their country?"

Arrival of Captains Lewis and Clark at St. Louis.

> This desirable and unexpected event, took place on Tuesday, the 23d of this of this inst. about the hour of 10 o'clock in the morning. On Monday evening the news reached this place, that Captains Lewis and Clark had arrived at the cantonment, near the mouth of the Missouri; and the great concourse of people that lined the bank of the river at the time of their landing at this place the next day, must be considered as a strong evidence of the respect entertained of those gentlemen for the danger and difficulties they must have encountered in their expedition of discovery. But the citizens of St. Louis, anxious to evince fully their joy at this event, (which cannot but be considered as very interesting to every American) united in celebrating their arrival by a splended dinner at Christy's Inn, on the 25th, which was succeeded by a Ball in the evening.

Courtesy of the Filson Historical Society, Louisville, Kentucky

The welcome home celebration. The Frankfort, Kentucky, *Western World* article on October 11, 1806. Courtesy of the Filson Society, Louisville, Kentucky.

If President Jefferson eschews toasts, it is fortunate that he had never planned to meet the Expedition after it reached its destination in St. Louis. Although a complete listing of the glasses raised in honor of the day is staggering, below are a few of the more significant ones recorded: "The following were the Toasts drank at the dinner. [To ...]
The President of the United States – The friend of science, the polar star of *discovery*, the philosopher and the patriot.
The Missouri Expedition – May the knowledge of the newly explored regions of the West, be the least benefit that we may derive from this painful and perilous Expedition.
The hardy followers of Captains Lewis and Clark – May they be rewarded by the esteem of their fellow citizens."

Gentlemen stand at the dining tables and raise their voices and glasses. Not all is praise. While not intended as such, one voice is ominous in his recollection of history, specifically as it regarded the explorer Christopher Columbus:

> "May those who imitate his hardihood, perseverance and merit, never have, like him, to encounter public ingratitude."

If "public" embraces something more official, what of George Rogers Clark's problems getting reimbursement for his military campaigns? Recall the Captains' fears of Congressional quibbling about provisioning purchases and costs at the front end of the trip. Lewis will shortly stage an auction to sell off the remaining goods and equipment to reduce total Expedition costs.

Only one other negative is raised – perhaps directed at the very government in power:

> "Our National Council – May the baneful influence of private ambition and political intrigue, be ever expelled thence by the genuine spirit of republicanism."

All other toasts are paeans of praise, ranging from "Peace with all nations; but submission to none," to tributes to America. Proud and patriotic statements are made on the Virtues of The United States, "Our fathers who shed their blood and laid down their lives to purchase our independence," George Washington, The Federal Constitution, the Capitol of the United States, Commerce, Agriculture, and Industry. They then toast the:

"The Territory of Louisiana,"

"Freedom without bloodshed," and

"The great river that Lewis and Clark charted: The Missouri – Under the auspices of America, may it prove a vehicle of wealth to all the nations of the world."

Finally, the men apparently run out of political steam and remember the gentler sex. With flushed faces and relaxing arms, they toast an affectionate gesture to the women, and an acknowledgment of what those frontier men consider most valuable:

"The fair daughters of Louisiana – May they forever bestow their smiles on hardihood and virtuous valour."

It remains for one final glass to be raised, the eighteenth on that brilliant starry night; and this is done after the two satisfied and fulfilled Captains have taken their leave.

To "Captains Lewis and Clark – Their perilous services endear them to every American heart."

Reference Section
Foods, Meals, and Menus of the Expedition

You will be pleased to purchase when requested by the Bearer
Captain Meriwether Lewis such articles as he may have occasion for ...

— JOSHUA WINGATE, MARCH 14, 1803 ^{L1:76}

An assortment of Expedition foods prepared for a re-creation of the Corps' cooking in June 2002.

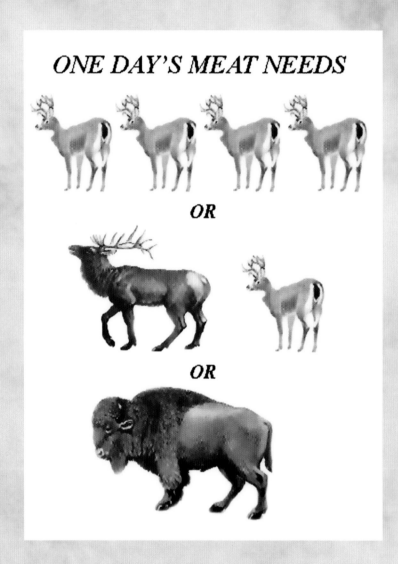

Meat of the Expedition

*We eat an emensity of meat ... it requires 4 deer, an Elk and a deer,
or one buffaloe, to supply us plentifully 24 hours*

— LEWIS, JULY 13, 1805, GREAT FALLS

IMAGINE LEWIS LOOKING DOWN A BANQUET TABLE with thirty-one hungry Olympians and one healthy, nursing female, seeing avid faces and upraised knives and spoons ready to dig in. It is a big party for every dinner – and breakfast, too. It is hard to imagine the immense quantities of food needed to support the Corps throughout those two years. No one writes on a daily grocery list: "elk – 190 pounds." Lewis, the consummate quartermaster, gives one formula for a happy, carnivorous crowd. And this propensity for meat is nothing new, for throughout history in England and France "prodigious feats of meat-eating" were customary and even expected when game was available.[181]

How Much Meat Per Day?

Perhaps the best way of looking at this entire question is to examine the activity level, as well as the hunting results for the week, and account for rations they are still carrying. During times of extreme activity the men eat more, a foregone conclusion – Lewis' *"emensity of meat"* at the Great Falls portage. This subject is analyzed in detail in *Appendix C: Food Requirements*, and considers the Corps' peak caloric requirements while paddling heavy dugout canoes ten hours a day upriver, or the exhausting work hauling those same heavy canoes uphill more than 360 feet over eighteen miles at the Great Falls portage. The conclusions support six to nine pounds of meat per day. Another perspective is the summary at the end of this chapter of total hunting kills over the whole trip, which yields just over six pounds per day per adult, averaged over the entire twenty-eight month Expedition. But, as the men are floating/paddling down the

Columbia, their main meal (dog) consists of perhaps four or five dogs. The weight of these curs nowhere approaches the amount of hoofed game noted on the Plains. So, views on consumption need to relate both what is consumed (simply meat, or meat plus carbohydrates), if it is fatty (like the dog) or lean (like venison), and how hard the men are working. If they are sitting in Fort Clatsop, sewing moccasins on a nasty day, their caloric needs would likely be only 40% of that required on peak upriver canoeing days, portaging, or when they are lowering heavy wooden dugouts down frothing, steep cascades.

Game of the American West

The following section describes game hunted and eaten by the Corps. By the time the Expedition is over, more than twenty-one different species of mammals are consumed by the Corps. The animals are grouped by broad family, then are listed alphabetically. At the end of this section is an unpublished tally that gives a rough idea of the actual animal count and distribution as the Corps crossed the Northwest.

Buffalo and Elk

Perhaps the most important thing to remember when imagining these animals – and the food they provide – is that they are not always fat with thick meat waiting to be cut into rib steaks or roasted up in huge hunks on the spit. From the time winter sets in, these animals depend on a diminishing food supply, and by spring they are often just barely alive themselves. Their condition will be *"pore," "verry meagre,"* or even *"unfit for use."* This disagreeable find is repeated over and over, but Lewis articulates it well on April 17, 1805: *"we met with a herd of buffaloe of which I killed the fatest as I concieved among them, however on examining it I found it so poar that I thought it unfit for uce and only took the tongue; the party killed another which was still more lean."* J4:55

It is only after the grasses green up and get thick and lush that these herbivores will begin to put on weight and become more substantial. The Expedition eats well going up the Missouri, has a very difficult winter and spring in North Dakota, feasts during the summer in Montana, starves crossing the Bitterroots, has a rough time in the winter spent on the Pacific coast, finds an abundance on the Plains, and then returns home amidst food shortages. All of this is part of the natural life-cycle, and man necessarily has to move with it as the calendar turns.

Buffalo, properly bison, sightings (▲) on the Expedition route, as noted by researcher Gary Pound.

Bison or Buffalo

Weight: Males 1500 lbs (680 kg); females 1300 lbs (590 kg).[a]
Meat: 400 pounds (USDA), likely choice cuts by Corps at 250 pounds.

"Saw great nos. of Buffalow ... " J3:186 Clark in October, 1804.

America's Eden is what the Expedition sees, for the relatively low population density of natives allows game to flourish. Literally millions of buffalo dot the landscape, and the explorers even see the mountain bison, a species now confined to Canada. The buffalo provide one of their favorite meats on the trip.

The first buffalo kill is early in the trip on August 23, 1804, near the Nebraska/South Dakota border. Joseph Field downs the animal and Lewis takes twelve men to

[a] All weights are from James C. Halfpenny, *Scats and Tracks of the Rocky Mountains.*

bring the carcass back to the boats. The huge consumption of buffalo starts after the Expedition departs from Fort Mandan, increasing during their 1805 summer in Montana. On the idyllic day of June 14, Lewis descends from the hills and sees, *"a herd of at least a thousand buffaloe."* And Clark's view of the Montana plains are even more staggering – on June 30 he tells Lewis, *"he saw at least ten thousand at one view."*

Lewis and the men thoroughly enjoy the boudin blanc sausage concocted by Charbonneau, as well as the fatty tongue. The huge humps they so love are part of a musculature that counterbalances the buffalo's heavy head. It also provides push-power for the males, which "snowplow" so that the entire herd can find forage in the winter. The Corps has two very different attitudes and approaches to the game they kill. If they are starving, they eat it all. If they are in the land of plenty, they take only the parts they want. *"... had killed 6 buffalow, and Saved only the tongues, & brains for to dress Skins."* J9:179

BUFFALO STEAK[182]

Render some fat in a hot skillet. Add sirloin of buffalo steak and sear on both sides. Cook as beefsteak at a lower heat until done. Thicken juices with flour, and cook gravy until thick. Thin with water or milk and bring to a boil with salt.
– Anonymous early recipe

This recipe is a fine use for the flour they carried, and the mess cooks might have prepared a hunk of meat in this fashion. A mess of cold stew would not carry well to the next day's mid-morning breakfast unless the kettle had a lid, or unless they simply topped it with a hide covering and tied it in place as a waterproof barrier.

By May 25, 1805, Lewis the gourmet is getting uneasy. *"buffalow are now scarce and I begin to fear our harvest of white puddings are at an end."* On July 3 the temporary reprieve they experience around Great Falls is giving out. Remembering the Indian warning, Lewis laments again that *"the white puddings will be irretreivably lost and Sharbono out of imployment."* Bison will not come back onto the menu until the Corps returns in the summer of 1806. What Lewis does not know is that his prognostication of *"fasting occasionally"* is about to become more than true. Like the natives, they have became dependent on the buffalo.

Buffalo Calves

Weight: approximately 160 pounds.

The calves are separate and distinct from their elders, tasting much like costly veal. On April 21, 1805, Lewis' party kills four calves which *"we found very delicious. I think it equal to any veal I ever tasted."* [J4:57] Clark calls it *"verry good veele."* Their fine state can be attributed to drinking milk, which depletes the mother and adds to the baby.

Elk or Wapiti

Weight: Males 700 lbs (320 kg); females 450 lbs (200 kg). Meat: 180 pounds (USDA); likely choice cuts by Corps at 120 pounds.

Bull elk

Wapiti is a native word for "white," denoting the white rump that is seen as the animal departs. These are big animals; a male bull can be 9½ feet in length and stand almost 5' high, a ferocious adversary when in rut. Lewis measures the largest buck elk he's seen at 5'3" at the shoulder. [J4:88] Once elk covered the continent, but by the early 1800s the elk range was reduced to primarily west of the Mississippi, as their eastern habitat became overpopulated and overhunted. Today these animals have retreated to mountain ranges and the nearby valleys.

One of the first kills is in 1804 in what is now Nebraska; Clark observes some elk on an island and shoots one on July 14. In another two weeks, it becomes apparent that the competitors on the food chain are in action – twenty native families are out hunting elk, as is the Corps. But perhaps the natives don't have to worry. The Corps is still having trouble shooting straight. Months after winter practice at Camp River Dubois, *"2 Elk Swam by the boat ... and was not killed, many guns fired at it."* [J2:502] As the hunters improve, Clark records with amazement that on August 2, the hunters bring in *"Three verry large & fat bucks ... the 4 qtr. of one Buck weigh'd 147 wt 1½ Inch fat on the ribs."*

In early spring of 1805, Lewis is moved to write that he has plenty of deer and beaver; *"the flesh of the Elk and goat are less esteemed, and are certainly inferior."* [J4:111] By the time they reach what is now Montana, the elk are in *"tolerable order"* and find their rightful place on the menu. The hearty meat will come later in the summer, after the browse greens

up and the winter-thin elk are nourished and become fatter.

The elk disappear by the time the Corps reaches Beaverhead Rock and begins traversing the Rockies, but these impressive animals reappear (a variant species – the Roosevelt Elk) along the hills of the Pacific coast. And, in fact, their presence is one of the deciding factors for the location of winter camp, *"The Elk being an animal much larger than Deer, easier to kiled better meat (in the winter when pore) and Skins better for the Clothes of our party ..."* [J6:85] Elk are the key; well-fed, clothed troops are far happier soldiers. The faith the men have in Drouillard is patently evident when Lewis scribes on December 1, 1805, *"heard him shoot 5 times just above us and am in hopes he has fallen in with a gang of elk."* Joseph Field is actually the fellow bringing in elk the next day, nice fatty marrow-bones. It is the first elk on the west side of the Rockies, and it *"revived the Sperits of my men verry much."* Good food now has moved beyond being just fuel, it is a morale booster.

Despite the difficulties of hunting in the sodden evergreen forests and carting home heavy quarters of elk through waist-deep bogs, the men do well with the elk. Gass counts more than 131 killed from December 1 to March 20, 1806,[183] and calculating a minimal 120 edible pounds each, this amounts to 15,720 pounds of meat, 140 pounds per day, 4½ pounds per person per day at a time when energy requirements are fairly low. This figure may be a bit high if spoilage and a winter weight loss is added in, but it indicates literally tons of meat being consumed.

Deer, Pronghorn, and Sheep

Eastern White-tailed Deer, also known as Common Deer, Fallow Deer, Long-tailed Deer

Weight: Males 130 lbs (60 kg); females 110 lbs (50 kg). Meat: about 50-70 pounds (USDA).

Lewis is familiar with this deer in his native Virginia. The first time he mentions this subspecies in the *Journals* is at the border between Illinois and Missouri, showing its widespread range at that time. It is truly a welcome side-dish for the men during the winter at Camp River Dubois: During January alone the hunters bring in nineteen deer, a supplement to commissary supplies. By the time the party is going up the Missouri, the hunters are bringing in big amounts. *"30th June ... Killed 2 Deer Bucks Swinging [swimming] the river ... Killed 9 Deer to day."*

Deer are so plentiful that Clark remarks on the multitude of tracks, likening them to hog tracks near a farm. Finally, on July 2, 1804, he becomes so blasé as to say, *"Deer Sign has become So Common it is hardly necessary to mention them."* At the end of the month (the 31st), they delight in a buck that amazingly and deliciously has *"one inch of fat on the ribs."*

Mule Deer, or Black-tailed Deer

Weight: Males 160 lbs (70 kg); females 130 lbs (60 kg). Meat: 60-80 lbs (USDA), choicer cuts are likely 40-50 pounds.

Mule deer

Shields is the first to spot mule deer near Ponca Creek, in what is now Nebraska. By the time the Expedition has reached Montana, the mule deer are plentiful. Reaching the western part of the state, the Corps is truly in the region where "the deer and the antelope play," for the buffalo are gone. The black-tailed deer provide much of the meat eaten, as well as the name *"Blacktail Deer Creek."*

Western White-tailed Deer, also known as Long-tailed Red Deer

This extravaganza of deer and elk continues as the Corp approaches Beaverhead Rock, a sure sign they are approaching Shoshone territory. *"The hunters all returned they had killed 8 deer and 2 Elk. some of the deer wer in excellent order."* J5:8 By July 29, 1805, not only is it full summer with grasses and browse at their height, but the deer are no longer either the mule deer or the common deer. The western white-tailed deer has become the predominant species, and *"we have killed no mule deer since we lay here."* Those they take are *"qu[i]te as large as those of the United States."* The hunters are bringing in more meat, *"very fine."* And Clark, who has been doing poorly, *"eate tolerably freely of our good venison."* In less than three days, the picture changes, *"Game being very scarce and shy. ... we had seen a few deer and some goats but have not been fortunate enough to kill any ..."*

Compared to domesticated, unchanging meat flavors (feedlot beef always tastes like feedlot beef), much of wild game's flavor is derived from the nutrients going in. While struggling in August to haul the canoes up the shallow river, Clark leaves the men to their work and brings back a buck with, regrettably, *"an uncommon bitter taist which is unpleasent."* Lewis takes a guess and supposes that it is due to the willow that forms their principal browse. J5:98 This is one of the final straws for the privates and sets off a round of serious complaints – their swollen feet are misery, they're bone-weary and exhausted, and the meat is disagreeable.

Would they have been in a far better mood with a big swig of whiskey and a round of beaver tail and boudin blanc? Definitely. A good satisfying meal is a psychological charm.

Even in the initial phase of crossing the Rockies, deer are found – not easily, but Drouillard continues bringing them in and the flavor improves. The men no doubt are grateful to have deer that tastes like deer.

Columbian Black-tailed Deer or Black-tailed Fallow Deer

The Pacific coast deer the hunters bring in are a subspecies of the mule deer.[184] They are bigger than the delicate eastern deer, with bigger bodies and shorter, sturdier legs, being jumpers rather than runners. The sick-'n'-tired-of-fish eaters no doubt make short work of the two deer that grace their cooking fire. On November 19, 1805, venison *"rosted on Stiks exposed to the fire"* forms *"a Sumptious brackfast."* This fawning over food is something new; the men are no longer spoiled by the plains abundance and their gratitude level is up.

Columbian White-tailed Deer, also known as Long-tailed Deer, Common Fallow Deer, Common Red Deer

Clark notes this species in discussions of western quadrupeds on February 15, 1806, and again on February 19 as: *"The common red deer we found under the rocky mts. in the neighborhood of the Chopunnish, and about the great falls of the Columbia river and as low down the same as the commencement of the tide water. these do not appear to differ essentially from those of our country [Eastern white-tailed deer] being about the same size shape and appearance in every rispect except their great length of tail ..."* They are noted again on the return trip: seven are killed on March 28, 1806, and another shot on April 15.

Pronghorn "Antelope" (also journaled as "goat")

Weight: Males 125 lbs (56 kg); females 110 lbs (50 kg).

In an identity confusion, Pronghorn is referenced in the *Journals* as both Antelope and Goat. In early spring, on May 5, 1805, the *Journals* read, *"the flesh of the Elk and goat are less esteemed, and are certainly inferior."* That doesn't stop Seaman from pursuing them, and he even outruns one in *"a fair race."* Eleven days later, the Captain's palate hasn't changed, and it is still *"not very pleasant food."* By August 9, 1805, in western Montana, deer and antelope are their only choices,

Pronghorn "antelope"

"*we killed two Antelopes on our way and brought with us as much meat as was necessary for our suppers and breakfast the next morning.*" Game is scarce, the animals fleet, and it takes three men to bring in two animals.

Bighorn Sheep or Mountain Sheep
Weight: Males 300 lbs (135 kg); females 200 lbs (90 kg).

Bighorn sheep

This is one of the more difficult species to hunt, for they are fast and agile and head for the most rugged terrain they can find. Despite the apparent difficulty, Drouillard, Clark, and Bratton all nail one each. These are stocky animals and far denser than deer; the horn is light brown and becomes almost white and very transparent when dressed. The horns are astonishingly heavy: the male's head and horns weigh in at 27 pounds. Natives use the horn on their hunting bows, "*watercups spoons and platters ...*" J4:194 Just upriver from Three Forks, Montana, the men with Clark are delighted to find bighorn on the menu – Sergeant Ordway writes, "*Capt.Clark killed a Mountain Sheep ... the one killed roled down Some distance when it fell. we got it and dined hearty on it.*" J9:193

Surprisingly Lewis, the food connoisseur, has nothing to say about the bighorn meat but Clark does. "*The flesh of this animal is dark and I think inferior to the flesh of the Common Deer, and Superior to the antilope of the Missouri.*" J4:198

Bears

Grizzly (formerly *Ursus horribilis horribilis*, something to think about.)
Weight: male 450 lbs (200 kg); female 350 lbs (160 kg).

Grizzly and prey

The grizzlies are the greatest animal challenge on the trip, both fearsome and awe-inspiring. On May 5, 1805, Clark and Drouillard close in for the kill: "*it was a most tremendious looking anamal, and extreemly hard to kill notwithstanding he had five balls through his lungs and five others in various parts he swam more than half the distance across the river to a* sandbar *& it was at least twenty minutes before he died ...*" Six days later, after another dying grizzly chases Bratton, the Captain is again ruminating on the griz: "*I must confess I do not like the gentlemen and had reather fight two Indians than one bear ...*"

Although there are several references to eating bear, it is generally boiled for its oil, which Lewis notes is "*hard as hogs lard when cool, much more so than that of the black bear.*"

Black Bear or Brown Bear
Weight: male about 300 lbs (135 kg); female 120 lbs (54 kg).

The first bears brought in by Drouillard are an unlucky family of a mom and two cubs on June 7, 1804. Throughout the trip, a continuous supply of bear graces the Corps menu.

Cats

Cougar, also called Panther or Mountain Lion
There are a number of panther kills made on the journey,

Cougar

and never once does it explicitly show up on the daily menu. Since these animals are high on the food-chain competition list, and fairly dangerous to humans, these would be good reasons to kill such a predator. On the other hand, these big cats are often killed when there is little meat on the menu and an extra supply of food would be welcome. On August 3, 1805, the party is struggling up the too-shallow Jefferson River and the men are exhausted from double-team hauling of the canoes. There is one deer for breakfast, another that Clark kills, and a few fish. Clearly they are short on food. Did they eat the panther that Reubin Field kills that day? The *Journals* note only its length as 7½ feet nose-to-tail-tip.

Wild Cat, also called Lynx or Bobcat
There are references to "*killed a cat*" in the *Journals*, such as: "*Drewyer also killed a tiger cat [Oregon bobcat]*" J7:24 but little information is provided.

Canine Family

Coyote or Prairie Wolf
Weight: 20-25 lbs (9-11 kg), males larger than females.

September 18, 1804: "*the hunters killed ... a Prarie wolf, had it all jerked.*" It must have been tasty enough, for on October 5, they kill another one. The coyote entrees continue on the menu, more off than on, throughout the next year, and on April 24, 1805, the hunters bring in *"Some young wolves of the Small kind."* On September 21, 1805, Lewis serves up a jumble of tastes to his crew: coyote, leftover horse, crayfish, and a few grouse. Another *"Prarie wolf"* is taken on October 2.

Wolf
Weight: 110-130 lbs (50-60 kg), males larger than females.

The first wolves are killed on July 20, 1804, when Clark and the hunters are stalking elk, but do not find any: *"I killed an emence large yellow Wolf ..."*

Is wolf really on the menu? Yes, Gass notes on January 3, 1805, *"... hunters going ... down the river, killed nothing for two days, but a wolf, which they were obliged to eat ..."* At Fort Clatsop the men eat dog and deem it delicious; wolf is a very close relative, and even bigger (therefore more meat, more servings). Furthermore it is *"fat,"* which translates in the *Journals* as tasty.[J4:217] Finally Lewis picks up his pen on January 5, 1806, and begins writing a rather dispassionate analysis of his diet. *"I get fat meat, for as to the species of meat I am not very particular, the flesh of the dog the horse and the wolf, having from habit become equally formiliar ..."*

A surprising use is made of the wolf skins; they are tested to cover the ill-fated iron canoe and are used in making *"sacks ... to transport my [Clark's] Instruments."*[J4:365]

Dog
Although an estimated 193 are purchased for food, there little information regarding species or size, except that previously noted: *"small ... party coloured; black white brown and brindle"* with long heads and pointy noses. First served by the Sioux, dog became a regular on the menu west of the Rockies. It is served either boiled or roasted. Clark never takes a liking to its flavor.

Small Mammals

Badger or Braroe
Weight: estimates from about 18 lbs (8 kg) to 26 lbs (12 kg).[185]

Badger

The first badger killed weighs 16 pounds, but it is a specimen, stuffed and sent back to Jefferson. This doesn't mean it's inedible. Another one is taken on October 7, 1804. Then there is an odd listing of gifts from the Salish; a chief gives them a *"Dressed Brarow"* as well as otter and two Goat and antelope skins.[J5:188] Is that badger dressed, as in to eat? Or is it a pelt and should join the skinned gifts? The language is unclear.

Beaver
Weight: *"largest rodent in North America, 30-60 lbs (14-27 kg)"*[186] Another range is 22-75 lbs (10-35 kg).[187]

The beaver's range in 1804 is widespread, and they first appear on the menu during the summer of 1804 – Seaman repeatedly dives in and brings back a denfull. The next beaver haul of five animals is on July 26. The

Beaver

weight of the tail (approximately 1 to 2 pounds) is appropriate for dinner *"a deux"* for the Captains, and although there isn't enough tail meat to go around, the men in the messes are quite pleased with the taste of the body.

Lewis likes beaver tail so well that he pens a gourmet review: *"... the flesh of the beaver is esteemed a delecacy among us; I think the tale a most delicious morsal, when boiled it resembles in flavor the fresh tongues and sounds of the codfish, and is usually sufficiently large to afford a plentifull meal for two men."*[J4:100] The fattiness of the meat can also stand up well to the taste-tempting, barbeque process. His comparison to cod tongue and air bladder is baffling, as they are parts of the fish no longer consumed, and today would constitute part of a scavenger diet rather than an East Coast delicacy. However, Thomas Jefferson's cookbook lists a recipe for "Tongues & Sounds" of codfish, something Lewis has eaten and is using as a taste comparison.

Not only does Seaman chase beaver but they are trapped by Drouillard. He even shoots these fat and plump swimming entrees, gunning one down on April 12, 1805. Compared to the skinny, *"pore"* winter-deprived herbivores, they are a welcome dish. April 17 – *"three beaver taken this moring ... the men prefer the flesh of this anamal, to that of any other which we have, or are able to procure at this moment. I eat very heartily of the beaver myself, and think it excellent; particularly the tale, and liver."* By May 24 beaver are becoming scarce, out of their preferred territory. Lewis notes that *"the beaver appears to keep pace with the timber as it declines in quantity they also become more scarce."* This makes sense for a rodent that gnaws down trees for dinner. But again, as with disappearing buffalo that reappear, so do the beaver. On July 26, 1805, the Captains note, *"emence number of Beaver and orter in this little river ..."* The animals come and go, depending on the habitat. And not all beaver live in the flat-lands; there are also mountain beaver.

Hare, also called White-tailed Jackrabbit
Weight: 7-13 lbs (3-6 kg). [188]

"*Shields Killed a Hare like the mountain hare of Europe, waighing 61/4 pounds (altho pore) ...*" [J3:71] Clark catches one of these in the middle of changing fur color from winter white to summer gray on April 12, 1805. These animals are noted in the *Journals* at various times both on the outbound and the return trip, but as isolated kills. Gass notes on October 17, 1805, that "*In the plains are a great many hares ...*"

Rabbit or Eastern Cottontail
Weight: about 1 lb (0.5 kg).

This small French entree, "*lapin,*" appears on January 14, 1804, "*the party Caught 14 Rabits to day & 7 yesterday.*" Thompson kills fourteen during the week, and Hall catches fourteen. Another fourteen are cooked up a week later on January 23. There are no diner's comments, but it seems strange that so many rabbits come only in bunches of fourteen. Finally, on the January 26, Clark breaks down and says, "*Rabits &. in great quantity,*" at least a change from his now-standard number.

Muskrat
Weight: up to 4 lbs (2 kg).

The men are reduced to eating the smallest of things when they snag a muskrat on April 18, 1805, but it is spring and they are hungry. The muskrat also lives in watery regions like the beaver and it is probably just a fortuitous snare by the hunter who brings it in. Normally it wouldn't be hunted.

Opossum
Weight: male: 14 lbs (6 kg); female: 8 lbs (4 kg). [189]

Again, another Virginia staple. This long and pointy-nosed, sharp-fanged mammal originally hailed from South America and found itself part of the diet of the Caribbean long before Columbus. This may indicate that it was intentionally carried along as a food source, since the Islands are quite distinct and distant from the continent. Long a staple of the South, its meat is termed "*succulent.*" [190] The first 'possum came back to camp for dinner on December 12, 1803, along with some turkeys. This species is part of the "*great appearance of Gaim*" that Clark notes as they begin building Wood River camp.

Otter
Weight: 10-30 lbs (5-14 kg), males slightly larger than females.

The entrance of otter onto the menu is prompted by clear water; the Great Falls made the water too frothy and disturbed down-stream. On July 12, 1805, Lewis observes that "*the otter are now plenty since the water has become sufficiently clear for them to take fish.*" It's a good observation, for most creatures want to see their food. This particular region of the upper Missouri is the only range for these animals, and they have an episodic appearance on the menu. River otters are not seen west of the Bitterroots.

River otter

Porcupine
Weight: 10-25 lbs (5-11 kg), basketball sized; maximum weight: 40 lbs. [191]

Naturalists cite not only their quills, but also their vocal variety, "*they ... make a number of strange sounding calls. Moans, whines, snorts, shrieks, barks, and sobs have all been described.*" [192] Lest we think that "*porkipine*" is some sort of culinary mistake, no – it's not. "*the flesh of this anamal is a pleasant and whoalsome food ...*" [J3:69] Nor does that comment mean it's a favorite. On May 3, 1805, Lewis notes "*an unusual number of Porcupines*" but since an elk is already brought in by Clark, the quilled beasts are safe.

Prairie Dog, or Whistling Squirrel or Burrowing Squirrel
Weight: 2-3 lbs (1-1.4 kg), "*about the size of a large guinea pig.*" [193]

Although this little animal is noted several times in the Plains, the most impressive sighting was on June 5, 1805, "*we saw the largest collection of the burrowing or barking squirrels that we had ever yet seen ... the territory of this community for about 7 miles.*" The only information regarding eating any is on the same day, "*we each killed a burrowing squirrel as we passed them in order to make shure of our suppers.*"

Raccoon
Weight: 8-20 lbs (4-9 kg).

"Enjoyed by the early Colonial settlers of the East and South ... and something of a delicacy," it is puzzling that there is no specific record of eating them; this may be a taken-for-granted food. Rather, the quality of their skins is noted, as on January 2, 1806, "*the fur of ... the rackoon in this countrey are extreemly good ...*" [J6:162] Homeward bound in September, 1806, the Corps spots raccoons on the riverbank, and "*one of the men killed a racoon which the indians [travel-ing with the Corps] very much admired.*" [J8:355]

Squirrels
Burrowing Squirrel – see *Prairie Dog*

Columbian Ground Squirrel

Confusion reigns when on June 10, 1806, at Camp Chopunnish, west of the Bitterroots, Lewis says *"we find a great number of burrowing squirrels about our camp of which we killed several; I eat of them and found them quite as tender and wel-flavored as our grey squirrel."* Lewis has used the term burrowing squirrel earlier to refer to the prairie dog – here, it is most likely the Columbian ground squirrel.

Gray Squirrel

This is the first squirrel species encountered as the Corps moves across the country. Lewis sends Seaman out to find a few tasty morsels, and shoots a few himself, even though *"they swim very light on the water and make pretty good speed ..."* J2:79 The vast number of these little animals has been decreased significantly over these past two centuries as the native forests have been cut down and the environment's natural food supply has been reduced to a fraction of its former abundance. This is also a case of food sharing along the food chain – many animals and humans tap into the same resource. Lewis reports on September 11, 1803, *"they wer fat and I thought them when fryed a pleasent food."*

Western Gray or Large Gray Squirrel

On October 26, 1805, just like magic, the scarcity of the Columbia plains gives way to coastal abundance. The hunters take, among other game, *"4 verry large gray Squirrels."* Whatever food review might have come of this happy find, the squirrels play second fiddle to the excellent salmon trout that gets all the attention and the raves.

Richardson Red Squirrel

May 14, 1806 – *"Shannon ... returned with a few pheasants and two squirrells."*

THE MAJOR GAME TALLIED
ANIMALS AND BIRDS KILLED ON THE EXPEDITION[b]

Primary Food		Other Animals		Birds	
Deer	1048	Fox	1	Geese	57
Antelope	80	Otter	11	Brant	59
Bighorn	41	Badger	4	Duck	68
Elk	382	Porcupine	5	Turkey	18
Bison	259	Rabbit/Hare	7	Grouse	54
Bear	28	Prairie Dog	10	Plover	48
Beaver	111	Panther	2	Eagle	5
Wolf/Coyote	28	Squirrel	6	Hawk	3
Native Dogs	193			Pigeon	9
Horse/colt	10			Others	9

The Carnivores' Menu in Summary

Typical twenty-first century meat markets stock their meat coolers with beef, pork, and possibly lamb. By contrast, the 1805 pantry included buffalo, elk, deer, antelope and bighorn sheep; plus small mammals ranging from rabbit to prairie dogs. (Poultry is not included and is discussed in the next section.) In all, the Expedition meats encompass twenty-five different tastes and textures: some that the men don't like (pronghorn), and some they love (buffalo veal and beaver tail). This great variety reflects the many different habitats crossed; the *Journals* detail an inventory of new animal species previously unknown in New England and provides an appreciation of the awe-inspiring American Serengeti. In speaking of the animals he is eating, Lewis philosophically leaves us an insight into his perceptions:

---

b Table and following chart are from an unpublished study by Raymond Darwin Burroughs, now held by The Lewis and Clark Trail Heritage Foundation in Great Falls, Montana. While there are noticeable errors in some counts (Gass says 131 elk at Fort Clatsop; Burroughs lists 105), the aggregate total weights are likely correct.

ANIMALS KILLED BY EXPEDITION SEGMENT

	Deer (a)	Elk (b)	Bison	Bear	Beaver Canine	Small Animals	Birds
Outbound - 1804–05							
St. Charles to Mandan	251	31	21	11	29	7	30
Winter at Fort Mandan	130	52	58		10	7	
Fort Mandan to Marias	70	34	43		52	1	23
Marias to Shoshones	212	55	58	11	23	11	9
Shoshones to Pacific	62	20			105 *	5	212
Winter at Fort Clatsop	9	105			11 *	2	14
Return Trip - 1806							
Pacific to Travelers' Rest	126	26		16	84 *		19
Lewis on Missouri	124	25	27	9	9		9
Clark & Ordway	115	26	43	5	7	3	11
Missouri to St. Louis	51	15	10			10	3
Total Kills	**1169**	**392**	**259**	**28**	**332**	**46**	**330**
Avg. Meat/Animal (lbs.)	50	150	200	200	18	5	1.5
Total Meat (tons)	**29.2**	**29.4**	**12.9**	**2.8**	**3.0**	**0.1**	**0.2**

(a) "Deer" includes 80 antelope and 41 bighorn sheep

(b) "Elk" includes the 5 horses/colts each way over Rockies

(*) "Beaver/Canine" includes 193 native dogs (*), 28 wolf/coyotes, and 111 beaver

---

"As for the species of meat I am not very particular ... I have learned to think that if the chord be sufficiently strong, which binds the soul and boddy together, it does not so much matter about the materials which compose it." [J6:166]

The meat obtained totals 77.6 tons, or 155,000 pounds. The Corps was gone 850 days – of these, 600 were active working "days on the road," burning on the order of 5100 Cal. per day; 250 were the over-winter camp days: Fort Mandan and Fort Clatsop, where the men burned perhaps 2000 Cal. per day, or 40% of high-energy output. Together, these form the equivalence of 700 full-working days. With 45 men going to the Mandans and 32 adults thereafter, there were 25,500 person-working-days to feed; resulting in an average of 6 pounds of meat per person per full-work-day for the entire trip. This does not include salmon or any other fish. Further, the time distribution of the meat is very non-uniform with periods of both extreme *Feasting*, then extreme *Fasting*.

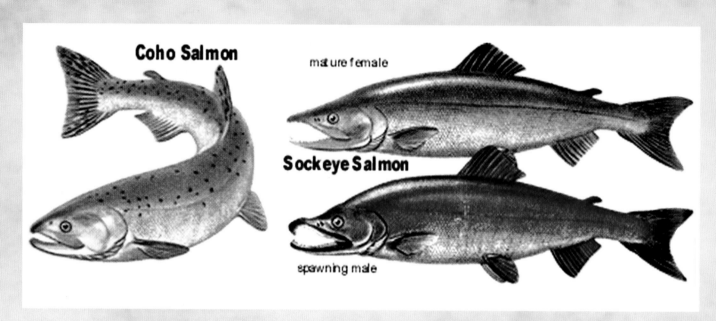

Of all the fish and fowl described and obtained by the Corps, these Columbia River salmon provid the greatest amount of food at the most critical times when game was scarce. These salmon form the food basis of the Columbia River valley native cultures.

Fish and Fowl of the Expedition

*We hawled and caught a large number of fine trout and
a kind of mullet about 16 Inhes long which I had not seen before ...*
— LEWIS, AUGUST 19, 1805

... for the first time for three weeks past I had a good dinner of Blue wing Teel ...
— CLARK, OCTOBER 14, 1805

THE COMMON NOTION OF FOODS EATEN by the Expedition begins with buffalo and ends with salmon. Little importance is given to other fish or fowl and these two categories appear to be overshadowed by the game animals. Several of the very largest specimens brought in as scientific wonders/discoveries of the day range from the immense catfish and western sturgeon (sometimes weighing more than a hefty male mule deer) to the largest bird on the continent, the California condor. If we forget these two realms of creatures, would their absence on the menu be noticeable? Yes. They add a variety of flavors, different textures and aromas at mealtime, and fill in for missing meat, allowing the irreplaceable pork to remain in the keg where it belongs – for last-chance dinners.

When everything really does disappear amidst the vast and dangerous ecological changes crossing *"this horrible mountain desert,"* an immense dietary shift occurs. Gone are the goods from St. Louis; now it is completely native foods, many of them new to white men. Gone, too, are the familiars from the midwestern Louisiana territories. So long, huge catfish and elusive turkeys. In their place are new fish, new fowl. What are these new *plats du jour* and what do the men think of them?

Fish

The Captains are not particularly good at keeping track of fish. In fact, they sometimes specifically ignore them, Clark even writing, *"it is not necessary to mention fish as we catch them at any place on the river ..."* J3:38 At least the *Journals* are fairly explicit about what types of fish they are eating, and even record some extreme catches. On the western trek there is one dedicated and brilliant fisherman, whom Lewis describes as *"remarkably fond of fishing."* He is Silas Goodrich, a fellow who can probably tickle trout right into the fry pan or toss out a line baited with a mosquito and bring in a 200-pound sturgeon. If the sergeants include trout on the menu, assume that Goodrich is nearby. Little is known about him, other than he was among the *"men transferred from other companies to his [Lewis']."* L2:425 He arrives at the onslaught of a bad winter, good only for ice fishing. The winter accounts don't mention fish until the following March, 1804, when it is noted that three large catfish, caught by George Shannon, show up. The next day *"several fish"* are brought into camp. More river fishing occurs, with a notation of *"rivr Catts,"* as a present to Clark on May 18. As fishing and fish are only occasionally noted, it would be easy to conclude that fishing is not a top priority, nor is there much time for it.

Fishing Techniques

How would the men have fished? In a wilderness world where mechanization doesn't exist, very primitive methods are used for catching little fish or snagging the big one. There are poles, but no spinning reels. There are traps and snares, but unlike the beaver traps carried, the fish traps are fashioned out of twigs instead of metal. By far one of the most common methods is spearing the fish, or *"guiging."* While this might seem related to some atlatl throwing contest, this technique is not so difficult, especially since most of the water is very clear.

Gigs – Even the dictionary definition of "gig" can be misleading, citing two different techniques: (1) a fish spear, and (2) a fish line with hooks designed to catch fish by jabbing their bodies.[194] The first use of spearing occurs as Lewis is just getting started down the Ohio, *"we fixed some spears after the indian method but have had too much to attend to of more importance than gigging fish."* [J2:71] The next use of gigs may be more suited to the hook-type design, although it isn't used for fishing. Lewis brings out gigs on July 23, 1805, and has the men wire them onto their setting poles which are slipping on the smooth-rock bottom. The gigs are suddenly converted to underwater grappling hooks, strong enough for Lewis to allow that they *"answered the desired purpose."* The downward thrust of a spear-type of gig would do the job, as would a big barbed hook snagging on rocks and allowing the men to pull against the bottom – either type would work.

"The Net" – Lewis finds fishing peaceful and more of a pastime than a mass-feeding technique. As he begins camping with the Shoshone, circumstances dictate that he change modes. Needing a greater number of fish, he says he *"had the net arranged and set this evening to catch some trout which we could see in great abundance at the bottom of the river."* It is wasted effort. The next morning, August 19, 1805, they pull it in but have *"caugt no fish."* They stow the net and try a different technique.

Brush Drag – Used first on August 15, 1804, this is an improvised net made of brush held together to form a sweep along the bottom of the stream, ending up with the fish being hauled out probably on some desirable sandy shore. Apparently this drag is composed of fairly fine brush and twigs because Clark catches a solitary shrimp, not something that can be accomplished with a large mesh.

After net-fishing fails, Lewis has a few of the men make a willow seine, which is as effective as Clark's drag had been the year before. *"we hawled and caught a large number of fine trout and a kind of mullet about 16 Inhes long which I had not seen before."* [J5:119]

Indian Methods of Fishing – The Expedition is close to totally reliant on native fishing as they come out of the Rockies. The Shoshone, who first introduce the Corps to salmon, *"employ wairs, gigs, and fishing hooks."* [J5:122] Natives used carved-bone hooks, which were being replaced by metal ones as trade goods from merchant ships on the Pacific coast, some of Western civilizations' more practical gear.

Fish by their Respective Drainages

Environmentally, individual species have either a broad adaptability and are found in waters ranging from muddy to clear, warm to cool, or they are quite specific and localized in where they choose to live. By looking at fish by their respective river drainages, there is an indication of the extent to which they are broad-ranging or localized.

Ambiguities exist in determining exactly what Lewis is describing and considering nobody's love of "rotten fish" there are obvious reasons he did not send any specimens back east for scientists to examine and methodically christen with scientific names.

The Ohio

Considering Clark's comment about not mentioning fish, what is known about the fish that graced the crystalline Ohio? Big fish, in water so clear that in Pennsylvania, Lewis writes, *"We see a great number of Fish of different kinds, the Stergeon, Bass, Cat fish, pike, &c."* [J2:71] It is a watery bounty.

Up the Missouri

On May 23, 1804, as the Corps begins its journey, the flotilla passes a small creek called Femme Osage River, and it is *"abounding in fish."* Fish are not uppermost on the Captains' minds however. They note sunfish in Kansas and *"great quantities of fish"* in Gosling Lake, but remember that these are "meat and potatoes" men, and fish aren't all that attractive. Goodrich, however, is irrepressible, and he brings in *"two verry fat Cat fish"* on July 17. Were those fish distributed throughout the messes or did they stay only in his mess? These fish are prevalent enough that Clark names one site, *"Camp White Catfish"* on July 22, on the Iowa side of

CHANNEL CATFISH
Ictalurus punctatus

Channel catfish

the river, facing what is now Bellevue, Nebraska. [J2:413n2] When the observant Captain goes on to describes this fish as having small eyes and a tail like a dolphin, he may be describing a newly discovered species, the channel catfish.[195]

Nature's abundance of one specific species with its own little niche graces the Missouri (near today's Pottawattamie County, Iowa). It is loaded with catfish – not much else, but while stopping to dine *"in a fiew minits"* they catch *"three verry large Catfish (3) one nearly white ... verry fat, a quart of Oile Came out of the Surpolous fat of one of these fish ..."*

The catfish continue upriver, *"so plenty that we catch them at any time and place ..."* [J3:39] The size of the catfish declines the farther upriver the Corps goes; the colder waters and diminished warm-water food supply may have something to do with it. By June 11, 1805, Lewis notes, *"the white cat continue as high as the entrance of Maria's R, but those we have caught above the Mandans never excede 6 lbs. I beleive that there are but few in this part of the Missouri."*

JEFFERSON CATFISH SOUP[196]

To 2 quarts of water add 4 or 5 catfish, according to size, a slice of lean ham, 2 onions chopped fine, 3 sprigs of parsley, a bunch of sweet herbs, half a dozen peppercorns, and a teaspoon of salt. Boil until the fish go to pieces, strain, put on the fire again with another fish that has been skinned and cut into pieces. Boil until the fish is tender. Add ½ pint cream, 1 tablespoon of flour, mixed to a paste with 2 tablespoons of butter, and the yolks of 4 eggs. Serve with chopped parsley.[a]

Another new species crops up: the buffalo-fish, with three possible varieties: the largemouth, smallmouth, or black. [J2:433n1] There are also many new fish the Captains record, surprisingly noted in the weather diary of July, 1804: northern pike, *"catt"* (channel catfish or black bullhead), perch (sauger, walleye, or yellow perch), and carp (probably the river carpsucker).

When Lewis comes across a pelican roosting spot and takes a specimen on August 8, 1804, the food chain is still operating. The men, scavenging fish left behind by these fisher-birds, take *"3 fish which was fresh and very good ..."* And as they paddle by the Little Sioux River, Clark makes the usual nebulous description of *"great Quantitys of fish Common to the Countrey."* [J2:458] They name this camp *"Fish Camp"* on August 13.

Two days later, on August 15, Clark rounds up ten men to build a fish trap with *"Some Small willow & Bark we mad a Drag and haulted up the Creek, and Cought 318 fish of diferent kind ..."* When they put their minds to it, they fish big.

---

[a] This historic recipe may be somewhat thin by modern tastes. Improvements can include: boiling to reduce the initial broth to half, and the addition of more butter and a teaspoon of sea-salt.

The inventory of fish caught lists pike, bass, salmon, perch, red horse, small cat, and silverfish (a kind of perch also found in the Ohio). They also discover *"large Mustles Verry fat, Ducks, Pliver of different Kinds"* living near beaver ponds, an interesting assortment of inter-dependent species. These mussels are a freshwater shellfish, not the saltwater variety. With this kind of abundance, they could fry up lots of fish as a welcome addition to their normal diet.

Apparently this vast catch prompts some sort of adrenalin rush or macho competition in fishing, for the next day Lewis and a dozen men go out dragging, and bring in *"about 800 fine fish ... 79 Pike, 8 Salmon, 1 Rock, 1 flat Back, 127 Buffalow & readHorse, 4 Bass & 490 Cat, with many Small and large Silver fish."* This appears to be very indiscriminate fishing, probably done for scientific survey purposes, but nonetheless quite wasteful.

Salmon? More Likely a Trout – Looking at the inventory above, there appears to be a case of mistaken identity, because salmon simply aren't found in Midwestern waterways. Guesses place it as a brook trout, a goldeye, or even a mooneye. [J2:484n4] Likewise, the *"Rock"* has been speculated as likely a white or rock bass. [J2:486n5]

Brook trout

Shrimp – Not only do the men find tasty shellfish on August 15, 1804, they get a shrimp. *"I cought a Srimp prosisely of Shape Size & flavour of those about N.Orleans & the lower party of the Mississippi."* [J2:483] This single item gives an insight into Clark – he has a more experienced palate than expected. In fact, from March to December of 1798, he traveled on a 4000-mile business trip that led him south to New Orleans, up to Baltimore, and back to Kentucky; and acquainted him with southern foodstuffs.[197] And, while saltwater shrimp are by far the most common variety available, freshwater shrimp are indeed found in inland rivers. The question remains: What variety of crustacean did Clark catch?

Crayfish – A very irregular item almost never found on the menu, but eaten several times, including one time just before emerging into the Nez Perce territory: *"... some crawfish which we obtained in a creek ..."* [J5:226]

Mussels – Certainly a treat. Clark happily says, on August 15, 1804, that he discovers *"large Mustles Verry fat,"* (Thurston County, Nebraska). These delicacies appear again in June, 1805, at the Musselshell River.

Goldeye – The goldeye resembles the "*Hickory Shad or old wife*" according to Lewis on June 11, 1805. He describes it as a fish that doesn't inhabit muddy waters, and that single fact may account for its flavor being the better of the two fish found in the same proximity (goldeye versus sauger).

Sauger

Sauger – White, round, about nine inches long and similar to a chub. The bait is meat or grasshopper, and it isn't a terrifically tasty fish. It is "*a soft fish*," Lewis also opines on June 11, 1805, "*not very good, tho' the flesh is of a fine white colour.*" "Soft fish" is not a complimentary term; most diners are not enamored with mushy texture in fish and will go to some lengths to camouflage it into a more appetizing form.

VOYAGEUR-STYLE MUSSEL AND FISH SUPE[b]

Filet fish into good size pieces and dredge in a mixture of flour (perhaps some cornmeal), salt, and pepper. Set aside. Heat the kettle and when hot, pour in bear oil (or pork lard). Stir in some chopped onions and a handful or two of flour; saute all until barely colored. Then add the fish to the sizzling mixture. When browned, add water and cook the simmering stew until done, about 10 to 15 minutes, throwing the mussels in for the last 5 minutes. Adding wild garlic while cooking or any of the cresses at the end will enliven the broth.

The Fishing Jag

Lewis and Goodrich make an unlikely pair, but both have the fisherman's trait of being solitary, and on June 12, 1805, they are whiling the evening away, fishing. The Captain seems to be in a cheerful mood: "*This evening I ate very heartily and after pening the transactions of the day amused*

---

[b] This is a period-style recipe – a common cooking concept that might have been used, but is not documented in the *Journals*.

myself catching those white fish mentioned yesterday; they are here in great abundance I caught upwards of a douzen in a few minutes; they bit most freely at the melt of a deer which goodrich had brought with him for the purpose of fishing." The bait is deer spleen, a successful choice.

Cutthroat trout

In this section of the Missouri there is enough time to fish as Lewis searches for and finds the Great Falls. On June 13, Goodrich's first reaction is to fish the falls, happily providing taste treats for the men, "*half a douzen very fine [cutthroat] trout and a number of both species of the white fish [sauger].*" Lewis, ever immersed in detail, notes that they are like the speckled trout back home but have specks of "*deep black instead of the red or goald colour of those common to the U.' States.*" These are gorgeous fish, generally 16-23" long, and having "*a small dash of red on each side ...*"

The third day of the fishing spree finds Lewis amusing himself again fishing after sleeping off a hard day's outing and a near-attack by a grizzly the day before. The Captain orders Goodrich to dry his [Lewis'] catch, "*a number of very fine trout,*" while the Private himself catches two dozen trout and a couple of channel catfish. On June 19, Lewis is still happily employed fishing at the Upper Portage Camp – this is actually one of the few times throughout the trip that he just seems to be relaxing. "*I amused myself in fishing several hours today and caught a number of both species of the white fish, but no trout nor Cat.*" Surprisingly, the next day the Captain is not fishing, but Sacagawea is. There's no report of whether or not she catches anything, but this is right after her prolonged illness and she is craving fish.

A week later, on Tuesday, June 25, Lewis is disheartened, "*I have made an unsuccessfull attempt to catch fish, and do not think there are any in this part of the river.*" Meanwhile, below the Falls, Clark brings in "*great quantities of Trout, and a kind of mustel, flat backs and a Soft fish resembling a Shad and a few Cat.*" It is Clark, who on July 3, notices that fish seem to be absent above the Great Falls. On July 10, while Lewis reconciles himself to the failure of his iron boat, he fishes – always a soothing balm. "*Having nothing further to do I amused myself in fishing and caught a few small fish; they were of the species of white chub ... small and few in number. I had thought on my first arrival here [above the falls] that there were no fish in this part of the river.*" He is, as he would phrase it, agreeably disappointed.

More Trout and One Salmonidae

As the river becomes more shallow (near today's Helena, Montana), a number of trout are spotted, but the only catch of the day is simply described as having *"a white colour on the belly and sides and of a bluish cast on the back."* Accidentally injured with a setting pole, it is hauled in and is probably a cisco or a whitefish. [J4:415n8] Meanwhile, Goodrich and all other fishermen are having problems: *"we see a great abundance of fish in the stream some of which we take to be trout but they will not bite at any bate we can offer them."* [J5:11] Apparently deer melt isn't working.

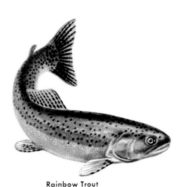

Rainbow Trout

Rainbow trout is an inland variety of the migrating steelhead (salmon) trout.

Goodrich's fishing experience comes in handy along the Jefferson River basin, because Lewis consults *"one of our men,"* and presumably the best fisherman is the one to be consulted. The new fish is probably the same as the Eastern bottlenose, a white, scaly fish with a *"remarkable small long mouth"* [J5:37] which gets its name from the neck of a bottle. The trout in the same stream are always considered good eating but at the time the bottlenose or sucker gets no taste review. Later this fish, probably a northern sucker, is deemed *"no means as good as the trout."* [J5:119]

Idaho Salmon – Lewis' first taste of actual salmon comes as a gift from the Lemhi Shoshone, who live by the waters leading down to the Columbia from the middle of May to the end of August and spend their time fishing as the migratory fish come upriver. [J5:122] On August 28, 1805, the Kentucky Captain begins his many-month tangle with the salmon, *"pleasent eateing, not with standing they weaken me verry fast and my flesh I find is declining."*

Salmon Roe – Not eaten with any frequency but at least tasted, for Clark says he *"purchased Some fish roe of those pore but kind people,"* referring to the Lemhi Shoshone. [J5:177]

Columbia Fisheries

Pacific fish are the salvation of the Expedition. As the arid Columbia plain leaves the Corps meatless, the salmon kingdom commences. The men observe great established fishing places, clear bottoms that are salmon-roe nurseries. It is the end of the fall breeding run and the two fish migrating upstream at this time are the coho (or silver salmon) and the sockeye. Later Lewis writes a perceptive description to Jefferson, aptly describing the conditons they encounter when fishing. *"At this season* [September] *the Salmon altho' abundant are so meagre that they are unfit for use in great measure."* [L1:339] Clark's culinary beliefs no doubt run contrary to the native approach when eating dried salmon, for they believe in *"mearly worming* [warming] *it and eating the rine* [skin] *& Scales with the flesh of the fish."* And he is appalled that sand is always present on the food. Not only does eating scales and sand sound wretched, but the civilized Kentucky gentleman believes it contributes to the dismal state of the inhabitants' gums and worn-down teeth. [J5:290]

Depending on whether it was fresh, air dried, or pounded makes all the difference in flavor perceptions and seemingly in health. Even Clark admits to boiled salmon being *"delicious."* [J5:288] The natives at the Deschutes River in Oregon store their pounded fish in beargrass baskets and pronounce this dried staple to be *"Sound and Sweet"* even after several years of storage. [J5:325] Whitehouse notes that *"the Natives ... brought us Some fish which had been roasted and pounded up fine and made up in balls, which eat verry well."* [J11:360]

Despite the seeming overabundance of fish, the natives don't want to part with it. Clark notes this hitch at The Dalles on Saturday, October 23. *"the Indians not verry fond of Selling their good fish, compells us to make use of dogs for food."* In amazement, he estimates that he sees close to ten-thousand pounds of dried fish, five tons of provisions.

Stranded and camping in the rain at their ocean-battered and rain-deluged outpost at Point Ellice, the Corps is relieved as the locals come canoeing by on November 11 in a floating store, selling red char (or sockeye salmon). In the midst of their suffering, the men enjoy these thirteen *"excellent fish."* For days they eat nothing but salmon – no dogs, no elk, no deer – just fish. And often there isn't enough. On November 14, they are fasting on the shores of maritime bounty, *"only 2 fish to day for the whole Party."* The continuous rain spoils their supply of pounded fish during *"the most disagreeable time I have experienced."* [J6:48] Hunting continues to be bleak, and different parties are dispatched in all directions, hoping for fowl or hoofed game. The troops will never be confirmed fish enthusiasts.

Salmon Trout (Steelhead) – This pink-fleshed salmonidae appears as a staple to the natives on the Columbia when the salmon are not running, and after gigging one, the Corps fries it in a little bear's oil. It is so good that it bowls Clark over, and he deems it *"the finest fish I ever tasted ..."* [J5:342] a high compliment from a meat and potatoes man.

Coastal Dining

The Starry Flounder – Despite coming across what should have been a good-eating fish, the eaters of the Corps are inclined to stick with what they know. An impressionistic line drawing of the flounder is inserted into the log, [J6:63] and then the men dine on brant and pounded fish. Why they pass up this fresh fish is a mystery.

Eulachon [ū´·le·kän] ***or Candlefish*** – The early run of candlefish sends Lewis into a gourmet tither. He is introduced to this little foot-long delicacy in February by Clatsop Chief Comowool, who comes by loaded with goods for sale, offering the largest and smallest fish around. The candlefish,[c] *"are taken in great quantities in the Columbia R. about 40 miles above us by means of skiming or scooping nets."* [J6:342] Lewis is so delighted with this exquisite new taste that he sends for more.

Sturgeon – Sturgeon, the other fish brought for sale at Fort Clatsop, is one of the fish giants that inhabit the great rivers of world, and the Corps is buying the Columbia River species. An immense fish growing up to thirteen feet in length, it can top out at weights of up to a full ton.[198] This is not something that Goodrich might expect to snag on his line. Unlike Clark's purchase of salmon roe from the Shoshone, there is no mention made of roe on the Columbia.[d] Since sturgeon can live up to a hundred years, it takes up to twenty years to reach maturity and begin producing eggs. The coastal natives prefer food now, which limits the fish's maturation. Lewis deems this seafood to be *"good of it's kind"* [J6:344] and regretfully there is no caviar on this visit to the Pacific Northwest.

Boneville Power Administration

Giant sturgeon

Sea Mammals and Gastropods

While they are not fish, sea mammals live in the same watery environment and can logically be placed here with their aquatic brethren. These maritime creatures that appear during the Fort Clatsop winter are just a small part of the Expedition's food supplies and include *"Whale, Porpus, Skaite, flounder, Salmon, red charr ... Clam, perrewinkle, common mussle, cockle."* [J6:407]

The Corps shoots several harbor seals, apparently a native delicacy, but the corpses sink, indicating either a lack of fat or deflated lungs. Eating whale is a new experience.[e] Porpoise is another native treat which is caught by gigging, and apparently some is brought to the fort – it isn't clear if it is a sale or a gift – and is sampled. Lewis finds the flavor *"disagreeable."* [J6:410] If this is the case, it's probably fortunate that Lewis didn't get a chance to try harbor seal.

While shellfish may comprise a segment of the native diet and the men have enjoyed mussels before, the small size of these mollusks and the unpleasant prospects of standing in the pouring rain harvesting them from frigid ocean waters leaves the Corps cold. There's no reason to be interested.

Fowl

Man the hunter has always looked for ways to make his life easier, and one of those ways was to shoot the largest birds available. When there is great variety and no hunting laws, this strategy is followed quite regularly. During the Middle Ages, aristocracy dined on *"swans, storks, cranes, peacocks, herons ..."*[199] This provides a backdrop for what the Corps will shoot if they can, or trade for if it becomes available. Many of the same birds will be eaten (swans, cranes), and fowl is on the platter many winter nights at Camp River Dubois. There are the large native turkeys so beloved by Ben Franklin (which he proposed as the national bird), grouse – *"many grous Caught to Day"* [J2:158] as Clark remarks over and over – and heath hens. Heath hens and grouse are terms which the Captains sometimes use interchangeably, but they are not quite synonymous.

Geese

On the Fourth of July, 1804, as the Corps paddles through what will become Kansas, Clark is so impressed with *"great numbers of Goslins to day ... which Were nearly grown"* and their attendant parents, that he christens their pond *"Gosling*

---

[c] The eulachon is so named the "candlefish" because the high oil content allows threading it with a wick and then burning it as a candle.
[d] American sturgeon caviar, "Malossol," was selling for $100 a pound in 2002.

[e] The full whale story is covered in *The Pacific Winter*, page 192.

Lake." This impressive scene doesn't mean that the food chain principle is not working, for on July 13, the stalwart commander goes for the kill, *"I Killed two Goslings nearly Grown, Several others Killed and cought on Shore, also one old Goose, with pin fethers, She Could not fly."* Hungry predators usually take advantage of a life-cycle misfortune like this.

About the same time the next year, on the Montana plains, there are *"great numbers of gees"* young and old – all without the wing feathers that allow flight and all literally grounded. *"my dog caught several today, as he frequently dose. the young ones are very fine but the old gees are poor and unfit for uce."* J4:411 Nearing Shoshone territory on August 4, 1805, Clark's canoe party is eating *"geese and ducks ... killed by those who navigated the canoes."* This is double duty, but if there's a hungry private who spots a goose while looking for water hazards, he may temporarily become a hunter.

Black brant

The goose entrees continue sporadically as the Corps marches into the Bitter-roots. After running the *"agitated gut"* of the The Dalles cascades, Clark shoots a goose J5:337 and then commandeers it and some venison as a compensatory dinner to congratulate himself on a successful run – a Captain's reward dinner.

By the time the Corps reaches the Cascades of the Columbia, they are into the habitat for the lesser Canada goose, the birds being *"Smaller than Common, and have white under their rumps & <abov> around the tale ..."* J6:8 The men alternately call them "gees" or "brant," more or less synonymous terms. The first haul is eighteen lesser geese and one brant of a different type. Pacific maritime lakes and waterways are an ideal habitat for bird life, and on November 16, York brings in Canada geese, white snow geese, and black (Western) and speckled (Eastern) brant. J6:59n3 The snow goose will provide the most meat, and the black brant the least, *"verry small, a little larger than a large Duck."* J6:53 There is also the white-fronted goose, weighing about 8½ pounds.

Goose and Eagle Eggs. Ordway records the first of the egg raids: *"Saw a Goose nest on a tree one man clumb it found only 1 egg."* J9:130 Their haul is never much; on April 18, 1805, *"one of the men clumb up and got 2 [bald eagle] Eggs (all there was);"* J9:133 and *"shot a Goose on hir nest we got 6*

eggs out of it ..." J9:137 May is the end of nesting, and the eggs appeared for only about a month. The *Journals* record a total of sixteen eggs, not many.

Swans

Swans are large birds and provide enough meat to make them a popular entree, far more practical than, for instance, quail. The French near St. Louis find this to be the case, and Clark is amused by the antics that follow a simple shot. On December 27, 1804, a wounded swan is making great headway downriver to escape, and the French are in hot pursuit. It takes more than two miles before the French win the race. Nearing the Three Forks of the Missouri in 1805, *"We saw three swans this morning, which like the geese have not yet recovered the feathers of the wing and could not fly we killed two of them"* J4:411

In the marshy terrain near the Sandy River in Oregon, fowling becomes a pleasure. On November 3, 1805, the combined hunting parties kill three swans, five ducks, and eight geese. Additionally, Collins brings in a large buck, and, finally convinced there is enough food for the party, Clark gives the Indians a goose. The next night, the concentration of birds is so dense that *"I could not Sleep for the noise."* In fact, it is far worse. Not only are ducks and geese present, but there are also swans and sandhill cranes, both of which have dissonant calls, and it results in a quacking, honking, trumpeting cacophony – *"their noise horrid."* J6:21

Wild Turkey

The clucking, gobbling wild turkey has a broad range, from the Atlantic seaboard across the country to the Missouri. The Corps first hunts it in the rich lands at Wood River. On December 21, 1803, the hunters again bring in turkey, *"7 ... verry fat."* Traveling upriver in early spring, 1804, turkey steadily remains on the menu. By midsummer, it makes infrequent appearances, and finally the Corps passes beyond its habitat and it is not seen again until late-summer, 1806, when on the return home, turkeys are again an infrequent but succulent entree.

Back on the Eastern seaboard, Virginians had long-since put the wily bird on their table, a

Wild turkey

feat in itself since it is a difficult fowl to bag. Since the Jefferson, Clark, and Lewis families were all from Virginia, preparing turkey for the table would have been commonplace and the roasting bird turning over glowing coals on the hearth would send savory, enticing aromas throughout the house. Here is a recipe from *The Williamsburg Cookbook* that demonstrates the versatility of preparation in Colonial America. From the Corps' supplies, a close replica of this recipe could have been produced – however, on the frontier the bird might simply have been kettle-cooked or roasted over the fire.

WILLIAMSBURG WILD TURKEY[200]

"Plunge the cleansed turkey into a Pot of boiling Water for five Minutes ... Make a stuffing of Bits of Pork, plenty of Celery, stewed Giblets, hard-boiled Eggs, pounded Cracker, Pepper and Salt, and a heaping Spoonful of Butter. Work this well and fill the Turkey. With another large Spoonful of Butter grease the Bird, and then sprinkle Salt and Pepper over it. Lay in a Pan, with a pint of Broth in which Meat has been boiled. Place in a hot Oven. When it begins to brown, dredge with Flour and baste, turning often, so that each Part may be equally browned. Put a buttered Sheet of Paper over the Breast to prevent Dryness. When thoroughly done, lay on a Dish, brown some Crackers, pound and sift over it, and serve with Celery or Oyster Sauce."

❧ ❧

In adapting the Williamsburg recipe, the proportions for stuffing a six-pound free-range turkey were:

1 C.	diced celery
2	hard-boiled eggs, chopped
1 C.	giblets and blanched Salt-pork
2 C.	pounded Hardtack (pounded to crumbs)
2 T.	butter

Grouse

There are five different types of grouse brought in by the Corps. Gracing the plate are birds named for their appearance – ruffed and blue (actually described as a *"large black species"*), as well as by their habitat – sage and spruce. The identification of these separate subspecies is particularly difficult because of the male/female distinctions as well as the

totally different appearance of the fledglings. Ruffed grouse are first seen on July 25, 1804, but taken two weeks later, on August 8, *"prarie hen or grouse, was seen in the praries between the Missouri and the river platte."* The environment changes to support sharp-tailed grouse, and they are at one point so plentiful that Clark names a roosting spot, *"Grous Island."* [J3:148]

Lewis continues his observations on the differences in grouse. While the emphasis is on hunting big game, he does see *"two fesants ... of a dark brown colour much larger than the phesant of the U' States."* This apparently is a new species, the blue grouse. [J4:415n6] By August 1, 1805, the grouse *"is almost grown we killed one of them. this bird is fully a third larger than the common phesant of the Atlantic states,"* and he continues with a final gustatory comment, *"the flesh of this bird is white and agreeably flavored."* It is cooked with parched corn and made into a soup.

GROUSE AND CORN SOUP

Dredge grouse in cornmeal and fry in bear grease (pork fat). Add water to cover.
Cover and simmer 15 to 20 minutes.
Add ½ cup parched corn per person after 10 minutes.[f]
Season with sage if desired; salt and pepper to taste.
Top with diced wild onion or chives, if available.

The sage grouse, which Clark bags on August 20, is dark brown, with a long pointy, tail and a fleshy protuberance, something like that of a turkey. The Captains call it various names: mountain cock, pheasant, or cock-of-the-plains. It is a rather large bird, *"as large as a small turkey,"* which feeds on sagebrush seed, greasewood, and grasshoppers. Ingested sage doesn't appear to season the flesh like externally applied seasoning twigs or

Prairie grouse

---

[f] To do this authentically requires ground parched corn (if available); or alternatively try finely ground Corn Nuts™ and adjust the salt.

Spruce grouse

leaves, but may have other affects. Clark later writes at Fort Clatsop that *"the flesh of this fowl is dark and only tolerable in point of flavour. I do not think it as good as wth the Pheasant or Prarie hen, or grouse."* J6:371

As the Expedition first progresses into today's Idaho, the *"prarie fowl"* remains on the menu, still within its ecological range. But, the species of grouse being bagged changes near Lolo Hot Springs. The *"pheasents"* look the same except they now have a black tail. It is the spruce grouse. J5:204n4 These *"large black and white pheasant"* are hardy birds, indeed they are the only thing bagged during the worst of the Bitterroots transit, and Lewis describes them as being small. Genetics or lack of feed? Their size is less important because of several favorable traits: *"when Supprised flies up & lights on a tree and is easily Shot their flesh is Superior to most of the Pheasant Species which we have met with."* J6:373 Perhaps their fine flavor comes from eating pine nuts and bearberry. Clark weighs in with a comment that their cooking techniques aren't giving the bird meat full credit and they *"were only tolerably flavoured tho' these birds <are> would be fine well cooked."* J6:376

By the time the Corps is river-running through the Columbia plains on October 17 , Clark gives us a clue that the region supports several types of grouse. *"I shot a large Prairie Cock [sage grouse] Several Grouse, Ducks and fish."* Since this is one of their favorite birds, it will continue on the menu anytime a hunter can get one. The Oregon ruffed grouse gets high diner recommendations as well, *"flesh of this is preferable to either of the others and that of the breast is as white as the pheasant of the Atlantic coast."* J6:375

Cranes

The mileage log for September 7, 1805, shows the Corps traveling between snow-covered mountains to the left and bald, stony hills covered with cactus to the right when someone shoots two cranes. Crane appears on the menu

again on October 19, Clark at the gun. Later he enjoys the fowl as Cruzatte plays dinner music on the violin. This doesn't sound like an Expedition environment; somehow it's more evocative of a fun-loving restaurant. This large bird is also taken on the Pacific coast, before Fort Clatsop is built.

Curloo (Curlew), Plover

On the eastern side of the Rockies, the Corps is very opportunistic when it comes to hunting. Young curloos have only pin feathers; they are grabbed for the pot. These birds are *"so shy and watchfull there is no possibility of geting a shoot at them ..."* J4:417 and so grabbing or using Seaman is the Corps' best recourse. The very thought of using ammunition on a bird of this size is indicative of a rising hunger level.

Long-billed Curlew

Golden Plover

fall

Curloo and plover

Along the Washington coast, Clark resorts to calling them *"pliver"* instead of plover, but it is still the same bird, or birds – for now there are actually two types, sporting *"yellow & black legs."* The men don't care; they just pluck the forty-eight birds and dine on them. Altogether there are at least three different plovers: the black-bellied, the lesser golden, and the mountain plovers; plus the long-billed curlew.

Ducks

Another menu item dating from antiquity, the duck is known for its excellent flavor. Surprisingly, the Corps is remarkably short on ducks for a very long time. They see them, they identify them, and they don't eat them. One of the first actual eating experiences is near Beaverhead, Montana, where Lewis is out alone, firing his gun and hallooing – he isn't sure if he's ahead of the party or behind it. In the midst of this uproar a duck lands *"about 40 steps of me and I killed it; having secured my supper I looked ... for a suitable place to amuse myself in combating the musquetoes ..."* J5:15 He cooks it up and despite wild duck's decidedly gamey flavor, he *"found [it] very good."* There is no indication of what type of duck it is.

Wild duck meat is very unlike the duck breasts served with sour cherries or a Cointreau sauce in the twenty-first century. The cultivated fowl crisp up nicely and have a wonderfully fatty, moist texture and mouth feel. Their wild cousins are extremely lean, gamey, and are definitely chewy. Since the breast meat is literally connected to the flapping wings, it is tough. The legs don't do as much work and are far more tender. And wild ducks may have only half as much edible meat as their cultivated brethren.

Various species comprise this group, varying in flavors and colors. In length they range from fourteen to twenty-four inches, and a good part of the time it isn't clear which species the Corps is eating, only that they are enjoying their meal. Clark's mess devours their ducks, which are *"of a delicious flavour."* J5:312

Blue-winged Teal – On October 14, 1805, when dog is the Expedition's main meat, a happy Clark writes, *"for the first time in three weeks past I had a good dinner of Blue wing Teel."* He is so elated that he also writes in the margin of his mileage log, *"killed 8 ducks, good dinner."* The teal are in this locale; another two are shot the next day, and on that day Labiche brings in: *"2 Ducks of the large kind"* as well

Blue-winged teal

as two geese. Fowl are supporting the Expedition. Lewis also enjoys teal, judging it to be *"a very excellent duck."* J6:398

Bufflehead Duck or Butterbox Duck – Clark: *"I take this to be the same species of duck common to the ohio, as also the atlantic coast."* Obviously the men know this duck already, and so it is a pure pleasure to find it again, for *"the flesh of this duck is verry well flavored I think Superior to the Duckinmalard."* J6:397

Duckinmallard – This appears to be 1800s slang for the mallard duck, *"Small*

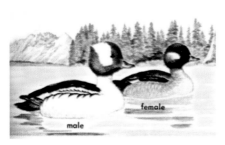

Bufflehead duck

ducks the flavour of which much resembles the Canvis back." J5:309 With a huge range, the mallard is common throughout the United States.[201]

Canvasback – A large population of these is found and hunted near the mouth of the Columbia. Lewis is besides himself gastronomically over this bird. *"One of the most delicious in the world,"* and *"nothing need be added in prais of the exquisit flavor of this duck,"* finally tripping over himself to declare the ones on the West Coast to be *"equally as delicious"* as those found on the East Coast. J6:397

Canvasback duck

Red-breasted Merganser – Lewis dissected this bird and found crayfish in its stomach, which leads to the conclusion that, despite being a duck, it probably isn't eaten. A food writer describes the bird this way, "A fish-eating duck, which frequently tastes like a duck which has eaten fish."[202] This description also fits the grebes, of which Lewis matter-of-factly declares *"the flesh unfit for uce."*

Red-breasted merganser

Coot and Cormorant

November 30, 1805, is a day for small birds, and coot is just that. It is otherwise known as a black duck but is not really duck. Clark is impressed by the *"emence large flocks in the Shallow waters …"* With these numbers, three birds is a rather small kill. But it might have been worth it, for on March 10, 1806, Lewis writes, *"they are usually fat and agreeably flavored."* As to the cormorant, Clark judges it to be, *"fat and tolerably flavoured."* J6:387

Crow

If "eating crow" has a bad connotation, starving men have no such qualms. This bird is brought in by Rueben Field on September 22, 1805, and served alongside *"fish roots and buries."*

Hawks

"my hunters killed three Hawks, which we found Fat and delicious," notes Clark on November 30, 1805, on the south shore of the Columbia estuary.

Fish and Fowl in Summary

These protein entrees work magic for the troops. Whether it is a fine batch of trout dipped in cornmeal and then sizzled in bear grease, or a goose splattering and cracking, turning golden as it roasts and drips over the fire, both would have wonderful, enticing aromas wafting out to tantalize the hungry young men as they anxiously await dinner, hearing the sounds of fat popping as it explodes against the orange-red and deep-crimson coals. They could enjoy new tastes as their tongues carried the dispersing flavors past the tastebuds, relaxing only after their hunger pangs ceased.

Despite culinary taste disasters like duck that tastes like fish or barely-tolerable sage grouse, most of the meals taken from these two disparate pantries are quite fine; and in fact, many of the happiest food entries in the *Journals* relate to the "Poultry Platter" or the "Fish Feast." Of course, with more than fifty different dishes to sample, there are high odds for success. Should the Corps not have had these many and varied options, they might have become *"verry verry"* tired of eating just the red-meat specials. Indeed, the very delicate balance between feasting versus fasting often depended on the fish swimming by or the fowl flying overhead.

Blue camas grows abundantly in the high Rocky Mountain meadows. Its root-bulb forms the carbohydrate basis of the Nez Perce diet.

Plant Food of the Expedition
Starches, Greens, Fruits, Nuts, and Berries

*... these roots [camas] are like onions, Sweet when Dried,
and tolerably good in bread ...*

— CLARK, SEPTEMBER 20, 1805

*the Chief informed us that they had nothing but berries to eat and gave us some
cakes of serviceberries and Choke cherries which had been dryed in the sun ...*

— LEWIS, AUGUST 13, 1805

WHEN LOOKING AT THE PLANTS featured on the Corps' menu, four distinct categories are possible. There are straight carbohydrates, primarily roots. A tiny percentage of true "greens" are gathered. Different fruits account for a substantial part of the summer and fall gatherings, and finally there are a few nuts, which are inconsequential.

Little note is made of starch consumption during the winter near St. Louis, and vegetable consumption is apparently nonexistent except for the wagon-load of turnips. But when the Expedition leaves St. Louis in the early spring of 1804, the keelboat and pirogues are loaded. For weeks the Captains have been working with the Army commissary to obtain literally tons of carbohydrates. The Captains are purchasing huge volumes of starches, starting with about five tons of corn, flour, dried peas, and beans. Three tons of corn are the backbone of their rations, with two tons of flour and hardtack a close second.[a] These supplies feed the men well, but as supplies are used, even more corn must be taken on at the Mandan villages.

While these are the cultivated crops and products, there is also an interesting admixture of native foodstuffs at the edges of the frontier.

---

[a] Today the U.S. Army advises that their troops consume 60 to 65% carbohydrates in their diet.

Native Carbohydrates on the Plains

The American West is an abundant pantry, with many edibles stocked throughout fourteen very different ecological regions. If the Corps runs out of prairie turnips, for example, it doesn't mean the end of that vegetable entirely. It may come onto the menu, disappear, and then reappear. Likewise, something may appear on the way out and reappear only after the Corps has returned to the same environmental niche where they found the plant before. A lack of familiarity with these new foods is where the natives will lend their expertise and keep the Corps running on new and unknown fuels.

The Three Sisters

Some Plains tribes cultivate the nutritional triumvirate of corn, squash, and beans. During the frigid winters when meat is scarce or unavailable, the inland natives rely on these valuable dried products to keep them in good health. The Corps eats their share, trading services for food-in-the-pot.

Jerusalem artichoke
is the root of the
sunflower.

Jerusalem Artichokes, or Sunchokes

"one of the men informed [us] that

the Menetares have plenty of artichokes ..." and from the *Journals* we know that the roots of these cheery yellow flowers are harvested as *"jerusalem artichokes,"* and are *"well tasted."* [J326, 27n10] In fact, Lewis later attributes the flavor of these to another sunflower that the Shoshone eat, but then remembers that the previous tuberosis roots he ate before were far larger than the little nutallii whose roots are *"about the size of a nutmeg ... and I found them preferable ..."* although he qualifies this, *"however there is some allowance to be made for the length of time I have been with-out vegetable food."* [J5:143]

Hog Peanut or Ground Bean

Coming upriver, the Arikaras introduce the Corps to *"a large Been,"* which Clark deems *"rich and verry nurishing."* [J3:159] It is the hog peanut or the ground bean, and the tribes have an interesting way of getting it. Meadow mice, it turns out, love this starch and carry it back to their holes. The Indian women come along and raid the mouse pantry, always with a pack-rat approach of leaving something else behind in trade that will keep the little mice alive and functioning.

While the men are paddling or sailing upstream on the Missouri through the prairies of North Dakota and Montana, Sacagawea walks, gathering roots and vegetables including the hog peanut and the Indian potato.

Hog peanut

Indian Potato or Groundnut

A pea-vine–type plant, this moisture-loving plant has perennial roots that are pried from the soil with a sharpened stick. Once harvested, they are boiled, an outer skin slipped off, and then dried. Lewis notes that *"these they boil with meat or pound and make an agreeable bread ..."* He continues with the observation that it can be cooked when fresh, *"without danger provided it be well roasted or boiled ..."* [J2:223]

Indian potato

Yellow Lotus

Yellow lotus is a vivid-yellow flowering

pond plant, which Lewis notes has twenty to thirty cells, each containing *"an oval nut much ... resembling a small white acorn smothe extreemly heard, and containing a white cernal of an agreeable flavor ..."* [J2:222] The nuts serve many on the food chain, and they are eaten roasted or raw. At Camp River Dubois, a man comes by offering nuts of the yellow lotus, and the engagés and their French families no doubt consider the *"graine de volaille"* as a valid entry on their dinner menu. Bears feast on the leaves, and the roots feed a number of wild birds, particularly the swan (hence the name Swan Root). As with other aquatic foodstuffs, this vivid-yellow flowering plant anchors deep in ponds. The native women go directly into the water and loosen the roots with their feet. It is commonly scraped and boiled, Lewis continues, *"when it is prepared for the pot it is of a fine white coulour boils to a pulp and makes an agreeable soupe ... it is esteemed as nutricius as the pumpkin or squash and is not very dissimilar in taste."* Like other edibles, it is preserved by drying.

Yellow lotus

Morels

On June 19, 1806, Lewis write that *"Cruzatte brought me several large morells which I roasted and eat without salt pepper or grease in this way I had for the first time the true taist of the morell which is truly an insipid taistless food."*

Onions and Garlic

Onions are a taste treat that sparkles the stews and sets the men's tastebuds tingling. Fields of white wild onions are found near the entrance to the Little Missouri in North Dakota and they *"had some ... collected and cooked, found them agreeable."* [J4:26]

Near Three Forks, Montana, at the juncture of the Madison, Gallatin, and Jefferson Rivers, Lewis is walking ahead and spots a patch of small onions, *"white crisp and well flavored ... and withall I think it as pleasantly flavored as any species of that root I even tasted."* [J4:416] Even though these aren't a true starch, they come close, and the flavor-starved Captain rejoices – and starts gathering. He has half a bushel picked even before the canoes pull up, and when they do, he calls a breakfast break. The men also get into the gathering mode, and Lewis collects seed to take back. Several different members of the allium family show up along the route, as well as a *"strong, tough and disagreeable"* wild garlic. J4:420

Wild Ginger
"it resembles that plant [ginger] somewhat in both taste and effect ..." J3:453 but Lewis, after tasting it, views it more as medicinal than a food. It becomes specimen #10 returned by the keelboat.

Sagebrush and Rye
The curious gourmet Captain amuses himself with smelling and tasting *"many aromatic herbs ... resembling in taste, smel and appearance, the sage, hysop, wormwood, southernwood."* J4:35 Although not eaten, Lewis remarks on a species of wild rye that appeals to him, something a miller or distiller might find interesting.

Breadroot, Pomme Blanch, *"Hankee,"* or Prairie Turnip

The French have a partiality for *pomme blanche.* Lewis has a remarkably flexible opinion of this food, deeming it on two occasions to be *"insipid"* and then turning around in the same sentence to declare that it would well suit *"our epicures,"* thinking that it could replace truffles in their ragouts. J4:126 Either this is an amazing discrepancy, or he doesn't think much of truffles. More than once Sacagawea goes out gathering breadroot. On the return trip, Clark's men again spot these prairie turnips and go on a digging spree, excavating a *"great parcel of the root which the Nativs call Hankee ..."* J8:288 This is in August, a time when the bulb is ripe and at its most nutritious

Prairie turnip

stage but before the fall winds and winter snows blow away or bury the tell-tale plant stalk.

Over the Rockies and Westward
The men are still eating plenty of corn as they reach the Shoshone, for on August 26 Lewis orders a ration of two cups each of corn for both his men and the baggage carriers as they begin their trek across the mountains. Parched and pounded, this makes up into a lot of soup per person.

From the time the Expedition and Shoshone part in the fall of 1805 until they return to the Mandan villages in the fall of 1806, the Captains must rely totally on the Far West purveyors. For one full year, the Corps is largely dependent upon native willingness to give or trade food.

Bitterroot

Bitterroot
Lemhi Shoshone eat bitterroot and on August 22 give some to their guest. Lewis probably tries to smile politely, but, in fact, he is so nauseated by the bitter taste that he returns the roots to the cooks after only one bite, who *"eat them heartily."*

Camas or Quamash or Pashequa
A bulb similar to a gladiola corm, this species loves a moist terrain and is often found at higher elevations. A staple of the Nez Perce, it is given to the starving men as they descend the Pacific slope of the Rockies. In 1806, eight natives leave on June 10 to begin *"gowing to the quawmash fields to hunt."* This is clearly a hunting party, not a camas-gathering foray because: (1) by Lewis' estimation the bulbs are not fully ripe and ready to pick until *"the middle of July ..."* J8:16 and (2) by tribal convention, women do the digging for bulbs and men stay away – they are considered bad luck. The bulbs can be safely harvested in the spring when bearing their blue-purple flowers, so as to not be mistaken with the white-flowering death camas; the confusion begins after the flowers die off. The real trick is to recognize the difference between a corm (the blue-flowered camas) and an onion-like bulb (the death camas). Even this trick won't work if a wild onion is picked first, for the smell of onions remains on the hands and the death camas is an onion look-alike. This is a case of not trusting smell, for the nose can be fooled if the plants are picked in the wrong order.203 Native harvesters, of course, know the subtle differences.

Wars are known to have been started over harvesting rights, and young

USFS, used courtesy of *We Proceeded On*

Camas root and a nickle for size comparison.

women are considered better spouses if they're good collectors. Collecting is labor intensive, the bulb being *"white ... the size of a nutmeg to that of a hens egg ... or about as large as an onion of one years growth from the seed."* [J8:14] The roots are dug from hard ground with a digging stick, never an easy chore. Traversing a plain on September 20, 1805, Clark notes *"grt quantities of roots have been gathered and in heaps."* There are a number of ways to prepare camas: raw like a crisp vegetable, roasted like a potato, sometimes stone-boiled, but usually baked pit-style until the sugars caramelize and what emerges is a brownish mass of super-sweet pulp, which is 43% fructose.[204] That same day Clark observes *"these roots are like onions, Sweet when Dried, and tolerably good in bread, ..."* [J6:219] Whitehouse describes pounding the pre-cooked camas to a fine consistency and continues: *"they dry the cakes and String them on Strings, in Such a way that they would keep a year & handy to carry, any journey."* [J11:327]

Camas is dug with a stick, one tiny bulb at a time.

CAMAS BREAD

"if the design is to make bread or cakes of these roots they undergo a second process of baking being previously pounded after the fi[r]st baking between two stones until they are reduced to the consistency of dough and then rolled in grass in cakes of eight or ten lbs are returned to the sweat intermixed with fresh roots in order that the steam may freely get to these loaves of bread. when taken out the second time the women make up this dough into cakes of various shapes and sizes usually from ½ to ¾ of an inch thick and expose it on sticks to dry in the sun, or place it over the smoke of their fires." [J8:17]

Wapato or Broad-leafed Arrowhead or Arrowleaf

During the winter with the Clatsops, the men trade what little they have left for more local starches. A big favorite is the egg-shaped wapato, a riverine inhabitant that is harvested by native women who wade in the water, sometimes up to their necks, loosening the roots with their bare feet and then tossing the floating plants into their canoes. When it is roasted, the white-men are reminded of their back-home favorite, the Irish potato, and the wapato is viewed as *"a tolerable Substitute for bread ..."* [J6:79] Lewis pinpoints its preference to avoiding salt; it grows inland *"about 15 miles on a Direct line from the Sea."* [J6:154]

Cattails

The review of cattails as a food is better than average: *"it is pleasantly taisted and appears to be very nutricious."* [J6:366]

Balsam Root

Another broad-ranging starch, the balsamroot resembles a sunflower. *"the stem is eaten by natives without any preparation."* Clark mentions it on the Columbia (April 14, 1806).

Yampah (Indian Carrot) and Western Sweet Cicily

In transit over the Rockies on August 26, 1805, Lewis sees the first yampah being gathered by the Shoshone women, who are harvesting it for their *"poor starved children."* He finds it *"white firm and crisp in it's present state, when dried and pounded it makes a fine white meal; the flavor of this root is not unlike that of annis-seed but not so pungent ..."*

In the spring of 1806, the party stalls out at the base of the mountains. After a long winter and anxious to leave for home, the Corps must wait for the snowy gates to melt open, wait to cross the terrible Rockies and be done with them. The snow is too deep; even on June 15, they are forced to backtrack. One recompense is that Lewis discovers western sweet cicily, *"A species of fennel root eaten by the Indians, of an annis taste; flowers white, Columbia River."* [b] This feathery, fine-leafed edible may have reminded him in flavor of two other licorice- or anise-flavored plants they had encountered: wild liquorice [c] and seashore lupin. Although these plants are all separate and distinct species, the human tongue is easily confused by the anise/fennel/liquorice triad. Lewis' description uses two of the terms in the same sentence without hesitation.

Yampah

---

[b] Lewis collects and presses a specimen of yampah with this label description, dated April 25, 1806, but does not make a *Journal* note of it until May 16, 1806, when he notes that Sacagawea has gathered *"a quantity of the roots"* [J7:264 and J7:266n]

[c] The "qu" in liquorice is the British spelling, still evident in the former colonies, and before Webster.

Wild Liquorice (Pacific silverweed)[d]

Clark on January 22, 1806, writes: *"This root when roasted possesses an agreeable flavour not unlike the Sweet potato."* [J6:229]

Seashore Lupin

The Chinooks bring seashore lupin to the Corps as a present on November 17, and Clark calls it *"Lickorish."* It is prepared by boiling the underground rhizome, and the only food notation on this plant is that it resembles *"the common liquorice in taste and Size."*

Biscuit Root

On May 6 – above Colter's Creek on the Clearwater – Lewis records, *"A root 5 or 6 inches long eaten raw or boiled by the natives."* He is referring to a different Nez Perce vegetable, the biscuit root – also tagged as "Lewis' Lomatium."

Chapelel or Cous (pronounced: cows)

Another Lomatium, this is a carbohydrate that Clark first encounters as a bread, the native phonics sound like Cha-pel-el, which is the name Lewis uses. This is a long white root that grows in a sandy soil and is prepared by pounding – the sound *"reminds me of a nail factory,"* Lewis wryly pens. [J7:239] The flavor reminds the gourmet Captain of American ginseng, and he prefers the porridge preparation to that of cous bread. [J7:234]

During their trek, the Captains do their best to ensure that their men have enough carbohydrates. Just as the Mandans have the Three Sisters, the Chinooks have their "three roots": the wapato, the edible thistle, and the seashore lupin – Clark describes these as their mainstay carbohydrates. Between the American Army supplies and all these native starches, the troops are fueled up. The rest of the roots and tubers mentioned are important because: (1) they are new to American botany, (2) they are initial observations of native foods in the ethnobotanical records, and (3) they are consumed by curious explorers who provide a working food review of these "new" edibles.

Greens

The French engagés may have suffered a total loss of what they considered a "healthy" lifestyle, for the amount of greens eaten on the trip is negligible. As they travel, the men find a type of kale [J3:452] and boil it – probably with some of the pork. It would be a complimentary flavor combination,

"and [they] *found* [it] *healthy and pleasant."* The privates certainly gathered greens when they had a chance; York swims over to an island on June 5, 1804, to collect cresses for the Captains' mess. Across the country they encounter four different members of this Rorippa family, always growing in wet environments. The young bucks go foraging for their own messes and *"find it a very pleasant wholsome sallad."* [J3:452]

Other greens are noted, such as wild chives and the two types of sorrel or dock, a bitter green much beloved by the French. Lewis eats roasted bracken fern. Clark observes the edible *"Lams quarter,"* on July 14, 1804, but it's unclear if they gather it. On June 25, 1805, Lewis notices, *"great quantities of mint also are here it resemble the pepper mint very much in taste and ap-*

Cress

pearance." Edible thistle and edible valeriana also appear, but only one or two times on the Corps' menu.

By combining authentic ingredients that were eaten on the Expedition (cresses, crab apple or green apple, honey, vinegar, and berries), a pleasant salad can be constructed.

WHOLESOME CRESS AND APPLE SALAD

Mix watercress and apple (chopped or slivered, fresh or dried) in desired proportion.

Combine a dressing of vinegar, honey, salt and pepper, and stir thoroughly.

Toss the greens in the dressing, and add fresh berries if available.

In short, the great nutritional benefits of greens are noticeably absent. Perhaps some of their physical ailments could have been prevented by a more consistent and constant diet of these plants, but towing boats upriver or careening downriver in dugout canoes doesn't lead to gathering plants; and a "salad" might appear somewhat anemic to hungry men craving protein.

Fruits and Berries

If the men don't eat many greens, then they overdo it with fruit. A quick snack, a sugary dessert, fruits fill the bill. The

---

[d] Pacific silverweed is a recent naming identification noted by Earle and Reveal, *op. cit*, page 106.

citizens of St. Louis had orchards of various fruits, but probably only the Captains got to eat "fruit preserves" while the troops had to wait for these sweets to come ripe the following summer. The townsfolk grow apples, the Corps pass "... wild apples ... the French Say is well flavered when ripe," J2:321 and on the Mandan Christmas Eve of 1804 the men receive apples, "Dryed apples," carried upriver and saved for a special occasion.

Grapes are another favorite, "Summer and fall Grapes," J2:452n6 a different nomenclature than is used today. The men take to gathering these and the "Blue Current Common in the U.S," as well as the common gooseberry, J2:433 so named by earlier cooks who noticed it went well with the goose. By the time the Corps is traveling up the Missouri, the vegetation is prolific and new plants appear. There is the buffaloberry, named for the huge animals that munch on them, which Clark describes as growing "in great abundance a[nd] makes a Delightfull Tart." J3:136 Being his birthday, Clark goes on with un-usual enthusiasm to say that the plains are lush with "Cheres, Apple, Grapes, Currents, Rasp burry, Gooseberris Hastlenuts"e as well as a "great Variety of Plants & flours not Common to the U.S." What a field-day for botanists and naturalists!

In tracing the Corps' consumption of fruits, the calendar indicates the degree of ripeness. If it's July, they're probably eating partially ripe, slightly sour fruit; and if it's August or September, the fruit is sweetening at the end of the season. On September 23 Clark declares "plumbs & grapes fully ripe."

A SEPTEMBER CHRONOLOGY

2nd: Service Berries dried on the bushes, abundant and very fine. black colour.
3rd: Choke Cherries ripe and abundant.
19th: Rose Raspberries ripe and abundant.

Plums

There are plums along the way out and plums on the return trip. Most of the time Lewis is very careful about the words he uses, and is meticulously correct. Clark, on the other hand, uses a few colloquial terms and sometimes neither man is clear about what botanical specimens he is seeing.

There is a plethora of names for the plum family –

several common names refer to just one species, and one common name ("wild goose plum") is used for two different species. There are the hortulan plums and the sandhill plums. There is also the Osage plum (not a plum at all), a fruit so delicious that Lewis sends some cuttings back to Jefferson. Additionally, Clark comes across a "Yellow Plumb," which he deems to be "deliciously flavored." Not only are they eating this delicious fruit, but Clark so impressed that on September 3, 1804, he collects, "three different kinds of plumb stones ... of a delicious flavor ... which I intend to Send to my brother." J3:44 This is about the biggest tribute given to any plant: that of preserving the seeds for some faraway recipient. As with all gardening prizes, hope for their viability abounds "but it is not known what happened to them, if they were raised and bore fruit, etc."[205]

Grapes

There are at least three different types growing along the Missouri, and Clark is seemingly a big fruit man. He adores the plums, finds fruit tarts to be delicious, and raves about the grapes: "Superior quallity large and well flavoured." J3:44 On August 1, 1804, Clark records "Several men geathering grapes &c" and they combine the gatherings into a fine dessert. Along the Columbia they come across two species specific to that locale: the Oregon grape and the Oregon dull grape. f

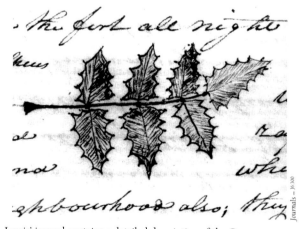

Lewis' journal contains a detailed description of the Oregon grape.

---

e See recipe in *Up the Missouri to the Mandans*, page 101.

f The Oregon grape was initially labeled *Berberis aquifolium*, in the Barberry genus, along with the oval, red-fruited Barberry. In 1818, Thomas Nuttall created a new genus, *Mahonia*, in honor of horticulturist Bernard McMahon and moved a hundred of the five-hundred *Berberis* species to it – those with thornless stems, spiked evergreen leaves, and flowers in distinct clusters, like the Oregon grape. Thus, today, botanists may still classify the Oregon tall grape as a *Berberis*, but most horticulturists call it *Mahonia aquifolium*. Similarly, the low Oregon grape (or Oregon dull grape) is either *Berberis nervosa*, or more recently *Mahonia nervosa*.

Cherries

Cherries, another perennial American favorite, abound. But the *Journals* don't mention cherry pie (as they did buffaloberry tart), even though there are at least three different types of cherries in St. Louis. Residents there have planted a sweet one for eating, a sour one for cooking, and the Mahleb, a hardy variety. Later, the very abundance of wild cherries and other fruit delights the men, *"thickets of Plumbs Cheres &c are Seen on its banks."* To carry the cherries along, Ordway notes that they gathered them at the noon stop and, *"put [them] in to the Whisky barrel."* J9:27

Chokecherry

Chokecherries

After reaching the Mandan villages, the Corps meets the chokecherry for the first time when it appears in Little Crow's wife's soup. The chokecherry and currants appear together, sharing the same terrain, and serviceberries come onto the menu. By August 13, 1805, berries have ceased being a dessert and have become the sole item for dinner. Lewis writes, *"the Chief [Cameahwait] informed us that they [the Shoshone] had nothing but berries to eat and gave us some cakes of serviceberries and Choke cherries which had been dried in the sun; of these I made a hearty meal."* On the way home in 1806, Lewis records *"the undergrowth is chooke cherry near the water courses"* J8:7 Regretfully, it is too early in the season and the fruit-deprived Corps has to wait.

The Fake Gooseberry

By early summer of 1805, the first of the berries are coming ripe. By June 13, *"goose berries are ripe and in great abundance, the yellow Current is also Common, not yet ripe ..."* Lewis also mistakenly identifies a now-ripe berry as a gooseberry, a good source for high Vitamin C, but it is *"pale red"* and a currant. Unfortunately this "gooseberry" is relatively unpalatable, at least to Lewis who isn't happy with either its texture or flavor, for on June 18, 1805, he writes, *"the pulp is a yelloish slimy muselaginous substance of a sweetish and pine-like tast, not agreeable to me."* He is obviously not going to make gooseberry pie. There may be several reasons for this mis-identification, starting with Lewis' very perception of the fruit, calling it *"about the size of the common gooseberry."* Then he is fooled by both its texture and the strange flavor, neither of which resemble the common currant.g On July 25, 1805, he writes, *"I have observed a red as well as a yellow*

species of goosberry." Again, Lewis is actually seeing a currant, the Squaw or Western Red. He is misled by two different colors (the best explanation being unripe fruit) and he calls it *"a very indifferent fruit"* but collects the seeds as a matter of obligation, *"as they form a variety of the native fruits of this country I preserved some ..."* These two red currants appear to be totally different in taste, but Lewis indicates that they are both the same plant, an interesting flavor phenomena.

More, still on Currants

The *Ribes* family illustrates some wayward plant descriptions rather well: blood currant, buffalo currant, garden currant, golden currant (purple, yellow), purple currant (wild black), red currant (aka squaw currant), red-flowering currant, squaw currant (aka red currant), sticky currant, and wild black (blue) currant. By July 17, all the currants and serviceberries are ripe *"and in great perfection"* as the Corps moves through hazy heat toward the Shoshone homeland, and when it gets down to edibility, the golden

Wild red currant

currant is the big favorite, *"vastly preferable to those of our gardens."* Lewis describes its flavor as *"not so ascid, & more agreeable flavored"* compared to the red currant with which he is familiar. But later the gourmet botanist is seduced by yet another variety, the black swamp currant, *"really a charming fruit"* which he no doubt would plant in his backyard, but he reverses himself on July 27, 1805, and finds *"this fruit ... extreemly asced."* Perhaps Lewis' palate is failing in its memory, or perhaps the fruit just simply isn't ripe. No matter. Not only are the men eating the berries, but Lewis is collecting: *"of each of these I preserved some seeds ..."* J4:406

Buffaloberry

One new berry that they encounter along the way is the buffaloberry, tumbling down the sides of a hill loaded with fruit, *"much richer and finer flavd [flavored]"* than a currant. From these berries they make a *"Delightfull Tart."*h Anyone unfamiliar with this thorny, spiky bush doesn't know what effort

---

g Lewis isn't the only one fooled, and his perception that the berry has a pine-like taste is the tell-tale key. *The Wild Berry Book* by Katie Lyle points out that certain members of the *Ribes* or currant family inadvertantly fall prey to the blister rust that kills white pines, that virus seemingly fooled by the same chemistry.

h Buffaloberry Tart recipe appears in *Up the Missouri to the Mandans*, page 105.

this entailed. Old timers used to arm themselves in long sleeves and gloves, and take a blanket and baseball bat when they went berrying. The blanket went under the bush as a catch-all, and the baseball bat was used to batter the bush until the berries fell off. It was a hazardous occupation tangling with the spines, but the berries were worth it.

Buffaloberry

Serviceberry

The serviceberries get a high rating, *"larger more luscious and of so deep a purple that on first sight you would think them black."* Or, *"the deep purple servicebury which I found to be excellent,"* and the gourmet Captain continues raving about the *"superior excellence of it's flavor and size."* [J5:31] On August 2, 1805, the men *"feasted sumtuously on our wild fruits particularly the yellow courant and the deep perple servicebury ..."* This abundance continues and the serviceberry actually becomes a major part of the diet, as men *"geathered cosiderable quantities"* of the fruit to accompany their trout and deer. They also are a major component of the Shoshone diet.

Serviceberry

Huckleberry

In crossing the Rockies, one of the berries Lewis discovers is the mountain huckleberry, then unknown. He describes it as resembling the chokecherry, bearing a black fruit with a single stone and having *"a sweetish taste."* [J5:218]

The Delicious Berries

"A large basket of mashed berries" is a welcome present from Chief Yelleppit of the Walla Walla or Walula Indians on October 18, 1805. Then a whole new series of berries appear as the Corps travels through the Columbian Plateau and down to the Pacific coast, plants unfamiliar to the Eastern botanists: nanny-berry, wolf-berry, Pacific blackberry, bearberry, and the salal berry. Wild strawberries, with their minuscule, delicate, and lusciously perfumed fruits are discovered several times. Remembering advice from his herbalist mother, Lewis might have gathered rosehips; he writes that

these bulbous red *"apples of this species ... [had been] more than triple the size of those of the ordinary wild rose ..."* [J8:10] These are impressive not only for their size but for their health-giving properties. There are other berries as well, bunchberries, cranberries (not the variety seen in markets today but a *"light brown bury"* [J6:235]), a high-bush cranberry and a squashberry (members of the *Viburnum* family), both quite durable compared to the tiny woodland strawberries or the rosy raspberries, which have a far higher water content and are very difficult to dry without molding.

By the time the Corps reaches the coast, it is time for a whole new repertoire of foods. Almost on the Pacific, they find a *"Small red Berry which grows on a Stem of about 6 or 8 Inches from the Ground, in bunches and in great quantity on the Mountains, the taste insipid."* [J6:44] This is the bunchberry, and it sounds like the men ignore it, for it certainly isn't any taste treat. In fact, the same *Journal* entry complains, *"nothing to eat but Pounded fish ..."* [J6:44]

Cranberries (the low-growing, not the high-bush variety) are bog dwellers, and those on the West Coast are no exception to the Eastern rule. They are in damp and ferocious mires which shake over great distances, and there is *"much Cramberry growing amongst the moss."* [J6:116]

In short, the vitamin-rich berries appear with enough regularity and variety that the men emerge healthier than they might have otherwise been. This is particularly true in the winter when fresh fruit is not available, but dried berries are kept at-the-ready. For all, this is a bounteous health blessing with the fruits not only pleasant to eat but loaded with vitamins and antioxidants.

Seeds and Nuts

Most of the nuts consumed on the trip are a rather sporadic snack – not much more. The *Journals* record a considerable use of sunflower seeds but limited consumption of hazelnuts, hickory nuts, filberts, and acorns.

Acorns

The first reference to the Corps eating acorns occurs on September 16, 1804, when the men harvest some from the bur or mossy-cup oak. This episode shows the food chain hard in competition, for the men find *"acorns of excellent flavor,"* and these feed not only deer and squirrels, but also *"Buffaloe Elk ... bear, turkies, ducks, pigegians, and even the wolves ..."*

Hazelnuts and Filberts

These two nuts are relatives and grow on shrubs and small trees which are part of the birch family. Although these names are often used synonymously, even in some dictionaries, they are two different species with different origins. The hazelnut (*Corylus americana*) occurs naturally in the eastern U.S. and was known to Clark before the Expedition; it was encountered along the Missouri. By comparison, the Corps first encountered the filbert (*Corylus cornuta* of Eurasian origin) on October 22, 1805, near the Great (*Celilo*) Falls of the Columbia when they were given as a gift by the local natives. Filberts continued to be seen in the lower Columbia through April, 1806.

Sunflower Seeds

Lewis find sunflowers blooming away on July 17, 1805, and he is reminded of eating sunflowers the year before. *"The Indians of the Missouri particularly those who do not cultivate maze make great uce of the seed of this plant for bread, or use it in thickening their soope. they most commonly first parch the seed and then pound them between two smooth stones untill they reduce it to a fine meal. to this they sometimes mearly add a portion of water and drink it in that state ..."* The ever-interested Captain also describes a Midwest "sunflower dough" and fondly remembers this native treat. He notes this preparation for the seeds is *"much the best and have eat it in that state heartily and think it a pallateable dish."*

RAW SUNFLOWER DOUGH

After pounding the seed between two smooth stones, take the fine meal and *"add a sufficient quantity of marrow grease to reduce it to the consistency of common dough and eate it in that manner."* J4:391

When Lewis comes across sunflower seeds again while with the Shoshone, the grinding of the seeds is identical, and *"this meal is a favorite food."* J5:172

Eating a Tree: A Native Use

A taste for pine is not confined to winter desperation. On July 19, 1805, Sacagawea clarifies her original tribe's use of the tree. The sap, the soft part of the wood, and the bark are all used as food. In September, trudging through what is now Missoula County in Montana, the Corps encounters more peeled Ponderosa. Clark comments that it is *"the under bark which they eate at certain Seasons of the year, I am told in the Spring they make use of this bark."* J5:201 Whitehouse logs an intriguing recipe.

PINE AND BERRY BARS

"... Pine trees, pealed as high up as a Man could reach, which we suppose the Natives had done in order to get the inside bark, for to mix with their dried fruit to eat; it being the manner in which they prepare it ..." J11:311

The fibrous matter would be sticky with sap, a fine medium for holding together fruit. It is not clear where Whitehouse came upon this bit of information, but it is one of the few native recipes recorded.

Pacific Provisions

From the time the Corps begins crossing the Columbian Plain until they reach the Pacific Ocean, the explorers are cataloging a new pantry of plant stuffs. Some come ripe early in the season, but more are gathered during late summer and fall, forming the backbone for winter sustenance and survival.

PACIFIC PANTRY

Among the vegetarian items eaten and/or offered for trade are:

Vegetables	Roots	Berries/Nuts
Sea lupin	Bread of roots	Oregon crabapple
Liquorice	Camas	Bearberry or saccomis
	Wapato	High-bush cranberries
	Fern root	Breadberry soup
	Horsetail rushes	Salal berries
	Edible thistle	Acorns

Stylistically, it is worth noting how the Philadelphia-trained Lewis approaches these new foods. A trained observer in both science and the art of eating, Jefferson's protégé generally gives a scientific description of the plant or animal, tells how it is harvested/hunted, the manner of cooking, and, finally, the table result. The words he uses to describe "texture" include: *"brittle," "strong liggaments," "thin membrencies like network," "consistency of gruel."* Creatively but accurately, he portrays a strong, unmistakable picture of hues: *"deep purple burry," "small pale red bury," "light brown bury."* If the identity of these berries is unknown, the discovery process could begin with an artist's palette.

Few people today are familiar with these edibles in the

Pacific vegetarian inventory, so listing them is an exercise in remembering forgotten foods, historic foods, or forager's specials.

Edible Thistle
Extolled by the ever-learning gourmet Captain: *"... the consistence when first taken from the earth is white and nearly as crisp as a carrot; when prepared for uce by the same process before described [fire roasting] ... , it becomes black [its name changes to 'black root'], and is more shugary than any fuit or root that I have met with in uce among the natives; the sweet is precisely that of the sugar in flavor; this root is sometimes eaten also when first taken from the ground without any preparation; but in this way is vastly inferior."* J6:226 Clark's tastebuds are a bit different: He doesn't find the raw vegetable *"inferior"* but *"well-tasted,"* commenting that it soon *"weathers and becoms hard and insipped."* J6:227

Bracken Fern
Lewis doesn't care for roasted fern root: *"... much like wheat dough and not very unlike it in flavour, although also it has a pungency which becomes more visible after you have chewed it some little time; this pungency was disagreeable to me, but the natives eat it very voraciously and I have no doubt but it is a very nutricious food."* J6:228 The flavor bothers him. Perhaps the fire-roasting brings out the acrid, slightly bitter taste, and he would have been happier with a gentler preparation of first simmering them and then seasoning with butter and salt.[i]

Giant Horsetail Rush Roots
For the judicious eater, the subtle nuances of flavor count a lot, as seen in Lewis' review: *"the pulp is white brittle and easily masticated either raw or roasted the latter is the way in which it is most usually prepared for uce. this root is reather insipid in point of flavour ..."*

Oregon Crabapple
Earlier in St. Louis, there appear to be crabapples, and later on the trip the explorers find the Oregon crabapple. It isn't sweet like the cultivated apples, but *"... when the fruit has been touched by the frost is not unpleasant, being an agreeable assed."* J6:103 Lewis' commentary on December 1, 1805, is

enthusiastic, like a produce manager or green grocer visiting a new locale: *"there is a wild crab apple which the natives eat ... the fruit consists of little oval burries which grow in clusters at the extremities of the twigs like the black haws. the fruit is of a brown colour ..."*

Bearberry
Lewis gourmet review of January 29, 1806, finds *"this fruit is a fine scarlet,"* but *"it is a very tasteless and insippid ..."* having only the advantage of remaining on the bushes all winter, and *"the frost appears to take no effect on it."* As for other diners in the neighborhood, *"the natives usually eat them without any preperation."* Lewis likely wrinkles his nose as he comments wryly, *"in their most succulent state they appear to be almost as dry as flour ..."* J6:246

Evergreen Huckleberry
Always on the lookout for familiar foods, Lewis discovers that he has identified a berry as being a relative of the native salal berry, when it was not. He corrects the identification as, *"a small deep perple berry like the common huckleberry of a pleasent flavor ... the natives eat this berry when ripe but seldom collect it in such quantities as to dry it for winter uce."* J6:297 But as it is December, it is unlikely he has eaten any of them. He then makes a similar observation comparing the Pacific blackberry with the blackberry common to the Atlantic states, again commenting on the use of only fresh, ripe fruit.

Vegetable Variety in Summary
In trying to determine what the Corps actually ate during their two-year journey, it's apparent that while their accumulated dining experiences are broad and wide-ranging, many details are lacking. If they saw it and could stop, they would, and they would likely eat it. However, if they're running the rapids and see snowberries, the fruit might later get logged, but not be eaten. Medicinal and nutritive uses of berries combine, as when *"Collins ... returned in the evening unsuccessfull as to the chase but brought with him some cranberries for the sick."* J6:330 There are only a few plants that they refuse, bitterroot and bunchberry for example; and the fruits range in quality from *"very tasteless and insipid"* to *"charming."* Nor has the homesick Virginian forgotten favorite Eastern foods, the mere sight of one becoming an emotional trigger, *"The Cranbury of this neighbourhood is precisely the same common to the U'States, and is the production of marshey or boggy grounds."* J6:243

---

[i] Be aware that fiddleheads can have an enzyme which disturbs vitamin B_1 metabolism; it can cause serious problems when eaten raw or lightly sauteed. The University of Maine suggests that they be boiled at least ten minutes.[206]

Beverages of the Expedition

Stopping a soldier from drinking was like stopping a dog from barking.

— BERNARD CORNWELL IN *THE WINTER KING*

THE TERM "BEVERAGES" brings to mind coffee, tea, and liquor. But for the Corps, by far the most common and important beverage is water, and this is not clean water from a tap, but wherever and however they find it.

Water

When traveling, getting and keeping enough water in the men's systems is a challenge.[a] The first troublesome warning comes on May 9, 1804, while the party is still at Camp River Dubois. Clark is serving as an able quartermaster, looking out for his troops' needs. "... *I send to the Missouries water for drinking water, it being much Cooler than the Mississippi ...*" This is a perplexing move because the Missouri is muddier at the confluence than the Mississippi. The Expedition is camped on the Illinois side and should have had the clearer Mississippi water right at the shore. But this is just the start. The litany of water woes continues across the west: "*the water is brackish,*"[J2:282] and the "*waters of the Kansais is verry disigreeably tasted to me.*"[J2:327]

From June 26 to 29, 1804, Clark is even weighing the water. "*Missourie Water weighs 78°. The Kansais weighs 72°* [units unknown, intent appears to be measuring specific gravity of the water]." The Missouri is denser with sediment (earth materials are about twice the density of water, so the weight indicates that the Missouri has 4% more sediment by volume); on the other hand, the Kansas has trace amounts of various dissolved minerals (hardness) giving it the disagreeable flavor. In another case, "*a small rivulet of clear water ... which on tasting, I discovered to be in a small degree brackish.*"[J4:41] None of these observations suggest a refreshing drink of water.

Other water sources have different drawbacks. "*These springs* [Lolo Hot Springs] *come out in maney places in the rocks and nearly boiling hot ...*"[J5:201] Or, the privates might risk losing their cups in water that is "*so terbid that no bird wich feeds exclusively on fish can subsist on it ...*"[J4:121]

If the frothing, rushing, gushing river is sometimes white, Milk River is especially so, having "*a peculiar whiteness, being about the colour of a cup of tea with the admixture of a tablespoonfull of milk.*"[J4:124] The sediments causing this whiteness are glacial till. Sometimes their cups are filled with a cherry-colored fluid – not juice, but the results of a gully washer. During the Great Falls portage, "*soon after the storm this evening the water on this side of the river became of a deep crimson colour which I pesume proceeded from some stream above and on this side. there is a kind of soft red stone in the bluffs and bottoms of the gullies ... which forms this coloring matter.*"[J4:336] Even black is part of the palette: "*all the Streams which head a fiew miles in the hills discharge water which is black & unfit for use.*"[J4:44]

Drinking water isn't supposed to be "*So muddy and worm* [warm] *as to render it very disagreeable to drink,*"[J8:248] but it's

---

[a] Today's Army guidelines place a huge emphasis on maintaining adequate hydration; commanders are urged to "enforce drinking" on a regular schedule, provide plenty of fluids, encourage a decreased intake of salt, and even have their troops monitor the color of their own urine (almost clear being the most desirable; dark yellow indicating inadequate hydration).

also not drinkable when it's frozen. And the frozen water can appear not only on ponds, or as snowfall, but also falls as stunning bullets of hail, dangerous to the human cranium. *"the hail was as large as musket balls and covered the ground perfectly. we hand [have] some of it collected which kept very well through the day and served to cool our water."* J4:364 In another instance, *"Capt. Lewis made a small bowl of Ice punch out of one [hailstone] they were 7 Inches in Surcumference ..."* J11:214

The water situation in the Bitterroots is vexing, but manageable. Ordway writes, *"we found a small spring before we came to the highest part of the mountain where we halted and drank a little portable Soup"* then, *"we travvelled untill after dark in hopes to find water. but could not find any. we found Some Spots of Snow so we Camped on the top of the Mountain and melted Some Snow,"* which they use to make more portable soup. J9:224 Gass echoes Ordway, *"There was here no water; but a bank of snow answered as a substitute ..."* J10:143 The next day ten inches of snow falls.

Either sheer curiosity or the commonly held belief that mineral waters are healthful prompts the men to imbibe at Lolo Hot Springs, *"Several of our party drank of the Water that was in this [Indian] Bath, it had strongly the taste of Sulphur, & was very clear."* J11:313 The telling criterion is clarity. Listen to the happiness it evokes from men who appreciate a good drink – a *"beatiful bold runing stream ... ; the water is transparent,"* J4:103 and even more satisfactorily, *"the water of this [Giant Springs] fountain is extremely tranparent and cold ... very pure and pleasent."* J4:340

When the Corps reaches the Pacific, winter storms are hurling seawater in all directions. The spume and swells cascade into already brackish water found in the coastal inlets, and even pots left out to catch pure rainwater are contaminated. Clark's disposition is turning bad-tempered when he balefully views the Columbia estuary and declares, *"Salt water I view as an evil in as much as it is not helthy –"* J6:84 It will take a move to the Oregon side of the estuary and a retreat inland to restore the harmony of man and water.

Liquor

A standard 1802–1812 Army daily ration of liquor is a gill – a half-cup, or four ounces. A gill of whiskey consumed by a 160-pound man will result shortly in a blood-alcohol level of .07% – not quite today's legal driving limit; and in the average man it would then be metabolized completely in about five hours. A gill, then, is the limiting amount a soldier may consume at one time, and not be likely to be materially

affected in his duties, and it appears that sometimes the alcohol was doled out, perhaps an ounce at a time. And, under various stress conditions, as well as on holidays such as Independence Day and New Year's Day, the Captains issued extra liquor rations.

But the *Journals* also refer to "drams." By definition, a dram is ⅛ of an ounce – ¾ of a teaspoon, or only 1/32 of a gill – a mere taste, if even that – not something men would line up to receive. The *Journal* references to *"drams"* are probably *not* the apothecary measure of a dram; but rather a colloquial reference to "a small portion," as in the Scottish phrase: "just a wee dram."

America has always had a tradition of drinking, and this is not quiet and polite "tippling." While some eschew liquor as an offense to both the body and God, alcohol in its various guises (whiskey, rum, gin, beer, cider, wine) played a substantial role in colonial America through the westward expansion. In 1733, it was estimated that per capita consumption of liquor in the Colonies was 3.75 gallons annually. Re-figuring this quantity, and eliminating women and children, the amount comes to a gill per man per day. Georgia tried banning rum and other liquors in 1735, but rum continued to seep in and the law was repealed after seven years. Up in Massachusetts, a meeting house was constructed in one week with common labor, logs, sixty-nine gallons of rum, several barrels of beer, and some cider. So accepted was alcohol as part of daily life that the "pastor and congregation alike drank it before Sunday church services, as well as at every meal." [207] And, alcohol could be safer to drink than polluted water.

Even the Founding Fathers adhered to the hard drinking ways of the public. Paul Revere held his patriotic and revolutionary meetings in Boston's taverns, and George Washington thought of liquor as voter insurance. He wooed the 391 voters of his county in his 1758 House of Burgesses campaign with politically correct spirits and slightly more benign punches, wines and beers. The grand total was 160 gallons, over 3 pints per man. He won the election.

So alcohol seeped through the fabric of the nation. Thomas Jefferson was enthralled and fascinated by wines – an elitist diversion and preoccupation. The landed gentry kept kegs of liquor stored away. George Rogers Clark found both violent outlet and fuzzy solace in whiskey after losing his fortune to pay debts incurred on behalf of the government of Virginia, which refused to reimburse him. Indians sloshed in the white man's poison, and soldiers drank to build up courage, relieve suffering, and forget.

So, what did the Corps drink besides water?

A country whiskey still on the early 1800s frontier.

Corn Likker, or Whiskey

The manufacture of whiskey was a result of, and cure for, several economic dilemmas. New England's distilleries made rum from Caribbean sugar and shipped it west, making it an expensive proposition for drinkers. This monopoly on hard liquor was broken by the development of corn whiskey. The formula begins with limestone-filtered, clear water that springs forth in abundance in Kentucky. The fermentable part of the beverage is corn, which American settlers were harvesting as soon as they cleared the land and could plant the crops.

Kentuckians began producing enough excess corn that they needed to reach the buyers' markets on the Eastern seaboard, and this meant a difficult transport across the Alleghenies. So, in 1783, a local solution arrived in the form of a distillery that turned the corn crop into a sour mash, which forms the basis of whiskey. The flavor of this new corn-fueled firewater (75-78% corn produces the typical sweet tang),[208] and its ultra-smooth taste was actually produced by a Baptist minister, one Elijah Craig, who had a keen sense of how to finesse mellowness out of rotgut. His tastes obviously extended beyond the "fruit of the vine," and he called his product Bourbon, after the emigrants who arrived from France.[209] Economically this new product was easier to transport and weighed far less than the cumbersome loads of corn cobs previously piled high in creaking wooden wagons.

By the time statehood was granted in 1792, more than two thousand whiskey distilleries were brewing away in Kentucky alone. Also in the 1790s, the Army switched from a "rum ration" to a "whiskey ration." The new taste was appealing and the product found a ready market.[b]

Brandy

The winter of 1803–04 at Wood River is cold, but the Corps is well-provisioned. The commander is assuring his men sufficient provisions, especially anti-freeze in the form of liquor. *"Mr. Cummins Came with meel & Brandy from Contractor ..."* [J2:166] While there are few references to brandy, there is another one on Christmas, 1804, at Fort Mandan. Patrick Gass writes, *"Captain Clarke then presented to each man a glass of brandy ..."* And at 10:00 AM they had another glass of brandy.

Rum or Tafia

The rum used as a ration comes out of the French Caribbean islands of Haiti, Guadeloupe, Martinique, and the other tiny islands held by the French Empire; it was shipped via New Orleans up the Mississippi to St. Louis. Rum was also a staple product of the British West Indies; and New England monopolized rum sold in the eastern states. Tafia (also called taffia or tafee) was described as "an inferior kind of rum, distilled from sugar refuse or from coarse molasses." The word itself comes from "a Malay word which we get from the French by way of the West Indies," and most paradoxically, "we call this liquor Jamaica."[210] Since Jamaican rum is historically a dark rum, this gives some idea of what tafia looks like, a nice deep amber running to brown.

Clark notes tafia's first use on November 30, 1804, and on that cold night *"gave a little Taffee."* After being out under extreme duress, *"the prarie being covered with*

Rum from the Caribbean islands.

---

[b] The federal government, in a move to assure edible food supplies as well as to protect eastern rum manufacturing interests, levied a 9¢ per gallon tax on the fragrant, golden liquid. It should be noted that whiskey, itself, was a form of cash, and this new tax was seen as another means of robbing the farmer. By 1794, irritation had reached an incendiary flash point and the Whiskey Rebellion broke out in the western states. It was put down without bloodshed, and production never ceased.

Snow and extreamly cold 2 of our men Got their feet frost Bitten & one Got his Ear frost bitten ... a half Gill of Taffee gave to the men," J9:101 *"Which we Stood in need off."* J9:100 Other references to tafia are on December 7 and 8, 1804. It is also a festive Christmas drink, along with good food. But again, there is a problem. While Clark and Ordway refer to tafia as the drink served on Christmas, 1804; both Gass and Whitehouse repeatedly indicate that three (yes, three) *"glass[es] of Brandy"* are issued to every man.

Rum as Grog

References to rum appear in another form: grog. That famous Naval drink, a mixture of rum and water was named after a famous British Admiral, Edward "Grog" Vernon, who wore a heavy grogram cloak.[211] Having problems with drunkenness on board, Vernon ordered the rum rations to be diluted with water.

In 1805, after the near-sinking of a pirogue when Charbonneau was at the helm (and Cruzatte threatened to shoot him if he didn't stop praying and take up the tiller) alcohol was used as a nerve soother. *"... We thought it a proper occasion to console ourselves and cheer the sperits of our men and accordingly took a drink of grog and gave each man a gill of spirits."* J4:153 Not only a tranquilizer for stress and fear, it also is a pain and misery reliever. The weather is highly unsettled this midsummer on the western plains and a ferocious hail, rain, and windstorm leaves the crew frozen and battered. Their sympathetic commander responds quickly, *"I refresh the men with a drink of grog ..."* J4:337 Two days later, on

A flash flood during the portage almost claims Sacagawea.

C. W. Russell, collection of the Russell Museum

June 29, 1805, a hellish storm nearly washes the Charbonneau family and Clark down a gully, and they barely escape with their lives. Sacagawea is just recovering from a severe illness and the baby loses all his clothes; both are dangerously chilled. A *"greatly agitated"* York succeeds in finding his master, who immediately instructs him to give some spirits to the small group, and that includes the native woman who does not drink. Clark feels it is salutary and then orders them to go back to camp, literally *"at the run"* for clothing. But the saga hasn't ended: The rest of the almost naked portage party are bloody and battered from the same huge hailstorm, *"some nearly killed, one knocked down three times ..."* and again Clark *"refreshed them with a little grog ..."* This refresher is important enough that a hydro-feature is named in its honor: Grog Spring.

Ordway provides another reference: *"they refreshed themselves with a drink of grog as they had a canteen of old Spirits with them."* J9:163 A canteen is mentioned on the inventory list. Apparently it was used for liquor rather than water and perhaps it is under the care of whichever Captain is ashore. There is no other evidence of canteens being carried.

If the references to "grog" imply the Navy dilution, it would make sense. By fall 1804, the original 120-gallon supply of liquor would have been running low; stretching it out by dilution with water is reasonable, as is reducing the ration. By November 1804, as winter sets in at Fort Mandan, the amount begins to be listed as *"gave the men a dram,"* and finally the ration is no longer daily, but only on occasion.

A Rambunctious Camp

As surely as the sun rises and sets, so will the troops get into liquor and alcoholic brawls. On December 31, 1803, Clark writes: *"I Issued certain [orders?] & prohibited a Certain [blank] Ramey from selling Liquer to the Party ... Colter ... Willard Leakens Hall & Collins Drunk."* The next day, two different men are drunk. On January 4, 1804, Clark appears to be seriously evaluating the men for their worthiness to continue with the Expedition. Among the notes: *"Howard – never Drink water"* and *"Hall + – + Drink"*

Day after day this continues. *"at Sun Set Maj. Rumsey the Comsy [commissary agent] arrived with Some provisions in a waggon of Mr. Todd, Seven or Eight men followd the waggon Intoxicated from the whiskey they receced [received] of R – [Ramey, Rumsey?] on the way out of the barrel which was for the Party, I ordered a Gill to each man a Cold night ..."* J2:156 Even with more incidents of alcohol disappearing, Clark never wavers on its necessity. His packing table *"To stow away in the Boat"* has a line listing 18 kegs of whiskey: 15" long by 12" diameter. [J2:165] This would be about 90 gallons of whiskey; eventually 120 gallons of alcohol is stowed.

Liquor is a reward for a hard day's work. Lewis deems the physical labor involved in manual sawing and smithing to be as valuable as rewarding a true-eyed sharp-shooter, and he directs that each sawyer, blacksmith, maple sugar–maker, and the winner of the daily target practice be given an "extra" ration. [J2:175] Since the standard Army ration is $\frac{1}{2}$ cup of alcohol, when the laborers are to receive an extra gill, the day's allotment goes up to a full cup, a portion of which apparently can be requested any-time during the day.[212]

But there are flagrant violations. On March 3, 1804, Lewis declares himself *"mortifyed and disappointed ... nor is he less surprised at the want of discretion"* for those who es-poused disobedience. He is chagrined, even more so at Shields, the party's oldest soldier at thirty-five, for having *"excited disorder and faction among the party,"* for Shields is one of the men who often carries messages to him in St. Louis. Not only is Lewis deeply disappointed, he is irate:

> *The abuse of some of the party with respect to the prev-elege heretofore granted them of going into the country, is not less displeasing; to such as have made hunting or other business a pretext to cover their design of visiting a neighbouring whiskey shop, he cannot for the present extend this prevelige; and dose therefore most positively direct, that Colter, Boyle, Wiser, and Robinson do not re-cieve permission to leave camp ... <u>for ten days.</u>*

If the early transgressions regarding liquor were treated mildly, the penalties turn fairly vicious once the Corps is un-derway. Clark states that the party is *"agreeable to the Sen-tences of a Court Mtl of the party who we have always found verry ready to punish Such Crimes– "* [J2:332] No more confine-ments to camp, now it is military discipline – enough to bring a man to his knees. In a surge of democratic justice, the men are not willing to hand over their share of alcohol to someone else without their specific permission. On June 29, 1804, Clark records:

> *The Court Convened ... to the trial of the Prisoners Viz John Collins Charged 'with getting drunk on his post this morning out of whiskey put under his Charge as a Sentinal and for Suffering <u>Hugh Hall</u> to draw whiskey out of the Said Barrel intended for the party' To this Charge the prisoner plead <u>not guilty</u>. ... Sentence him to recive <u>one hundred Lashes on his bear Back</u>. Hugh Hall was brought with [']takeing whiskey out of a Keg this morning which whiskey was Stored on the Bank (and*

> *under the Charge of the guard) Contrary to all order, rule, or regulation' To this Charge the prisoner 'Pleades Guilty.' The Court find the prisoner guilty and Sentence him to receive <u>fifty</u> Lashes on his bear Back.* [J2:329-30]

Drunken rages and brawls are part of Clark's memories of the past winter. If lashing seems a harsh penalty for im-bibing, he probably has no sympathy whatsoever – there is no tolerance for disobeying military orders.

But the psychological factors are what drives the drink-ing – tension tamer; pain killer; relief inducer; pleasure and enjoyment; celebration and elation. All of these aspects are part of the drinking scene of the Corps of Discovery.

Breakfast Drinks

Coffee

The British happily exported tea to America until the Rev-olution, after which the habit of brewing the Chinese drink waned. Rebellion was one reason; another was the faddish new beverage becoming deeply ingrained on the continent: coffee to the English-speaking, café to the French. Although the beans originally grew in tropical Ethiopia, the Arabs took it home and brewed it, where it was discovered by European travelers. Its astonishing ap-peal was so great that raiders from a number of countries mounted a series of clandestine operations to smuggle the beans out of the Middle East, miraculously skirting the penalty for exporting them – the death sentence. The English, French, and Dutch were in fevered competition to establish coffee-plantation empires in their colonies, profit from expanding the coffee sales, and socialize in coffee houses.

By the 1630s the English were running coffee houses and the French weren't far behind with their sociable gathering spots. The *Coffea* tree was so fussy that when one destined for Louis XI was shipped, Captain Gabriel Mathieu de Clieu drenched the specimen on deck with his own drinking water, becoming a culinary hero for his efforts.[213] The appeal of the black, bitter brew as a quick breakfast with a caffeine jolt came as the heavier medieval plowman's diet of soup and later corn or potatoes was fading into the agrarian past. It was an urban drink, something that could hold you over if you ate a croissant with it, a habit that began with the rich and spread slowly to the poor.

In 1804, Lewis is buying coffee, fifty pounds of it. On April 16, Clark packs the heavy bag away, and a month later notes that it is ready for the upriver trip. Coffee appears again (no quantity) when the Corps re-inventories at

Fort Clatsop. The beans are sold green; they are not pre-roasted for that is done at home in a skillet, and the longer the roasting, the darker the bean, and the more pungent the brew. Then the beans must be ground. Jefferson's kitchen has a coffee grinder, but there is not a mention of one on the Expedition inventory; they do have three corn mills – two twenty-six pounders and a lighter twenty pounder. One is given to the Mandans, and one is buried at the cache in Montana. Although never mentioned, the third one remains a mystery. Possibly it is just carried along to mill their remaining supply of corn ... and perhaps the coffee?

A recipe from the *1844 Kitchen Directory and American Housewife* recommends the proportions of 1 tablespoon coffee to 2 cups of water, [c] boiled together for 20 to 25 minutes and then (because of the muddy grounds) clarified with either an egg shell or a piece of fish skin.[214]

A coffee grinder is a necessary implement after the beans are roasted.

Thomas Jefferson Memorial Foundation

Coffee is touted as a pick-me-up, and perhaps it is this semi-medicinal effect an ailing Clark is seeking, for this is one of the few occasions that Clark pampers himself. During the Great Falls portage, he writes, *"June 25th Tuesday 1805 – I feel my Self a little unwell with a looseness &c &c. put out the Stores to dry & Set Charbonah &c to Cook for the party against their return – he being the only man left on this Side with me I had a little Coffee for brackfast which was to me a riarity as I had not tasted any Since last winter."* [J4:332] Even his own estimation of coffee consumption indicates a spartan approach.

But something does not add up. If the recipe above is used, then the fifty-pound sack would make five thousand cups of coffee, but Clark suggests a minimal use. So, where did it go? There are no answers; but perhaps the process of brewing coffee was so "ordinary" (except for Clark) that none of the journalists thought to mention it.

Tea

Tea bags are newcomers on the culinary scene. As long as twelve-hundred years ago, blocks of tea (a relative of the camellia) began to be distributed in China.[215] Pieces from the smooth block, or brick, were then boiled and poured into fine china tea cups. These molded bricks of tea are still sold, beautiful dark slabs into which intricate designs and symbolic leaves are pressed. The problem of carrying bulk tea leaves in a watery world would be monumental but this "condensed tea" is easy to transport. There is scant evidence of Chinese-style tea

In the 1800s tea comes in compressed bricks rather than as loose-leaf tea.

being used, most teas being herbal and associated with medicinal cures; however, the inventory lists two pounds of "English" tea being taken and the assumption is that tea-drinking Lewis and Clark most likely use it from time-to-time – hardly something to write in a journal when the day's main event was a grizzly attack.

Frontier medicine prescribes tea. On January 20, 1805, in camp at Fort Mandan, Clark kindly sends stewed fruit and tea to one of Charbonneau's sick wives. Teas as cures are also concocted from various plants, especially by Lewis, whose mother was an herbalist. Horsemint tea, a rather pleasant beverage, also falls into this category, especially since it was being administered to the invalided William Bratton who *"is so weak in the loins that he is scarcely able to walk <four or five steps>, nor can he set upwright but with the greatest pain."* Finally resorting to a sweat hole, Bratton is given *"copious draughts of a strong tea of horse mint."* The menthol in the tea works as a redeeming anaesthetic.[216, d] While some botanists have proposed that the plant is giant hyssop, the medicinal qualities of that herb don't seem to line up with what were needed in this case. The next day, May 24, 1806, *"Bratton feels himself much better and is walking about today and says he is nearly free from pain."* [J7:283]

Chocolate

Cacao, "the drink of the Gods" is one of the oldest beverages of the Americas, traced as far back as perhaps two thousand years ago in Mexico. It was introduced to Europe by the Spanish, beginning somewhere in the 1520s, and it quickly

---

[c] Note that the usual modern proportions use about twice as much coffee: 1 tablespoon to 1 cup, but brewed about half as long.

[d] Today it is used (in a cream form instead of liquid) in Solarcaine, Unguentine, Ben Gay, etc.

migrated northward. The French were dropping by their local "chocolate house" by the mid 1600s. About this time the Dutch conquered the market from the Spanish, becoming the central suppliers for Europe. Frothing the drink was a technique that the Spanish learned from the Aztecs through Cortez. By the early 1700s the base for the drink was a thick paste or block containing "vanilla, sugar, cloves, and other spices. About this time, some drinkers began to add milk or wine. Frothiness was still appreciated."[217]

Surprisingly the Americans considered cacao a medicine and carried it about in a tin box. The Captains did not take this on the trip, but upon returning and near civilization, Clark avails himself to this remedial known as a stomachic, an anti-dysenteric.[218] While it is soothing, it also contains a substantial amount of caffeine, making it a stimulant. "*I felt my Self very unwell and derected a little Chocolate which Mr. McClellen gave us, prepared of which I drank about a pint and found great relief ...*"[J8:359] McClellan, the generous Army buddy, has also given the Corps some gifts:"*Buisquit, Choco-late Sugar & whiskey ...*"[J8:363] No wonder the red-headed Captain feels better. Maybe he even added some bourbon and dipped the biscuit into the piping hot brew.

The chocolate carried by McClellan might have come upriver from New Orleans, purchased from the Spanish in Mexico – i.e., Mexican chocolate. Or, it might be the flavored Dutch bars. In either case, the preparation would be similar. Unlike the hot cocoa drink popular today, which is very high in milk and sugar, this earlier chocolate was water-based. Diane Kennedy, probably the foremost Mexican food authority, says "The drinking chocolate of Mexico ... [is] lighter bodied, and it has a definite texture." Here is her recipe.[219]

HOT CHOCOLATE

1½ C. (375 ml) water
1½ oz. (45 g) Mexican chocolate

Heat water in an earthenware pot. As it comes to a boil, break the chocolate into it and stir until the chocolate has melted. Let it boil gently for about 5 minutes so that all the flavor comes out, then beat it ... until frothy.

Ciders

There were mild fresh ciders made from plentiful crops of cherries and apples, and hard ciders resulting from a light fermentation of the fresh juice.[e] Jefferson himself was strongly opinionated about his fruits and raised Hewes's Crab, "the best cyder apple existing."[220] While making apple cider is almost a lost art because home presses have been dethroned by large-scale, bottled juice commercial presses, it is eminently simple to make.

APPLE CIDER

Gather windfall apples or crabapples. Put through a cider press or grate, and strain the juice. Boil for 5 minutes, and put aside.

Malt Liquors – Beer and Porter

The process of making malt liquors had trickled down through the ages, starting with the ancient Middle Eastern cultures known in the Bible. Pliny, the early Greek philosopher, remarked that the barbarians drank beer while the Romans drank wine.[221] Serving as the foundation to these ales were the essential starches and sugars released after barley had been dried and later soaked in warm water. The frail ales, made solely with barley, tend to go off or spoil after a short period of time. Beer, on the other hand, is ale with hops added – the specific qualities of hops adding preservative factors, flavor, and reducing the sweetness of the ale. Beer's shelf life is far longer. As for alcoholic content, these beverages are quite mild: a weak ale might run 3%, malt liquor at 5.6%, and a hefty strong ale at 7%.

On two occasions beer is mentioned. At Camp River Dubois the Army commissary arrives on "*28th Jany, 1804 – at 6 oClock [pm] 14° abov 0, Porter all frosed & several bottles broke ...*" Porter at this time is considered to be "a premium brew," a heavy, dark beer loaded with hops and left to age for an extra half year.[222] A *Journals* footnote states that its color derives from charring the grain and that it had a very low 4% alcohol content.[J2:167n4] Behind the sad occurrence of broken beer bottles is the English discovery that the bubbles in beer can be preserved in a bottle with a cork. Previously, beer was

---
[e] Freezing a hard cider pulls most of the water from it and produces an arctic blast called "Jersey Lightning."

stored in kegs and served flat. When bottled and very cold, the low percentages of alcohol are a problem – the water in the beverage freezes, its volume increases as it expands into ice, putting too much pressure on the bottle, and pow! It shatters.

The second reference is unusual. As the Corps rides the cascading Columbia River near the mouth of the John Day River on October 21, 1805, an immense surprise awaits them as they crawl out of their canoes for a rest. John Collins, whom Clark had earlier described as a *"blackguard,"* and who had been court-martialed for being drunk on post previously, has accidentally come up with some alcohol: *"Collins made Some excellent beer of the <u>Pasheco quar mash</u> bread of roots which was verry good ..."* [J5:315] The camas bread, which has been carried downriver from the month before when the Nez Perce greeted them with food, fermented from *"being frequently wet molded & Sowered &c."* [J5:319]

This harkens back to the Egyptians who, more than 3700 years ago, preserved their malted grain by baking it into a flat bread, and then soaking it in water when beer was to be made.[223] Comparing Clark's description with the process described above, they are identical except the starch is different – nonetheless, the end result is beer, very good beer.

"Eight bottles of wine" – January 29, 1804

While the troops like their whiskey, the gentlemen Captains have a more sophisticated palate. The eight bottles sent by Lewis to Camp River Dubois on January 29, 1804, are perhaps a gift, a little indulgence sent to compensate his friend William for holding down the boys in the wood. Nothing more is known about this mysterious delivery: where it came from, who manufactured it, was it local, Eastern, or French?

Wine is also for celebrating. Ordway writes that upon hailing the returning party, Army Captain Robert McClellan *"gave our officers wine and the party as much whiskey as we all could drink."* [J9:361] In a following entry Ordway clarifies the wine to be a take-with-you gift of three bottles. Here is an example of an expected class distinction: ordinary men drink whiskey, gentlemen officers savor their wine. It is a fine gesture by McClellan to think of what a traveling fellow officer might need to accompany his lean venison.

Appendix A
Index of Recipes and Menus

Some Known Meals and Food Gifts

Breakfasts –

July 19, 1804, Clark: *"rosted Ribs of a deer ... and a little Coffee"*

August 19, 1804, Clark: *"the main [Oto] Chief Brack fast with us naked [less than fully dressed]; & beged for a Sun glass."* The strategy of appearing with minimal clothing is to indicate neediness. The sun glass he wants concentrates the sun's rays and focuses them for building a fire, a handy and intriguing tool in a time without matches.

June 12, 1805, Lewis: Grizzly bear.

June 13, 1805, Lewis: *"venison and fish"*

June 25, 1805, Lewis: says his friend Clark is somewhat unwell. Clark himself says, *"I had a little Coffee for brackfast which was to me a riarity as I had not tastd any Since last winter."*

July 16, 1805, Lewis: *"Drewyer killed a buffaloe this morning ... we halted and breakfasted on it.   here for the first time I ate of the small guts of the buffaloe cooked over a blazing fire in the Indian stile without any preperation of washing or other clensing and found them very good."*

August 3, 1805, 11 AM, Lewis: *"Drewyer killed a doe and we halted and took breakfast."*

Comfortable Dinners

April 11, 1804: Venison steak, beaver tail, hardtack.[J4:22]

June 13, 1805, Lewis: *"my fare is really sumptuous this evening: buffaloe's humps, tongues and marrowbones, fine trout parched meal pepper and salt, and a good appetite; the last is not considered the least of the luxuries."*

Teton Sioux Feast – September 26, 1804

Cooked dog – The Sioux like theirs raw

Pemmican

Ground potato on several platters, *"Good"*

Arikara Meal – October 11, 1804

Bread of corn and beans

Corn and beans boiled

Hog-peanut or ground bean

Squash

Shoshone Meals

August 13, 1805, Lewis:

Cakes of serviceberries and dried chokecherries

Boiled antelope

Fresh salmon, roasted

August 20, 1805, Clark:

One salmon and cakes of dried berries

3 fresh salmon

Nez Perce – September 20, 1805

Dried salmon, buffalo

Camas and red haws

Nez Perce – September 23, 1805: Chief Twisted Hair dinner

Broiled dried salmon

Chinook Chief – October 26, 1805

Gifts of: Deer meat

White bread made of roots

Bear oil

Klickitat Chief – October 29, 1805

Gifts of: Bearberries

Filberts

Pounded fish

Bread made of roots

Chilluckittequaws (Wishram – Wascos)

"Friendly Village" – November 1, 1805:

Gifts: Fish, berries, nuts, root bread, dried berries

Chief's Dinner – October 29, 1805:

Pounded fish

Root bread

Filberts

Bearberries

Deschutes – November 4, 1805

Wapato

Wahkiakums – November 7, 1805

Fish to *"eate"*

Chinooks –

November 17, 1805: Wapato and seashore lupine

November 20, 1805: Sturgeon, dried sturgeon, salmon, and wapato

Young Clatsop Chief's Dinner – December 9, 1805.

Manners are important. Table is set with new mats.

Fish

Licorice

Black roots

In horn bowls: *"cramberies & bearberries"*

Salal berry syrup

In a *"neet wooden trencher,"* soup of berry bread with roots, served with a cockleshell spoon

Appendix B
Foods Eaten by the Expedition

EWIS DOCUMENTED EVERY NATURAL FEATURE encountered as a report to Jefferson, whether or not the items were edible. For a full discussion of all botanical entries, please refer to *Lewis and Clark: Pioneering Naturalists* by Paul Russell Cutright. Following is a subset of that list for which there is some evidence that the plants and animals were actually eaten, all but a few of which are discussed throughout this book. Included are the more common foods brought as provisions, or eaten at Camp River Dubois; and various preparations (e.g. portable soup). Where several names were used for the same species (e.g., prairie dog = barking squirrel), the names are cross-referenced. There has been no attempt to categorize these foods – discussion of them in the text can be pursued using the Index. (Foods referenced in the *Journals* and listed below but not further discussed in the text are marked "+")

acorns
antelope
apple, white = breadroot
bacon
badger
beans
bear, brown
bear, grizzly
bear oil
bearberry
beaver
beef
beer
berry, salal
berry, salmon
berry, purple
berry, red
bighorn
biscuit
bitter cherry +
bitterroot
bituminous matter
black roots
black walnut +
blackberry
blackberry, Pacific
bottlenose = northern
sucker
boudin blanc
brant
brant, white = snow goose

brandy
bread
bread of roots
breadroot = pomme blanch
   = prairie turnip
buffalo
buffaloberry
buffalo-bean = ground
plum
bunchberry
burrowing squirrel
butter
camas = pashaquaw
carp
carrot-root = edible thistle
cat, wild = tiger cat
catfish
catfish, white
cattail
cheese
cherry
chives, wild
chocolate
chokecherries
chub, white
cisco
coffee
coots
cormerants
corn
corn, lyed

corn meal
corn, parched
corn, soft
cous
coyote
crabapple
crabapple, Oregon
cranberries - bog &
   high-bush
crane
crawfish
cresses
crow
cucumber, wild
currants
deer, blacktail
deer, common
deer, fallow
deer, mule
dock, narrow
dog
dog oil +
duck, bufflehead
   = butterbox duck
duck, canvasback
duckinmallard
   = mallard duck
dumplings
eagle
eggs, chicken
eggs, goose

elk
eulachon = candlefish
fennel
fern, western bracken
filbert
fish, green
fish roe
flour
flour & berry paste
fruit, stewed
garlic
geese
goats
goldeye
goose, snow
goose, spruce
goose, goslings
gooseberries
grape
grape, Oregon
grape, Oregon dull
grog
ground bean = hog peanut
groundnut = Indian potato
ground plum
   = buffalo-bean
ground potato
grouse, blue
grouse, Oregon ruffed
grouse, ruffed
grouse, sage

grouse, spruce
gull, speckled
guts, deer and buffalo
hail
hare = jackrabbit
hawk
haws, black and red
hazelnut
heath hen = sage grouse
honey
horse
horse, colt
horsetail rush
huckleberry
hump, buffalo
Indian potato
jaybird +
jerky
Jerusalem artichoke
    = sunchoke
lamb's quarter
liquorice
lotus, yellow
lupin, seashore
marrow bones
meat – dried horse
milk
mint
morel
mountain bison
mountain sucker +

mullet
muskrat
nettle
onion, wild
opossum
otter
parched meal
pashequar = camas
pawpaws
pelican
pemmican
perch
pheasant
pheasant, dark brown
pin cherry
pliver or plover
plum, wild
plums
porcupine
pork
porpoise
portable soup
porter
potatoes
potatoes, wild
prairie dogs
prairie fowl = grouse
prairie hen = grouse
pronghorn
pumpkin
quail, mountain

quamash + = camas
rabbit, cottontail
raccoon
raspberry
red charr
root bread
rush roots
sagebrush
salmon, coho
salmon, sockeye
salmon, trout = steelhead
salmon, trout, white
salt
sauger
seal
service berries
shappapell = cous
sheep, mountain
soup
spirits
squash
squirrel, burrowing,
    barking, whistling
    =prairie dog
squirrel, Columbian
ground
squirrel, fox
squirrel, gray
squirrel, Richardson's red
strawberries
sturgeon

sucker
sugar
sunflower root (bread)
sunflower seed
swans
taffia = rum
tallow
tart
tea
teal, blue-winged
thistle, edible
tongue, buffalo
train oil = whale oil
trout, cutthroat
trout, salmon
turkey
turnips
valeriana
wapato (arrowhead)
watermelon
western spring beauty
whale blubber
whale oil = train oil
whiskey
whitefish
wine
wolf
yampah

Appendix C: Food Requirements

Caloric Needs

Fueling the body requires processing adequate calories from foods. There are 3 components:

1. Basal Metabolism: This is the requirement for a basic, sedentary life and is about 10 Calories [a] per pound of body weight.

2. Activity Energy: This need, added to the above, is the energy required for various activities and ranges from 1 to 4 Cal per hour per pound of body weight:

Activity	Cal/hr/lb
Walking briskly	1.0
Sawing wood	1.7
Canoeing vigorously	2.0

3. Specific Dynamic Action: On top of everything else, there is another 10% requirement just used in digesting the food eaten to meet the needs above.

The "average man": While the Corps men's weights are not known, the work of C. E. S. Franks, *The Canoe and Whitewater,* reports that the average French boatman weighed 155 pounds.

Combined Needs: Combining the Specific Dynamic Action with the other requirements, and using a 155-pound man, yields:

Function	Calories
Basal Metabolism	1705/day
Walking Briskly	170/hr
Sawing Wood	290/hr
Canoeing vigorously	340/hr

Examples: (i) A 155-lb. man canoeing vigorously for 10 hours [b] in a day requires: 1705 + 340 x 10 = 5105 Calories.

(ii) A 155-lb. man sitting in winter camp, but walking 4 hours to hunt requires: 1705 + 170 x 4 = 2385 Calories. Note that neither of these figures are exact: 5000 and 2400 Calories respectively are just as valid.

Reported Dietary Needs: In addition to the above calculations, the following are two other references: (a) *U.S. Army Nutritional Guidance for Military Field Operations in Temperate and Extreme Environment,* and (b) C. E. S. Frank's book noted above on canoeing regarding the Canadian French Voyageurs (paddling 15 hrs/day)

Reference	Calories/day
(a) U.S. Army basic diet	3000
Corps of Discovery canoeing	5000
(b) Canadian Voyageurs	6990

Food Energy Values

Foods eaten provide both energy (calories) and other vital nutrients. While a proper food balance is needed to supply amino-acids for tissue growth, vitamins for proper body chemistry, and fiber for good digestive function, the critical need for the hard-working Corps was energy. The three food components to consider are:

Proteins: meats and some beans. Provides 5½ Calories per gram of protein. Meats average about 20% protein, which gives 520 Calories per pound of cooked lean buffalo.[c] Army daily recommendations are: ½–1 gram of protein per pound of body weight, and 12-15% of daily calories from proteins.

Carbohydrates: grains, roots, fruits, sugars. Carbohydrates are the primary energy source, providing 5 Calories per gram. Digested carbohydrates store as glycogen in liver and muscles, and as glucose in the blood; these stores deplete in 2 hours of hard exercise or 8 hours of fasting and can take 20 hours to replenish. Grains (cornmeal and flour) are 80-85% carbohydrates providing 1800 Calories per pound. Army daily recommendations are: 2-3 grams of carbohydrate per pound of body weight, and about 60-65% of daily calories.

Fats: meat-fats, vegetable-oils, nuts; also, greases,

---

[a] This book uses "Cal" or "Calorie" to measure calories. As in common usage, this Cal (or Calorie, always capitalized) unit is the heat required to heat one kilogram of water one degree Centigrade, and is equivalent to the more exact scientific term "Kcal." Note that the generic reference to food energy (rather than as a quantity unit) is "calorie", lower-case.

[b] Although total elapsed canoeing time during midsummer is likely to have been more like 14-15 hours/day, actual paddling is estimated at 10 of these hours at a net forward progress of 2 mi/hr, also a good net walking rate for the hunters and a Captain (one usually walked). This would give the reported upriver progress of about 20 miles per good day. Assuming an average river flow of 2 mi/hr, the "over-water" speed is then 4 mi/hr. Then on the return journey downstream, the same effort would yield a progress speed of 6 mi/hr, or 60 miles per 10-hour day – about what was reported.

---

[c] Figures derived from USDA Nutritional Analysis.

whale-blubber, candlefish, fresh salmon, and the well-loved boudin blanc sausage. Army recommendations are: 20-25% of daily calories.

Combined Army Diet: The Army diet of 3000 calories is recommended to be 60-65% from carbohydrates, or 1900 Calories; and 35-40% proteins and fats, or 1100 Calories. This can be generally met with standard rations:

2 pounds of meat, lard, beans	1040 Calories
18 ounces of bread/grain	2000 Calories

Corps' Diet: The Corps' average 5000 Calorie diet can be derived by looking at overall meat killed, and the stated ration plan:

6 pounds of meat and fat	3120 Calories
1 pound of grains or roots	1800 Calories
Various fruits, berries, vegetables	80 Calories
Total	5000 Calories

Thus, the Corps' diet starts with the Army basic diet, then adds another 4 pounds of meat to get to 5000 Calories. When the diet shifts almost entirely to meat, it changes to:

9 pounds of meat	4680 Calories
Some grains and fruits	320 Calories
Total	5000 Calories

The Volume of Meat

During times when game is plentiful, Lewis withdraws the carried rations (conserving for tougher times ahead) and relies on hunted game. On July 13, 1805, he writes, *"meat now forms our food prinsipally as we reserve our flour parched meal and corn as much as possible for the rocky mountains which we are shortly to enter ..."* [J4:379] Without the grain component, the meat requirement rises to 9 pounds per man per day – much in line with his listing in that same entry of, *"it requires 4 deer, an Elk and a deer, or one buffaloe to supply us plentifully 24 hours."* The likely harvested meat weight for each of these game sources is:

Deer: USDA guides suggest 60-80 pounds of usable meat per deer, using modern meat-market cutting. For the Corps' hunters who are on the go, and with game on the Plains plentiful, it is likely that they bring back only 60 pounds of select ribs, loins, rumps, etc.

Elk: USDA lists 180 pounds. This is consistent with Lewis' statement that equates an elk to 3 deer.

Buffalo: Here is even greater guessing game – the USDA suggests 400 pounds of marketable meat, but the Corps prefers to use the hump and tongue, although they probably also take the more tender loins and ribs – say, 250 pounds.

Using the Lewis' hunting list and the assumptions above, we arrive at 240-250 pounds of meat per day. That breaks down to about 8 pounds per adult per day – a large bulk quantity to prepare and cook in a 24-hour period. And, since the biggest meal is the afternoon dinner, it would suggest a consumption of at least 3-4 pounds of cooked meat in one sitting!

This issue of how much meat is consumed by the Corps is one subject to spirited debate, with many of the Lewis &Clark scholars jumping into the fracas. Estimates start at 2-2½ pounds of meat per day on the low side and go to the whopping high-side figure of 9 pounds a day.[d]

Now the question, "How can one eat 9 pounds of meat?" An answer is not easy to visualize in the twenty-first century. To some serious experts it seems totally inconceivable that anyone could eat more than 2-2½ pounds of meat per day – yet another expert remembers back to his mother feeding the harvesting crews, and he has no doubt that 9 pounds per day is entirely possible, an amount consistent with the figure published by Stephen Ambrose in *Undaunted Courage*.[e] Franks in *The Canoe and Whitewater* indicates that for the voyageurs, the daily food ration actually eaten was 7 pounds of salmon or 10 pounds of whitefish.[f] Another example of meat needs is recorded by Lewis on June 12, 1805: *"we had killed a buffaloe, an Antelope and three mule deer, and taken a sufficient quantity of the best of the flesh of these anamals for three meals ..."* Yes, this is **A Lot of Meat,** and a lot of food for discussion.

---

[d] Commentators on this controversy include: L and C researcher Dr. Ken Walcheck; professor emeritus Dr. Jack Taylor; the late Don Nell, past president of the Lewis and Clark Trail Heritage Foundation; and late author and researcher Stephen Ambrose – among many others.
[e] Ambrose, page 217.
[f] Franks, page 142.

Additional Resources

THE FOLLOWING BOOKS, GROUPED BY SUBJECT MATTER, are suggested for further reading. This is by no means an exhaustive list and contains books likely to be found in bookstores and libraries. Articles appearing in other publications, research papers, and pamphlets are not in this listing, but may be found in the *Bibliography* section, as may the publication details of the books listed below. Inclusion or absence from these listings does not constitute an endorsement, or lack thereof, by this author.

The Expedition

Undaunted Courage by Stephen Ambrose

The Lewis and Clark Journals (1-volume version) edited by Gary Moulton

Or Perish in the Attempt: Wilderness Medicine in the Lewis & Clark Expedition by David J. Peck

Members of the Corps of Discovery from the Lewis and Clark Bicentennial Foundation

The Saga of Lewis and Clark by Thomas and Jeremy Schmidt (DK Books)

Along the Trail with Lewis and Clark by Barbara Fifer and Vicky Soderberg, maps by Joe Mussulman – exploring the route today

A Lewis and Clark Companion by Stephenie Ambrose Tubbs and Clay Jenkinson

History

Exploring the West from Monticello: A Perspective in Maps from Columbus to Lewis and Clark by Guy Meriwether Benson

Tailor Made, Trail Worn: Army Life, Clothing & Weapons of the Corps of Discovery by Robert J. Moore and Michael Haynes

Colonial St. Louis: Building a Creole Capital by Charles E. Peterson

Food History and Historic Cookbooks

So Serve It Up: Eighteenth Century Foodways by Clarissa F. Dillon

Thomas Jefferson's Cookbook by Marie Kimball

The Virginia Housewife, with Historical Notes & Commentaries by Karen Hess by Mary Randolph

The Williamsburg Cookbook by Helen Bullock

Foods, Food-Science, and Cooking

On Food and Cooking: The Science and Lore of the Kitchen by Harold McGee

The Encyclopedia of American Food & Drink by John Mariani

Pickled, Potted, and Canned: How the Art and Science of Food Preserving Changed the World by Sue Shephard

Tools and Gadgets by Bobbie Kalman

Native American Foods and Traditions

Lewis and Clark among the Indians by James Ronda

The Native Americans: An Illustrated History by David Hurst Thomas

Roots of Survival: Native American Storytelling and the Sacred by Joseph Bruchac

Enduring Harvests: Native American Foods & Festivals for Every Season by E. Barrie Kavasch

Buffalo Bird Woman's Garden by Gilbert L. Wilson

Uses of Plants by the Indians of the Missouri River Region by Melvin R.Gilmore

Salmon and his People: Fish & Fishing in Nez Perce Culture by Dan Landeen and Allen Pinkham

The Feast is Rich: A guide to traditional Coast Salish Indian food gathering and preparation by Carol Batdorf

Plants and Animals

Lewis and Clark: Pioneering Naturalists by Paul Russell Cutright

Lewis and Clark's Green World: The Expedition and its Plants by A. Scott Earle and James L. Reveal

Scats and Tracks of the Rocky Mountains by James C. Halfpenny

The Fruits and Fruit Trees of Monticello by Peter J. Hatch

Guide to Wild Foods and Useful Plants by Christopher Nyerges

Edible and Medicinal Plants of the Rockies by Linda Kershaw

Web Sites

There are many internet web-sites addressing Lewis & Clark topics which can be found using any search browser. A general index can be found at: www.lcarchive.org   A few are listed here for reference and as a start for further browsing:

Lewis and Clark

General overview	www.lewis-clark.org
National Historic Trail	www.nps.gov/lecl
Trail Heritage Foundation	www.lewisandclark.org
Bicentennial (2003-2006)	www.lewisandclark200.org
PBS film	www.pbs.org/lewisandclark
The trail today	www.lewisandclarktrail.com
In the footsteps	www.sierraclub.org/lewisandclark
Ethnography	www.peabody.harvard.edu/lewis_and_clark
Food	www.lewisandclark-food.com
Artworks	www.lewisandclarkpaintings.com

Other Sites

Monticello - Jefferson's home	www.monticello.org
Jefferson National Expansion Memorial	www.nps.gov/jeff
Food history	www.foodhistorynews.org
Plant references - national database	http://plants.usda.org
Plants and animals	www.natureserve.org

Resources and Suppliers:

For every topic in the food and social history of the Lewis & Clark Expedition, there are numerous additional resources and suppliers. Here are just a few:

Music

Pierre Cruzatte: A Musical Journey Along the Trail with Lewis & Clark with Daniel Slosberg.
    Native Ground Music, (800) 752-2656, www.nativeground.com
Fiddle Tunes of the Lewis & Clark Era by Howard Marshall and Vivian Williams.
    Voyager Recordings, (206) 323-1112, www.VoyagerRecords.com

Cookware

Cast-iron cookware – America's original cookware. Now buy it new, pre-seasoned, and ready for stove or campfire.
    Lodge Manufacturing Company, (423) 837-7181, www.lodgemfg.com

Provisions

Sour mash whiskey: Labot & Graham, Kentucky's oldest – since 1812, (859) 879-1812, www.woodfordreserve.com
Wines: On-line, search under "Hermanoff MO wineries," Hermann, Missouri – just up the road from St. Charles
    Canoe Ridge Winery, WA (label has Lewis & Clark in a canoe), (509) 527-0885, www.canoeridgevineyard.com
Meats (a wide variety of meats eaten by the Corps)
    Niman Ranch (pork and beef), (510) 808-0340, www.nimanranch.com
    Prairie Harvest (wild game), (605) 642-5676, www.prairieharvest.com
Smoked Salmon (from present-day Washington)
    Just Smoked Salmon, (866 toll-free) 716-2710, www.justsmokedsalmon.com
    Kasilof Fish Company, (800) 322-7552, www.iLoveSalmon.com
Stone Ground Grains and Parched Corn Meal
    Bob's Red Mill, (800) 349-2173, www.bobsredmill.com
    Corn Meal from Spring Mill State Park, Mitchell, Indiana 47446 (see a working mill and buy the products).
    "Brinser's Best" manufactured by Haldeman Mills, (877)787-9657, www.theamishcountrystore.safeshopper.com
Fruits and Vegetables
    Frieda's Specialty Fruits and Vegetables (Jerusalem Artichokes, "Sunchokes", (800) 241-1771, www.friedas.com
    Melissa's (check for "sunflower chokes"), (800) 588-0151, www.melissas.com
    Trader Joe's Markets (dense dried fruits and vegetables foods), (800) 746-7857, www.traderjoes.com
    "Just Corn" and "Just Cherries" (light-textured dried corn and cherries), www.justtomatoes.com
    Integration Acres (Pawpaws, the Missouri variety, not papaya), (740) 698-2124, www.integrationacres.com

Notes

The following abbreviations have been used for frequently cited works; more complete entries for them may be found in the Bibliography:

LLCE   Jackson, *Letters of the Lewis and Clark Expedition* - also as superscript ᴸ vol:page in the text.

JLC   Mounton, *Journals of the Lewis and Clark Expedition* - also as superscript ᴶ vol:page in the text.

WPO   *We Proceeded On,* a quarterly journal publication.

1. Stanton, "Non-Monticello Accounts of Food and Drink", p. 1.
2. Beldon, p. 13.
3. Ticknor, p. 64.
4. Stanton, "Jeffersonian Dinners - Specific Dishes Mentioned", p. 1.
5. Kimball, p. 16.
6. Mitchill, as referenced in Stanton, "Non-Monticello Accounts of Food and Drink", p. 3.
7. Stanton, "Jeffersonian Dinners", p. 1.
8. Robbins, p. 38.
9. Trager, p. 195.
10. Visser, p. 23.
11. Trager, pp. 189, 199.
12. Kiple, Vol. 2, pp. 1134-35.
13. American Institute of Wine & Food.
14. From *The Ladies Home Companion*, a 1753 cookbook. Reprint provided by the Lewis and Clark Trail Heritage Interpretative Center, Great Falls Montana.
15. Advertisement by James Burmester, Rare Books, in Bath England. Catalogue 48, book review for #225, A broadside advertisement for various portable soups.
16. Shepherd, p. 181.
17. Ann Shackleford, as referenced in Walcheck (in publication in WPO). A very similar recipe appears in Chuinard, pp 160-161; which Chuinard attributes to Cutbush, p. 314-315. However, the Shackleford version appears much earlier. The identification of the Shackleford recipe as matching the Chuinard/Cutbush recipe is attributed to Ken Walcheck.
18. Mendell, p. 72.
19. Bullock, p. 6-7, which quotes Byrd, *History of the Dividing Line.*
20. WPO, "The Ladies Companion", Vol. 9, no. 4, p. 11.
21. Walcheck, "Soup", p. 1, referencing Shackleford; and Chuinard, p. 162.
22. Randolf, p. 19.
23. Randolf, p. 13.
24. Aidells, pp. 343-344.
25. Randolf, p. 19.
26. Aidells, p. 343.
27. Rees, p. 2.
28. Moore, "The Army Mess".
29. Mariani, *The Dictionary of American Food and Drink*, p. 215.
30. Kiple, Vol. 1, p. 451.
31. Society for Range Management, *Trail Boss's Cowboy Cookbook*, p. 196.
32. McGee, p. 104.
33. JLC, 3:120, note 10, attributed to Edward Wentworth.
34. JLC, 3:120, note 10, attributed to Edward Wentworth.
35. Grodinsky, p. 2.
36. Bleeker, p. 103.
37. Caduto, p. 125.
38. Charles Peterson, pp. 30-31.
39. McGee, pp. 170-171.
40. Bennett, p. 473.
41. Lewis, Camp Equipage document from National Archives.
42. Kiple, p. 61.
43. Warren, pp. 23-24.
44. Robert Hunt, p. 27, note 22.
45. Large, WPO (2/90), p. 6.
46. All material relating to the rations, quantities, and varying caloric requirements by locale are derived from "The United States Army Rations."
47. Private correspondence with Bob Moore, historian at Jefferson National Expansion Memorial. He cites, "Standing Orders, 1803, Record Group 98, National Archives and Records Administration (NARA), No.10 Records of the Garrison at Fort Independence, Boston Harbor, 1803-1815, p. 68.
48. Private correspondence with Bob Moore, citing "General Orders, Fort Wayne, Indiana, August 18, 1802, in Indiana Historical Collections, Vol. XV, Fort Wayne, Garrison Orderly Book, edited by Bert Griswold, p. 93.
49. Private correspondence with Bob Moore, citing Fort Belle-fontaine Orderly Book, 1808-1810, Missouri Historical Society.
50. Franks, p. 124.
51. U.S. Army, *Nutritional Guidance*, p. 21.
52. U.S. Army, *Nutritional Guidance*, p. 5-6.

53. Franks, p. 46.
54. Kane, p. 114.
55. Foxfire 5, p.210-211.
56. Foxfire 5, 212-214; also see JLC 2:213f1 for further amplification.
57. Schmidt, p. 44.
58. Karsmizki, a presentation, September 2001.
59. Walters, p. 166.
60. Mansfield, p. 82 for starting ingredients proportions only; author for adapted recipe and preparation instructions.
61. Thwaites, Vol. III, p. 274.
62. Mariani, p.1
63. Gunther, p. 19-20.
64. Mennell, p. 72 (referring to La Varenne).
65. October 2001, *Nation's Restaurant News*.
66. Maria Baker-Fulco, private conversation, 2000.
67. Kiple, vol. 1, pp. 991, 993.
68. Moore, "The Army Mess".
69. Goude, www.edibleplants.com/month/minerslet.htm.
70. David Worley, Lewis and Clark Medical Conference, Bozeman, MT, October 2001.
71. Kershaw, p. 204.
72. Ronda, *Lewis and Clark Among the Indians*, p. 8.
73. Thomas, p. 166.
74. Turner, p. 260.
75. Holland, "What was Money Worth in 1804".
76. Stofiel - quoting Alexander Henry, a contemporary of Lewis and Clark.
77. Balch, p. 68.
78. Cambridge, p. 1540.
79. Guillard Hunt, pp. 38-39.
80. Kimball, p. 36.
81. Simmons, p. 69.
82. McGee, p. 280.
83. Glasse, p. 151.
84. Dillon, p. 166.
85. Recipe courtesy of John Toenyes, Lewis and Clark Honor Guard.
86. Flandrin, p. 354.
87. Stoddard, p. 214.
88. JLC, 1:Maps 3A & 3B.
89. Kiple, Vol. 1, p. 440.
90. Walters, p. 144.
91. Jim Holmberg, private correspondence, 11/26/02.
92. Stadler, p. 14.
93. Liljegren, as quoted in Charles Peterson, p. 21.
94. Info@kanniskorner.com
95. Stoddard p.219 – Extrapolated from the figure of 180 houses in 1766.
96. Charles Peterson, p. 8-9.

97. Charles Peterson, p. 8 n9.
98. Charles Peterson, p. 30.
99. Charles Peterson, p. 39.
100. Charles Peterson, p. 36.
101. Carley, p. 203.
102. Stoddard, p. 216.
103. Charles Peterson, pp. 35-36.
104. Nasatir, Vol. II, pp. 647-48.
105. Oglesby, p. 18.
106. Stoddard, p. 231.
107. Moore, private correspondence.
108. Kimball, p. 81.
109. Stoddard, p. 229.
110. Stoddard, p. 229.
111. Moore, private correspondence, September, 2002.
112. Stadler, p. 12 – referring to a letter of Stoddard to his mother.
113. Stadler, p. 12.
114. Kubik, p. 10.
115. Stadler, p. 12.
116. Clark letter, Missouri Historical Society files.
117. Stadler, p. 12.
118. Dennis White, Montana Mandolin Society, private communication.
119. Stoddard, p. 228.
120. Leaf and Leeman, p. 186.
121. Kalman, *Tools and Gadgets*, p. 10; and Stadler, p. 14.
122. Charles Peterson, p. 30.
123. Leaf, p. 186.
124. Dillon, p. 105.
125. Kalm, p. 55, as referenced in Dillon, p. 105.
126. Dillon, p. vii.
127. Stoddard, p. 228.
128. David Wallace, Textual Archives Services Division, National Archives and Records Administration. Private correspondence, June 17, 1998.
129. Holland, "The Corps of Discovery Inventory".
130. Moliere, The School for Husbands (1661), in International Thesaurus of Quotations.
131. Biddle, pp. 31-32.
132. Stevens, pp. 10-13.
133. Ronda, *Lewis and Clark Among the Indians*, p. 12.
134. Wilson, p. 97.
135. Henry, p. 328.
136. Catlin, p. 143.
137. Catlin, pp. 148, 151, 153.
138. Ronda, speech at Portland, OR, March 2002.
139. Bruchak, p. 29.
140. Gilbert, p. 27.
141. Catlin, p. 168.

142. Arden, p. 118.
143. Bruchak, p. 71.
144. Wilson, p. 36.
145. Wilson, p. 42.
146. Wilson, p. 88.
147. Rhonda, ... *Indians,* p. 72.
148. Bruchak, p. 40.
149. Will, pp. 32-33.
150. Wilson, p. 75.
151. Henry, p. 329.
152. Nordblom, p. 1.
153. Chriswell, xxxiii.
154. Canduto, p. 128.
155. United Tribes Technical College, p. 19.
156. Kavasch, p. 80.
157. Randolph, p. 26.
158. Ronda, ... *Indians,* p. 152.
159. From a pageant by Johnny Arlee (Salish), reported by Rebecca Robbins, p. 26.
160. McGee, pp. 594-95.
161. McGee, p. 617.
162. Kershaw, p. 64.
163. Kershaw, p. 105.
164. Ronda, ... *Indians,* p. 172.
165. Ronda, ... *Indians,* p. 162.
166. Thwaites, Vol. III, p. 136, note 1.
167. Pat Cole (Chinook), from a presentation at *Confulunce of Cultures,* Missoula, MT, May 29, 2003.
168. Furlong, p. 38.
169. Ronda, ... *Indians,* p. 34..
170. Fifer, p. 156.
171. Kimball, pp. 76-79.
172. Thwaites, Vol. IV, pp. 102-103.
173. Trager, p. 169.
174. Thomas, p. 237.
175. Jenkinson, p. 89.
176. Rogers, p. 17.
177. Calloway, "Pawpaws ...".
178. Winckler, p. 29.
179. Ronda, "St. Louis Welcomes ... ," p. 19.
180. Handwritten page from a Lewis personal diary of 1796, writing not necessarily verified as Lewis himself, Missouri Historical Society files.
181. Mennell, p. 62.
182. Luchetti, p. 18.

183. Gass, p. 228.
184. Cutright, p. 242.
185. Streubel, p. 140.
186. Halfpenny, p. 50.
187. Streubel, p. 102.
188. Streubel, p. 83.
189. Internet: www.animaldiversity.unmz.umich.edu/accounts/dipelphus
190. Root, p. 303.
191. Streubel, p. 124.
192. Streubel, p. 124.
193. Halfpenny, p. 58.
194. *New World Dictionary,* p. 589.
195. Cutright, p. 74.
196. Kimball, p. 47.
197. Holmberg, p. xxviii.
198. http://has.er.usgs.gov/fishes/accounts
199. Kiple, Vol. 2, p. 1211.
200. Bullock, pp. 69-70.
201. Kiple, Vol. 1, p. 517.
202. Root, p. 256.
203. Dr. Jack Taylor, Private conversation, July 2002.
204. Kershaw, p. 105.
205. Jim Holmberg, Filson Historical Society, private correspondence, June 7 and July 16, 2001.
206. Internet, www.emext.maine.edu/onlinepubs/htmpubs/4198.htm.
207. Kiple, Vol. 1, p. 1308.
208. Gabányi, p. 53.
209. Mariani, p. 39.
210. Thwaites, Vol. 1, p. 232.
211. Kiple, Vol. 1, p. 660.
212. Karsmizki, "Doling it Out".
213. Heise, pp. 19-20.
214. McGee, p. 223.
215. McGee, p. 215.
216. Castleman, p. 255.
217. Kiple, Vol. 1, p. 638.
218. Kiple, Vol. 2, p. 1540.
219. Kennedy, p. 453.
220. *Monticello: A Guidebook,* p. 86.
221. McGee, p. 466.
222. McGee, p. 469.
223. McGee, p. 429.

Bibliography

Ackerman, Diane. "The Bloom of a Taste Bud." *Wine, Food & the Arts: Works Gathered by the American Institute of Wine and Food,* Volume 1. San Francisco, CA: American Institute of Wine and Food.

Aidells, Bruce and Denis Kelly. *Hot Links and Country Flavors: sausages in American Regional Cooking.* New York: Alfred A. Knopf, 1990.

Ambrose, Stephen E. *Undaunted Courage.* New York: Simon and Schuster, 1996.

American Institute of Wine & Food. *Wine, Food & the Arts: Works Gathered by The American Institute of Wine & Food,* Vol 2. Belvedere, CA : Swan Island Books, 1997.

Arden, Harvey and Steve Wall. *Wisdomkeepers: Meetings with Native American Spiritual Elders.* Hillsboro, OR: Beyond Words Publishing, 1990.

Arnold, Samuel P. *The Fort Cookbook: New Foods from the Old West from the Famous Denver Restaurant.* New York: HarperCollins Publishers, Inc., 1997.

Balch, James M. and Phyllis Balch. *Prescription for Nutritional Healing.* New York: Avery Publishing Group, 1997.

Batdorf, Carol. *The Feast is Rich: A Guide to Traditional Coast Salish Indian Food Gathering and Preparation.* Bellingham, WA: Whatcom Museum of History & Art, 1980.

Belden, Louise. *The Festive Tradition: Table Decoration and Desserts in America, 1650–1900.* New York: Norton, 1983.

Bennett. *Chemical Formulary.* New York: Chemical Publishing, 1935.

Benson, Guy Meriwether. *Exploring the West from Monticello: A Perspective in Maps from Columbus to Lewis and Clark.* Charlottesville: Department of Special Collections, University of Virginia Library, 1995.

Beveridge, N.E. *Cups of Valor.* Harrisburg, PA: Stackpole Books, 1968.

Biddle, Nicholas, ed. *The Journals of the Lewis and Clark Expedition.* Reprint: New York: Heritage Press, 1962.

Bleeker, Sonia. *The Sea Hunters: Indians of the Northwest Coast.* New York: William Morrow and Company, 1951.

Bowers, Alfred. *Hidatsa Social and Ceremonial Organization.* Lincoln & London: University of Nebraska Press, 1992.

Brown, Jo Ann. "New Light on Some of the Expedition Engagés." WPO (Aug 1996).

Bruchac, Joseph. *Roots of Survival: Native American Storytelling and the Sacred.* Golden, CO: Fulcrum Publishing, 1996.

Bullock, Helen. *The Williamsburg Cookbook.* Colonial Williamsburg, 1938, distributed by Holt, Reinhart, 1951.

Burmeister, James. Dealer in Rare Books, Catalogue 48 (English Books 1675–1900). Single sheet flyer by Vigor (first name unlisted) to His Majesty's Royal Navy, London, circa 1790–1800, re: portable soup.

Burroughs, Raymond Darwin. *The Natural History of the Lewis and Clark Expedition.* East Lansing: Michigan State University Press, 1961.

———. Unpublished study of the animals hunted by the Corps of Discovery.

Byrd, Max. *Jefferson.* New York: Bantam Books, 1993.

Byrd, William of Westover, Virginia. *History of the Dividing Line.* n.p., 1729.

Caduto, Michael J. and Joseph Bruchac. *Native American Gardening: Stories, Projects and Recipes for Families.* Golden, CO: Fulcrum Publishing, 1996. (Recipient in 1998 of National Parenting Publications Awards)

Calloway, M.B. "Pawpaw (*Asimina triloba*): A 'tropical' fruit for temperate climates." J. Janick and J.E. Simon (eds.). *New Crops.* New York: Wiley, 1993, pp.505–15.

Carley, Eliane Amé-Leroy. *Classics from a French Kitchen.* New York and Canada: Crown Publishers, 1983.

Carlin, Joseph M. "Weights and Measures in Nineteenth Century America." *The Journal of Gastronomy,* Vol.3, No.3 (Autumn 1987).

———. "Pleasures of the Table: Eating and Drinking in the Early Republic." *Nutrition Today,* Vol.33, No.2 (March/April 1998).

Castellino, Nicolo and Pietro Castellino and Nicola Sannolo, eds. *Inorganic Lead Exposure: Metabolism and Intoxication.* Boca Raton, FL: CRC Press, Inc., 1995.

Castleman, Michael. *The Healing Herbs: The Ultimate Guide to the Curative Power of Nature's Medicines.* Emmaus, PA: Rodale Press. 1991.

Catlin, George. *Manners & Customs Letters and Notes on the North American Indians,* edited by Michael MacDonald Mooney. New York: Clarkson N. Potter, (no date listed).

Chuinard, E.G. *Only One Man Died: The Medical Aspects of the Lewis and Clark Expedition.* Fairfield, WA: Ye Galleon Press, 1979.

Clark, Charles G. *Men of the Lewis & Clark Expedition: A Biographical Roster of Fifty-one Members.* Spokane: Arthur H. Clark Co., 2001.

Clayton, Bernard, Jr. *The Complete Book of Soups and Stews.* New York: Simon & Schuster, Inc., 1984.

Craft, Roy D. "Lewis and Clark's Wapato - Endangered Plant- Fights for Survival." WPO (2/82).

Criswell, Elijah Harry. *Lewis & Clark - Pioneering Linguists.* A Xerox copy of the above titled work produced by the Headwaters Chapter of the Lewis & Clark Trail Heritage Foundation, Box 577, Bozeman, MT 59715; with the knowledge and consent of the University of Missouri Studies, Columbia, Missouri, April 1991.

Cornwell, Bernard. *The Winter King.* New York: St. Martin's Press, 2000.

Cutbush, Edward. *Observations on the Means of Preserving the Health of Soldiers and Sailors.* Philadlphia: Fry and Kannerer, 1808.

Cutright, Paul Russell. *Lewis and Clark: Pioneering Naturalists.* Lincoln and London: Bison Books, 1989.

———. "Well Traveled Plants of Lewis and Clark." WPO (2/78).

Cutler, William Parker and Julia Perkins Cutler. *Life Journals and Correspondence of Rev. Manasseh Cutler.* Cincinnati, 1888.

Danforth, Randi, ed. *Culinaria: The United States.* NY: Könemann Publishers USA, 1988.

Dillon, Clarissa F. *So Serve It Up: Eighteenth Century Foodways.* Self-published, 1999.

Dillon, Richard. *Meriwether Lewis: A Biography.* New York: Coward-McCann, 1965.

The Discovery Writers. *Lewis and Clark in the Bitterroots.* Stevensville, MT: Stoneydale Press Publishing Company, 1998.

Duncan, Dayton. *Lewis & Clark: The Journey of the Corps of Discovery.* New York: Alfred A. Knopf, 1997.

Earle, A. Scott and James L. Reveal. *Lewis and Clark's Green World: The Expedition and its Plants.* Helena, MT: Farcountry Press, 2003.

Encyclopedia of Textiles. 3rd Edition. Englewood Cliffs, NJ: Prentice-Hall, 1980.

Erickson, Martin. "Historian: Lewis and Clark Fulfilled Nez Perce Dream." News Update in WPO (2/98).

Erickson, Martin. "No Merry Weather for Lewis and Clark." News Update in WPO (5/98).

Evenson, Teri, Lauren Lesmeister and Jeff Evenson. *The Lewis & Clark Cookbook with Contemporary Recipes.* Bismarck, ND: Whisper'n'Waters, 2000.

Ewers, John. *Indian Life on the Upper Missouri.* Norman, OK: University of Oklahoma Press, 1968.

Fazio, James R. *Across the Snowy Ranges.* Moscow, ID: Woodland Press, 2001.

Fifer, Barbara and Vicky Soderberg, with maps by Joseph Mussulman. *Along the Trail with Lewis and Clark.* Helena, MT: Montana Magazine, 1998.

Flandrin, Jean-Louis and Massimo Montanari. *Food: A Culinary History from Antiquity to the Present.* New York and Cichester, West Sussex: Columbia University Press, 1999.

Foley, William E. and Rice, C. David. *The First Chouteaus.* Urbana and Chicago: University of Illinois Press, 1983.

"Food of the Mandans." Orin Grant Libby Collection, State Historical Society of North Dakota Collection of Manuscripts. A85, Box 29, Folder 20.

Franks, C.E.S. *The Canoe and Whitewater.* Toronto and Buffalo: University of Toronto Press, 1977.

Frieda's "Sunchokes." Product page at www.friedas.com/detail.cfm?ID=199

Furlong, Marjorie and Virginia Pill. *Wild Edible Fruits and Berries.* Naturegraph, 1974.

Gabányi, Stefan. *Whisk(e)y.* New York: Abberville Press, 1997.

Garavaglia, Louis A. *Firearms of the American West, 1803–1865.* Niwot, CO: University Press of Colorado, 1998.

Gass, Patrick. *A Journal of the Voyages and Travels of a Corps of Discovery under the Command of Capt. Lewis and Capt. Clarke of the Army of the United States.* Edited by David McKeehan. Minneapolis: Ross and Haines, 1958.

Gatliff, Jason W. "How I Made My Oilcloth" at www.HistoricalTrekking.com. Supplemented by personal correspondence.

Glasse, Hannah, *The Art of Cookery, Made Plain and Easy.* London: Printed for the Author, 1747; facsimile reprint, London: Prospect Books, Ltd., 1983.

Gilmore, Melvin R. *Uses of Plants by the Indians of the Missouri River Region.* Enlarged Edition. Lincoln & London: University of Nebraska Press, 1991.

Goodwin, Mary. *Lighting in Colonial Virginia.* Colonial Williamsburg Foundation Library research report series; RR-108, 1961.

Goude. *Dining on the Wilds.* A video course and an internet synopsis: www.edibleplants.com

Gravaglia, Louis A. *Firearms of the American West, 1803–1865.* Niwot, CO: University of Colorado Press, 1998.

Grodinsky, Peggy, ed. "Eat These Words," *The James Beard Foundation Calendar and Newsletter.* September 2000.

Halfpenny, James C. *Scats and Tracks of the Rocky Mountains.* Guildford, CT: The Globe Pequot Press, 2001.

Hallock, Thomas. "Literary Recipes from the Lewis and Clark Journals: The Epic Design and Wilderness Tastes of Early National Nature Writing." *Journal of American Studies,* 38:3, (Fall 1997), pp.43-66.

Hamady, Mary. *Lebanese Mountain Cookery.* Boston: David R. Godine, 1987.

Hart, Jeff. *Montana Native Plants and Early Peoples.* Helena, MT: Montana Historical Society Press, 1976, reprint 1996.

Hatch, Peter J. *The Fruits and Fruit Trees of Monticello.* Charlottesville and London: University Press of Virginia, 1998.

Heise, Ulla. *Coffee and Coffee Houses.* West Chester, PA: Schiffer Publishing Ltd, 1987.

Henisch, B.A. *Fast and Feast: Food in Medieval Society.* University Park and London: Pennsylvania State University Press, 1976.

Henry, Alexander. *New Light on the Early History of the Greater Northwest.* New York: F.P. Harper, 1897.

Holland, Charles H., Jr. "The Corps of Discovery Inventory." unpublished.

————. "What was Money Worth in 1804." unpublished.

Holmberg, James J. *Dear Brother: Letters of William Clark to Jonathan Clark.* New York: Yale University Press, 2002.

Howard, Ella Mae. *Lewis and Clark: Exploration of Central Montana.* Great Falls, MT: Lewis and Clark Interpretative Association, 1993.

Hunt, Gaillard, ed. *The First Forty Years of Washington Society in The Family Letters of Margaret Bayard Smith.* New York: Frederick Ungar Publishing Co., 1965.

Hunt, Robert P. "Gills & Drams of Consolation." WPO (8/91 & 11/91).

————. "Matches and Magic. " WPO (8/2000).

————. "Merry to the Fiddle." WPO (11/88).

Jv:ppp, see JLC below and Moulton. Inline superscript references to the *Journals* appear in this abbreviated format, referring to Volume (v), Page (ppp).

Jackson, Donald, ed. *Letters of the Lewis and Clark Expedition with Related Documents 1783–1854.* Urbana, IL: University of Illinois Press, 1962. This work is abbreviated as LLCE in the endnotes (see entry below).

Jackson, Donald. "Jefferson, Meriwether Lewis, and the Reduction of the United States Army." *Proceedings of the American Philophical Society,* Vol.124, no.2 (April 1980).

————. "Meriwether Lewis Comes Home." WPO (12/76).

Janick, J. and J.E. Simon (eds.). *New Crops.* New York: Wiley, 1993.

JLC, see Moulton (the "Definitive" 13-volume edition). The many references to the *Journals* will be abbreviated as 'JLC, vol:page', and spellings will be presented as in the *Journals* without numerous distracting [sic.]. All *Journal* references are italicized in this book, while italicizing and underlining in the *Journals* is shown here as italicized text with underlining.

Jenkinson, Clay Straus. *The Character of Meriwether Lewis: Completely Metamorphosed in the American West.* Reno, NV: Marmarth Press, 2000.

Kalm, Peter. Trans. by John Reinhold Forster. *Travels into North America.* Barre, MA: The Imprint Society, 1972.

Kalman, Bobbie. *The Kitchen.* Historic Community Series. NY, Canada, U.K.: Crabtree Publishing Company, 1990 and 1993.

————. *Tools and Gadgets.* Historic Community Series. NY, Canada, U.K.: Crabtree Publishing Company, 1992.

Kane, Paul. *Wanderings of an Artist: Among the Indians of North America.* Reprinted Edmonton: Hurtig, 1968.

Karsmizki, Ken. "Doling it Out." An address to the Lewis & Clark Trail Heritage Society, Bozeman, MT, September, 2001.

Kavasch, E. Barrie. *Enduring Harvests: Native American Foods & Festivals for Every Season.* Old Saybrook, CT: Globe Pequot Press, 1995.

Kennedy, Diane. *The Essential Cuisines of Mexico.* NY: Clarkson Potter Publishers, 2000.

Kershaw, Linda. *Edible and Medicinal Plants of the Rockies.* Renton, WA: Lone Pine Publishing, 2000.

Kimball, Marie. *Thomas Jefferson's Cookbook.* Charlottesville, SC: University Press of Virginia, 1976.

Kiple, Kenneth F. and Kriemhild C. Ornelas, eds. *The Cambridge World History of Food.* 2 volumes. Cambridge: Cambridge University Press, 2000.

Könemann, Ludwigg, P. Feierabend, G. Chassman, and R. Danforth, eds. *Culinaria: The United States.* New York: Könemann Publishers USA, 1998.

Kubik, Barbara. "Coulter" in WPO, Vol.9, no. 1, p. 10.

Kuhnleim, Harriet V. and Nancy Turner. *Traditional Plant Foods of Canadian Indigenous Peoples: Nutrition, Botany and Use.* Philadelphia, PA: Gordon and Breach Science Publishers, 1991.

Lv:ppp, see LLCE below and Jackson. Inline superscript references to the *Letters* appear in this abbreviated format, referring to Volume (v), Page (ppp).

Landeen, Dan and Allen Pinkham. *Salmon and his People: Fish & Fishing in Nez Perce Culture.* Lewiston, ID: Confluence Press, 1999.

Lange, Robert E. "Christmas Came Three Times - 1803-1804-1805 to the Corps of Discovery." WPO (12/76).

———. "The Expedition and the Inclement Weather of November-December 1805." WPO (11/79).

———. "Private George Shannon: The Expedition's Youngest Member." WPO (7/82).

Leaf, Alexandra and Fred Leeman. *Van Gogh's Table at the Auberge Ravoux.* Artisan, 2001.

Lewis, Meriwether. "Camp Equipage." Original handwritten document from National Archives.

Liljegren, Ernest J. "The Commission of Lieutenant Colonel Carlos Howard to Defend the Upper Mississippi Valley Against the English." Quoted in Charles Peterson.

LLCE. See Jackson, Donald. ed. *Letters of the Lewis and Clark Expedition with Related Documents.* The many endnote references to the *Letters* will be abbreviated as "LLCE, vol:page". All writings of Lewis or Clark are italicized in this book; while italicizing and underlining in *Letters* is shown here as italicized text with underlining.

Lyle, Katie. *The Wild Berry Book: Romance, Recipes, & Remedies.* Minocqua, Wisconsin: NorthWord Press, Inc., 1994.

Luchetti, Cathy. *Home on the Range: A Culinary History of the American West.* New York: Villard Books, 1993.

McGee, Harold. *On Food and Cooking: The Science and Lore of the Kitchen.* New York: Charles Scribner's Sons, 1984.

Mains, Jesse. "Dealing with Dead Deer Critters" January 19, 2001. http://historicaltrekking.com/tips/messages/73.shtml.

Mansfield, Leslie. *The Lewis & Clark Cookbook: Historic Recipes.* Berkeley: Celestial Arts, 2002.

Mariani, John F. *The Dictionary of American Food and Drink.* New Haven: Ticknor and Fields, 1983.

———. *The Encyclopedia of American Food & Drink.* New York: Lebhar-Friedman Books, 1999.

Martin, Paul and Christine Szuter. "War Zones and Game Sinks in Lewis and Clark's West." WPO (2/99): p.36–45. This article further references Paul Martin and Christine Szuter, *Conservation Biology*, p.673.

Matson, Madeline. *Food in Missouri: A Cultural Stew.* Columbia and London: University of Missouri Press, 1994.

Mennell, Stephen. *All Manners of Food: Eating and Taste in England and France from the Middle Ages to the Present.* Urbana and Chicago: University of Chicago Press, 1996.

Members of the Corps of Discovery. Washburn, ND: North Dakota Lewis & Clark Bicentennial Foundation, 1999.

Missouri Historical Society. "Description of St. Louis." *Missouri Historical Society Bulletin* (March 1934), p.20–27.

———. "The Library of John Hay of Cahokia and Belleville." *Missouri Historical Society Bulletin,* Vol. IX, No.2 (January 1953).

Monticello: A Guidebook. Charlottesville, SC: Thomas Jefferson Memorial Foundation, 1997.

Moore, Robert J. and Michael Haynes. *Tailor Made, Trail Worn: Army Life, Clothing & Weapons of the Corps of Discovery.* Helena, MT: Farcountry Press, 2003.

Moore, Robert J. "The Army Mess." WPO, not yet published.

———. *The French Heritage of St. Louis.* Unpublished training document for the National Park Service, Jefferson Memorial, St. Louis.

———. "The Making of a Myth: Did the Corps of Discovery Actually Eat Candles?" WPO (5/99).

Morse, Eric. *Fur Trade Canoe Routes of Canada/Then and Now.* Ottawa: Queen's Printer, 1969.

Moulton, Gary, ed. *The Journals of the Lewis and Clark Expedition.* 13 Volumes. The "Definitive Journals." Lincoln and London: University of Nebraska Press, 1986–2001. This work s abbreviated as JLC in the endnotes (see entry above).

Moulton, Gary. *The Lewis and Clark Journals: An Epic of Discovery.* A one-volume abridgement of the 13-volume "Definitive Journals." Lincoln: University of Nebraska Press, 2003.

Nasatir, A.P., ed. *Before Lewis and Clark.* 2 volumes. St. Louis, 1954.

National Park Service. *Lewis and Clark.* Government Printing Office, 1975.

Nell, Donald. "Where Is the Salt?" WPO (5/91).

Nell, Donald and John E. Taylor. *Lewis and Clark in the Three Rivers Valleys, Montana 1805–1806.* Sponsored by Headwaters Chapter- Lewis and Clark Trail Heritage Foundation, Inc. Tucson, AZ: The Patrice Press, 1996.

Nordblom, Katri. *The Nutritional Value of Wild Plants Is Far Superior to that of Cultivated Plants.* A pamphlet (npd).

Nyerges, Christopher. *Guide to Wild Foods and Useful Plants.* Chicago, IL: Chicago Review Press, Inc., 1999.

Oglesby, Richard. *Manuel Lisa and the Opening of the Missouri Fur Trade.* Norman, OK and London: University of Oklahoma Press, 1963.

Olson, Susanne M., "Dining at Monticello," Charlottesville, VA: Thomas Jefferson Memorial Foundation, Inc, pamphlet, 1994 (revised 12/7/94).

Oxford Dictionary of Quotations. New York & Oxford: Oxford University Press, 1992.

Peck, David J. *Or Perish in the Attempt.* Helena, MT: Farcountry Press, 2002.

Peterson, Charles E. *Colonial St. Louis: Building a Creole*

Capital. St. Louis: Missouri Historical Society, 1949; re-issued in new format at Tucson, AZ: The Patrice Press, 1993. [Citations use the pagination in the 1949 edition].

Peterson, Merrill D., ed. *Visitors to Monticello.* Charlottesville: University of Virginia Press, 1989; a discussion of T. Jefferson to Dr. Vine Utley, March 21, 1819, as reported by Francis Calley Gray.

Plamondon, Martin. *Lewis and Clark Trail Maps: A Cartographic Reconstruction.* 3 Volumes. Pullman, WA: Washington State University Press, 2000 and 2002.

Primm, James Neal. *Lion of the Valley.* Boulder, CO: Pruett, 1981.

Randolph, Mary. *The Virginia Housewife, with Historical Notes & Commentaries by Karen Hess.* Washington: Davis and Force, 1824; a facsimile of the first 1824 edition, with material from the 1825 and 1828 editions, used from the collections of, and with permissions from, the American Antiquarian Society, Worcester, MA. Columbia, SC: Univ. of South Carolina Press, 1984.

Rees, John U. "'Our pie-loving..stomachs..ache to even look:' Salt Meat for Armies, 1775–1865." *Food History News,* Vol. IX, No. IV (Spring 1998), p.2.

Robbins, Peggy. "The Presidential Cheeses," *Early American Life,* Vol.VI, No. 6 (December 1975).

Robbins, Rebecca. "Setting the Record Straight." *Tribal College Journal of American Indian Higher Education,* Vol. 14, No. 3 (Spring 2003), p.24.

Rogers, Ann. "Was it the Pawpaws?" WPO (2/87), p.17.

Roget's International Thesaurus. New York: Thomas Y. Crowell Company, 1946.

Ronda, James. "A Most Perfect Harmony." WPO (11/88).

———. "Imagining the West Through the Eyes of Lewis and Clark." WPO (5/92), pp. 21-26.

———. *Lewis and Clark Among the Indians.* Lincoln and London: University of Nebraska Press, 1984.

———. "St. Louis Welcomes Lewis and Clark." WPO (2/87), p.19.

Scharf, J. Thomas. *History of St. Louis City and County.* Philadelphia: Louis H. Everts & Co., 1883.

Schmidt, Thomas and Jeremy. *The Saga of Lewis and Clark: Into the Uncharted West.* New York: DK Publishing, 1999.

Schullery, Paul. *Lewis and Clark Among the Grizzlies.* Guilford, CT: Globe Pequot Press, 2002.

Scullin, Michael. "Try Your Hand at Hidatsa Gardening." A leaflet. Mankato, MN: Minnesota State University, (1998); and at http://kroeber. anthro.mankato.msus.edu/Scullin/index.htm.

Shakleford, Ann. *The Modern Art of Cooking Improved; Or Elegant, Cheap, and Easy Methods, of Preparing Most Dishes Now in Vogue.* 1767; Reproduction - no re-publication details.

Shephard, Sue. *Pickled, Potted, and Canned: How the Art and Science of Food Preserving Changed the World.* New York: Simon & Schuster, 2000.

Simmons, Amelia. *American Cookery.* Second Edition. Albany, NY, 1796; Facsimile re-production with an introduction by Karen Hess. Bedford, MA: Appleford Books, 1996.

———. *American Cookery, 1796.* Facsimile re-production *The First American Cookbook.* New York: Dover Publications, Inc., 1984.

Smithers, Jim. "The Realities and Complexities of Food for Sir Alexander Mackenzie." WPO (2/89).

Snyder, Gerald. *In The Footsteps of Lewis and Clark.* Washington, D.C.: National Geographic Society, 1970.

Society for Range Management. *Trail Boss's Cowboy Cookbook.* Society for Range Management, Third Printing, 1988.

Stadius, Martin. *Dreamers: on the Trail of the Nez Perce.* Caldwell, ID: Caxton Press, 1999.

Stadler, Frances H. "St Louis in 1804." WPO (Feb. 1994), p.11–16.

Stanton, Lucia C. "Jeffersonian Dinners - Specific Dishes Mentioned in the Documentary Record." Charlottesville, VA: Thomas Jefferson Memorial Foundation, Inc, Monticello Research Department, document vii.89.

———. "Jeffersonian Dinners." Charlottesville, VA: Thomas Jefferson Memorial Foundation, Inc. Monticello Research Department, document vii.89 rev.viii.94.

———. "Non-Monticello Accounts of Food and Drink." Charlottesville, VA: (Thomas Jefferson Memorial Foundation, Inc. Monticello Research Department, document 1.V.87/rev.27.V.88.

Stevens, Serita D. *Deadly Doses: A Writers Guide to Poisons.* Cincinnati: Writers Digest Books, 1990.

Stoddard, Maj. Amos. *Sketches, Historical and Descriptive of Louisiana.* Philadelphia: Mathew Carey, 1812.

Stofiel, John H. "The Mystery of the Third Corn Mill." WPO (5/92).

Streubel, Donald. *Small Mammals of the Yellowstone Ecosystem.* Boulder, CO: Roberts Rinehart, Inc, 1989.

Thomas, David Hurst ... [et al]; Betty & Ian Ballantine, eds. *The Native Americans: An Illustrated History.* Atlanta: Turner Publishing, Inc, 1993.

Thwaites, Reuben. *Original Journals of the Lewis and Clark Expedition 1804–1806.* Re-publication, New York: Arno Press, 1969.

Ticknor, George. In *Visitors to Monticello,* Merrill D. Peterson, ed. Charlottesville: University of Virginia Press, 1989. Quoted in Susanne M. Olson,"Dining in Monticello," *op.cit.*

Trager, James. *The Food Chronology: a Food Lover's Compendium of Events and Anecdotes from Prehistory to the Present.* Ontario, Canada: Henry Holt and Company, 1995.

United Tribes Technical College Office of Public Information, ed. *Indian Recipes.* Bismarck, ND, 1992.

US Army Military History Institute, PA. "United States Army Rations." Miscellaneous Files: Food 0-1608.

US Army Research Institute of Environmental Medicine. *Nutritional Guidance for Military Field Operations in Temperate and Extreme Environment.* Natick, MA, circa1990s.

Verrill, A. Hyatt. *Foods America Gave the World.* Boston: L.C. Page & Co, 1937.

Visser, Margaret. "Soup of the Evening, Beautiful Soup." *Wine, Food & the Arts: Works Gathered by The American Institute of Wine & Food,* Vol.2. American Institute of Wine & Food, 1997.

Walcheck, Kenneth. "Lewis's Portable Soup." WPO (August 2003); Pre-publication manuscript received as personal correspondence, 1999.

Waldman, Carl. *Atlas of the North American Indians.* New York: Checkmark Books, 2000.

Walters, Lon. *The Old West Baking Book.* Flagstaff AZ: Northland Publishing, 1996.

Warren, Christian. *Brush with Death: A Social History of Lead Poisoning.* Baltimore and London: Johns Hopkins University Press, 2000.

We Proceeded On, The official quarterly publication of the Lewis & Clark Trail Heritage Foundation, Inc. This publication is abbreviated as WPO in other citations herein.

Weatherford, Jack. *Indian Givers: How the Indians of the Americas Transformed the World.* New York: Ballantine Books, 1988.

Weatherwax, Paul. *Indian Corn in Old America.* New York: Macmillan Co., 1954.

Wedel, Waldo. "Notes on the Prairie Turnip (Psoralea esculenta) Among the Plains Indians." *Nebraska History,* Vol. 59, Number 2 (Summer 1978).

Wentworth, Edward N. "Dried Meats – Early Man's Travel Rations." *Agricultural History,* no. 30 (January 1956), pp. 2-10.

Wigginton, Eliot, ed. *Foxfire 4.* Anchor Press, 1977.

———. *Foxfire 5.* Anchor Press, 1979.

Will, George Francis. *Corn for the Northwest.* St. Paul, MN: Webb Book Publishing Co., 1930.

Williamson, Darcy and Lisa Railsback. *Cooking with Spirit: North American Indian Food & Fact.* Auburn, CA: American River Traders, 1993.

Wilson, Gilbert L. *Buffalo-Bird Woman's Garden.* St. Paul, MN: Minnesota Historical Society Press - Borealis Books, 1987.

Winckler, Suzanne. "Over the Moon About Cows." NY Times (May 3, 1998), p.29.

WPO, see *We Proceeded On,* above. Articles in WPO are referenced for convenience in other citations and bibliographic entries as WPO (date).

Yellowstone Today. Yellowstone National Park Official Newpaper, Spring 2002.

Index